# Treason
# the New World Order

# by Gurudas

Cassandra Press

San Rafael, Ca

Cassandra Press
P.O. Box 150868
San Rafael, CA. 94915

Printed in the United States of America

ISBN 0-945946-14-7

Other books by Gurudas

*Flower Essences and Vibrational Healing*
*Gem Elixirs and Vibrational Healing*, Vol. I
*Gem Elixirs and Vibrational Healing, Vol II*
*The Spiritual Properties of Herbs*

# Table of Contents

# Acknowledgments

I would like to express my sincere gratitude to all the people who contributed to the writing of this book.

# Preface

I originally was drawn to write this book because of my years of involvement in alternative health. In the 1980s I founded and later sold Pegasus Products, Inc. a firm that produces and distributes flower essences, gem elixirs, and homeopathic remedies. I was also a health practitioner for some years and have written four book on alternative health. FDA abuses have become the norm, and gradually I came to understand how dangerous the federal government has become to our freedoms.

My purpose in writing this book is to awaken more people to the fact that these are very dangerous times for America. More and more of the rights we take for granted are being lost. Too many politicians have sold out to the special interests, and most people are too busy watching TV to notice or take responsibility for what is happening. In the name of stopping illegal drugs and crime our rights are gradually being forfeited, as the federal government tightens control over the people.

I have also written this book so that people can more easily look at the whole picture. I have focused my research on extracting information from hundreds of books, newspapers, and magazines so that people can more easily understand what is taking place in America. Some might say that several stories of government abuse that are heard in one part of the country don't appear too threatening. Yet when you look at many different incidents all across the country and grasp the full picture it is clear that something is very wrong.

# Chapter I

# Introduction

"In our country the lie has become not just a moral category, but a pillar of the state."

Alexander Solzhenitsyn

"Is life so dear, or peace so sweet, as to be purchased at the price of chains and slavery? Forbid it, Almighty God—I know not what course others may take; but as for me, give me liberty or give me death?"

Patrick Henry

America today exists in a twilight zone, not a democracy or a Republic but not yet a police state. America has become an elitist corporate oligarchy. We as a people clearly do not have the freedoms that the Founding Fathers had and that they envisioned for future generations. The many cases of government abuse described in this book are no longer rare or unique, they are increasingly the norm. Especially since the late 1960s, numerous American political activists have been murdered, maimed, framed, kidnapped, bombed, and spied on by government agents. We now have camouflaged police that look like terrorists, undercover police in the schools, curfews, roadblocks, urine tests, and informer networks. Government terrorism against the people continues to grow.

While I discuss the secret, or invisible government, that controls America, I also show how society is changing as the new world order dictatorship gradually takes hold. The cultural, economic, social, and political trends that are creating the new world order are discussed in detail. Over many years the large corporations have taken control of our society, and we are all worse off because of this. In the 1930s the banking/corporate elite attempted to establish a dictatorship while their agent Roosevelt was in power. Now, with an out-of-control intelligence community, the situation is more dangerous. Presidential edicts establish secret laws, while Congress has little say as federal power grows. The dictatorship of the new world order would be much worse than Nazi Germany and the Soviet Union, because the technology to control people is much more advanced today. The *U.S. News & World Report* was quite accurate to present an article on North Korea with a caption under a photo entitled new world order.[1] That type of extreme control is what awaits America.

Historians have shown that one reason Hitler took control in Germany was because people were too busy with their own personal and professional lives to get involved in politics. Many felt that if Hitler took power he would become a good German because his advisors would control him. By the time people awoke, it was too late. A former Berlin businessman "blamed his own group, people with the time and money and the opportunity to know better, for what happened to

Germany. We ignored Hitler. We considered him an unimportant fellow....We considered it just a bit vulgar to bother with him, to bother with politics at all."[2]

In certain respects America today is like Germany in the 1930s. In the later days of the Weimar government, key leaders were assassinated just as in America. George McGovern said, as in the Weimar period many people today are angry and distrust the government.[3] As happened in Germany we have turned away from our Constitution. Hitler introduced gun control just as is happening today. Our 1968 gun control law is taken almost word for word from the 1938 German gun control law. As in Germany there are people in America today trying to warn the public that we face a disastrous turn away from our heritage if the people don't wake up. Germany had a developed culture, so the people did not believe the warnings. In America we have a democratic heritage and people are uneducated as to what is happening to our society partly because of a corporate-controlled press. Most people quietly go about their professional and personal lives not understanding that our way of life is gravely threatened by the coming new world order.

Many readers will read this material and think it foolish to say a dictatorship is coming. Unfortunately, that cavalier attitude is one reason why a Republic can be lost. Daniel Webster said: "God grants liberty only to those who love it, and are always ready to guard and defend it." If every one sits back complacently who will protect the Republic? Edmund Burke said, "All that is necessary for the triumph of evil is that good men do nothing." Many issues discussed in this book are ignored by the national press. People need to get more involved and study what is really happening in America. *Newsweek* published a letter from someone after the congressional Ruby Ridge hearings who said: "It concerns me that people I had believed to be paranoid extremists and lunatics may actually have a point."[4]

When decent people are confronted by evil, it can be difficult for them to accept it. This is one reason why people find it difficult to accept conspiracies. A few years ago the Texas Attorney General visited the place where people had been sacrificed in satanic rituals. On national television, this official said he wouldn't believe it except that he had seen it. In World War II after the Soviet army captured Treblinka, one of the first major death camps to be overrun, Western reporters were brought in. They reported the gas chambers and mass killings to the West, but it wasn't initially believed. It was considered to be anti-Nazi propaganda because supposedly even the Nazis couldn't kill people like cattle. Indeed, normal people have a right to ask why should people so thirst for money and power. It can be a sickness that decent people cannot understand.

Some people who hear this information laugh or get very upset because it disturbs their perception of reality. If you only get news from the national media, this book will be quite shocking. The truth is so scary that many people don't want to confront it. Patrick Henry said: "It is natural for man to indulge in the illusions of hope. We are apt to shut our eyes against a painful truth....For my part, whatever anguish of spirit it may cost, I am willing to know the whole truth; to know the worst; and to provide for it."

In recent years millions of Americans have learned that special interest groups now control the political process and own this country. Various banking groups and business leaders, along with rogue elements in the military and intelligence communities behind the scenes, are the dominant special interest group in America. Many politicians are controlled by these people, sometimes without politicians even realizing it. With great power, unlimited funds, occasional threats, and numerous contacts, this elite force secretly controls many special interest groups which actually serve as front organizations. Second, just as many politicians have sold out to special interest groups, there is today in America a systematic avoidance, distortion, and suppression of news in the national media, which today is controlled by a handful of bankers and corporations allied to this corporate elite. While I often refer to corporations in this book, behind the large corporations are large banks. David M. Kotz said banks generally control the large U.S. corporations by exerting outside pressure, placing their representatives on the board of directors, or through stock ownership.[5]

One doesn't have to believe in the power of the banking groups to understand that a dictatorship is coming. The bankers and corporate elite in hundreds of books, articles, and speeches openly write of their plans to disarm the U.S. military and end our sovereignty, while creating a one world government led by the UN with a powerful new army. Much of this literature is discussed in this book. Consider the actions of the UN, various U.S. government agencies, current laws, and how they are being enforced against the people. Numerous presidential edicts often nullify the Constitution.

One of the scary things about this book is that much of the material contained here was obtained from reading various newspapers and magazines or by just watching television. Many of the things discussed in this book accurately portray in frightening detail a growing trend towards the future society depicted in *Brave New World* by Huxley and *1984* by Orwell. In December, 1978 in *The Futurist*, David Goodman listed 137 predictions made by George Orwell. Over 100 of them had already come true. Goodman said: "The possibility of Orwell's *1984* becoming reality...is clear....Though 1984 has failed as a warning, it has been succeeding brilliantly as a forecast." In recent years, especially in doing the research for this book, I have notice over and over again people asking "How could this happen in America?" It will keep on happening, unless we the people take back the government.

In recent years the press has released much shocking information. If I had written a book years ago just listing the many exposes released in shows like *60 Minutes* on how the government has abused its citizens, few people would have believed such things could happen in America! If I had written several years ago that thousands of Americans had been secretly exposed to radiation, including even plutonium, without their knowledge or consent and that some of these people were pregnant, who would have believed this. When this was reported in late 1993, some said this only occurred in dictatorships like the former Soviet Union. It is time to understand that, in many respects, we are already living in a dictatorship. It is just very sophisticated. As Rousseau said: "There is no subjugation so perfect as that which keeps the appearance of freedom, for in that way one captures volition itself." When you control what people think, without people even realizing this is being done, it is possible to control and transform a society without using force. We are all blinded by propaganda.

Over 400,000 people have had their assets forfeited, the majority without even being accused of a crime. Many lose their property after they are found innocent of a crime. Your assets are guilty until proven innocent. No free society would allow such laws. Prosecutors openly harass criminal attorneys, and there is increasingly harsh anti-crime legislation with an attempt to remove guns from the people in the phony war on drugs. Law enforcement agencies act with increased aggressiveness against all citizens.[6] The traditional rights of a juror have been greatly weakened, while surveillance cameras are becoming common. Millions of Americans were exposed to open air nuclear tests which the government said were quite safe knowing this was a lie. America today has one of the largest prison populations in the world, and all signs indicate that population will greatly expand in the next few years, with many new prisons now being built.

The contents of this book may be new to many. However, Americans increasingly understand the vast treason and corruption now taking place. It is just that the national media will rarely discuss these issues, or they are discussed in a very biased manner, so many readers will not appreciate how widespread is the discussion and understanding of these problems. What if the information in this book is true? What if only part of it is true? Isn't it time to stop blindly believing the propaganda we are fed in the national media, ignoring politics or just pressing the lever at the polling station concluding that you have fulfilled your responsibility as a citizen. The present dangerous state of affairs has taken place partly because we as citizens have shirked our responsibilities. We must all get involved in the political process if we are to reverse the overwhelming power of the federal government and Wall Street.

Last year I listened to a conservative radio announcer attack the conspiracy views of the Christic Institute and *The Secret Government* by Bill Moyer. What the announcer didn't add is that many on the right also strongly attack the national security apparatus and the hidden power of the banking groups. Pat Robertson in the *New World Order* is not the only conservative attacking these forces. When Pat Robertson and Bill Moyers can agree that our nation is today threatened by certain internal forces, this is one more sign that people should take a closer look at what is happening today. Over the months I read and found relevant information in conservative publications, such as *The American Spectator* and the *National Review*, and in progressive publications, such as *Z Magazine* and *In These Times*. This book is not meant to be liberal or conservative; it is meant to support restoring constitutional government.

Across the political spectrum there are voices trying to warn the people that the country is gravely threatened. Some, like Gore Vidal, Stewart Udall, and Bill Moyers, talk about the nefarious activities of the national security state. Noam Chomsky describes the one world government in various books and articles. Others, like Buckminister Fuller in *Critical Path*, present a broad history of how the invisible corporate government has long controlled and manipulated the people. People like William Domhoff and C. Wright Mills describe the elite that have long ruled America from behind the scenes. Barry Goldwater and Pat Robertson describe the dangerous activities of certain bank controlled groups. Christopher Lasch and Gerry Spence feel our constitutional form of government has been seriously weakened by the corporate elite.

All these people say there are powerful groups threatening our way of life. Some sources identify the bankers and corporate elite as the source of our problems, while others feel the national security state is the threat. The power of Wall Street is now obvious to many. So much is happening today that it is increasingly clear a police state is no longer some distant event to fear. The American people must awaken and join together to restore constitutional government and diminish the power of the large corporations and their agent, the federal government, so that we can again be a free people.

# Chapter II

# Freedom Is Being Lost

"The only maxim of a free government ought to be to trust no man living with power to endanger the public liberty."

John Adams

"We hold these truths to be self-evident, that all men are created equal, that they are endowed by their Creator with certain unalienable Rights....When a long train of abuses and usurpations, pursuing invariably the same Object evinces a design to reduce them under absolute Despotism, it is their right, it is their duty, to throw off such Government, and to provide new Guards for their future security."

Declaration of Independence

Right from the founding of the Republic, the people have been controlled and ruled by an elite group of wealthy people. As students of the Constitution are well aware, the constitutional convention was conducted by men of means, determined to protect themselves and their class from the people. This is why the Senate and president were elected by separate representatives to protect society from dangerous democratic impulses. Alexander Hamilton said: "It is admitted that you cannot have a good executive upon a democratic plan....The people, sir, are a great beast." John Quincy Adams said: the framers of the Constitution did not profess to be "slavish adorers of our sovereign lords the people." Most who attended the constitutional convention feared and distrusted the political involvement of the people. Some, like Benjamin Franklin, initially disliked the Constitution believing it cheated the people.

While the constitutional convention was held because of dissatisfaction with the Articles of Confederation, the greater inspiration was the growing Shays Rebellion. Farmers and townspeople were revolting against the increased tax burden and political repression by the ruling elite. "It is clear that Shays rebellion played an integral part of the genesis and formation of the U.S. Constitution."[1] James Madison said this rebellion "contributed more to that uneasiness which produced the Convention...than those...from the inadequacy of the Confederation." Delegates at the convention wanted a strong central government to weaken the local power of the common people and to promote commerce. John Jay, the first Chief Justice of the Supreme Court, said: "The people who own the country ought to govern it." The intention was to establish the rule of law, not the rule of the common people.[2]

The Constitution established America as a Republic, not a democracy. James Madison said: "The two great points of difference between a democracy and a Republic are the delegation of the government in the latter, to a small number of citizens elected by the rest; secondly, the greater number of citizens and greater sphere of country over which the latter may be extended." In 1828 Noah Webster's *Dictionary* defined a Republic as "A commonwealth: a state in which the exercise of the sovereign power is lodged in representatives elected by the people. In modern usage, it differs from a democracy or democratic state in which the people exercise the powers of sovereignty in person."

In a Republic the rights of all citizens are protected; in a democracy there is a danger of tyranny from the majority. A Republic exists under the rule of law, while a democracy is threatened by tyranny from the majority. Tocqueville said: "A democracy cannot exist as a permanent form of government. It can only exist until the voters discover that they can vote themselves largess from the public treasure. From that moment on, the majority always votes for the candidate promising the most benefits from the public treasury, with the result that a democracy collapses over loose fiscal policy...always followed by a dictatorship." We have a limited democracy, in that the people are today allowed to directly elect members of Congress and to serve as jurors and on a grand jury. However, those who today think we are a democracy, not a Republic, should remember that the "Pledge of Allegiance" is to the Republic, not to the democracy. The word democracy isn't even in the Constitution.

Last year I heard a radio speech by a president from the early 1920s. He called America a Republic; this was the first time I had heard a politician use this word to describe America. Today, as the people's rights are being replaced by false external trappings, we are constantly assured that America is a democracy. Before the New Deal, America was rarely referred to as a democracy. The Constitution, in Article IV, Section 4, says: "The U.S. shall guarantee in every State in this Union a Republican form of government...."

Many people were aware that the new Constitution was prepared by the ruling elite. This is partly why many felt the constitutional convention had gone too far. In Rhode Island, where small farmers controlled state politics, the proposed Constitution was passed out to the people and, unlike in other states, they were allowed to directly vote on it. The result was 237 for and 2,708 against the Constitution. Two states rejected the Constitution, and intense pressure including secrecy and deceit were used to ratify it. Delegates to the Pennsylvania legislature were dragged to the assembly by a mob and forced to vote. In most states the Constitution was approved because the state legislatures were from the ruling class. The *Federalist Papers* were written to ease the concerns of many, and some states ratified the Constitution with the understanding that a Bill of Rights would be added.

The Bill of Rights was not originally in the Constitution, partly because the delegates were not overly interested in protecting the people's right, and the federal government was to have very limited powers, so many felt it wasn't needed. Pennsylvania delegate James Wilson said there was no need for a federal Bill of Rights because the new federal government would only have the powers expressly delegated to it. Many felt that state sovereignty and each state's Bill of Rights would be sufficient to protect the people, because governing would mainly be done by state and local authorities.

The difference between people today and those in the Revolutionary War is that then the average person understood they were trading rule by England for rule by the moneyed interests. And the people weren't always willing to accept this new rule. This is partly why the Shays and Whisky rebellions took place. Taxes were only part of the problem, despite what historians claim. In contrast, today there is a myth that America is a democracy and there is no ruling elite, and until recently people have not been willing to defend their rights. In the 1930s the oppressive actions of the federal government would have caused riots in most cities if the people had been as determined as our forefathers to defend their rights.

The myth that America is a real democracy has existed for many years, partly because the people have enjoyed certain rights lacking in most nations. At the turn of the last century, Brooks Adams said the choice of the ruling class was to coerce or bribe the majority. Now the federal government is owned by the large corporations, and our rights are increasingly vanishing. Adam Smith in the *Wealth of Nations* warned that throughout history there are always forces attempting to control the people to gain increased wealth and power. Smith said governments must act to control these forces or there would be dreadful consequences. Smith identified the "merchants and manufacturers" as the "principle architects" of government policies that brought great harm to the English people. Max Weber warned: "The question is how are freedom and democracy in the long run possible at all under the domination of highly developed capitalism? Freedom and democracy are only possible where the resolute will of a nation not to allow itself to be ruled like sheep is permanently alive."

That so few people today participate in the political process is cause for great concern. Not only is there a vacuum in political leadership, but that void is being filled by a corporate elite with the ready approval of a controlled press. James Q. Wilson, past president of the American Political Science Association, said: "Elections have become less important, because the real policy-making is now done by courts, bureaucracies and legislatures operated by an ambitious political class with very little orientation towards public preferences." These people represent their own interests, not that of the people.[3] The very legitimacy of government is now at stake with so few people voting. People understand that they are no longer part of the decision-making process.

In the 20th century many people have discussed the ruling elite. Gaetano Mosca said: "All political regimes are of necessity ruled by...an organized minority controlling a disorganized majority....The first class, always the less numerous, performs all political functions, monopolizes power and enjoys the advantages that power brings, whereas the second, the more numerous class, is directed and controlled by the first, in a manner that is now more or less legal, now more or less arbitrary and violent." Noam Chomsky said in America "the specialized class are offered the opportunity to manage public affairs by virtue of their subordination to those with real power in our societies, dominant business interests....These ideas...have an unmistakable resemblance to the Leninist concept of a vanguard party that leads the masses to a better life that they cannot conceive or construct on their own...." Lippmann's specialized class and Lenin's vanguard of revolutionary intellectuals will lead the way to a better society, however many must be sacrificed along the way.[4]

Supposedly there must be the manufacture of consent because the elite cannot trust public opinion because only certain capable people can manage society. Harold Lasswell said when elites cannot use force to compel obedience, social managers must turn to "a whole new technique of control, largely through propaganda." We must acknowledge "the ignorance and stupidity (of)...the masses" and not succumb to "democratic dogmatism about men being the best judges of their own interests."

These doctrines "and others are entirely natural in any society in which power is narrowly concentrated but formal mechanisms exist by which ordinary people may, in theory, play some role in shaping their own affairs—a threat that plainly must be barred." America does have more freedom for the people than in other western societies "so the ignorant and stupid masses are more dangerous....As the state loses the capacity to control the population by force, privileged sectors must find other methods to ensure that the rascal multitude is removed from the public arena." The people "can be permitted, even encouraged, to ratify the decisions of their betters in periodic elections."[5]

Gerry Spence, one of America's most respected criminal lawyers, said: "In this country we embrace the myth that we are still a democracy when we know that we are not a democracy, that we are not free, that the government does not serve us but subjugates us. Although we give lip service to the notion of freedom, we know the government is no longer the servant of the people but, at last, has become the people's master...for the ultimate enemy of any people is not the angry hate groups that fester within, but a government itself that has lost its respect for the individual. The ultimate enemy of democracy is not the drug dealer or the crooked politician or the crazed skinhead. The ultimate enemy is the New King that has become so powerful it can murder its own citizens with impunity.[6]

"A new tyranny has cast its cold and ugly shadow over the nation, a nation where the rights of the people, criminals, and citizens alike exist mostly in myth, where the police have become the handmaidens of power, where trials have become mere window dressing and mockeries of justice, and where the corporations are left free to pillage and ravage the people with utter impunity....Entrapped in our concrete reservations, indentured to our corporate masters, impoverished of our land, separated from the earth, and at last placed at odds with nature herself, many no longer see the issue of freedom as relevant.[7]

"It is a tyranny supported by the people...,one that enslaves the people while it convinces the people they are free....We have delivered our power to our oppressors in exchange for their promise that we will be safe....We have accepted the myths of freedom as fact in the place of freedom itself. We love our servitude. But why not? It often feels as good as freedom and we can enjoy it without the risk that always accompanies the struggle for freedom."[8] Too many Americans are willing to give up their freedom to feel safe. We speak about our rights as long as we don't have to sacrifice for them. We are free as long as we don't too vehemently express our beliefs. Then we may be labeled a political activist, terrorist, or racist and paranoid extremist and may be harassed by the police.

William Greider said: "The decayed condition of American democracy is difficult to grasp....Symptoms of distress are accumulating freely in the political system and citizens are demoralized by the lack of coherent remedies....The things that Americans were taught and still wish to believe about self-government—the articles of civic faith we loosely call democracy—no longer seem to fit the present reality...American democracy is in much deeper trouble than most people wish to acknowledge. Citizens are cut out of politics surrounding the most important governing questions. The representative system has undergone a grotesque distortion of its original purpose." Instead of a real democracy, we get false promises and many new laws. The corporations control both political parties, and the people have become powerless in the political process. The elite decision makers are too cut off from the people to really understand or represent the people. "The mutual understanding between citizens and government necessary for genuine democracy is now deformed or neglected....A genuine democracy will not likely develop until the two realms are reconciled—the irregular citizens and the formal structure of power....Modern representation has assumed a different purpose—taking care of clients, not the larger public interest."[9]

According to Ferdinand Lundberg, "The general public in most instances is completely helpless because it is disorganized and very much at odds within itself—lacking knowledge, single-minded leadership and staying power. The national public must at all times also deal with many local and personal problems. It is, therefore, always easily defeated by determined entrenched interests."[10]

Lewis Lapham said: "In the name of making the world safe for democracy, the United States revised its own democratic traditions and constitutional principles. By presidential fiat and Defense Department decree, the newly appointed guarantors of the world's peace suppressed the turbulent and newly un-American habits of free speech....The government learned to define freedom as freedom for the state, not for the citizens. The national interest became the parochial interest of the ruling class, not the multifarious interests of the individuals subsumed under the rubric of 'the American people.' The question was one of how a government by the judicious few could best control and improve the instincts of the foolish many.[11]

"The Constitution was made for the uses of the individual...and the institutions of American government were meant to support the liberties of the people, not the ambitions of the state. It was the law that had to give way to the citizen's freedom of thought and action, not the citizen's freedom of thought and action that had to give way to the law." Today, "the government reserves to itself unenumerated powers and seeks to limit the freedoms of the individual to a list of enumerated rights. The increasingly punitive uses and interpretations of the law support the ambitions of the state, not the liberties of the people."[12] Gore Vidal said: "Political decadence occurs when the forms that a state pretends to observe are known to be empty of all meaning. Who does not publicly worship the Constitution? Who, in practice, observes it at all? Congress has only two great powers under the Constitution: the power to declare war and the power of the purse."[13] Both have been largely lost to the national security state and the corporations.

As Charles Beard demonstrated in *Economic Basis of Politics*, our Constitution is firmly based on private economic interests. The Framers saw their task as preserving liberty, but they also wanted to protect property rights as basic to liberty. Widespread ownership of land gave people an economic stake in their freedom and in the system. The Founders were concerned with property rights and abstract rights because they wanted to protect "the real rights of real people." The Founders felt that along with a separation of powers in society, if a Republic was based on commerce and industry, it would be easier to prevent a tyranny of the majority. And it would be easier to achieve material gain in such a Republic, so the people would be more satisfied.[14]

However, increased use of maritime or commercial law has encroached upon constitutional and common law. Corporations attained rights but not the responsibilities of citizens. Corporate welfare became more important than citizen's rights. The corporate elite appointed their representatives, the lawyers and judges, to flood the country with thousands of complex laws, often too long for even Congress to read or understand. Gradually, judges enforced these laws and forgot about the Constitution and common law. Today government is controlled by the large corporations, and federal tyranny is growing. When our Republic was founded, wealth was tied to assets like property, and even the wealthy were generally cash poor. Everyone benefited from a good infrastructure. Today wealth is more purely monetary and can easily be moved between nations. Wealth is no longer tied to what also benefits the people. This is partly why the ruling elite has turned against the people.

Perhaps the greatest blessing of the Declaration of Independence, Constitution, and Bill of Rights is the recognition that people have natural rights that come from God; they are not delegated by the government. William Blackstone said: "This law of nature being coeval with mankind, and dictated by God himself is, of course, superior in obligation to any other....No human laws are of any validity if contrary to this...." Thus the power of a government must be limited, which was a fundamental principle of the Founders. The state was to respect and not interfere with the free exercise of natural rights.

In more recent years certain natural rights, like the right to property, are ending as the asset forfeiture laws seize people's assets, often when people aren't even charged with a crime. In addition, the state now grants the people many rights such as in the welfare state. Instead of being a passive observer that did not grant or even interfere with people's rights, the government has created and granted rights such as providing food and housing. For millions addicted to government support, all needs are provided by the state, which greatly increased government power because the state needed many new laws and regulations to fulfill its new obligations to the people. If the government has the power to grant rights, it will inevitably limit those rights and commit crimes against the people as we see today. What a government grants, it can take away. Citizens have the legal and moral right to resist unjust laws. This is why the right to jury nullification was widely accepted for over 100 years before the founding of the Republic. People have a right and duty when on a jury to reject unjust laws.

While it may be possible to improve the Constitution, I do not attack it, especially since the Bill of Rights was added. I agree with the Founders, like Benjamin Franklin, who felt that by establishing a Republic with a Bill of Rights they were also protecting the people's rights. The problem is not the Constitution, it is the nature of the human condition. Thucydides said: "Of the Gods we believe, and of men we know, that by a necessary law of their nature they rule wherever they can." Most communist nations had a Constitution with clauses protecting human rights. Such words had little value. Our Constitution will only work if the people actively strive to protect their rights and if the rule of law prevails. If the large corporations aren't soon stopped, our Republic will one day become a distant memory. Already most Americans think we are a democracy when, in fact, we are a Republic. The Republic should be reestablished with democratically-orientated institutions.

# Chapter III

# The Secret Government

"I sincerely believe...that banking establishments are more dangerous than standing armies."
Thomas Jefferson

"For what is a man profited, if he shall gain the whole world, and lose his own soul? Or what shall a man give in exchange for his soul?"
Matthew 16:26

Many books written by political and social scientists describe the corporate elite. While many consider America a pluralist society, too many well-researched books, such as *Who Rules America Now?* by G. William Domhoff and *The Power Elite* by C. Wright Mills, have shown that there is a cohesive upper class ruling America, a power elite consisting especially of corporate executives which dominates public policy, the electorial process, and government through numerous organizations and the expertise of foundations and think-tanks. These political scientists do not speak of conspiracies; yet what they write is often similar to what many on the right and left say about the corporate elite that controls America. Domhoff and many others have presented considerable evidence about the power and influence of the Trilateral Commission (TC) and Council on Foreign Relations (CFR) over our lives.

*FDR My Exploited Father-In-Law*, by C.B. Dall is a very important book because it provides an inside look at how certain people have controlled our political destiny throughout the 20th century. Dall describes how the corporate elite ruthlessly advance their objectives at the people's expense, grooming phony politicians, creating wars and then phony peace treaties to mislead the public. Dall said CFR control of our political destiny had created a "subtle dictatorship by the few." Dall called people like Colonel House, a key aide to President Wilson, "early one-worlders." Bernard Baruch guided Wilson, "leading him like one would a poodle on a string." Before Wilson could become a presidential candidate he had to support establishing the Federal Reserve, the direct election of senators, introduce the income tax, follow orders if a war started in Europe, and follow recommendations for cabinet posts. Dall called Baruch the number one political operative behind FDR. For some time Dall was confused by FDR's policies, but he came to understand that "Most of his (FDR's) thoughts, his political 'ammunition,' as it were, was carefully manufactured for him in advance by the CFR-One-World Money group." Gradually, Dall became rather dismayed at these events, because FDR supported the one worlders and the "UN hoax."[1] As R. Buckminister Fuller has also noted, the push for world government is a poison that has quietly existed among the ruling elite throughout the 20th century.

FDR's son Elliott Roosevelt wrote *The Conservators* in which he declared: "There are within our world perhaps only a dozen organizations which shape the courses of our various destinies as rigidly as they regularly constituted governments....The impact of their decisions reach...into every home and office building in the modern world." These groups are "the creme de la creme of global planners." Roosevelt proceeded to describe the elite groups discussed in this book.[2] On August 23, 1993 Christopher Hitchens, the writer and Oxford friend of Clintons, on C-Span said: "It is, of course, the case that there is a ruling class in this country, and that it has allies internationally." On August 28, 1994 Cokie Roberts said on ABC's *This Week With David Brinkley* that "Global bankers are really running the world."

Just as we now have one national political party with two branches, we have a secret government divided into four factions. The ruling faction includes the superrich, corporate and bank leaders, foundation heads, European aristocracy, and certain managers. The managers are often brilliant and ambitious people with few morals. These people generally belong to the TC, CFR, and the Bilderbergers. The secret government primarily includes the elites of Europe and America, although in recent years elites, from other regions have joined the corporate front groups discussed below. George Seldes said: "If it is true that money prevails in national and state elections, then it must also be true that the men who put up the money, the handful including the Du Ponts, Pews, Mellons, Rockefellers and others...also control our political life, our Congress, and the Presidency itself. A conspiracy of silence has always existed on this subject."[3] In the July 26, 1936 *New York Times* Joseph Kennedy, father of the future president, said: "Fifty men have run America, and that's a high figure." The second faction includes those in the national security state. The bankers and corporate elite are slightly more captivated by money, while the rogue military/intelligence groups are more drawn to power. The bankers and large corporations comprise the dominant force in control of the secret government. All CIA heads have been CFR members.

These factions form an extremely powerful special interest group determined to destroy the Constitution and establishing a one world government. People in this group created World Wars I and II and many other conflicts in this century. Human life has no meaning to these people. Remember, only a few people around Hitler really understood his plans; yet consider the destruction that resulted. From this group come the dedicated fanatics determined to kill however many people it takes to establish the planned world dictatorship. It is difficult to put into words just how ruthless these people are. There are probably no more than several hundred people actually directing events. These people are supported by dedicated operatives including hit squads and people in the local, state, and federal police who carry out orders. Many of these operatives understand that a police state is planned, but they do not understand the ramifications and details.

The execution of President Kennedy shows the determination of these fanatics. Fletcher Prouty, former officer in the Defense Intelligence Agency and author of *The Secret Team*, said the assassination of JFK was the work of the "Secret Team," an elite group that operates behind the scenes inside and outside the government. While in the service, Prouty served as liaison officer between the Pentagon and the CIA. He said since World War II "more and more control over military and diplomatic operations at home and abroad" was assumed by elites "whose activities are secret, whose budget is secret, whose very identities as often as not are secret...." He also said this group has always controlled the CIA.

In *High Treason*, members of the "Secret Team," or "The Club," were identified as some of the wealthiest and most powerful people in America. "The Secret Team runs the U.S., and to a large extent, they have circumvented the Constitution. They are highly suspicious of the democratic process, and they have consistently tried to control and manipulate elections." These people felt that Kennedy threatened their power. "The Secret Team did things to each President to make him understand that the power did not lie with the Presidency. His mandate may come from the people, but the power—and policy making—came from outside, from this shadow government....John Kennedy's murder was an example to all who followed, telling them to toe the line, and to do as they were told....Flag waving, super-patriotism, defense and 'national security' was the cover for these men to enrich themselves and entrench themselves in power. This Club, a loosely knit, informal organization, has gradually established a shadow government with a secret, institutionalized covert action capability outside the official government."[4]

The third faction of the secret government are the utopian dreamers or idealists who use slogans like "world peace through world law." Here are the scholars and think-tank experts and many members of the World Federalist Association (WFA). I once heard two such people being interviewed. They were smug in their belief that the nation state must end. Some of these people understand that many will die to create a world government, but they accept this as a necessary transition stage. Some in this faction have deluded themselves into believing that this new society will help the people. This may be from a sense of superiority that they, as the elite, know what is best for the people or from a belief that one world government will prevent war, promote peace, protect the environment, and raise the people's standard of living. History has shown that there are always some utopian dreamers who delude themselves into presenting a grandiose totalitarian scheme such as communism to improve or save humanity. Behind these dreamers always lurk those determined to enhance their power and wealth however many people must be killed along the way.

The fourth faction of the secret government includes opportunists who don't really care what a new world order means, but they believe that joining groups like the CFR provides career advancement, prestige, contacts and a means to earn more money. These members give the secret planners another layer of protection and respectability. Many CFR members in the media are in this category. Carroll Quigley, a professor and former teacher of President Clinton, wrote *Tragedy and Hope: A History of the World in Our Time*, describing in 1,348 pages the behind-the-scenes influence of bankers like the Morgans, Rothschilds, and Rockefellers.[5] Quigley, the official biographer of the CFR, said there was an inner circle who directed things, partly by manipulating a larger, outer circle through persuasion, patronage, and social pressure. C.B. Dall said: "Few members of the CFR know the long-range plans of its small top-management group."[6] While membership in these organizations doesn't mean there is monolithic servitude to the objectives as set forth by the leadership, all members of the groups described in this chapter support certain objectives like world government, NAFTA, and GATT.

However much money and power these people obtain, it is never enough. It is difficult for normal people to understand the deep insecurity in those promoting the new world order. In 1776 Benjamin Franklin wrote: "Sir, there are two passions which have a powerful influence on the affairs of men...the love of power and the love of money....When united in view of the same object, they have in many minds the most violent effects." The *Bible* warns: "For the love of money is the root of all evil...."[7] The drive to control people for money and power is relentless. Disagreements sometimes occur in these factions, but arguments are settled behind the scenes. Such disagreements are usually based on the means, not on the end goal of world domination and greater wealth. However, there are also communist and Catholic factions pushing plans for world domination that are in sharp agreement with the corporate plan for a world government

In speaking about the plans of the secret government, one is describing treason. A second, often unrelated factor is the vast corruption that has overtaken America because the rule of money has replaced the rule of law. Organized gangs steal whatever they can, usually with no participation by the secret government, although there may be an occasional alliance as for example when the CIA and mafia raided certain banks during the S&L scandal. As Ambrose Evans Pritchard, the Washington, D.C. based reporter for the London *Telegraph*, said there is so much corruption in America that it is now like many third world countries he has reported from. A third factor to consider is the bureaucracy and the slow but inevitable growth of government. Those who want the federal government to dominate all aspects of our lives are adept at using the bureaucracy to assist in achieving their goals. In *The Twilight of Democracy*, released in 1995, Patrick Kennon, a former CIA official, said democracy "has become marginal as a system of government" so we should turn to bureaucratic experts.

Some may ask why there is little information about the secret government in the press if they really rule America. It is because the corporate elite owns the national media. Many books like *None Dare Call It Treason* and *None Dare Call It Conspiracy*[8] list the owners of the national media in the CFR and TC. The interaction of the press, intelligence community, government, and our corporate masters is exemplified by the career of Leslie Gelb. In 1984, the *Washington Post*, and then the *New York Times*, said *New York Times* reporter Leslie Gelb had cooperated with the CIA during the Carter administration in 1978 to recruit reporters in Europe to publish stories that would encourage people to support development of the neutron bomb. Gelb worked in the State and Defense Departments under Johnson and Carter. Today he is president of the CFR.

Over the years the national media has issued brief reports on the corporate elite acknowledging their influence. In the September 1, 1961 issue of the *Christian Science Monitor*, the CFR was described as "probably one of the most influential, semipublic organizations in the field of foreign policy....It has staffed almost every key position of every administration since FDR." In a May 1962 article in *Esquire*, Richard H. Rovere said: "The directors of the CFR make up a sort of Presidium for that part of the Establishment that guides our destiny as a nation." On November 21, 1971, Anthony Lukas said, in the *New York Times*, "For the last three decades American foreign policy has remained largely in the hands of men—the overwhelming majority of them Council members (CFR) ....One of the most remarkable aspects of this remarkable organization...is how little is known about it outside a narrow circle of East Coast insiders." On October 30, 1993, the *Washington Post* assured us that the CFR is in charge and all is well. A column by CFR member Richard Harwood acknowledged that many government leaders are in the CFR and this organization manages foreign affairs and the military-industrial complex. Harwood said 10 percent of the CFR now come from the media, and he listed key people in the national media who are CFR members.[9]

Quigley described the early influence of Cecil Rhodes in establishing certain secret societies, usually called Round Table organizations in various countries. Rhodes also established Rhodes scholarships for people to attend Oxford University. The groups kept in touch through correspondence, visits, and the quarterly magazine, *The Round Table*, which was established in 1910. In 1919 the Royal Institute of International Affairs (Chatham House) was founded in London. They controlled many university chairs and newspapers like *The Times* of London and *The Observer*. On December 14, 1992 Christopher Hitchens in *The Nation* described how the Rhodes alumni work together as part of a ruling elite. Many of these people became very influential in government.

With a British perspective A.K. Chesterton, in *The New Unhappy Lords*, described how the secret government has dominated the major events of the 20th century. Chesterton first learned of the secret government in England when, as a journalist, he discovered that they could bring people from throughout the world to London to attend conferences during World War II. Even the British government couldn't do this. The CFR, established in 1921, was an outgrowth of this early British influence. From the start the CFR controlled The *New York Times, Herald Tribune, Christian Science Monitor*, and *Washington Post*. Controlling the national media was always understood to be crucial.

According to Quigley, "There does exist, and has existed for a generation, an international Anglophile network which operates, to some extent, in the way the radical Right believes the Communists act. In fact, this network, which we may identify as the Round Table Groups, has no aversion to cooperating with the Communists, or any other groups and frequently does so. I know of the operations of this network because I have studied it for twenty years and was permitted for two years, in the early 1960's, to examine its papers and secret records. I have no aversion to it or to most of its aims....In general my chief difference of opinion is that it wishes to remain unknown, and I believe its role in history is significant enough to be known.[10]

"The powers of financial capitalism had another far-reaching aim, nothing less than to create a world system of financial control in private hands able to dominate the political system of each country and the economy of the world as a whole. This system was to be controlled in a feudalist fashion by the central banks of the world acting in concert, by secret agreements arrived at in frequent private meetings and conferences." The privately owned Bank of International Settlements in Basle, Switzerland played a key role in this interaction of central banks. "The growth of financial capitalism made possible a centralization of world economic control and a use of this power for the direct benefit of financiers and the indirect injury of all other economic groups."[11]

In his next book, *The Anglo American Establishment*, Quigley had trouble finding a publisher. His first book was withdrawn after 9,000 copies were sold, despite its popularity, and the negatives were destroyed. The corporate controllers were displeased with what Quigley revealed. In this new book Quigley said: "It is not easy for an outsider to write the history of a secret group of this kind, but...it should be done, for this group is...one of the most important historical facts of the twentieth century." Quigley admitted "In this group were persons whose lives have been a disaster to our way of life." The front cover of this book shows the U.S. flag upside down which has long been a sign of distress. The cover also shows the U.S. flag inside the British flag. For decades England has controlled the U.S. far more than people understand.

The corporate elite hoped to establish a world government using the League of Nations, but this failed partly because the U.S. wouldn't join that organization. Colonel Edward House helped establish the CFR, and in *Philip Dru*, he said his goal was for "socialism as dreamed of by Karl Marx." The book described a "conspiracy" to capture both political parties and use them to create a socialist world government. The plan included electing a president by using "deception regarding his real opinions and intentions." Written in 1912, the book called for a graduated income tax and establishing a state-controlled central bank. These laws were passed in 1913, and many other goals outlined in the book also became reality. House called for a one-world government, one-world army, and one-world economy ruled by an Anglo-Saxon financial oligarchy with a dictator served by a 12 man council. Our Constitution would be greatly changed. President Roosevelt wrote Colonel House on November 23, 1933 "The real truth of the matter is, as you and I know, that a financial element in the large centers has owned the government ever since the days of (President) Andrew Jackson—and I am not wholly excepting the Administration of W.W. (Woodrow Wilson). The country is going through a repetition of Jackson's fight with the Bank of the U.S.—only on a far bigger and broader basis."[12]

The CFR is based in New York with a branch in Washington, D.C. In recent years it has grown to over 3,000 members. David Rockefeller was chairman of the board from 1970-1985, and Henry Kissinger is a prominent member. The 1952 CFR annual report said its members sometimes suspend their membership when they join the government, and the Reece congressional investigation said there were secret CFR members. As suggested by the writings of its members, its goal is to condition the people to rely on government as the solution to all problems and to pull the country into a one world government directed by the UN. The CFR position of promoting free trade and a world government controlled by the elites of the U.S., Europe, and Japan with limited democracy is well expressed in *The Management of Interdependence: A Preliminary View*, by Miriam Camps.

The CFR has dominated U.S. foreign policy and the State Department for decades through its publications, meetings, and private study groups. Kraft, in a July, 1958 *Harpers* article, said its study groups played a key role in shaping the UN charter. Weekly in the news, CFR experts discuss foreign affairs as guest experts. Rear Admiral Chester Ward, a CFR member for 16 years, said: "Once the ruling members of the CFR have decided that the U.S. Government should adopt a particular policy, the very substantial research facilities of CFR are put to work to develop arguments, intellectual and emotional, to support the new policy, and to confound and discredit, intellectually and politically, any opposition."[13] Just recently a CFR panel proposed ending a 19-year policy that prevented the press from working for the CIA, and this is probably what will happen. The CFR announces policy and the U.S. government follows orders.[14]

"The most powerful clique in these elitist groups have one objective in common—they want to bring about the surrender of the sovereignty and the national independence of the U.S." They want to end national boundaries and racial and ethnic loyalties, supposedly to increase business and ensure world peace. What they strive for would inevitably lead to dictatorship and loss of freedoms by the people. The CFR was founded for "the purpose of promoting disarmament and submergence of U.S. sovereignty and national independence into an all-powerful one-world government....This lust to surrender the sovereignty and independence of the U.S. is pervasive throughout most of the membership...."[15]

FBI Bureau File 62-5256 shows that the FBI has investigated the CFR several times since 1931 especially for Nazi and communist activities. CFR headquarters is near the old Soviet Embassy to the UN. Obtained through a Freedom of Information Act request, the 371-page file, with 336 pages released, had 263 instances of censoring. The record shows that, starting with Roosevelt, various presidents have blocked FBI investigations of the CFR citing national defense. It is quite unusual for a president to intervene in such investigations, and this is one more sign of the CFR's power. Over the years two ex-FBI agents have written books strongly attacking the CFR for its treasonous activities. Dan Smoot wrote *The Invisible Government*, and W. Cleon Skousen wrote *The Naked Capitalist*. Ted Gunderson and other ex-FBI agents also strongly attack CFR activities. Days after Hoover started another major investigation of the CFR, he died mysteriously. His successor, Patrick Gray III, started another investigation of the CFR, and he was forced to resign eight days after receiving detailed information about a CFR conspiracy against the U.S. government. The next FBI director, Clarence Kelley, was a CFR member. On March 15, 1974 he lied and wrote to Senator Hartke that the FBI had never investigated the CFR.[16]

The Trilateral Commission was established in 1973 by David Rockefeller after he read Zbigniew Brzezinski's book, *Between Two Ages*, which praised socialism and said the U.S. is becoming obsolete so we should join a one world government. National sovereignty was no longer a viable concept. The U.S. Constitution should be rewritten while the existing federal system of having sovereign states was no longer necessary. He called for an alliance among North America, Western Europe, Japan, and ultimately, the communist countries. He said: "Marxism represents a further vital and creative stage in the maturing of man's universal vision....Though Stalinism may have been a needless tragedy for both the Russian people and communism as an ideal, there is the intellectually tantalizing possibility that for the world at large it was...a blessing in disguise."[17]

These were strange words for a man who became President Carter's National Security Advisor; however, this was magic to David Rockefeller. He hired Brzezinski to direct the TC and brought in Carter as well. Comrade Rockefeller in 1972 made the remarkable statement: "The social experiment in China under Chairman Mao's leadership is one of the most important and successful in human history."[18] Over 60 million Chinese died in Mao's experiment. Based in New York City, the TC has several hundred members from Western Europe, Japan, Canada, and the U.S. with a goal of fostering closer cooperation among these regions to establish a global government.

The TC published *The Crisis of Democracy*, which claimed there was a crisis and excess of democracy because citizens had become too politically active. The democratic surge had created a "democratic distemper....A pervasive spirit of democracy may pose an intrinsic threat and undermine all forms of association, weakening the social bonds which hold together family, enterprise, and community....An excess of democracy means a deficit in governability...." Thus there was a need to restrain the American people. It was deemed necessary to protect the elites and restore a more equitable relationship between government authority and the people. Since the media had become too critical of government policy, there was a need to restrict freedom of the press and change the way officials are elected in order to weaken the people's influence.[19]

The Bilderberg group was founded in 1954 in Europe. According to TC-approved sources, its first meeting in 1954 was financed by the CIA.[20] It has an annual meeting, usually in Europe, and the Rothschilds play a major role in its affairs. In 1990 *American Hegemony and the Trilateral Commission*, by Stephen Gil, explained the activities of the TC and the Bilderbergers. Many members are in the European aristocracy, while American members are often also in the CFR. Its 1995 meeting in Switzerland was guarded by the Swiss army, which is strange for a private group. A recent member is William Kristol, editor of Rupert Murdocks' *Weekly Standard*. A relative unknown Kristol suddenly became an expert on many talk shows. When Kristol speaks he often represents the Bilderberg group. After Dole won the nomination, Kristol attacked him in the *Weekly Standard* because the Bilderberg group wants Clinton reelected. Kristol should register as a foreign lobbyist.

In a private June, 1991 Bilderberg meeting David Rockefeller said: "We are grateful to the *Washington Post*, the *New York Times*, *Time* magazine, and other great publications whose directors have attended our meetings and respected their promise of discretion for almost forty years....It would have been impossible for us to develop our plan for the world if we had been subject to the bright lights of publicity during those years. But the world is now more sophisticated and prepared to march towards a world government. The supernational sovereignty of an intellectual elite and world bankers is surely preferable to the national auto-determination practiced in past centuries."

The Carnegie Endowment for International Peace (CEIP) is another corporate group. Officially it is another Washington think-tank. For several years it was directed by Alger Hiss, the former senior State Department official found guilty of perjury for denying he'd copied government papers for the Soviet Union. And Councils on World Affairs groups exist in many cities across the U.S. Allied to the CFR and the State Department, these groups hold lectures to promote an international outlook.

There is also the World Federalist Association (WFA) based in Washington, D.C., which was previously called the United World Federalists, with members like Ronald Reagan and George Bush. Founded in 1947 its membership has dwindled to around 9,000 from a peak of 40,000 in the 1950s. Unlike the other corporate fronts, this group has openly called for immediate world government. One of its early brochures, *Beliefs, Purposes, Policies*, said its aim was to "create a world federal government with authority to enact, interpret and enforce world law adequate to maintain peace....World law should be enforceable directly upon individuals." Nations in a world government should have no right of secession, direct taxes should be paid by individuals, and there should be a world police force with nations being disarmed except for light arms to deal with internal matters.

The first WFA head Cord Meyer, Jr., who later became a senior CIA official, in 1947, wrote *Peace or Anarchy*, in which he called for a world government, full national disarmament, and a UN army that controlled all nuclear weapons. If a nation attempted to overthrow the UN, it would be crushed. The sovereign-nation state was called the great threat to peace, and individual citizens must submit themselves to world law and UN courts. The cold war required "total preparedness" which meant "totalitarianism for American citizens....This brutalization of life must be extended even to the control of the mind. Propaganda will be substituted for fact, and official ideology will supplant the free search for truth. Every source of public information...must be perverted. Those who dissent will (ultimately) face arrest."[21]

The journal, *Foreign Affairs*, with a circulation of 115,000, is the mouthpiece of the CFR. Over the years it has introduced important new foreign policies that became official U.S. government policy. For instance, George Kennan's containment of communism and Richard Nixon's position about reopening relations with Communist China were first announced in this journal. The journal, *Foreign Policy*, is published by the CEIP, while the quarterly, *World Federalist*, is published by the WFA. Also, if you want to see what is planned for our future, read *Futurist* magazine. From describing a cashless society to implants to control people, this publication reveals much.

These organizations have interlocking members with a common goal of establishing a one world government by dividing the world into three regions: Europe, North and South America, and the Pacific Union under the UN. Members comes from the economic, political, charitable, media, religious, educational, and academic elites. A recent book, *Who's Who of the Elite* by Robert G. Ross, Sr., lists most members in these groups.

Every administration since 1920 has included members of the CFR which has dominated the federal government, especially the Departments of Defense, State, and Treasury, since World War II. Thomas Dewey, the Republican presidential candidate in 1944 and 1948, was a CFR member as was Eisenhower, Nixon, Bush, Stevenson, Kennedy, Humphrey, and McGovern. Over 70 of Kennedy's appointments were members of these organizations. At the end of *None Dare Call It Conspiracy*, by Gary Allen, is a list of 110 members of the CFR Nixon appointed to his regime. Most key officials in Carter's administration were members of these groups, while Bush had 380 CFR members in his government. Clinton is a member of the CFR and TC. The May 21, 1995 *Arkansas Democrat Gazette* discussed Clinton's attending the 1991 Bilderberger convention and his alignment with Rockefeller. Over 80 percent of the heads of the federal government executive branches since World War II have been members of these groups.

CFR members in Clinton's regime include Secretary of State Christopher, Secretary of Interior Bruce Babbitt, Secretaries of Treasury Lloyd Bentsen and Robert Rubin, Secretary of Health and Human Services Donna Shalala, Secretary of Housing and Urban Development Henry Cisneros, Deputy Secretary of State Strobe Talbott, Under Secretary for Political Affairs Peter Tarnoff, Assistant Secretary of State for East Asian and Public Affairs Winston Lord, National Security Advisor Anthony Lake, UN Ambassador Madeleine Albright, recent CIA Director James Woolsey and current CIA head John Deutch (also in TC), Council of Economic Advisors Chairman Laura Tyson, and White House Science Advisor John Gibbons. This is only a partial list.

Former House speaker Foley and present House speaker Newt Gingrich, as well as former Senate majority leader George Mitchell, and former House majority leader Gephardt are members of the CFR, as are Supreme Court justices Stephen Breyer, Sandra O'Connor, and Ruth Ginsburg. Breyer and Ginsburg were only two of three U.S. Circuit Court of Appeals judges in the CFR. This nation of about 255 million people is more than capable of producing many dedicated public servants outside these elite groups yet they continue to dominate the government and the press rarely discusses this.[22]

Over the decades many heads of state and leaders of international organizations like NATO and the World Bank visit CFR headquarters in New York. In 1990 Nelson Mandela visited the CFR, as did Yeltsin soon after. Jean-Bertrand Aristide of Haiti gave a speech at the CFR on September 25, 1991. In 1995, when Castro visited New York, he promptly went to CFR headquarters to meet corporate leaders. U.S. foreign policy has been manipulated for decades to promote world government.

Leaders of various governments understand where real power resides, so representatives of the secret government are allowed to intervene in world affairs. In April, 1994 a private group led by Henry Kissinger and Lord Carrington, the former British Foreign Secretary, went to South Africa with "some private citizens" to settle things. Officially the mission was not labeled a success; however, shortly after this visit Chief Buthelezi finally agreed to bring his party into the electorial process, and peaceful elections took place with a transition of governments. In the spring of 1994, Selig Harrison from the CEIP visited North Korea to mediate the quarrel over North Korea obtaining nuclear arms. In mid-June, 1994 former President Carter also visited North Korea. In December, 1994 Rep. Richardson, another CFR member, visited North Korea. Even the North Koreans understand who really controls America, so they are willing to meet corporate representatives. Richardson went to Burma, and the imprisoned Burmese leader Aung San Suu Kyi was soon released. He also visited Iraq, and brought home two imprisoned Americans. Journalists like Cokie Roberts wondered in amazement how Richardson was so effective! In July, 1995 Kissinger met with senior U.S. and Chinese officials to improve the worsening relations.

*National Security and the U.S. Constitution* declared that "post-World War II and pre-Vietnam foreign policy operated in the context of an establishment consensus, brokered by major East Coast diplomatic and financial figures active in the CFR."[23] In 1994 Clinton said he would renew the most-favored trade status for China without tying it to human rights concerns. Shortly before this announcement, the TC released Triangle Paper number 45 "An Emerging China in a World of Interdependence" urging that China be allowed into existing regional organizations and be involved in security matters. If you want to learn what is in store for U.S. foreign policy, read CFR and TC reports.

The great danger to our Republic is that the traitors, although small in numbers, are a dedicated, well-financed, and well-organized group of utterly ruthless fanatics with no morals, who will use any method to establish a world government police state. While this is happening, most people ignore the evidence and watch football. This is how the communists and Nazis took control. In the 20th century, some have understood this danger.

John F. Hylan, Mayor of New York City, said on March 26, 1922: "The real menace of our Republic is the invisible government which like a giant octopus sprawls its slimy length over our city, state, and nation. Like the octopus of real life, it operates under cover of a self-created screen....It seizes in its long and powerful tentacles our executive officers, our legislative bodies, our schools, our courts, our newspapers, and every agency created for the public protection....At the head of this octopus are the Rockefeller-Standard Oil interests and a small group of powerful banking houses generally referred to as the international bankers. (They) virtually run the U.S. government for their own selfish purposes. They practically control both parties, write political platforms, make catspaws of party leaders, use the leading men of private organizations, and resort to every device to place in nomination for high public office only such candidates as will be amenable to the dictates of corrupt big business. They connive at centralization of government on the theory that a small group of hand-picked, privately controlled individuals in power can be more easily handled than a larger group among whom there will most likely be men sincerely interested in public welfare."[24]

In 1954 Senator Jenner said: "Today the path to total dictatorship in the U.S. can be laid by strictly legal means, unseen and unheard by Congress, the President, or the people....We have a well-organized political-action group in this country, determined to destroy our Constitution and establish a one-party state....The important point to remember about this group is not its ideology but its organization. It is a dynamic, aggressive, elite corps, forcing its way through every opening, to make a breach for a collectivist one-party state. It operates secretly, silently, continuously to transform our Government without suspecting that change is under way....If I seem to be extremist, the reason is that this revolutionary clique cannot be understood, unless we accept the fact that they are extremist. It is difficult for people governed by reasonableness and morality to imagine the existence of a movement which ignores reasonableness and boasts of its determination to destroy, which ignores morality, and boasts of its cleverness in outwitting its opponents by abandoning all scruples. This ruthless power-seeking elite is a disease of our century....This group...is answerable neither to the President, the Congress, nor the courts. It is practically irremovable." The senator's two page speech should be read by every American.[25] Over the decades, many in Congress have attacked the power of the secret government.

In 1953 and 1954 the Reece Committee investigated the tax-exempt foundations and their relationship to left-wing groups. At that time Congress said CFR "productions are not objective but are directed overwhelmingly at promoting the globalistic concept." The CFR had become "in essence an agency of the U.S. government...carrying its internationalist bias with it." However, little changed and the investigation soon ended, because the foundations were too powerful. These foundations work together supporting common goals like transforming education, supporting the UN, and supporting foreign aid to promote the new world order. Ford Foundation chairman John J. McCloy was also chairman of the Chase Manhattan Bank and the CFR. The Ford, Rockefeller, and Carnegie Foundations and others were established to restore the reputations of big bankers and large corporations which were criticized harshly before World Wars I and II. They also avoided paying taxes while taking others' money as they attained great power and influence.[26]

In 1958 Rene Wormser the general counsel of the Reece Committee wrote *Foundations: Their Power and Influence* revealing how the tax-exempt foundations were used by the corporate elite to secretly shape and influence American life through social manipulation and political power. From research grants to universities to influence in government these foundations are an unchecked power that is "interlocking and self-perpetuating." The author said more public control should be exerted over how these foundations spend their money, and they should be banned from participating in political activities. Public trustees should be required in foundations, courts should examine their activities, and some foundations should lose their tax-exempt status.[27]

Certain popular books contributed to attacks on the corporate rulers. *None Dare Call It Treason* by John Stormer and *None Dare Call It Conspiracy* by Gary Allen sold millions of copies. Both books described in detail the corporate elite and their alignment with communism. *A Choice Not An Echo* and *The Grave-diggers* by Phyllis Schlafly said the Republican party was secretly controlled by the Bilderberger group and global communist domination was the goal.

For years conservative factions of the Republican party, especially in the West, attacked the CFR. Barry Goldwater said: "The CFR...believes national boundaries should be obliterated and one-world rule established."[28] "The TC...is intended to be the vehicle for multinational consolidation of the commercial and banking interests by seizing control of the political government of the U.S....In my view, the TC represents a skilled, coordinated effort to seize control and consolidate the four centers of power—political, monetary, intellectual, and ecclesiastical....What the Trilaterals truly intend is the creation of a worldwide economic power superior to the political governments of the nation-states involved. As managers and creators of the system, they will rule the future."[29]

R. Buckminster Fuller, a widely respected observer of our culture, also understood the great power of what he called the invisible government. In *Critical Path*, in the chapter "Legally Piggily," Fuller describes how large corporations and their lawyers control the U.S. "The U.S.A. is not run by its would-be 'democratic' government. All the latter can do is try to adjust to the initiatives already taken by (leaders of the) great corporations. Nothing could be more pathetic than the role that has to be played by the President of the United States, whose power is approximately zero. Nevertheless, the news media and most over-thirty-years-of-age U.S.A. citizens carry on as if the President has supreme power." The invisible power groups manipulate us through "its enormous media control and its election-funding and lobbying power of the American political game."[30]

On May 22, 1975 Fuller testified before the Senate Foreign Relations Committee stating, when asked where our country and people were going, "Not only have all the big corporations become transnational and taken all the former U.S.A. gold and other negotiable assets with them....Today most of the people in America still think of their nation as being the most powerful of the world nations—ergo, free to make its own most constructive moves. Quite the opposite is now true....The U.S. is both internally and externally bankrupt." In the 1960s and 1970s various sources such as C.B. Dall in *FDR, My Exploited Father-in-Law*,[31] said most of the gold in Fort Knox had been taken by the bankers because the U.S. was bankrupt. Fuller also said the second great gasoline shortage of June, 1979 was created by the invisible government to divert the public from concern generated by the Three Mile Island radiation accident.

In 1980 the American Legion (AL) passed Resolution 773 at their national convention demanding that Congress investigate the TC and CFR. This resolution was introduced into the House February 4, 1981 by Rep. McDonald, but Congress did nothing. In 1981 the AL introduced Resolution 243 again asking Congress to investigate the CFR and TC. The Veterans of Foreign Wars introduced a similarly worded Resolution 460 at their national convention in 1981.

The influence of the secret government has also been discussed in several elections. Christopher Lydon, in *The Atlantic Monthly*, said conspiracy theories are banned in mainstream American journalism and then, to his surprise, described how Rockefeller and the TC got Carter, a member of the TC and a man from a small southern state with no base in the democratic party, elected president. For months no one except the press took Carter's candidacy seriously. *Time* put Carter on the cover in 1971 and continued to present him in glowing terms.[32]

A chapter in *The Carter Presidency and Beyond* describes how the TC promoted Carter. The Rockefellers had old business ties in Atlanta; David Horowitz, co-author of *The Rockefellers*, said "Atlanta is Rockefeller South." Rockefeller intervened with the black leadership in Atlanta to get national black support for Carter. As president, Carter promoted the agenda of the corporate elite. Robertson, in *The New World Order*, describes how Carter and his administration were dominated by the New York banker groups, especially through the CFR. One reporter said: "It would be unfair to say the TC dominates the Carter administration. The TC is the Carter administration."[33] On the same morning I read the *Atlantic Monthly* articles about Carter, I also read several articles in the *Nation*[34] which described how the media, especially *Time*, had distorted the news to protect Clinton, especially concerning his involvement with money laundering, the CIA, and drug running in Arkansas. I could have been reading about the same candidate except for the 19 year difference.

It was fairly common, up to the early 1980s, to attack the power of the TC and the CFR. Reagan and Connally harshly attacked them during the 1980 election campaign partly because they got Carter elected President. Bush resigned from the CFR over the uproar but his CFR membership helped cost him the Republican nomination. However, once elected, Reagan brought many TC and CFR people into his administration.

By the mid 1980s these corporate groups had come to so dominate the national media and both political parties that they were rarely discussed. It was as if they never existed, despite the fact that they have dominated every White House for decades. In 1988 former Interior Secretary James Watt was a lone voice when he said the Reagan government was greatly influenced by the TC, which was using its influence to "protect their fortunes and preserve their political clout."

Congress and the president are increasingly irrelevant to the secret government. The CFR uses money and lobbyists to control Congress, as shown by the passage of NAFTA and GATT. The bankers are quite sophisticated, using lobbyists so some politicians have sold out to them without even realizing it. Many politicians do what they are ordered to do by various special interest groups which are secretly controlled by the corporations with their unlimited funds and influence.

These organizations have enormous economic and political clout. For instance, the Business Roundtable is a lobbyist group for major corporations and banks that played a major role in getting NAFTA and GATT passed. Both political parties have key leaders who are members of these elite groups. The parties often disagree because, if the Democratic and Republican leadership supported every bill, it would become too obvious that we really have only one national political party. Joseph Kraft said: "The Council (CFR) plays a special part in helping bridge the gap between the two parties, affording unofficially a measure of continuity when the guard changes in Washington."[35] The present dominant power of the corporate elite represents a decline of American pluralism.

Labor, farmers, small businesses, professionals, environmentalists, and consumers now have little say in the affairs of the nation, because big business controls both political parties. Money rules all.

Many believe one can trace the roots of the corporate elite and the secret government back to the late 1700s with the influence of the Illuminati. However, to go into that here would go beyond the scope of this book. There are many excellent texts that readers can study, and some of these books are listed in the bibliography. Other groups in the secret government such as the Order of Skull and Bones,[36] the Club of Rome, and 33rd degree Masons should be studied by the serious student to understand our present predicament. *Conspirators' Hierarchy: The Story of the Committee of 300*, by Dr. John Coleman, is a good review on the broad reach of the secret government into many areas of society.

# Chapter IV

# The New World Order

"We can have democracy in this country or we can have great wealth concentrated in the hands of a few, but we cannot have both."

Justice Louis D. Brandeis

"The money power preys upon the nation in times of peace and conspires against it in times of adversity. It is more despotic than monarchy, more insolent than autocracy, more selfish than bureaucracy. It denounces, as public enemies, all who question its methods or throw light upon its crimes."

Abraham Lincoln

In hundreds of books, articles, studies, and speeches in the 20th century, many influential and powerful people including many in Congress have called for a new world order and the surrender of U.S. sovereignty and individual freedoms to a one world government usually, involving the UN. People who attack these plans are called paranoid conspiracy theorists, extremists, or racists, but the national media ignores this extensive literature. Consider this, and you will begin to appreciate how the press deliberately and maliciously uses propaganda to lie to the people. When confronted with this evidence, elitists deny the existence of this literature or lie and say this is no longer the policy. Some, like Kenneth S. Stern in *A Force Upon the Plain*, make a brief comment about one part of this literature, downplaying and making fun of it to fool the public. People who think it is paranoid to be concerned about those who call for a world government should ask why this literature exists and why critics of the right almost never discuss this material. When you carefully study this literature and the events of the 20th century, the threat to our rights and way of life in a one world government with a new corporate-inspired Constitution is obvious.

During the 20th century many prominent leaders have supported the new world order and world government. For instance, on May 13, 1947 in London Winston Churchill said: "Unless some effective world supergovernment, for the purposes of preventing war, can be set up and begin its reign, the prospects for peace and human progress are dark and doubtful....Without a United Europe there is no prospect of world government."[1] Elsewhere Churchill said: "The creation of an authoritative world order is the ultimate aim toward which we must strive." Charles De Gaulle said: "Nations must unite in a world government or perish." Nehru said: "We have arrived at a stage where the next step must comprise a world and all its states, each having economic independence, but submitting to the authority of world organization."[2]

Secrecy is very important to these people. While many leading politicians support a world government, they refuse to openly discuss this topic with voters. In a 1976 interview in *Transition*, Senator Cranston warned against publicly promoting world government since "the more talk about world government the less chance of achieving it, because it frightens people...."[3] Jeffrey A. Baker said: "They camouflage their actions through the actions of others, constantly hiding behind people or institutions of purported good intent." When information leaks out, like the *Report From Iron Mountain*, it is always attacked by the media and corporate-approved experts. These experts hide their plans by denial or by claiming they are protecting the people's rights. In 1931 Arnold Toynbee said: "We are at present working discreetly with all our might to wrest this mysterious force called sovereignty (from) nation states....All the time we are denying with our lips what we are doing with our hands, because to impugn the sovereignty of the local nation states of the world is still a heresy...."

The Brandt Commission, a multinational group of national leaders and international financiers, defined the new world order as "A supra-national authority to regulate world commerce and industry; an international organization that would control the production and consumption of oil; an international currency that would replace the dollar; a world development fund that would make funds available to free and communist nations alike; an international police force to enforce the edicts of the New World Order."

The goal of the new world order is for the large corporations and superrich to totally control the world's population, resources, communications, finances, trade, and labor. This involves manipulating economics, politics, society, and religion on a global level. Lincoln Bloomfield wrote "Arms Control and World Government" in the July, 1962 journal *World Politics*. The article began: "The notion of a world government is today—and perhaps for all time—a fantastic one." Walter B. Wriston, ex-chairman of Citicorp, wrote *The Twilight of Sovereignty*, explaining how the information revolution was ending nation-state sovereignty. He said: "A truly global economy will require concessions of national power and compromises of national sovereignty that seemed impossible a few years ago and which even now we can but partly imagine." World citizenship is to become the standard. Already the Boy Scouts of America have a citizenship of the world merit badge.

Individuals in all nations must submit to international law and a world court. World law, not our Constitution, will rule supreme, and a world parliament is planned. On June 14, 1992 on ABC's *This Week with David Brinkley*, ex-Reagan adviser Michael Deaver said: "In five years we're going to have a World Parliament." Free trade with a stable system of payments is part of the plan, as is controlling the central bank in many countries like our Federal Reserve. These elitists believe the only way to make big money is through a monopoly. John D. Rockefeller once said "Competition is a sin." The free market myth is perpetuated by the giant corporations that strive to increase government regulation to limit competition, to enhance their profits and power. The plan is to also establish a new world religion and to remake the education system.

To reach these goals requires the destruction of the nation state, sovereignty, patriotism, nationalism, property rights, and the family unit. In the book *Experiences*, Toynbee, who spent many years working at the Chatham House discussed in Chapter III, said: "We are now moving into a chapter of human history in which our choice is going to be...between one world and no world....In the field of politics, nationalism is going to be subordinated to world-government...."[4] Elsewhere Toynbee said: "The cult of sovereignty has become mankind's major religion. Its God demands human sacrifice." On September 29, 1988, on ABC's *Nightline* Ted Koppel referred to nationalism as a virus. By controlling people, world government can be established.

There is an intimate relationship between socialism and those promoting the new world order with a one world government. Many early Fabian socialists like H.G. Wells, Bertrand Russell, and George Bernard Shaw supported world government and an end to sovereignty. Fabian socialists established the London School of Economics to train government bureaucrats to enhance central government control. Ultimately socialism is a greater threat than is communism, because socialism uses a gradual and insidious approach to achieve total control over the people, while the objectives of communism are more obvious. In the early 1900s when plans for a world government were further developed, businessmen like Cecil Rhodes provided money and influence while socialist intellectuals contributed ideas to achieve world government.

A constant strategy is to claim that governments must work together to solve the major problems of today. Supposedly, it is beyond the ability of individual nations to solve todays problems, so there must be a co-ordinated world strategy. A global approach with world government is needed to solve global problems, especially as the world gets more complex. Arnold Toynbee said: "In all developed countries a new way of life—a severely regimented way—will have to be imposed by a ruthless authoritarian government."[5] The plan is to create a world army, world court, world currency, world bank, and world tax. Each state will have only a lightly armed police force, while private gun ownership will end.

Previously, the nuclear threat was stressed. Jonathan Schell, in *The Fate of the Earth*, said world government was essential to avoid nuclear destruction. Today environmental concerns, third world poverty, food shortages, hunger, and national debts are more often used as an excuse for a world government. At a recent conference of the James A. Baker III Institute for Public Policy, the German Chancellor said: "The stability of the new world order and the new global challenges require cooperation between all global players" to fight organized crime, international terrorism, fundamentalism, and nationalism. *The First Global Revolution A Report By the Council of the Club of Rome* presented similar views. The Club of Rome is one of the corporate groups pushing for world government. Maurice Strong, a senior UN environmental official, said: We may get to the point where the only way of saving the world will be for industrial civilization to collapse."

Supposedly, if certain steps aren't taken by the elites of the world, conditions will continue to deteriorate so the poor will inherit the earth and live in misery. The U.S. standard of living is being deliberately lowered to the lowest common denominator to match that of many other nations to promote world government. It is claimed that democracy, or rule by the people, has too many limitations to really work especially in the current grave crisis. "Democracy is no longer well suited for the tasks ahead....Few politicians in office are sufficiently aware of the global nature of the problems in front of them and have little if any awareness of the interactions between the problems."[6] Supposedly, the people need the wise hand of the elite, even if they don't realize this. The elite have decided this on their own and believe they must act to save the world, also making themselves rulers to save the people who have no say in the matter. The people must continue believing they have a say in government, although that is a lie. CFR member George C. Lodge has just released *Managing Globalization in the Age of Interdependence*, in which he called for world "convergence and integration." If necessary, this convergence will be created by autocratically imposed fiat. Government will decide what the people need, and the people will be reeducated to accept this new ideology.

*Fateful Visions*, edited by CFR members, reviews from many sources what a world government will entail. For instance, some declare a world government will have the right to militarily enter a nation when there is just a rumor that a nation will take disruptive action, or to support world government policy. A nation's leaders could be arrested and direct rule imposed as in Somalia. The world government army, at least 500,000 strong, will control all nuclear weapons, and extensive international inspection will be required to maintain control. Admittedly, there may be a misuse of international police powers. As the debate to establish world government intensifies, civil war might occur in some countries as local patriots try to block their nation from joining a world government, and foreign troops will be used to defeat the patriots and support the pro-world government faction. Bloomfield explains how a UN international military force would be used to invade various countries.[7] In other words, if the U.S. government continues moving towards world government and widespread violence starts with the militias trying to save our Republic, UN troops would be brought in to destroy the militias. In addition, once world government is established, secession will not be allowed. Once a consensus has formed to establish a world government, all nations will have to join it. If some nations refused to do this, it supposedly would threaten peace, so force would be used against them.[8]

While most people remain asleep, elitists have for decades had deadly serious debates about how to create a one world government. The Institute for World Order, Inc. (now the World Policy Institute) through its newsletter, numerous books, and lectures has promoted world government for years. Richard Falk, in the *Yale Law Journal*, reviewed four proposed strategies to create a world government. The first is the Utopian legalism of Clark and Sohn, as discussed in *Introduction to World Peace Through World Law*, and *World Peace Through World Law*. A second approach is Kissinger's geopolitical power politics, while a third school of thought involving the multinational corporations and Trilateral Commission is more geoeconomic. A fourth view involves global populism and human dignity. Falk rejected the first approach as too unrealistic and the second and third approaches for being too ruthless and exploitative. As a utopian dreamer, he believes the fourth approach will best serve the people. Falk and others also seriously debate the importance of time and a transitional period for the claimed paradigm shift into a world government.[9]

Paul Warburg, testifying before the Senate Foreign Relations Committee on February 17, 1950, said: "We shall have world government whether or not you like it—by conquest or consent."[10] Warburg was a prominent Wall Street financier and CFR leader. His father helped establish the Federal Reserve. In 1959 he wrote *The West in Crisis* saying: "A world order without world law is an anachronism; and that, since war now means the extinction of civilization, a world which fails to establish the rule of law over the nation-states cannot long continue to exist. We are living in a perilous period of transition from the era of the fully sovereign nation-state to the era of world government...."[11] The *Economist* June 22, 1991 called for a global police force, an international court, and said the U.S. must submit to "a collective world order."

The second Humanist Manifesto in 1973 said: "We deplore the division of humankind on nationalistic grounds. We have reached a turning point in human history where the best option is to transcend the limits of national sovereignty and to move toward the building of a world community...a system of world law and world order based upon transnational federal government."

Several strategies are being used to create a world government. One plan is to gradually strength the UN and related international institutions. The UN has published many documents calling for its expanded role, and *Global Bondage* by Cliff Kincaid is a good reference on this. Second, regional governments and institutions are developing. Third, economic union is being used to create a political union.[12] The plan is to make people more dependent on each other, to become comfortable with international institutions and control. Richard N. Gardner said, in *Foreign Affairs* in April, 1974, "The hopeful aspect of the present situation is that even as nations resist appeals for 'world government' and 'the surrender of sovereignty,' technological, economic and political interests are forcing them to establish more and more far-ranging institutions to manage their mutual interdependence." David Korten of the People-Centered Development Forum, a pro-UN group, presented a paper at the 1995 International Development Conference revealing part of the strategy to create world government. He said, led by multinational banks, global consolidation was being promoted from above with NAFTA, GATT, and the Maastricht treaty, and it was being promoted from below by environmentalists, activists, and indigenous people.

The plan to create a one world government using a UN type body has existed for decades. About the League of Nations in 1922 *Foreign Affairs* declared: "Obviously there is going to be no peace or prosperity for mankind so long as it remains divided into fifty or sixty independent states....The real problem today is that of world government."[13] *The United Nations: Planned Tyranny*, by V. Orval Watts, was published in 1955. In great detail, Watts described the coming one world government and the UN's role in it. One person I spoke to in researching this book told me her father, who worked in defense in the 1950s, learned of these plans. Another contact working in the U.S. military in the early 1980s was ordered to provide highly classified documents to the Soviets. When he refused, he was told that by the end of this century the U.S. and the Soviet Union would join in a one world government. When he still refused to commit treason, his career was ruined.

Right from the start, the elite always planned for the UN to be a vehicle towards a one world corporate dictatorship. On September 7, 1948, *The Philadelphia Inquirer* quoted Senator Alben Barkley as stating: "The time is not yet mature for what we mean by world government....We must strengthen the UN before we can achieve our goal of world government." John Foster Dulles, in 1950, wrote *War or Peace* saying: "The UN represents not a final stage in the development of world order, but only a primitive stage. Therefore its primary task is to create the conditions which will make possible a more highly developed organization....Then, perhaps, a world police force could work."[14] On September 17, 1990, *Time* magazine said: "The Bush administration would like to make the UN a cornerstone of its plans to construct a New World Order." On March 6,

1991, Bush told Congress: "Now, we can see a new world coming into view. A world in which there is a very real prospect of a new world order....A world where the United Nations, freed from cold war stalemate, is poised to fulfill the historic vision of its founders." On February 1, 1992, Bush said: "My vision of a New World Order forsees a UN with a revitalized peacekeeping function. It is the sacred principles enshrined in the UN charter to which we henceforth pledge our allegiance." A president should only pledge his allegiance to the U.S. and the Constitution. The UN Secretary General Boutros Boutros-Ghali recently said: "The time of absolute and exclusive sovereignty has passed; its theology was never matched by reality."

A constant issue raised by elitists is a concern about overpopulation, food shortages, and the environment. Especially since the turn of the last century, various scientists have said overpopulation threatened economic growth and our very existence. George Bernard Shaw, a Fabian socialist and early supporter of world government, in 1928 wrote *The Intelligent Woman's Guide to Socialism and Capitalism.* He said people would be forcible fed, taught, and employed even if they didn't like this but "If it were discovered that you had not character and industry enough to be worth all this trouble, you might possibly be executed in a kindly manner...."

In *Anticipations of the Reaction of Mechanical and Scientific Progress Upon Human Life and Thought,* H.G. Wells said: "The ethical system which will dominate the world state, will be shaped primarily to favor...beautiful and strong bodies, clear and powerful minds...and to check the procreation of base and servile types....The new ethics will hold life to be a privilege and a responsibility...and the alternative in right conduct between living fully beautifully, and efficiently will be to die....The men of the New Republic (one world government) will have little pity and less benevolence....They will hold...that a certain portion of the population exists only on sufferance...and on the understanding that they do not propagate, and I do not foresee any reason to suppose that they will not hesitate to kill when that sufferance is abused....The men of the New Republic will not be squeamish either in facing or inflicting death....They will have an ideal that will make killing worth the while;....They will have the faith to kill....If deterrent punishments are used at all in the code of the future the deterrent will (be) good scientifically caused pain."[15]

Franklin Roosevelt closely followed and supported Well's views on having a world government. On December 4, 1933 he wrote Wells saying: "I have read, with pleasure and profit, almost everything that you have written....You are doing much to educate people everywhere, and for that I am grateful." On February 13, 1935 he wrote Wells: "How do you manage to retain such extraordinary clear judgements?...I believe our (the New Deal) biggest success is making people think during these past two years. They may not think straight but they are thinking in the right direction—and your direction and mine are not so far apart...."

Born into an English aristocratic family, the philosopher Bertrand Russell played a role in the British branch of the secret government. In various books like *Fact or Fiction, The Impact of Science on* Society, and *The Prospects of Industrial Civilization,* Russell called for world government. On July 11, 1955, he and others presented a manifesto claiming that nuclear war threatened humanity's survival, so national sovereignty must be limited. At times, Russell openly expressed his contempt for the common man. In *The Impact of Science on Society* he discussed the planned terror: "I do not pretend that birth control is the only way in which population can be kept from increasing....War...has hitherto been disappointing in this respect, but perhaps bacteriological war may prove more effective. If a Black Death could be spread throughout the world once in every generation survivors could procreate freely without making the world too full....The state of affairs might be somewhat unpleasant, but what of that? Really high-minded people are indifferent to happiness, especially other people's. "There are three ways of securing a society that shall be stable as regards population. The first is that of birth control, the second that of infanticide or really destructive wars, and the third that of general misery except for a powerful minority....These considerations prove that a scientific world society cannot be stable unless there is a world government....Unless...one power or group of powers emerges victorious and proceeds to establish a single government of the world with a monopoly of armed force, it is clear that the level of civilization must continually decline...."[16]

In 1948 Julian Huxley, the first head of UNESCO, wrote *UNESCO: Its Purpose and Its Philosophy*. He spoke of "the implications of the transfer of full sovereignty from separate nations to a world organization....Political unification in some sort of world government will be required....Even though...any radical eugenic policy will be for many years politically and psychologically impossible, it will be important for UNESCO to see that the eugenic problem is examined with the greatest care, and that the public mind is informed of the issues at stake so that much that now is unthinkable may at least become thinkable."[17] Ex-Senator William Benton said: "In its education program (UNESCO) can stress the ultimate need for world political unity and familiarize all peoples with the implications of the transfer of full sovereignty from separate nations to a world organization....Political unification in some sort of world government will be required."

In 1968 the Club of Rome concluded that civilization would collapse unless the death rate was increased and the birth rate was lowered. Various investigators, like John Coleman, report the Club of Rome developed a plan Global 2000 to kill several billion people by 2050. The mass killings in Cambodia and Africa are early stages of this operation. Paul Ehrlich, famous for his work on the population threat, said it might be necessary to add "a sterilant to the drinking war or staple foods" to sterilize the entire population, giving the antidote to a select few.[18] The forced sterilization programs of India and China may be the wave of the future in a corporate controlled society. In *The Population Bomb*, Ehrlich said: The population will drop from one of two solutions. The birth rate will be lowered or the "death rate solution" will be used through "war, famine, pestilence." Ehrlich's wife is a member of the Club of Rome.[19] He also said the "time of sugar coated solutions is long gone," and in a recent PBS documentary Ehrlich said: "If you don't solve the population problem the environment will collapse and our civilization will go along with it."

The UN Fund for Population Activities praised China's "exceptionally high implementation rate" and "high commitment" to population control methods such as abortion. The liberal *New Republic* recently said the UN acted with extreme slowness in Ethiopia regarding that nation's famine and then supported the government so many more died. Much UN food aid went to the military instead of the people. In Somalia, the UN stayed away when other relief agencies tried to help. When the UN finally got involved there were many problems. In Rwanda, the UN helped the armed militias, which had killed almost a million people, take control of numerous refugee camps. One private aid official said the UN took the lead in supporting these militias.[20]

In 1969, U Thant said: "I do not wish to seem overdramatic but I can only conclude that from the information that is available to me as Secretary-General (of the UN) that the members of the UN have perhaps ten years left in which to subordinate their ancient quarrels and launch a global partnership...to defuse the population explosion, and to supply the required momentum to development efforts." In 1987 the UN released a report, *Our Common Future*, claiming that in order to achieve sustainable development, lifestyle habits must be radically altered and closely regulated by government at all levels. Central planning was necessary under the UN's environmental bureaucracy.

In *Ecology and the Politics of Scarcity Revisited*, William Ophuls called for a world government with coercive powers. In *Preparing For the Twenty-First Century*, Paul Kennedy described how the global outlook is causing a weakening of the nation state. Overpopulation represented a threat to the nation state and the large transnational corporations. Former Washington governor Dixy Ray said, in *Environmental Overkill*, "The future is to be world government, with central planning by the UN....If force is needed, it will be provided by a UN green-helmeted police force." Already there are the UN Commission on Sustainable Development, UN Global Environmental Facility, and the UN treaty Agenda 21. The UN is ready to regulate the world to have a sustainable environment. Jacques-Yves Cousteau, in his journal *Calypso Log*, said it was necessary to create "an international environmental police, 'green helmets,' who would be under the direction of the UN. Our planet needs guardians...free of the constraints of...national sovereignty."

*Foreign Affairs* published an article with the ominous title "The Population Threat."[21] In *Living Within Limits: Ecology, Economics and Population Taboos*, Garrett Hardin said: "The issue of coercion must be faced....Loss of freedom is an inevitable consequence of unlimited population growth." Jacques-Yves Cousteau said: "It's terrible to have to say this. World population must be stabilized and to do that we must eliminate 350,000 people per day."[22] In one year that would equal 128 million people. At the UN Earth Summit in Rio, Cousteau said we have 10 years to solve the overpopulation problem, and he urged "drastic, unconventional decisions." The horrible truth is that there are individuals behind the new world order who plan to exterminate vast numbers of people, so the elite will have a world that meets with their approval. *Covert Action* and other sources report that AIDS is really germ warfare.[23] I discuss many population-extermination programs in Chapter XIX.

To end overpopulation, many elitists call for controlling the family. Warren Bennis and Philip Slater said, in *The Temporary Society* "One cannot permit submission to parental authority if one wishes to bring about profound social change....In order to effect rapid changes, any such centralized regime must mount a vigorous attack on the family lest the traditions of present generations be preserved." The state must "create an experiential chasm between parents and children to insulate the latter in order that they can more easily be indoctrinated with new ideas. The desire may be to cause an even more total submission to the state....One must teach (children) not to respect their tradition-bound elders, who are tied to the past and know only what is irrelevant."[24] As shown in Nazi Germany and the Soviet Union, totalitarian governments weaken the family unit in order to transfer loyalty to the state.

In the February, 1946 issue of *Psychiatry*, G.B. Chisholm said: "We have swallowed all manner of poisonous certainties fed us by our parents, our Sunday and day school teachers, our politicians, our priests....The re-interpretation and eventual eradication of the concept of right and wrong which has been the basis of child training, the substitution of intelligent and rational thinking for faith in the certainties of the old people, these are the belated objectives...for charting the changes in human behavior....Freedom from moralities means" to be "free from outmoded types of loyalties...."[25]

Garrett Hardin said: "It should be easy to limit a woman's reproduction by sterilizing her....People need to recognize that population control is needed to protect the quality of life for our children. The 'right' to breed implies ownership of children. This concept is no longer tenable. 'My' child's germ plasm is not mine; it is really only part of the community's store. I was merely the temporary custodian of part of it. If parenthood is a right, population control is impossible."[26]

In the April, 1981 issue of *The Futurist* magazine, Gene Stephens said to lessen crime by 2000 much more control will be needed. "The movement to license or certify parents may be well under way." Usually couples will be allowed to raise their own children; however, certain parents will be forced to surrender "superior babies" to be raised by others the state deems more appropriate to be the parents. "Child breeding and rearing...may be considered too important to be left to chance...." Drugs and genetic engineering will be used so that "controlled breeding will result in fewer biological reasons for crime."

In *The Case for Compulsive Birth Control*, Edgar R. Chasteen proposed subverting the traditional family by promoting alternative lifestyles. He said the birth rate would be lowered if citizens were made "politically insecure" through arrest and imprisonment with no right of appeal, no free speech, and invasion of the home. For compulsory population control, the public must be convinced that "parenthood (is) a privilege extended by society, rather than a right inherent in the individual. Accordingly, society has both the right and the duty to limit population when either its physical existence or its quality of life is threatened....There are no natural rights conferred upon man....Rights are derived from the law and the law is man-made."[27] The British surgeon Sir Roy Calne recently wrote *Too Many People*, in which he called for adopting many of China's birthing policies such as state-approved licensing to have children. The *Manchester Guardian* endorsed this saying: "If we don't sacrifice some freedoms we may be left with none."

The UN Convention on the Rights of the Child places the state over the family. Already in some countries where this convention has passed, UN representatives are interfering in traditional family practices, supposedly to protect children. Clinton is pushing to get this treaty passed in the Senate. Hillary Clinton's book *It Takes a Village and Other Lessons Children Teach Us* is a thinly veiled attempt to increase state authority over the family in the name of protecting the state's investment in children. Home visits by government agents will be required in a world government. Ultimately, human births may only occur through artificial means, when the state gives permission.

The Ford and Rockefeller Foundations, The World Research Institute, Resources for the Future, and the Worldwatch Institute, led by members of the CFR, donate large sums to support population control and ecology groups. Under CFR member Adele Simmons, the MacArthur Foundation leads the way in donations to these groups. Over the years, these foundations have issued many reports calling for central planning and world government to save the environment. For instance, CFR member Lester R. Brown, head of the Worldwatch Institute declared, in *World Without Borders*, that a world environmental agency was needed because protecting the environment was not "possible within the existing framework of independent nation-states." He called for developing "supranational institutions" to create a world government. Many environmental organizations have little interest in protecting the environment; they have been subverted to support the corporate agenda. These groups have even covered up Clinton's strong anti-environment policy.[28]

Laurance Rockefeller, in *The Reader's Digest*, warned that humanity must follow a simpler path, more in tune with the environment, or "authoritarian controls" may be used.[29] Barbara Marx Hubbard, supported by Rockefeller's Fund for Enhancement of the Human Spirit, wrote *The Revelation: A Message of Hope for the New Millennium.* She said humanity may chose a "gentle path" surrendering rule to an elite, but a sharp reduction of the world's population was necessary, which may require a "violent path." In the early 1980s, some of this material was distributed privately but was not publicly published, because the corporate controllers don't want the public to learn what is coming. Hubbard said: "Out of the full spectrum of human personality...one-fourth is destructive....They are defective seeds....In the past they were permitted to die a 'natural death.'..." Now "the elders" have decided that "the destructive one-fourth must be eliminated from the social body" in order to save everyone else. "Fortunately, you...are not responsible for this act. We are. We are in charge of God's selection process for planet Earth. He selects, we destroy. We are the riders of the pale horse, Death....We come to bring death....The riders of the pale horse are about to pass among you. Grim reapers, they will separate the wheat from the chaff. This is the most painful period in the history of humanity."[30] Population and environment concerns are considered a valid excuse for the elite to ultimately seize control, act like Gods, and kill huge numbers of people.

I do not fully agree with those who attack the entire environmental movement. There are serious environmental concerns that should be dealt with, but it is also essential to respect people and private property. There must be a spirit of compromise to solve real environmental problems. The millions of people involved in the environment movement have no understanding or interest in promoting world government. Most people in the environmental movement don't understand the new world order. Environment and overpopulation concerns have been manipulated by key environmental leaders who use the media to shape the environmental agenda and increase government control over the people. People in the wise use movement should understand that large corporations supporting this movement are often closely allied to the corporate elite promoting the new world order, and the corporations usually support both sides to manipulate events. *Covert Action* provided an excellent article on this involvement by the transnational corporations and Trilateral Commission.[31]

Another constant theme raised in the rantings of those promoting the new world order is to use technology and economic power to achieve social engineering. A typical book is *Changing Images of Man*, edited by Markley and Harmon.

The authors said there must be important changes in industrial man and industrial society if we are to survive. To deal with the growing scarcity of resources such as food and the population explosion, various methods of social control are explored. Zbigniew Brzezinski, in *Between Two Ages*, described a shift from an industrial to a technetronic society shaped by the impact of technology and electronics. "Both the growing capacity for the instant calculation of the most complex interactions and the increasing availability of biochemical means of human control augment the potential scope of consciously chosen direction, and thereby also the pressures to direct, to choose, and to change." This new society will "give rise to difficult problems in determining the legitimate scope of social control. The possibility of extensive chemical mind control, the danger of loss of individuality inherent in extensive transplantation, the feasibility of manipulating the genetic structure will call for the social definition of common criteria of use and restraint."[32]

World War II was seen as a great opportunity to move towards world government. The CFR formed study groups and started working directly with the State Department in 1939, to work for world peace and union after the war. Clarence K. Streit formed the Federal Union in 1940 to promote world government. Supported by prominent people like John Foster Dulles, a founder of the CFR and later Secretary of State, it placed ads in major newspapers on January 5, 1942 urging Congress to support union with certain foreign governments. This new union would directly tax people, control all armed forces, and make and enforce all laws. Streit wrote *Union Now, Union Now With Britain*, and in 1961, *Freedom's Frontier Atlantic Union Now* calling for world government.

In 1942, Dulles while chairman of the Federal Council of Churches Commission, issued a report calling for "a world government, strong immediate limitation on national sovereignty, international control of all armies and navies, a universal system of money, world-wide freedom of immigration, progressive elimination of all tariff and quota restrictions on world trade and a democratically-controlled world bank." The report said "a new order of economic life is both imminent and imperative."[33] In 1946 Dulles, in a Federal Council of Churches Report, said changes in the U.S. and the Soviet Union would make it possible to merge the two systems into a world government.[34]

After the UN was formed, the United World Federalists (UWF) got 27 state legislatures to pass resolutions supporting a constitutional convention to change the U.S. Constitution to join a world government, but voters got most of these resolutions repealed. Recently, the North Carolina general assembly rescinded, by a 92-11 vote a 1941 resolution supporting participation in a "Federation of the World," a "new world order," and an international convention to create a world Constitution.

In 1954 Rowan Gaither, head of the Ford Foundation, told Norman Dodd, a senator on the Reese Committee: "We operate here under directives which emulate from the White House. The substance of the directives under which we operate are that we shall use our grant making power to alter life in the U.S. so that we can comfortably be merged with the Soviet Union." On December 4, 1985, World Federalist Association (WFA) vice-president John Logue told a subcommittee of the House Foreign Affairs Committee: "It is time to tell the world's people not what they want to hear but what they must hear. What they ought to hear is that if we really want to have peace and promote justice, we must...strengthen the

UN....The UN must have taxing power....It must have a large peacekeeping force....It must be able to make and enforce law on the individual."[35]

Over the years, especially after World War II, many in Congress worked to surrender U.S. sovereignty to a world government, while others harshly attacked such proposals. In 1947, Rep. Richard Nixon introduced a world government resolution, and he wanted a UN police force. In June, 1952 the Senate held a hearing on the push for world government and global citizenship. On July 10, 1952 Congress passed what became Public Law 495, Section 112 which said: "None of the funds appropriated in this title (Department of State Appropriation Act, 1953) shall be used...to pay the U.S. contribution to any international organization which engages in the direct or indirect promotion of the principles or doctrine of one world government or one world citizenship." This law remained in effect until it was deleted in 1987. Obviously Congress is not filled with racists, anti-Semites, or conspiracy nuts.

In 1949, about 40 senators and 105 representatives introduced the Atlantic Union Resolution which called for a convention to strengthen the UN and establish a world government. For 10 years, this resolution was continually introduced, and one can read the *Congressional Record* to see the bitter debates on this topic. The Atlantic Union Committee included many CFR members, while Rockefeller provided rent free space for its headquarters. Its first head, former Supreme Court Justice Owen J. Roberts, said national sovereignty was a "silly shibboleth." Back in 1943, in the May 2 issue of *The Philadelphia Inquirer*, Roberts said: "An international government, with police power over every individual citizen in the nations belonging to it...is the only way...." In a change of strategy, the NATO Citizens Commission Law was passed in 1960. Later, pushed by the World Affairs Council on January 30, 1976, 124 members of Congress signed a Declaration of Interdependence: "Two centuries ago our forefather brought forth a new nation; now we must join with others to bring forth a New World Order...."

Those promoting the new world order are now trying to influence more people. In *Time*, July 20, 1992, Strobe Talbott, Deputy Secretary of State, CFR and TC member, and Clinton's roommate at Oxford, said in the next century "nationhood as we know it will be obsolete; all states will recognize a single, global authority....National sovereignty wasn't such a great idea after all." He said that GATT and IMF are the future world government's "protoministries of trade, finance and development for a united world."[36] This senior government official wants to surrender U.S. sovereignty to a world government. Read this two-page article and you may appreciate how dangerous things are. In response to this article, Clinton wrote to the WFA expressing his congratulations. He said: "Norman Cousins (past head of the WFA) worked for world peace and world government....Best wishes for an enjoyable reception and for future success."

The November, 1994 issue of *The Rotarian* had an editorial calling for world government.[37] The March/April, 1995 issue of *Sojourners* magazine had an ad promoting world government, and *Harper's* magazine had a full page ad promoting world government in its January, 1995 issue. This ad was promoted by a group that has a world Constitution ready to replace our current Constitution.

The Western corporate elite have long worked closely with the communists to promote world government. In 1916 Lenin said: "The aim of socialism is not only to abolish the present division of mankind into small states and all-national isolation, not only to bring the nations closer to each other, but also to merge them." In 1936 the Communist International formally described three stages for achieving world government. Speaking in Missouri in May, 1992, Gorbachev said: "This is a turning point on a historic and worldwide scale and signifies the incipient substitution of one paradigm of civilization for another....An awareness of the need for some kind of global government is gaining ground, one in which all the members of the world community would take part....Many countries are morbidly jealous of their sovereignty, and...of their national independence and identity....Here the decisive role may and must be played by the UN....The new world order will not be fully realized unless the UN and its Security Council create structures...authorized to impose sanctions and make use of other means of compulsion. All members of the UN must recognize the acceptability of international interference (in a nations internal affairs)....Under certain circumstances it will be desirable to put certain national armed forces at the disposal of the Security Council, making them subordinate to the UN military command."

In 1993 Gorbachev said: "This has been a period of international transition." He spoke about the need for "international institutions acting on behalf of all....Clinton will be a success if he manages to use American influence to accomplish this transformation of international responsibility and increase significantly the role of the UN." While many feel this would limit U.S. independence "accepting the aegis of a higher institution that operates on a consensus such as the UN, would have many advantages....Clinton...will be a great president—if he can make America the creator of a new world order."[38]

In late September, 1995, Gorbachev and his foundation hosted a world forum in San Francisco to promote a new world order and a council of wise men to solve the worlds problems. Jim Garrison, head of the Gorbachev Foundation, told the *San Francisco Weekly* in the May 31-June 6, 1995 edition that the ultimate purpose of the meeting was to shape the "next phase of human development....Over the next twenty to thirty years, we are going to end up with world government. It's inevitable." Zbigniew Brzezinski said: "Finally, I have no illusions about world government emerging in our lifetime....We cannot leap into world government through one quick step....The precondition for eventual and genuine globalization is progressive regionalization because by that we move towards larger, more stable, more cooperative units." Sam Keen declared that if the world population was cut 90 percent this would protect the ecology.

Many corporations and foundations like UPS, United Airlines, and Archer-Daniels financed and participated in this gathering, because they support the new world order. They feel that free trade will increase profits, and the Constitution doesn't show up in the balance sheet. In many ways, the large corporations are working to increase federal government power and tighten control over the people. Many people in government and the large corporations feel that world government is inevitable, so they support it. Norman Cousins wrote in 1985 in *Human Events*, "World government is coming, in fact, it is inevitable. No arguments for or against it can change that fact." Cousins was head of the WFA and Chairman of Planetary Citizen. The debate to have a world government was concluded decades ago, although most Americans were not allowed to take part in this discussion.

In 1984, in *New Lies For Old*, Anatoliy Golitsyn, an ex-KGB officer and defector, described the coming collapse of the Soviet Union and the liberalization policy, which he called a phony deception to mislead the West. He said the West has generally understood the communist military threat, but not its political threat. He said the coming collapse of the Soviet Union was part of a long-range disinformation campaign to fulfill long-range communist goals for world domination. By the end of 1993, 139 out of 148 of his predictions had been fulfilled for a 94 percent accuracy rate, while 46 predictions were yet to be fulfilled.[39]

Golitsyn is not psychic; he just leaked plans that have existed between the East and West for decades. Some communists, like Gorbachev, actually support working with Wall Street to create a world government. As long as working with the corporate elite brings Russia and China money, technology, and trade, most communists will support having a one world government someday, but they will never actually surrender their sovereignty unless they are in control. The cold war is over, but the communist threat remains. In the future, it will be a wolf in new clothes. They are playing the corporate elite for fools, and as with General Butler in the 1930s, the corporate elite stupidly think they can bribe everyone to accomplish whatever treason they want. The CFR does not control Russia and China to the degree that they think. In 1994 in *Soil, Tied to Our Blood*, Gennadi Zyuganov, head of the Russian communist party, said: "We (Russians) are the last power on this planet that is capable of mounting a challenge to the New World Order—the global cosmopolitan dictatorship. We must work against our...destroyers, using means as carefully thought-out and as goal-orientated as theirs are." Reportedly, Russian nationalist Vladimir Zhirinovsky, said on November 9, 1994, at the UN: "There has long been a hidden agenda to merge America and Russia under the new world order."

Over the years, many have attacked the new world order. In *The Open Conspiracy, Blue Prints For A World Revolution*, H.G. Wells called for world government. G.K. Chesterton analyzed this work and said "Internationalism is in any case hostile to democracy....The only purely popular government is local, and founded on local knowledge....To make all politics cosmopolitan is to create an aristocracy of globe-trotters."[40] Ralph Nader testified before a House subcommittee that GATT "formalized a world economic government dominated by giant corporations, without a correlative democratic rule of law to hold this economic government accountable."[41]

On June 26, 1995, former British Prime Minister Margaret Thatcher spoke at the National Press Club in Washington, D.C. She attacked the new world order and defended state sovereignty, warning against turning British rule over "to European institutions and non-elected bureaucracies." She was also against transferring the power of British courts to a European court. She said the agenda of European federalists would damage U.S. interests, and she was very critical of the attacks on national sovereignty that have become so common in the "forced internationalism." At the Gorbachev conference, Thatcher warned, "Do not use the UN for something for which it was not founded. We cannot put executive decisions into its hands." These views explain why she was removed from office.

The Catholic Church and the Pope understand what is coming. As an archbishop in 1976 the Pope said: "We are standing in the face of the greatest historical confrontation humanity has gone through...a test of 2000 years of culture and Christian civilization....Wide circles of American society and wide circles of the Christian community do not realize this fully...."[42] In *The Keys of This Blood*, Malachi Martin, with a decidedly Catholic Church influence, described how certain elite groups are striving towards global unity and world domination in a one world government. He identified certain groups involved, such as the internationalists—political bureaucrats that focus on agreements between nations and unity through politics, and transnationalists—business men who use cash to achieve their goals of increased international trade. Reportedly, some elements of the Catholic Church are quietly working to stop the coming world dictatorship, while others support it, determined to preserve a strong position for the Catholic Church.

A clue to what is coming was revealed in 1967, when *Report From Iron Mountain on the Possibility and Desirability of Peace* was published. Some 15 Americans from various fields took over two years to do this think-tank study for the government. It was never supposed to be published, which is understandable when one reads it. Translated into 15 languages, it was on the best seller list, so naturally its validity was denied, because it revealed so much about the coming terror. When you plan to destroy a society, it is not wise to acknowledge this. I read five reviews of this book, with the best one in the March, 1968 *Bulletin of the Atomic Scientists*. It admitted the report might be false, but then explained why it might be true. The report was written when ending the cold war was considered possible and when there were many private government studies. In November, 1967, the president of Dial Press, the publisher, defended the book's authenticity in the *New York Times*, while John K. Galbraith, in a review, defended its authenticity admitting he was asked to be part of the study group. Reportedly, the report was leaked by a guilt-ridden participant to Leonard C. Lewin. In 1972, Lewin, who wrote the book's introduction, claimed that he wrote the book, and it was a satirical attack on the military.[43] Simon & Schuster recently republished this book.

According to this report, the war system has worked quite well and peace is not desirable, because there would be many problems converting from a war economy. Poverty is necessary and desirable, while the war system must continue until new institutions can be developed to maintain social stability and political control. War is also supposedly a necessary means of population control, because disease no longer sufficiently reduces the population. Undesirable genetic traits were self-liquidating but now continue because of medical advances, so new methods of eugenics are needed. Most medical advances were considered a problem and birth-control drugs might be added to food and water to limit population growth. Teams of experimental biologists in the U.S., Mexico, and the USSR were working to create life to make it much easier to limit population growth.[44] A world without war must ultimately turn to universal test-tube procreation to limit population growth. In 1968 Brzezinski wrote of genetic manipulation to maintain social control and "the creation of beings" that will function and reason like men.[45] George Bernard Shaw said: "If you want better people you must breed them as carefully as you breed thoroughbred horses and pedigree boars."[46]

Without war, new institutions and alternate enemies must be created to maintain control. Many substitutes for war were considered but each had serious limitations. Space research and an outer space UFO menace were deemed to not be sufficiently credible. It would be difficult to deliberately damage the environment so that nations would surrender their sovereignty. A credible substitute for war must create an omnipresent and readily understood fear of personal destruction, and this fear must be sufficient to ensure adherence to society's values. The report suggested "the reintroduction...consistent with modern technology and political processes, of slavery." Noting the works of Wells, Huxley, and Orwell, the report said that slavery might be essential in the future to maintain social control.

The book concluded that war is a good excuse to control and expand the economy, control antisocial tendencies, establish standards for the arts, provide motivation for scientific and technological progress, and help maintain political authority, class distinctions, and ecological balance between the population and raw materials necessary for survival. War helps maintain a stable government "by providing an external necessity for a society to accept political rule." Bertrand Russell, in *The Impact of Science on Society*, said: "War has been throughout history, the chief source of social cohesion...." This is the sick mentality of the secret government. This vile report has to be read to be believed.

There are many who call the new world order socialist or communist. Certainly there are leftist elements in these groups, but there is also a strong neo-Nazi faction in the corporate elite. In the 1930s, the corporate elite used fascist ideas to promote a police state; in more recent years, they turned to communist principles. In truth, the philosophical views of these people is not the key issue. Their common ideology is an unrelenting lust for money, power, and control. Any ideology is acceptable towards that end. Barry Goldwater correctly said of the CFR and other elitist groups: "They have no ideological anchors. In their pursuit of a new world order they are prepared to deal without prejudice with a communist state, a socialist state, a democratic state, monarchy, oligarchy—it's all the same to them."[47]

People who attack the view that there is a conspiracy involving the wealthy and powerful to achieve world government are attacked for presenting a conspiracy view of history. This is done partly because critics are unable to refute these claims. When the message cannot be refuted, the messenger is attacked. "One of the things we most need to understand—and one of the things historians most often fail to discuss—are the precise means by which the dominant class and those who serve it go about accomplishing their goals in politics."[48] Michael Parenti said: "It should be noted that there are conspiracies among ruling groups, things done in secrecy with the intent to sustain or extend power—as Watergate, the Pentagon Papers, the FBI's COINTELPRO campaign against the left, and the CIA's daily doings have demonstrated."[49] Thomas Jefferson warned: "Single acts of tyranny may be ascribed to the accidental opinion of a day, but a series of oppressions, begun at a distinguished period, unalterable through every change of ministers, too plainly prove a deliberate, systematical plan of reducing us to slavery."

At the same time, William Cooper has a point in saying there isn't a conspiracy, because so much is published about the coming new world order. The move towards world government involves the quiet networking of thousands of individuals. If there is a conspiracy to establish a one world government, it is an open one. Remember the title of H.G. Well's book, *The Open Conspiracy, Blue Prints For A World Revolution*. The corporate elite reveal much about their plans, because they look at the people with contempt and they have had their way for many years. President Nixon told the *New York Times* on November 10, 1972: "The average American is just like the child in the family." Averell Harriman said the American people wanted nothing better than to "go to the movies and drink Coke." In 1996, Ted Turner, head of CNN, said before an international forum: "The U.S. has got some of the dumbest people in the world. I want you to know that. We know that."[50] These elitists are too blinded by their arrogance to understand just how angry and educated more and more Americans are becoming.

The elites have traditionally had an extremely negative attitude towards the people they ruled and have always had problems accepting the involvement of the people in government. Charles Lasch, in *The Revolt of the Elites and the Betrayal of Democracy*, said the elites "regard the masses with mingled scorn and apprehension." Jose Ortega y Gasset, in *The Revolt of the Masses*, said the masses cannot rule and their involvement in government has created a grave crisis. Walter Lippmann said the "omnicompetent citizen" was no longer possible in the age of specialization. He believed public opinion was no better than gossip and that real governing should be left in the hands of experts.

While many dismiss the view of a corporate elite creating a one world government as left or right wing extremisms, the reality is that the new world order is increasingly here. While most people ignore the motives behind the coming one world government, and some debate whether or not such a government is coming and if there is a conspiracy, the new world order is unfolding before our eyes. You don't have to believe what I and others write; study the literature noted above and the laws passed by Congress and other governments.

Stopping the corporate traitors from establishing a world dictatorship is the foremost issue of our time. Many of the concerns people have today from labor rights, to ending abortions, to having a balanced budget however important these issues are will be irrelevant if we live in a police state. Many conflicts in our society have been deliberately created to divert the people's attention so the corporate elite can quietly and gradually shift this Republic into a world dictatorship. However, with many people awakening to these plans and a freer flow of information, I believe the one world government dictatorship will never occur. In the end, the new world order crowd will join Hitler's Third Reich in the ash heap of history.

## Chapter V

# Fooling the People

"The people never give up their liberties but under some delusion."
Edmund Burke

"Political language...is designed to make lies sound truthful and murder respectable, and to give an appearance of solidity to pure wind....The first step in liquidating a people is to erase its memory."
George Orwell

There are many reasons why most people do not understand that our rights are being lost. People think we have a democracy with the people in charge, because this is what the controlled national media tells us. Certain agencies like the CIA use public relations firms, authors, and journalists to fool the public and to perform roles the government cannot legally do.[1] In the 1970s it was revealed that the CIA had hired hundreds of journalists to shape public opinion.[2] It would be extremely naive to not appreciate that such disinformation continues to manipulate and confuse the people.

This propaganda along with various mind control techniques over the years created a paradigm as described by the philosopher Thomas S. Kuhn in *The Structure of Scientific Revolutions*. A paradigm represents a model or shared beliefs of the way the world works for most people. Theories help create facts, and people who exist inside a paradigm are quite comfortable with the facts they are told. People who present information outside the existing paradigm are initially called silly, but gradually as different views become a threat to the status quo, people with new ideas are demonized as crazy, extremist, or racist. Conflicting paradigms are sharply resisted.

This helps explain why almost no one in the Western intelligence community foresaw the collapse of the Soviet Union. Everyone believed this would never happen so the possibility was ignored by all but a few people, like Senator Moynihan. One intelligence officer said in the late 1980s he would have been put in a mental hospital if he had said the Soviet Union was soon going to collapse. Despite growing contrary evidence inside the paradigm everyone felt the Soviet Union remained a powerful and dangerous enemy. Other evidence was ignored or disbelieved.[3]

A crisis may cause the formation of a new paradigm as many people work to reconstruct society with new institutions. Then society is divided into separate factions, one defending the old paradigm, while the other group seeks to establish new ideas and institutions. Once this happens normal political interaction may fail, and serious conflict is possible. Political revolutions may occur when groups in the population realize that existing institutions have ceased to properly meet the needs of the people. Then the question is, can the new paradigm solve the problems that created a crisis in the old paradigm?[4] Millions remain in a state of denial today, thinking all is well, while the Patriot movement is getting stronger partly because many people have broken out of the corporate managed paradigm of America.

Previously propaganda and controlled elections were sufficient to control the people. Now, along with controlling the media and subverting society, a key part of the strategy of the secret government is to keep the people distracted with issues that will not interfere with their goal of establishing tighter control and a one world government. This is done by using various propaganda techniques to redirect the people's actions. Emotional debates and conflicts are created so many people are too busy to notice what is happening to our constitutional rights. The object is to keep the people stupid and ignorant, watching television and sports or other amusements diverting attention and keeping people from organizing. In certain respects our country is like the Roman Empire in its dying days. Then citizens watched people being eaten by lions; today, we are fed hundreds of stories involving crime, sex, and sports. Eduardo Galeano said "The majority must resign itself to the consumption of fantasy. Illusions of wealth are sold to the poor, illusions of freedom to the oppressed,...dreams of victory to the defeated and of power to the weak." Arthur Miller in *Democratic Dictatorship* called this process the tyranny of technology. Franz Neumann said: "The higher the state of technological development, the greater the concentration of political power." People will be made to enjoy their enslavement.

A classic example of this strategy is the abortion debate. America is the only nation where the abortion issue is such an intense focus for many. In no other country, even where the Catholic church is much stronger, is there such an intense abortion debate. The secret government often places provocateurs on opposing sides of an issue to arouse the people. Whether the issue is child abuse, racial tension, the environment, capital punishment, affirmative action, or women's right, there are many intensely debated issues in our society where this quiet manipulation proceeds. I do not question the sincere beliefs that people have regarding abortion and these other issues, but it is also obvious that millions of people are so involved in these debates that they have little time to examine what is happening to our Constitution and the government. I also do not claim that the secret government is at work in every issue debated in our society, but at times this is a key hidden factor.

The corporate elite will sometimes set up front groups that supposedly support a cause while they work to weaken the entire movement. Money is donated and provocateurs are planted in various groups the secret government wants to control. A classical example of this is corporate infiltration of the environmental movement. Large corporations and foundations support certain environmental groups like the Wilderness Society. The David and Lucile Packard Foundation supports the Wilderness Society, which never challenged Hewlett-Packard's poor land management in the Challis National Forest. One member of the board of the Wilderness Society is Walter Minnick C.E.O. of a multinational timber company, T J International, which is partly owned and allied with other timber companies that are constantly cutting timber with little regard for the environment.

An obvious diversion for many years was the communist threat. The result was and is that anything could be done to justify the national security state. Historically, after each war America substantially dismantled the military and related industries that supported it, but this did not occur after World War II and the cold war. Some try to justify continuing the defense/security apparatus by speaking of nuclear proliferation, militias, war on drugs, and third world terrorism, or by using the military for national emergencies to stay on a permanent war footing. On the CBS *Evening News*, March 19, 1995, there was a report on growing Muslim fundamentalism and its threat to the U.S. Senator John Glenn and the NATO Secretary General described Islamic fundamentalism as even more dangerous than communism. At least one reporter called this "absurd" and suggested that NATO needed a new threat to justify its existence.[5]

Bertram Gross, in *Friendly Fascism*, said technology and corporate central government power were gradually shifting the U.S. towards totalitarianism. Buttressed by constitutional restraints and splits among the elites, he felt that fascism would come gradually through silent encroachments, and the great danger would be that this slow process would be unnoticed by most Americans. It is essential to preserve the facade of democracy while gradually shifting to a police state. The goal is to "accustom the American people to the destruction of their freedoms." By the time people realize what is happening it could be too late. In America, fascism will come from "powerful tendencies within the Establishment," not from the right or left. The American model of fascism will be "pluralistic in nature" with "no charismatic dictator, no one-party rule, no mass fascist party, no glorification of the state, no dissolution of legislatures, no discontinuation of elections...." William Shirer, author of *The Rise and Fall of the Third Reich*, said America may be the first country in which fascism takes power through democratic elections.

The forces that have prevented friendly fascism from developing, such as strong labor unions and a free press, have been subverted by the large corporations. Many labor leaders have become bureaucrats unable to represent their members. Through "mind management and sophisticated repression" incentives, punishments, and escape valves are provided to pave the way for friendly fascism. Widespread diversions such as sex, drugs, cults, mental illness, and sports are used to control people, so they will accept servitude and not oppose government policies. The "soma pills" described by Aldous Huxley, in *Brave New World*, have arrived.

In *Brave New World*, Aldous Huxley said the especially efficient totalitarian state would be one in which the political bosses and managers control a population of slaves who do not have to be coerced, because they love their servitude. To make people love their slavery is the task today assigned to totalitarian states. We accept our bondage partly because we don't even realize that we have become enslaved by the addiction of television and other forms of modern-day propaganda. To become free, we must first recognize our entrapment.

A major strategy to delude the people is to transform the country gradually into a dictatorship, not upsetting the people. CFR member Henry Morgenthau, who was FDR's Secretary of the Treasury, said: "We can hardly expect the nation-state to make itself superfluous, at least not overnight....The transition will not be dramatic, but a gradual one." CFR member Philip C. Jessup, in *The International Problems of Governing Mankind*, said: "I agree that national sovereignty is the root of the evil....The question of procedure remains. Can the root be pulled up by one mighty revolutionary heave, or should it first be loosened by digging around it and cutting the rootlets one by one?" The Fabian Socialist H.G. Wells said Roosevelt's New Deal was "the most effective instrument possible for the coming of the new world order....He is continuously revolutionary in the new way without ever provoking a stark revolutionary crisis."

In 1955 Milton Mayer wrote a remarkable book, *They Thought They Were Free*. Ten dedicated Nazis, people from the middle class, for example a policeman and cabinetmaker, were interviewed to explain how Hitler took control. People should study this book especially the chapter entitled "But Then It Was Too Late" to understand how the tactic of gradualism can transform a free people to slavery. Daniel Webster cautioned: "If this Constitution be picked away by piecemeal, it is gone as effectively as if a military despot had grasped it, trampled it underfoot and scattered it to the winds."

An important strategy the secret government uses to maintain control is to support ambitious people early in their careers. People are promoted if they have demonstrated intelligence, ambition, leadership, and few morals. These people are corrupted though sex, money, and drugs with evidence of criminality gathered to blackmail them, if necessary. They must follow orders, or their careers will be ruined and they may go to jail. This principle is applied to many politicians, but is applied with special care to senior officials, like presidents. Once the invisible government chooses someone to become president, the instruments of corporate power distort the news to protect the chosen one. The people are only allowed to participate by voting, which is why many no longer bother. Who will win is decided long before election day. The CFR and TC don't care which party elects the president, as long as they control each candidate and the people continue to be fooled. This system guarantees a corrupt leadership and a disillusioned populace.

In *FDR, My Exploited Father-In-Law*, C.B. Dall said: "Politics is the gentle art of having to pretend to be something that you know you are not, for vote-catching purposes, while being aided by our press....Usually, carefully screened leading 'actors' are picked well in advance of election day by a small group, picked for *both major parties*, thereby reducing the promotional risk to just about zero....It is desirable for such a candidate to have great *personal ambition* and, perchance, to be *vulnerable to blackmail* for some past occurrences; hence, someone not apt to become too independent in time, but always amenable to 'suggestions' on the policy level." Colonel House, the chief aide to Woodrow Wilson, knew that, along with great personal ambition, Wilson was vulnerable to blackmail. Dall said Wilson appointed Brandeis to the Supreme Court because he was being blackmailed and couldn't obtain $250,000 to get back certain letters.[6]

While President, Eisenhower made a speech at a park Bernard Baruch had founded. He said: "Twenty-five years ago as a young and unknown major I took the wisest step in my life—I consulted Mr. Baruch." When the war started Eisenhower was promoted over at least 150 senior officers to head the allied war effort in Europe. For many years Baruch protected the interests of Wall Street in Washington.[7]

In 1969 Alexander Haig was a colonel, but within several years he became a senior White House aide and later head of NATO, because he hitched his career to Henry Kissinger. Colin Powell and Jimmy Carter were promoted by the CFR beginning in the early 1970s. Lamar Alexander turned one dollar into $620,000. Even Hillary Clinton couldn't match such corruption. General John M.

Shalikashvili was advanced over many officers to become chairman of the Joint Chiefs of Staff. Hillary Clinton's commodities trade was an obvious set-up. The massive corruption of Clinton is clear to many as are his drug and sexual appetites.

On November 18, 1993 in *The Wanderer*, a national newspaper, James K. Fitzpatrick a prominent journalist revealed that while he has never believed in stories of a secret government or the Illuminati, Clinton's support of NAFTA made him wonder, especially because of statements made by Clinton. During his acceptance speech when nominated by the Democrats, Clinton spoke about the influence his old professor Carrol Quigley, author of *Tragedy and Hope*, had on his life. After his election Clinton told reporters how Quigley had spoken and written about a secret shadow government of powerful businessmen and bankers who controlled our political agenda. Clinton said, while a student, he decided to work with this secret group to enhance his political career. Fitzpatrick, not understanding how controlled our news is, was shocked that this interview wasn't discussed in the media. That this technique of controlling our leaders has long existed helps explain why attention should be directed to stop the corporate leaders. The politicians are just agents who can easily be replaced.

In recent years, the growing use of computerized vote machines has provided new opportunities to control elections. There have been dozens of instances of vote fraud throughout the country such as in Florida, Wisconsin, and California; and sometimes judges throw out election results. The growing problems with these machines is being documented by Computer Professionals for Social Responsibility in Palo Alto, Election Watch in Pacific Palisades, California, and Cincinnatus in Cincinnati. Even the national media, including the *New York Times* and *Wall Street Journal*, have discussed the dangers of computerized voting machines.[8] On November 7, 1988 the *New Yorker* had a 23 page report on the dangers of computerized voting machines. *Science News* explained how modern vote machines help steal elections.[9] Amazingly, when vote results are challenged the computer programs usually aren't analyzed because the manufacturers have successfully claimed they are proprietary. Private corporations increasingly own our elections. Computer scientist Peter G. Neumann, in *Computer-Related Risks*, said: "The opportunities for rigging elections (are) childs play for vendors and knowledgeable election officials." In the 1988 New Hampshire primary, Dole won the precincts that used paper ballots while Bush won the computerized ones.

Even more threatening is the fact that, in many states, election results are reported to the New York City based News Election Service (NES), a private company owned by ABC, CBS, NBC, and the Associated Press (AP). The book *Votescam: The Stealing of America* documents the dangers of this operation.[10] There is no system to challenge the announced results. For instance, each caucus in the Iowa primary reports the results to the NES. In Dubuque County, Iowa, Buchanan got 870 votes, but the next day the *Cedar Rapids Gazette* quoted the AP saying Buchanan got 757 votes and Dole's total was increased. When people complained, they were told there could be no final count until April. Numerous other instances of suspicious behavior occurred, and Buchanan may have been cheated out of victory in Iowa, Arizona, and South Carolina. This is why thousands came to see Buchanan, while only a few voters came to see Dole. It is rather suspicious that Buchanan refused to complain about this.

The most dangerous scam used against the people are presidential edicts. Every president has issued orders and directives which are often called Executive Orders (EO); however, in the 20th century the use, scope, and authority of EOs greatly increased. These edicts have the force and effect of law; however, there is no constitutional basis for a president to make laws. Congress should make the law and the president should administer and enforce it. There is much room for abuse of presidential power with these edicts. Nowhere does the Constitution say that a president can issue an EO, nor do any federal statutes exist defining the purpose or permissible subject matter of EOs.

Previously, most EOs dealt with routine administrative issues such as land use and civil service regulations. EOs now exist for the Feds to seize all communications (EO 10995), to takeover all food supplies and farms (EO 10998), to control all transportation (EO 10999), to force all civilians into work brigades (slave labor) (EO 11000), to takeover all health and education activities (EO 11001), and for the post office to register everyone (EO 11002). These and other EOs have been combined into EO 11490, which Carter signed in 1979. This is a dictatorship in waiting. One can only image the horrors of the secret EOs that have never been published or leaked.

The greatest abuse of presidential authority lies in presidents declaring a national emergency and martial law. Presidents have already signed EOs declaring national emergencies because of events in the Middle East, Yugoslavia, South Africa, Kuwait, and chemical/biological problems. How these events require a national emergency in the U.S. defies reality. In 1985 the *New York Times* asked why there had to be a national emergency in the U.S. over South Africa.[11] Having a national emergency with a weakened Constitution has become the norm to gradually get people used to the conditions of a police state.

EO 9066 issued February 19, 1942 by President Roosevelt caused the internment of 120,000 Japanese Americans in glorified concentration camps. Along with being imprisoned for several years, these people, 75,000 of whom were American citizens, lost most of their assets. For this to happen just because a president signed one piece of paper shows how dangerous things are. If a phony emergency is declared, Clinton could then call for the surrender of all arms and the arrest of his political opponents who would be called a threat to national security. Passing especially dangerous EOs started March 9, 1933 when Roosevelt weakened the Constitution by declaring a national emergency that put us into a state of war.[12] On June 17, 1995 the Texas Republican party issued Resolution 5 calling for a return to constitutional government and an end to Roosevelt's emergency rule and weakening of the Constitution. The press responded with a resounding silence.

Recent EOs have become absurd. On October 21, 1994 Clinton issued an EO requiring schools to expel students who bring a gun to school. Such students should receive serious punishment, but Clinton has no constitutional authority to decided how schools deal with local problems. Clinton is only the president. Clinton's speech announcing this policy received wide publicity yet no one in the media complained about this abuse of power. Must we now get used to a president announcing new laws on the most minute details of our lives. Just after the November, 1994 elections, *The Washington Post* reported that Clinton and his staff planned to govern more with executive orders and regulations.[13] Clinton was elected president, not king or dictator.

When Rep. Jack Brooks in March, 1987 asked presidential aide Frank Carlucci to provide a list of all presidential edicts issued since 1981 he refused to comply. Speaker of the House Jim Wright said: "Congress cannot react responsibly to new dictates for national policy set in operation by the executive branch behind closed doors." Presidential edicts are often classified with no one in Congress even aware of their subject matter.

Control by Congress over executive rule making has been replaced by a powerful executive branch which is destroying the checks and balances designed by the Constitution. In *Myers v. U.S.* (1926) the Supreme Court said: "The doctrine of the separation of powers was adopted by the Convention of 1787, not to promote efficiency but to preclude the exercise of arbitrary power. The purpose was, not to avoid friction, but, by means of the inevitable friction incident to the distribution of the governmental powers among three departments, to save the people from autocracy....Speed and efficiency, however, are not the proper ends of government. If they were, the framers would have created a dictatorship." Rule by executive edict means that a president can sign a piece of paper and pass unpopular laws that are totally against the will of Congress and the people, as we saw when Clinton used an EO to loan money to Mexico.

Those promoting the new world order are deliberately changing our history and culture. A good book that describes how history books are confusing and distorting our history is *Lies My Teacher Told Me*, by James W. Loewen. Text book publishers avoid controversies, only present a positive tone, and ignore much American history. Schools socialize students to be good and obedient citizens. The racial prejudice of people like President Wilson, the contributions of women, and the role of militias in founding our Republic are removed from history. Issues such as General Butler and the planned military coup, the munitions hearings in the 1930s, and corporate treason during World War II are rarely discussed in history books. Loewen, to his credit, said there may be an upper-class conspiracy "manipulated by elite white male capitalists who orchestrate how history is written as part of their scheme to perpetuate their own power and privilege at the expense of the rest of us."[14] State-controlled curricula promote corporate-influenced distortions of our heritage.

It will be much harder for the younger generation to stand up for constitutional government because of the distortions being taught in the schools. In November, 1995 the U.S. Department of Education released a report based on questioning 22,000 school children about our history. Fifty percent of the children weren't even aware that the cold war existed! A 1994 study by the National Assessment of Educational Progress revealed that 57 percent of public high school seniors lack a basic understanding of U.S. history. With poor schooling and TV addiction, for many history started with the New Deal. People no longer remember the values of our Republic and the wisdom of the Founders. The shift to outcome based education, Goals 2000, and multiculturalism means that if the corporate controllers aren't stopped, one day few people will defend the Constitution because few will even remember that it once existed. Multiculturalism has played a key role in destroying Canada[15] as a nation state, and this is also why it is being pushed in the U.S. It is one more strategy being used to weaken national sovereignty, to move towards a world government.

Multiculturalism is also being used to separate us from our Christian heritage and Western culture. Other cultures are highlighted while ours is undermined. The

California Teachers Association released a calendar that doesn't identify July 4th. It includes Buddhist Nirvana day and Ramadan but not Christmas or Thanksgiving. The National Educational Association passed out millions of calenders to teachers that listed UN day and various Buddhist and Moslem holidays but did not mention Christmas. Listing various religious holidays is fine, but to remove traditional American religious and patriotic holidays is outrageous.

Increasingly, basic American constitutional and political history is not being taught. Under the new world order, within a few generations our history will be forgotten, because it will be banned. On May 16, 1993 *Parade Magazine* published an article about putting false words in the mouth of dead people. It cited as an example the supposedly false words of Patrick Henry "Give me liberty or give me death."[16] In fact, Henry said these noble words, March 23, 1775, at St. John's Church in Richmond Virginia in conjunction with the second Virginia convention.[17] Karl Marx said: "If you can cut people off from their history they can be easily persuaded."

An important book is *The Rewriting of America's History* by Catherine Millard. A librarian at the Library of Congress, she documents many instances where our Christian heritage and memorial to the Founding Fathers are being erased or distorted. Independence Square in Philadelphia, where the Constitution and Declaration of Independence were signed, had a National Museum which was taken over by the Independence National Historic Park in 1951. The museum was disbanded with its contents dispersed to different buildings and many of the exhibits are no longer available to the public. Important Christian markers and plaques around Philadelphia have been replaced with humanistic plaques. The Liberty Bell has been moved from its original site and it is now called a "symbol of world freedom." An important painting "The First Prayer in Congress" has been lost. In Christ Church in Philadelphia, often called the Nation's Church, famous stained glass such as "Patriots Window" and "Liberty Window" were moved, supposedly to be cleaned, but instead they have been replaced by plain glass.[18]

Sections of the Library of Congress have been closed for renovations, but the "improvements" made it much harder for librarians and researchers to use the facilities. The main card catalogue was almost deliberately destroyed except that the librarians and their union prevented this by threatening to sue. The computerized replacement has an error rate of 50 percent. The new head librarian in October 15, 1987 fired many people with no replacements, leaving various departments disorganized and understaffed. In an especially disgusting display of what is happening, religious scenes in the Library of Congress were replaced during renovations by grotesque gargoyle paintings. This exemplifies how Christ will be replaced by atheism or worse in the new world order.

In the Library of Congress rare books pertaining to our Christian heritage and the Founding Fathers are now listed as "missing in inventory" and "changed to the rare book collection," which means the public cannot see these books. In some instances, Millard found that books listed as missing were in their correct place. Millard listed groups of books that were all removed from circulation at the same time. There is an organized campaign to remove from public reach rare books on Christianity and the Founding Fathers. In some historical and religious exhibits, American history has been greatly altered and falsified. Millard was refused promotions and salary raises when she fought these changes.

Deborah Maceda works for the Library of Congress as a police detective in its Protective Services Office. For several years she complained about many books being damaged and stolen. One would expect that she would have been thanked for doing her job. Instead her many memos, which also included ways to improve security, were ignored until she was transferred. There were proceedings to fire her until Congress intervened. Now several agencies, including the FBI are investigating the Library of Congress which a union called "out of control."[19] On July 6, 1996 CBS *Evening News* said the Library of Congress was often using psychiatrist testing, which are generally illegal in the workplace, to harass and fire whistleblowers.

"If people are stripped of the ability...to make their own things and their own history, they may continue to act properly, but they lose the capacity to learn for themselves about their own rightness. They stagnate or surrender....Those who steal their right to make their own history...can be condemned, for they steal from people the right to know what they know, the right to become human....History is culture."[20] Our history is being cleansed to fit what our corporate controllers want.

Since 1670 when a jury refused to convict William Penn, it has been part of our heritage that juries have a right to decide a case based on the law as well as the facts of the case. In 1794 Chief Justice of the Supreme Court John Jay said in *Georgia v. Brailsford*: "The jury has a right to judge both the law as well as the fact in controversy." Alexander Hamilton said: "Jurors should acquit, even against the judge's instruction...if exercising their judgement with discretion and honesty they have a clear conviction that the charge of the court is wrong." The Constitutions of four states—Maryland, Indiana, Oregon, and Georgia—specifically guarantee the right of jurors to "judge the law." Today 23 states declare the right of jury nullification (the right of a jury to judge a law) in freedom of speech regarding libel and sedition. Throughout the 1800s this principle was primarily challenged only once when Congress passed an anti-slave law which northern juries refused to support. Then the government was close to the people, so laws were rarely passed that were against the people's wishes. However, in 1895 in *Sparf and Hansen v. U.S.*, the Supreme Court ruled that while juries still had the right to judge the law a judge didn't have to inform a jury of this.[21]

In the 1900s we have been swamped with laws that many are against because government often no longer represents the people. The Fully Informed Jury Association (FIJA) informs citizens of the right to reject a law while on a jury despite what a judge states.[22] People informing perspective jurors of this right have been harassed by the authorities, and some have been arrested and tried for jury tampering. In other words, people just quoting the words of the Founding Fathers like Thomas Jefferson are being arrested. The authorities are getting desperate, because increasingly juries in various cases are voting not guilty as word gets out. Perhaps next people telling perspective jurors about the right to free speech and freedom of worship will also be arrested. Where will it stop? On June 19, 1995 CBS *Evening News* completely distorted our history. A judge said letting a jury decide the law would create anarchy and this would be taking the law into their own hands. The head of the FIJA was interviewed and while he discussed the views of the Founders supporting the right of jury nullification, this was censored from what appeared on TV.

After the Oklahoma bombing, the *Wall Street Journal* wrote a propaganda piece defining jury-power activism as a racist and anti-Semitic militia plot. That the Founders and many justices have long supported this right, which exists to this day, was ignored.[23] The *Village Voice* quoted this article suggesting that jury rights people may well be extremists and racists.[24] It was stated in the *Wall Street Journal*, so it must be true! Disinformation creates more lies and our heritage is gradually forgotten. A few public trials like the O.J. case are now being used as an excuse to attack and change the jury system to further weaken our civil rights.

Another strategy is to create more crime and a false war on drugs by deliberately flooding the country with illegal drugs. "U.S. officials had undercut the war on drugs for so long, and exposes had dribbled out so sporadically, that public outrage never reached critical mass."[25] This is being done to scare people into giving up certain constitutionally protected rights such as the right to bear arms. Chaos and fear have historically been used to create a totalitarian state. Rather than trying to seize all guns, a far better solution to crime would be to resolve the issues that have turned people to criminal activity and to stop the government from flooding the country with illegal drugs.

On one radio show, a student quoted his college professor as saying the main reason why the Founders wanted people to own a gun was to prevent government tyranny. The "expert" on the show, who had written a book on gun control, said this was a myth. Most historians and legal scholars understand that the student and his professor are correct, but many now say otherwise. One reason we no longer have constitutional government is because our constitutional heritage is being relegated to the level of a myth. On May 9, 1994 ABC ran *Day One: America Under the Gun*. A reporter said with so much crime the Constitution is becoming a luxury.

The media constantly tells us that crime keeps getting worse when that is not true. The Washington Center for Media and Public Affairs found that between 1992 and 1993 the number of crime stories reported on ABC, CBS, and NBC had doubled. The drug scare is being used as an excuse to tighten government control over the people and to strengthen the national security state. Crime is being used as an excuse to federalize and militarize state and local police into a unified national police force.

An obvious example of how drugs have been used to control and demoralize the people is exemplified by the black ghettos being flooded with illegal drugs. Ample supply helped create demand. The radical black movement of the 1960s became submerged in a drug haze. Louis Farrakhan was quite right to state, when being interviewed by Barbara Walters on ABC in 1994, that in the mid-1960s the black community was suddenly flooded with illegal drugs and this was done by the government. Norval Morris, a law professor, interviewed almost 100 experts in law enforcement and they called the war on drugs a war against blacks. White people buy and sell most illegal drugs, but most people imprisoned are black.[26]

It is much easier to control and manipulate a society that loses its will to drugs. Drug use weakens will power and the ability for independent thinking. This can be illegal drugs like cocaine or legal drugs like Prozac or Valium. Many schools post "Drug Free Zone" signs and proceed to drug the children with Ritalin to control them. The end result is that people have difficulty thinking clearly and defending their rights, which are slowly being lost. When Japan ruled China during World War II, it flooded China with opium, as did England in the 1800s, to control the populace and raise money for government operations.[27]

Besides these key strategies, many other techniques are used to fool the people. Reasonable goals are proclaimed that most would support, while hidden objectives are promoted that support the one world government. Noble objectives are promoted that also provide more wealth and control for the corporate elite while weakening the rights of the people. False promises of greater material wealth, jobs, and environmental protection were used to promote NAFTA and GATT, while these treaties actually foster the destruction of the middle class and U.S. sovereignty. Under President Carter there was a call to help third world nations with their debt crisis. Many decent people wanted to raise the standard of living in these nations, so they supported a plan to provide assistance. Instead that money was used to pay interest on multinational bank loans.

Asset forfeiture laws show that laws are passed, supposedly to protect the people against criminals, and then the laws are enforced well beyond their original intent or language to remove the people's rights. These laws were originally passed to seize the property of drug dealers and mafia leaders, but today they are often applied to innocent citizens while the criminals hide their assets so they cannot be seized. These laws are being enacted supposedly to protect the people, when in fact constitutional rights are violated.

Another strategy is to introduce an especially egregious law or program in a less-populated state where there is less media coverage. If the law passes, it is introduced in other states. If there is great resistance, the government backs down, always watching how the people react, perhaps presenting the same law in another state with certain changes. In 1989 Oklahoma passed a law requiring everyone to register their assets, with a heavy fine if you refused or hid any assets, so similar laws may be passed in other states. As discussed in Chapter XV, today the National Guard has basically established martial law in parts of Puerto Rico. This has been going on for several years with little press coverage. It is done in the name of protecting the people from crime, as the people lose their rights. How long will it be before this occurs in many states?

Very long laws are passed that include obscure clauses that are difficult to find and that few would support. These clauses are rarely discussed by the press or in Congress. After Senator Brown read NAFTA, a 2,000 page document, he was shocked enough to reverse his vote and reject it. The GATT treaty establishing the World Trade Organization contains 22,000 pages. Provisions in GATT make it harder for Americans to save for retirement. The amount U.S. employees can contribute to 401(k) plans has been reduced to compensate for lost revenue due to tariffs being reduced. A UN food safety and trade commission will help set GATT standards, which may lower or remove many U.S. consumer safety laws such as pesticide use. We may soon be flooded with radiated products because other nations will insist on this under GATT. Under the Constitution, Article 1, Section 8 Clause 3, Congress shall "regulate Commerce with foreign Nations...." This has been illegally surrendered by GATT—to a foreign entity.

GATT created a new commission, CODEX, under the UN World Health Organization. It is now in the process of establishing strict international standards which will require a doctor's prescription to obtain supplements, because this is what the large drug companies want. This will cause many problems in the alternative health movement, and many health food stores will close. Politicians like Clinton and Dole will complain for five minutes, and then pass more laws destroying U.S. sovereignty.

After the Oklahoma bombing, I constantly read and heard the right wing attacked in the national media as being conspiracy nuts, partly because it felt the UN was a serious threat to the U.S. Never once was there a discussion of the huge body of evidence supporting such concerns. A classic example of this propaganda took place in late October, 1995 on *Talk of the Nation*, a PBS talk radio show. The topic was the UN and the three guests were all pro-UN. Sure enough, as the show began, the announcer asked about right-wing concerns over the UN controlling the U.S. The three guests immediately agreed this was foolish. This was like asking a Marxist to criticize communism. When you debate a topic and have three guests, at least one should take an opposing position. Otherwise, you just get propaganda.

It is not that the UN alone is a threat, it is the large corporations that have always controlled the UN, and the concern is what they plan to do with it. Right from the start the UN has been a corporate front. The CFR, led by the Soviet agent Alger Hiss, played a key role in establishing the UN, and its headquarters are built on Rockefeller-donated land. The U.S. delegation to form the UN included many CFR members. The press declares that the UN is quite disorganized and incompetent, and an example of this is the failed UN peacekeeping operations. This is a convenient excuse to hide the future plans for the UN to be the center of a one world government. C.B. Dall, *FDR, My Exploited Father-in-Law*, said: "The UN is but a long-range, international-banking apparatus neatly set up for financial and economic profit by a small group of powerful One-World Revolutionaries, hungry for profit and power."[28]

Truman signed the UN Participation Act on December 20, 1945. Under this act "The President shall not be deemed to require the authorization of the Congress" to provide troops to the UN security council as the president desired. The constitutional requirement that only Congress can declare a war was illegally weakened by this treaty. Rep. Frederick Smith said: "This measure strikes at the very heart of the Constitution. It provides that the power to declare war shall be taken from Congress and given to the President. Here is the essence of dictatorship, and dictatorial control over all else must inevitably tend to follow." Time is proving him correct. Congress has little influence over how the U.S. votes at the UN. The UN, not Congress, approved the Korean War. At the UN on October 24, 1950 Truman said: "The men who laid down their lives for the UN in Korea...died in order that the UN might live." Are you prepared to die for the UN? Ask the relatives of the 54,000 soldiers killed in that "nonwar" if we should be concerned about the UN. To this day U.S. troops serving in Korea serve under the UN. When U.S. serviceman David Hilemon was killed over North Korea in 1994, his body was returned in a casket covered with a UN flag. On April 25, 1996, Anthony Lake, Clinton's national security adviser, said in a lecture we need to be a "global 911" to manage the world's crises.

While many criticize the actions of UN peacekeepers, people don't understand that NATO is a military arm of the UN. NATO and SEATO were created as collective defense organizations under Article 51 of the UN charter. Articles 1, 5, 7, and 12 in the NATO treaty show the reliance of NATO on the UN for its legitimacy. On December 15, 1995, the UN Security Council approved the NATO mission to Bosnia. This approval was necessary for NATO to act. Supporting the policy of the UN being used to create a one world government, the new head of NATO is a Spanish Marxist. Rep. Funderburk and 35 others in Congress attacked this appointment.

Led by members of the CFR in 1961, the U.S. State Department issued a publication, *Freedom From War*, outlining in detail plans to disarm the U.S. military and establish a UN army. The U.S. Arms Control and Disarmament Agency, also established in 1961, is working towards this goal. Books like *A World Effectively Controlled By the UN, Introduction to World Peace Through World Law*, and *World Peace Through World Law* describe these plans in great detail. Aside from local police who will carry small arms, the entire world is to be disarmed except for a powerful UN army and police force. In 1992, UN Secretary General Boutros Ghali presented *An Agenda for Peace* calling for a permanent UN army. The report said: "The time of absolute and exclusive sovereignty has passed," and it listed reasons that would justify the UN using its army to intervene in a nation. Senator Boren, in the *New York Times* August 26, 1992, said the world needs a UN army to create the new world order. On June 27, 1995 the *New York Times* called for a UN world army that could be paid for by people paying dues as UN citizens. Articles 42 and 43 of the UN charter provide the basis for creating a UN army under the UN Security Council.[29] In the April 11, 1993 *Washington Post,* the prominent journalist George Will said "Article 43 is the law of the land—our land." Why weren't the American people asked to approve this change?

For years there have been calls for ensuring UN domination by transferring all nuclear weapons to a UN army. No nation will be allowed to have nuclear weapons. On December 17, 1995 the *Rocky Mountain News* said Clinton transferred a ton of plutonium at Rocky Flats and 199 tons of nuclear material in Oak Ridge, Tennessee to the UN. Done without congressional approval, this represents 20 percent of U.S. strategic nuclear reserves.

*Foreign Policy*, a corporate mouthpiece, presented an article that actually listed nations to be taken over by the UN.[30] The use of UN troops in Somalia and Haiti exemplifies the coming trend. Clinton used U.S. troops to enter Haiti after receiving UN permission; he refused to seek the approval of Congress as required by the Constitution. Strobe Talbott, a CFR member and Deputy Secretary of State, said "once a country utterly loses its ability to govern itself, it also loses its claim to sovereignty and should become a ward of the UN."[31] Under the Dayton Accord, Bosnia got a new Constitution which surrendered sovereignty and required that it become a UN protectorate. Foreign judges will be appointed and a UN representative will be "the final authority in theatre."[32] Rep. Duncan Hunter, in the January 26, 1996 *Human Events*, said Bosnia will be controlled for five years and that our commitment to reshape this society is much deeper and longer than the American people understand. Already the *New York Times* reported on June 13, 1996 that U.S. troops may have to remain in Bosnia beyond 1996. The Bosnia horror may have been deliberately created so the UN solution could be provided as a test case to end a nation's sovereignty. William Pfaff in the *International Herald Tribune*, which is owned by the *Washington Post* and *New York Times*, said: "The principle of absolute national sovereignty is being overturned....The civil war in Yugoslavia has rendered this service to us."

Another example of this pattern occurred in late July, 1991 on CNN. Stansfield Turner, ex-head of the CIA, said about Iraq: "We have a much bigger objective. We've got to look at the long run here. This is an example—the situation between the UN and Iraq—where the UN is deliberately intruding into the sovereignty of a sovereign nation....Now this is a marvelous precedent (for) all countries of the world...." In 1933 H.G. Wells, in *The Shape of Things to Come*, said the new world order would develop in around 50 years out of a conflict near Basra, Iraq when "Russia is ready to assimilate." With the Gulf War, he was almost correct.

Already an international police force has formed and is serving in Bosnia. The *Daily Universe* quoted Kissinger associate Lawrence Eagleburger's speech at Brigham Young University on November 8, 1994. He said: The U.S. "can either become the world policeman, or an international policing force must be established with adequate authority and force to maintain world peace....We have to be the world's thought policemen to create a world police force." In 1995 the U.S. contributed millions of dollars to establish an international police training center in Hungary.

The *Chicago Tribune*, on September 29, 1993 presented an editorial by Bob Greene describing the many problems in the U.S. He said a UN multinational force is desperately needed in the U.S. On April 16, 1996 NBC *Evening News* said "5,000 police officers from around the world" will protect the Olympics in Atlanta. *Newsweek* on June 24 said "foreign law enforcement agencies" would protect the Olympics. *The Economist* said on June 22 that over 2,000 international police would be on hand. Obviously, the U.S. has enough trained people to provide proper security, but this exercise will help get Americans used to foreign troops patrolling our streets.

The unofficial word in the U.S. military is that, to get ahead in their careers officers must promote working under the UN in various peacekeeping missions. Traditional patriotism is no longer sufficient. This new role was described by James J. Schneider in the April, 1995 military journal *Special Warfare*. Schneider teaches at the U.S. Army Command and General Staff College. He said: "The U.S. Army of the future will face its greatest challenge since the end of the Civil War....The future will be dominated by a single overwhelming presence—the United Nations. The resurgence and growing influence of the UN will not only affect our soldiers but may change the very structure of the nation-state...." There is growing pressure on military officers to adjust to the new world order or to resign.

On May 24, 1994 the UN Disarmament Commission adopted a working paper proposing the control of guns in the U.S. and other nations to limit international arms trafficking. Clinton supports this objective. *Foreign Affairs* called for the prompt global control of small arms and weapons, because such weapons allow militias to challenge UN and U.S. troops. There may one day be a treaty requiring strict gun control in the U.S.[33]

There are growing calls for a world UN tax. In 1993 the Ford Foundation financed a study, *Financing an Effective United Nations*, by TC and CFR members. This report called for a UN tax. The UN's *Human Development Report*, in 1994 called for a UN tax. A global UN tax was discussed at the UN conference in Copenhagen in 1995. Sweden's Prime Minister Ingvar Carlsson, Australia's Foreign Minister Gareth Evansand, and Pakistan's Prime Minister Benazir Bhutto have called for a UN tax. Jon Stewart wrote a column that appeared in many newspapers calling for a UN tax. Reportedly the International Court of Justice may force Congress to pay this future tax.[34] On January 15, 1996 and in the March/April 1996 issue of *Foreign Affairs*, Boutros Ghali called for a UN tax and said ultimately such a tax would be applied. On May 13, 1996 *The Nation* called for a world flat tax to support the UN and other global institutions. According to this article "A global flat tax...would be in the interest of working and middle-class Americans." If you prefer to think that concern about a new world order is foolish fantasy, you will one day look back and think how low your taxes once were. In the new world order, there will be a new direct tax to support the world government. The U.S., which strongly supports the UN, could easily pay the money it owes the UN. However, using congressional resistance, the government may be deliberately creating a crisis, so that the UN will be given the authority to tax people directly.

In 1994 the Congressional Research Service published a revised version of a 1990 report "An International Criminal Court" stating that the UN is gradually trying to establish a permanent criminal court. In the future U.S. citizens may be tried before such a court for many different crimes. *Foreign Affairs* called for the examination of bank deposits in all nations and to establish a Global Bank Police to enhance banking security and limit money laundering.[35] Certain sites, like Yellowstone, have been declared World Heritage Sites by the UN. Park rangers in certain Colorado parks admit off the record that some land is now controlled by the UN. In other countries the UN has intervened in how land is used. The recent book *Our Global Neighborhood* in 410 pages outlined in great detail the coming world government. The plan, in the next few years, is to quietly sign treaties that will force all nations to join a world government. There are many books that explain how dangerous the UN is. As with many of the issues discussed in this chapter, this is a complex topic I will discuss in more detail in a future book.

Manipulating statistics is another widely used gimmick to fool the people. Clinton said domestic violence is the number one "health risk for women between the ages of 15 and 44 in our country" as he announced federal grants of $26 million to prevent this violence. According to the AP on March 22, 1995, the government released shocking statistics such as a claim that three to four million women a year are victims of domestic violence, to support Clinton's claim. Various authorities challenged this claim with some questioning what the government defines as violence. *Detroit News* columnist Tony Snow said typically in Washington "When you want to persuade people to do something that they see no need to do, don't reason with them. Make up a statistic so stunning that they will feel obligated to go along." Naturally, one result is more government control over our lives.

Other statistics are hidden from the people. We are constantly told that gun control is essential to ease the crime problem, yet when statistics suggest otherwise they are hidden or denied. Since Florida passed a law in 1987, 100,000 people have obtained a license to carry concealed handguns. There have been few abuses with only 17 licenses revoked because of a crime committed with a licensed gun. The national murder rate increased 12 percent between 1987 and 1992 but it dropped 21 percent in Florida. In this same period, Florida crime rose 17.8 percent but nationally it rose 24 percent.

Typically when a scandal surfaces and the public is aroused, an investigation is held but the people doing the investigating are carefully chosen, so that some information is released to satisfy the public but the full story is suppressed. This is done to convince people that the system still works. And officials may lie or not call certain witnesses during an investigation to cover-up unpleasant facts. After the Ames case broke, the CIA director said he would propose that Brent Scowcroft and Harold Brown should head a committee to review U.S. intelligence operations. It is business as usual with these CFR members. In the recent Whitewater hearings, Congress refused to question key people like Larry Nichols. Bo Gritz was only called at the last minute at the end of the Randy Weaver hearings with little press coverage.

The Task Force on Radiation and Human Rights tried to get people who were more sympathetic to the victims added to the government's recent investigation of secret government radiation experiments on people, but the White House was not responsive. Key people on the government's committee have links to the radiation experiments they are now investigating. Some panel members were from the same institutions being investigated.[36] One member of the government's investigation, Jay Katz, a medical ethics specialist said: "We don't want to pass severe moral judgments, because it's really more important to look at the present."[37] The standards have changed little from the 1940s, when the 1946 Nuremberg Code was established which required the agreement of people in experiments.[38] Already the Clinton regime is showing signs of wanting to get done with this story without revealing too much. The investigating committee released an Interim Report in October, 1994, and reported that various government agencies including the CIA are not providing the required information.

The three events that provided a convenient rationale for big government, and thus greater corporate power in the 20th century, were the two world wars and the great depression, with the resulting New Deal. In each instance the large corporations manipulated the people by using the Hegelian principle of creating a problem, then creating opposing views, and finally providing solutions that the people would otherwise never have accepted. Often one position has definite weaknesses, so the people will unknowingly accept the choice of the corporate elite.

During these emergencies, the government needed to borrow money which allowed the bankers to gain influence and profit. In such emergencies, the government surrendered more of its sovereignty to the large banks as collateral. This strategy has been used many times to create wasteful bureaucracies further enhancing federal corporate power. During a national crisis, normal constitutional restraints are forgotten, and once the federal government gets new powers it rarely gives them up. The constitutional scholar, Edward S. Corwin, said the New Deal and World War II greatly increased presidential powers and was leading to the dissolution of constitutional government and law. Our constitutional system of dual federalism and the doctrine of separation of powers has been radically altered as tremendous power shifted to the central government.[39]

During the great depression many like, Charles A. Beard in *The Open Door At Home*, felt the U.S. would best develop though regional trade, high tariffs, and self-sufficiency. The CFR used the depression to claim that it was partly caused by limiting trade and that global free trade would help solve the depression.[40] It is a deliberately created myth that the Hawley-Smoot Tariff Act of 1930 and "*laissez-faire* capitalism" of the 1920s caused the 1929 crash and great depression, so that big government was needed to control the excesses of capitalism. In previous depressions, the government didn't intervene, and the depression was settled much sooner and with far lower unemployment than in the 1930s. Extensive government intervention in the New Deal guaranteed a long and deep depression.[41]

Business cycles, especially depressions, are very influenced by government monetary intervention. Murray N. Rothbard and the Ludwig von Mises Institute have provided ample evidence that government intervention with loose bank credit during the 1920s played a key role in creating the great depression. There was a major increase in money supply from 1921 until July, 1929 primarily from an increase in bank deposits and bank credits. A House hearing on stabilizing the dollar disclosed, in 1928, that the Federal Reserve was working closely with European central banks and a major crash was planned.[42] The Federal Reserve followed a policy of continuous credit and a low discount during the 1920s causing inflation and foreign lending. By manipulating interest rates they inflated stock prices and then a tightened money supply caused a collapse in stock prices. Even Alan Greenspan, current head of the Federal Reserve admitted in *The Objectivist* July, 1966, that Fed excess credit policies in the 1920s "nearly destroyed the economies of the world."

Various bankers, such as J.P. Morgan, deliberately created several artificial panics to pressure the formation of a central bank. In the panic of 1893, Senator Robert Owen testified before a congressional committee about the Panic Circular of 1893 that his bank received. It said: "You will at once retire one-third of your circulation and call in one-half of your loans...." *Life* magazine on April 25, 1949, discussed the role of the Morgan bank in creating the panic of 1907.[43] William Bryan in *The United States Unresolved Monetary and Political Problems* described how the New York banks methodically called in broker call loans which meant stocks had to be sold which helped start the market collapse. After the Federal Reserve was created Rep. Charles Lindberg said: "From now on depressions will be scientifically created."

Rep. Louis McFadden, Chairman of the House Banking Committee, said: "It (the depression) was not accidental. It was a carefully contrived occurrence....The international bankers sought to bring about a condition of despair here so that they might emerge as the rulers of us all." On November 21, 1971 the *New York Times Magazine* quoted Rep. McFadden as stating the Federal Reserve Act established "a world banking system...a super-state controlled by international bankers and international industrialists acting together to enslave the world for their own pleasure." Every American should read McFadden's nine page statement about the Fed in the *Congressional Record* on June 10, 1932.

People were fooled into buying more stocks so they desperately needed government help after the market crashed. The Fed encouraged short-term borrowing then, at the appointed time, it called in the loans. Wealthy individuals aware of this manipulation sold stocks short or stayed out of the market and then made a fortune during the depression by buying stocks at sharply discounted prices. In *FDR, My Exploited Father-In-Law*, C.B. Dall said: the depression "was the calculated 'shearing' of the public by the World-Money powers, triggered by the planned sudden shortage of the supply of call money in the New York money market. Dall worked on the New York stock exchange floor during the depression. He said each day Ben Smith, supported by Tom Bragg and Joe Kennedy and their brokers, sold stocks short to undercut the entire market.[44]

In 1913 just before Christmas with only a few members present, Congress passed the Federal Reserve Act. No one challenged the false claim that the states had ratified this act. The Ninth Circuit court held in *Lewis v. U.S.* (1982) the "Federal Reserve Banks are privately owned, locally controlled corporations." Title 12 U.S. C. 283 and Title 12 U.S. C. 287 even list stock valuation information for this private corporation. The Fed is owned by various U.S. and European banks, yet under the Constitution, Article 1, Section 8, only Congress has the power "To coin Money, regulate the Value thereof...." If the U.S. Treasury prints money, there is no interest. Instead the government borrows billions of dollars a year paying about $250 billion a year just in interest for Federal Reserve notes that have no real value, while the media perpetuates the myth that the Federal Reserve is part of the U.S. government. The federal debt developed after the Federal Reserve was established, while gold and silver certificates were replaced by Federal Reserve notes. Congress cannot even investigate the daily activities of the Fed. This fraud worked because the politicians committed treason, and the people were asleep. In *FDR, My Exploited Father-in-Law*, C.B. Dall said: "The One-World Government leaders and their ever-close bankers...have now acquired full control of the money and credit machinery of the U.S....,via the creation...of the *privately owned* Federal Reserve Bank."[45]

Like any private corporation, the Fed takes actions to protect its stockholders; it does not represent the American people or even the federal government. This is why so many criticize Fed policies over interest rates. Your IRS checks are deposited into this private bank not in the U.S. Treasury, with no real accountability as to where the funds actually go. President Kennedy was assassinated partly because he printed U.S. Treasury notes along with the usual Federal Reserve notes. The Fed is the only profit-making corporation in the U.S. that isn't taxed. The talk about balancing the budget is an attempt to deflect the people's attention about the illegal activities of the Federal Reserve and the fact that the U.S. is bankrupt. Someday people will look back and wonder in amazement that so many people could have been so fooled for so many years by this scam.

The New Deal reforms were originally presented to extend and share governing power to assist the weak and unrepresented. The proclaimed goal was to create new forums and agencies for decision making, to provide a vehicle for citizens to be more involved in a representative government. Instead the New Deal enhanced government power over the people, created a national emergency that continues today, and allowed the power of the moneyed interests to spread. The federal government that has existed since the New Deal is an aberration that is anathema to our political heritage. Constitutional restraints were removed in the name of more democracy and greater equality. In 1936 former Senator James A. Reed, previously a supporter of the New Deal, attacked it as a "tyrannical" measure "leading to despotism, sought by its sponsors under the communistic cry of 'social justice.'" On the Senate floor he said Roosevelt's family "is one of the largest stockholders in" GE, and FDR was a "hired man for the economic royalists" on Wall Street.

The New Deal welfare state was set up with the intention of having a free people become addicted to big government. The welfare state represents government addiction. The process was like drug dealers who go to schools and give away free drugs, so people will become addicted and buy more and more. Then it is that much easier to manipulate and control the people. The myth was created that big government is good and that it should take care of everyone. The foremost principle of the Founding Fathers was that people should be allowed to lead their lives without government interference. With the New Deal we achieved the exact opposite. Our tradition of limited constitutional government with a system of checks and balances was forgotten. The mythology that Roosevelt saved America from the great depression and helped lead us through the second world war covers up the fact that we were once a free and independent people with little government interference except in clearly delineated areas. In the New Deal people sacrificed freedom and a belief that our rights come from God for a false sense of economic security. The paternalistic welfare system perpetuates dependency and weakness while robbing us of self-reliance and citizenship. A primary goal today should be not just to reinvent government but to restore responsible citizenship.

Numerous historians have pondered why there weren't more radical changes during the New Deal. William E. Leuchtenburg, author of *Franklin D. Roosevelt and the New Deal 1932-1940* and a widely respected scholar of the New Deal, called it a "halfway revolution." He concluded that Roosevelt carefully prevented challenges to vested interests, while the unorganized people rarely benefited. The National Recovery Administration did little to speed recovery and probably hindered it, the Agricultural Adjustment Agency curbed farm production when people were hungry which also hurt tenant farmers, and the Home Owners Loan Corporation helped refinance homes but also foreclosed on 100,000 mortgages.

Walter Karp in *Indispensable Enemies* has perhaps presented the best summary and analysis of Roosevelt's phony policies. "Roosevelt almost never fought for reform until it was forced upon him by overwhelming popular pressure, whereupon he saw to it that the reform enacted was as minimal as he could make it....Roosevelt's duplicity was a heinous act of bad faith and betrayal."[46] For instance, the Emergency Banking Relief Act was a very conservative document that restored the bankers' power at public expense, despite what reformers wanted.

Richard Hofstadter in *The Age of Reform* criticized the New Deal for opportunism and stressed the discontinuity of the New Deal with the populist reform tradition. Howard Zinn said Roosevelt was cautious about supporting candidates who wanted bold economic and social change, and he never created new political forces among the poor and disadvantaged who would have helped bring about a more complete economic transformation and redistribution of wealth.[47]

Barton J. Bernstein said most New Deal reforms accomplished far less than many claimed. "Though vigorous in rhetoric and experimental in tone, the New Deal was narrow in its goals and wary of bold economic reform." The "maneuvers in social reform were limited to cautious excursions." The New Deal reforms did not transform the American system; there was no real redistribution of income. Corporations did not become more responsible, and the political power of businesses was never weakened. Instead it grew stronger. Many Americans received no assistance in the 1930s, and while most ultimately didn't starve, there was little improvement in the economic lives of people aside from the rhetoric.[48]

I have discussed the New Deal partly because of another gigantic hoax called the Contract With America. This is another sophisticated plan to give the large corporations more money and power,[49] and it is another diversion to distract the people and Congress while more of our rights are removed. Amazingly many consider this contract revolutionary. Arthur Schlesinger, Jr feels the Republican attempts to dismantle the federal government is bringing the country back to the Articles of Confederation.[50]

*Money* magazine explained how, under the guise of attacking greedy lawyers, both houses with the aid of powerful financial lobbyists approved a law that seriously cripples the rights of investors to be protected against fraudulent financial advisors. The Republicans also strengthened federal controls and eliminated state laws that protected individual investors, supposedly to help the people. The representatives pushing this received large sums of money from groups like J.P. Morgan, Citicorp, and Merrill Lynch. The people want less federal control, but Congress won't really listen because the bankers and corporate elite control the Democratic/Republican party.[51] Tort reform includes corporate friendly clauses that limit punitive damages and the amount that can be collected in personal injury cases. In addition, tax money still goes to Washington, and the push for more federal control over crime continues.

The National Security Restoration Act was supposed to prevent U.S. troops from serving under UN command. On January 26, 1995, Secretary of State Warren Christopher lied before the House International Relations Committee declaring this provision unconstitutional. The resulting bill was so watered down that it is worthless. If the president certifies that service under the UN is in the vital national interest of the U.S., it is allowed, despite the Constitution. Article 1, Section 8 grants Congress the exclusive authority to declare war and raise and support the military.

The Brookings Institution released a report, *Fine Print*, saying the Contract With America is not a radical break with big government. Instead it "represents the final consolidation" of federal power; it will not significantly lessen federal government control over our lives. "The Contract preserves the national government's role in making, administering, and funding the vast and varied array of post-New Deal and post-Great Society domestic policies and programs."[52]

The contract and other Republican policies have been handled so poorly perhaps because there is a deliberate plan to defeat the freshmen members of the House. The corporate controllers don't really care who is in power in the Democratic/Republican party, unless there are individuals who threaten their influence as is the case with many of the new Republicans. An obvious move for Wall Street is to bring back the big government Democrats. Unfortunately, these new Republicans are too naive to understand who is really in control. In 1936 Roosevelt had a serious problem when so many liberal democrats were elected. Not wanting real reforms that would help the people and injure corporate power, Roosevelt took steps that rolled back the liberal tide in 1938. We may be seeing the same maneuver today.

The principle of providing government benefits to make the people more dependent on the government has been applied in hundreds of programs. Rep. Lamar Smith and Senator Simpson introduced bills to control immigration by creating a new federal computer system to identify every American hired. This would create a vast new federal bureaucracy and tighten federal control over the people despite GOP rhetoric. A national identification system is part of the plan.

The Clinton health plan was supposed to benefit the people's health but it would have increased federal control with a smart card introduced for better surveillance over our lives. A universal Health Security Card would have become a national ID card, and it would have been harder to use alternative healing methods under Clinton's plan. Presently smart cards can store 1,600 pages of information.

In 1992 candidate Clinton said: "Everyone will carry a smart card, encoded with his or her personal medical information."[53]

There is a serious risk that our Constitution will be replaced with a corporate approved version. Several new Constitutions have already been prepared. For instance, in 1964, the Ford and Rockefeller Foundations spent millions of dollars preparing the Proposed Constitution for the New States of America. In it the Bill of Rights was replaced by the grant of certain privileges. Our God given rights would be assigned and granted by the state when it deemed appropriate. The World Constitution and Parliament Association in Lakewood, Colorado has already prepared a world Constitution for the planned world government. Steven Boyd in *Alternative Constitutions for the U.S.* presents 10 proposed new Constitutions. If the one world government takes over, the present Constitution will be banned as a subversive document. Phil Marsh a tax protester was brought to trial. One count involved him sending the Constitution through the mail. When McVeigh's sister was initially questioned about the Oklahoma bombing, the press said she was found with extremist literature like the Constitution.

For years there have been attempts to hold a constitutional convention under the guise of weakening federal power and restoring state rights. In May, 1994 Utah Governor Mike Leavitt, a leader of the National Conference of State Legislatures which is supported by the Rockefeller and Carnegie Foundations, called for a Conference of States (COS). Leavitt said: "Our national government...is outdated and old-fashioned....There is a much better way." According to the May 25, 1994 *Salt Lake Tribune*, Governor Leavitt called for a constitutional convention but people were so angry at this that he soon denied making such a statement. In 1995 the National Governor's Association joined in the call to hold this meeting in Philadelphia October 22-25, the 50th anniversary of the UNs founding. With little public awareness, attending this convention was approved in various states, often with no debate, because of pressure by local political leaders.

In each state people quietly promoted this convention, denying it would be a constitutional convention despite the gathering evidence. It was claimed that the meeting would not have the force of law, so why was each state legislator required to pass a Resolution of Participation? They required that two-thirds of the states pass the resolution which is what is required to hold a constitutional convention. The conference would make its own rules and, per the Constitution, could petition Congress to hold a Constitutional convention and do whatever they wanted, even though the American people would have no idea the meeting was even taking place. This would have been the first meeting of all the states since the original Constitutional convention, but the national media rarely discussed this plan.

Senators Helms and Brown introduced Resolution 82 asking the states to convene a COS to add amendments to the Constitution "and that such states then consider whether it is necessary for the states to convene a constitutional convention pursuant to Article V of the Constitution of the U.S., in order to adopt such Amendment." Some people promoting COS, like Charles Cooper, openly call for changing our constitutional form of government. Paul Weyrich founder of the American Legislative Exchange Council which is also pushing COS said in a March 8, 1987 editorial in the *Washington Post* "Our national strategy is outdated, dysfunctional and insupportable....If we are going to be a serious nation, we need a serious system...we need some type of shadow government...." The clearest expression of subversion came in the book *Reforming American Government* released by the Committee on the Constitutional System, another CFR controlled group pushing for parliamentary government in America. One of it directors James M. Burn's, using text from *The Power to Lead*, said: "Let us face reality. The framers have simply been too shrewd for us. They have outwitted us. They designed separated institutions that cannot be unified by mechanical linkages, frail bridges, tinkering. If we are to 'turn the founders upside down'...we must directly confront the constitutional structure they erected."[54]

The Patriot movement got numerous state legislators to reject attending this convention, so the necessary number of states required for it to convene was not attained and it was cancelled. There was an intense debate in about 25 states. The Philadelphia city council voted unanimously March 16, 1995 not to support holding the meeting. The *Wall Street Journal* pushed for a constitutional convention,[55] while the *New York Times* in frustration announced that extreme right wing conspiracy theorists had blocked the meeting.[56]

This is a classic example of how the corporate view decides what is politically correct in America. The states rejected this phony conference because so many Americans complained to their state legislators. When America speaks and it doesn't reflect the corporate view the left or right is slandered. The canceling of this phony convention demonstrated the patriotism and influence of the Patriot movement. It also angered and scared the corporate elite. The call for this conference is coming from the large corporations, not from the people.

Before, the plan was to quietly get the states to agree to hold this meeting without anyone noticing. Now the plan is to use money. The corporate elite, including Mobile, Chevron, and Philip Morris, have already announced plans to redouble their efforts and to donate millions of dollars to various legislators to hold this convention, which is now called a Federalism Summit, in 1996. A meeting was held in Cincinnati October 22, 1995 to plan the strategy. Contact your local representatives and tell them not to allow this convention, which would change the Constitution and remove many of our rights.

James Weinstein, in *The Corporate Idea in the Liberal State, 1900-1918*, described how the liberal social reforms of the 20th century, from the New Deal to the New Frontier and the Great Society, ultimately were developed and managed by the corporations, not by progressive elements. The purpose always was to prevent anti-corporate sentiment and to control the marketplace. Weinstein describes "a conscious and successful effort to guide the economic and social policies of federal, state, and municipal governments by various business groupings in their own long-range interest as they perceived it."

The special interest groups, especially the large corporations, remain in control of the federal government and various schemes are used to fool the people about this. As shown in the 1994 election many people are fed up with the overwhelming power of the federal government; yet there are few attempts by Congress to return power to the states and the people. Programs by the states to make changes in welfare still require money to come from the federal government. The Contract With America didn't even include lobbying and campaign-finance reforms. Most people remain convinced that the source of many problems is the government, when in fact it is that the large corporations control the government. This reality has been deflected by careful propaganda. We have all been lied to for so long that that we are losing sight of our heritage and the truth can be quite shocking.

# Chapter VI

# State Rights and the Federal Government

"I believe there are more instances of the abridgment of freedom of the people by gradual and silent encroachments of those in power than by violent and sudden usurpations."

James Madison

"When all government, domestic and foreign, in little as in great things shall be drawn to Washington as the center of all power, it will...become as venal and oppressive as the government from which we are separated....I believe the states can best govern our home concerns and the general government our foreign ones."

Thomas Jefferson

The first attempt at federation occurred in 1643. For defense purposes four New England colonies formed the United Colonies of New England which was called a firm and perpetual union. In 1686 the union was disbanded. The original Articles of Confederation were abandoned because the central government was too weak. Now we have gone to the other extreme. As stated in the Declaration of Independence July 4, 1776, "That whenever any Form of Government becomes destructive of these ends, (described freedoms) it is the Right of the People to alter or abolish it, and to institute new Government...." Our Constitution does not state that the federal government shall exist in perpetuity, partly because the Articles of Confederation were four times declared to exist in perpetuity yet that agreement soon failed.

The federal government was created by 13 sovereign and free nations. Great Britain recognized the sovereign independence of each state at the 1783 Paris peace treaty. In *Sturges vs. Crowninshield* (1819), Chief Justice of the Supreme Court Marshall said at the beginning "we were divided into independent states, united for some purposes, but in most respects sovereign." These independent states decided on their own to accept the new Constitution. Before the Civil War the words used in various federal documents were "the U.S. are" but than that was changed to "the U.S. is." In older versions of the Bill of Rights the word "State" was always in capital letter but that is no longer true. Each of the 13 colonies performed the duties of sovereign states such as having a legislature to raise taxes and conduct war, raise a militia, and have relations with other states. To this day many states have economic relations with foreign nations to increase commerce.

Before accepting the new Constitution, Massachusetts demanded "that it be explicitly declared that all powers not delegated by the aforesaid Constitution are reserved to the several States, to be by them exercised." According to the New Hampshire Constitution, "The people of this Commonwealth have the sole and exclusive right of governing themselves as a free, sovereign, and independent

State; and do and forever hereafter shall exercise and enjoy every power, jurisdiction, and right which is not, or may not hereafter be, by them, expressly delegated to the U.S."

When Virginia joined the new Union on June 25, 1788, it declared "the powers granted under the Constitution, being derived from the people of the U.S., may be resumed by them whensoever the same shall be perverted to their injury or oppression...." When New York joined the Union on July 25, 1788, it said: "That the powers of Government may be re-assumed by the people, whensoever it shall become necessary to their happiness...." Rhode Island and North Carolina did not join the Union for over a year after the Union had been approved. They were considered independent sovereign nations by the other states. Upon joining the Union, Rhode Island declared: "That the powers of Government may be resumed by the people, whensoever it shall become necessary to their happiness...." Other state constitutions, like Texas, have similar protections.

William Rawle wrote *Views of the Constitution* in 1825, stating: "It depends on the State itself to retain or abolish the principle of representation, because it depends on itself whether or not it will continue a member of the Union. To deny this right would be inconsistent with the principle on which all our political systems are founded, which is, that the people have in all cases, a right to determine how they will be governed....The secession of a State from the Union depends on the will of the people of such a State." Rawles, born in Philadelphia, was a friend of Benjamin Franklin and George Washington. His book was widely used in constitutional law courses at various colleges throughout the country, including at West Point.

Before the Civil War, the states sometimes challenged federal authority. Many patriots today would draw inspiration from the debates in the late 1700s. The Alien and Sedition Acts angered many, and if Jefferson hadn't become president in 1800 and rejected these laws, the country might have split apart. Many considered the federal government the enemy of the people, and newspaper criticism was widespread. In 1797 Jefferson said the federal government represented "foreign jurisdiction."

The right of nullification was initially proclaimed in 1798, with the Virginia and Kentucky Resolutions, which were written by Madison and Jefferson. The doctrine of nullification is based on the understanding that the Union is an agreement among sovereign states, that the states have the right to judge violations of the Constitution, and the states don't have to follow the laws set forth by their agent, the federal government. Kentucky said nullification was the "rightful remedy" for violating the Constitution. Madison said federal inherent or implied powers were "creatures of ambition" which would ultimately "swallow up the State sovereignties." Since the states and the people created the Constitution, a state had a right to nullify or reject an unconstitutional federal law.[1] The federal government is an agent for the states that created it and who are its principals. Congress does not have the right to pass laws that violate the Constitution. Any such laws are invalid, because the federal government is not above the Constitution.

The U.S. did poorly in the War of 1812 partly because some states refused to provide a militia. They felt this was strictly a war between England and the federal government. In 1814 the New England states met in Hartford to consider seceding from the Union because the war had cost them considerable trade losses. They proclaimed the right of nullification.

In 1831 John Calhoun said: "The great and leading principle is that the general government emanated from the people of the several states, forming distinct political communities, and acting in their separate and sovereign capacity, and not from all the people forming one aggregate political community." Calhoun also said: "The object of a Constitution is to restrain the government, as that of laws is to restrain individuals." In the 1830s Georgia refused to follow several Supreme Court decisions regarding the Cherokee Indians. In 1832 South Carolina declared certain federal tariffs null and void. President Andrew Jackson, on December 10, 1832, called nullification rebellion and treason, but both sides backed down. In the 1850s various northern States nullified the 1850 Fugitive Slave Law by passing personal liberty laws. Slavery was a constant source of tension before the Civil War.

In 1848 Abraham Lincoln said: "Any people anywhere being inclined and having the power have the right to rise up and shake off the existing government, and form a new one that suits them better." In 1860, when confronted with these words, Lincoln defended his view of maintaining the Union by turning to God and the mystical belief that the Union must be saved at all costs. The power of the federal government increased tremendously during and after the Civil War. Supreme Court Chief Justice Salmon P. Chase said state sovereignty died at Appomattox.

In 1868 the Fourteenth Amendment was passed unconstitutionally. This act created a new class of citizenship. The Senate then consisted of 72 members, including 22 southerners. Since the Senate did not have the required 48 votes to pass the Fourteenth amendment, it would not seat the southerners. As a result, only 34 votes were needed. However, they were still one vote short, so, without a hearing, they illegally unseated a New Jersey senator who was against the amendment because he had only been elected by a plurality. Such an election was legal in New Jersey and in other states so this act was illegal but the conspirators used this strategy because they did not have the required two-third vote needed to expel a seated senator. The Fourteenth Amendment was passed by 33 of 49 senators. In a similar manner, the House would not seat 58 southern representatives, so the 182 northern members only needed 122 votes to pass the amendment. Although the vote was two short of the two-thirds required, the amendment was declared passed with 120 votes.

By March, 1867 only 17 of 37 states had ratified the amendment. Then the Reconstruction Act was passed, legalizing military occupation of all southern states except Tennessee—which had approved the new amendment. Under the military occupation most southern whites lost the right to vote, and six southern states were forced to pass the Fourteenth Amendment. This insured that the required 29 states were reached. Although Ohio and New Jersey repealed their earlier approval, disgusted with these events, they were still counted and the amendment was ratified.[2]

In *Dyett v. Turner* (1967) the Utah Supreme Court attacked the method by which the Fourteenth Amendment was passed. In *State v. Phillips* (1975) the Utah Supreme Court said: "No court in full possession of its faculties could honestly hold that the amendment (Fourteenth) was properly approved and adopted." The Fourteenth Amendment has been used to expand federal power "not only not granted to it, but expressly forbidden to it....History is strewn with other examples which demonstrate that undue, uncontrolled and unwieldy concentrations of power in any individual or institution tends to destroy itself. It is our opinion that this is the evil which the founders feared so keenly and tried so zealously to guard against, but which is now rife upon us." Although the Fourteenth Amendment has often been used to expand federal power, the Supreme Court has never ruled on its constitutionality.

Until early this century people still felt primarily loyal to their state. The federal government was a distant body that had little direct impact on people's lives. This is a key reason why so many southerners left the Union during the Civil War. It is difficult for us to appreciate such state loyalty today. The federal government was greatly enhanced when the Sixteenth Amendment, to collect income taxes, was falsely passed in 1913. This directly linked the federal government to every taxpayer and gradually played a further role in weakening state sovereignty.

The Ninth and Tenth Amendments strictly limit the federal government to those powers defined in the Constitution to protect state sovereignty and the people's rights. The evidence clearly shows that "the ratifying States regarded this statement of reserved powers as a vital, indeed an absolutely necessary addition to the Constitution."[3] And the first article of the Constitution states: "All legislative Powers herein granted...." which means the federal government only has the powers granted to it by the Constitution. That these amendments have been greatly weakened in this century, in violation of the Constitution, is the heart of our problem. The federal government has a role to play but it should be strictly within the Constitution.

Under the Constitution, the states agreed to give certain of their sovereign powers to the federal government. However, these few powers were specifically outlined with all other powers reserved to the states and the people. During the debate over ratifying the Constitution, this principle was widely understood, so many wondered in amazement how anyone could ever imagine that the federal government would usurp state sovereignty. Alexander Hamilton said in, *The Federalist Papers*, number 9: "The proposed Constitution so far from implying an abolition of the state governments, makes them constituent parts of the national sovereignty, by allowing them a direct representation in the Senate, and leaves in their possession certain exclusive and very important portions of sovereign power." In *The Federalist Papers*, number 17, Hamilton added: "Allowing the utmost latitude to the love of power which any reasonable man can require, I confess I am at a loss to discover what temptation the persons entrusted with the administration of the general (federal) government could ever feel to divest the states of the authorities of that description....It will always be far more easy for the state governments to encroach upon the national authorities, than for the national government to encroach upon the state authorities."

James Madison said in *The Federalist Papers*, number 45: "The state governments may be regarded as constituent and essential parts of the federal government; whilst the latter is nowise essential to the operation or organization of the former....The powers delegated by the proposed Constitution to the federal government are few and defined. Those which are to remain in the state governments are numerous and indefinite. The former will be exercised principally on external objects, as war, peace, negotiations, and foreign commerce....The powers reserved to the several states will extend to all the objects which, in the ordinary course of affairs, concern the lives, liberties, and properties of the people, and the internal order, improvement, and prosperity of the state." This hardly sounds like our present government. Leaving most powers including those undefined to the states and people and only a few defined powers to the federal government was a deliberate system of checks and balances to prevent the tyranny that is so common in concentrated government power. Today Washington has forgotten that the ultimate purpose of separate government powers is to protect the people from government tyranny.

During the ratification debate in Virginia, Patrick Henry and George Mason opposed the new Constitution. Henry said: "Be extremely cautious, watchful, and jealous of your liberty. Instead of securing your rights, you may lose them forever. There will be no checks, no real balances, in this government."[4] George Mason said having a central government "is totally subversive of every principle which has hitherto governed us. This power is calculated to annihilate totally the State governments....These two concurrent powers cannot exist long together; the one will destroy the other...." Mason was also very critical of the taxing power which he said "must carry everything before it."[5]

In 1816 Thomas Jefferson wrote: "The way to have good and safe government is not to trust it all to one, but to divide it among the many....Let the national government be entrusted with the defense of the nation and its foreign and federal relations; the state governments with the civil rights, laws, police and administration of what concerns the state generally; the counties with the local concerns of the counties....What has destroyed the liberty and the rights of man in every government which has ever existed under the sun? The generalizing and concentrating of cares and powers into one body."[6]

State and federal governments have legitimate functions, but the Constitution should be used as a guideline to set proper boundaries. This is rarely done today. The federal government has no legal authority to intervene in the affairs of states, except in the areas delegated under the Constitution. "The genius of the U.S. Constitution is that it's the world's only anti-government Constitution. The Founders understood clearly that the principle threat to the American people was then, and would always be, our own government."[7]

The states created a federal government partly because they found that a few issues such as diplomacy, interstate commerce, defense, and disputes among the states could best be settled by a national government. However, since the New Deal, it has been believed that all problems must be solved on a national level. The Constitution is supposed to be a system of restraints against the natural tendency of government to continue growing, but the federal government has gone way beyond its constitutional mandate; it has violated the rights of the states and the people. The New Deal represented a fundamental change in federal authority, but the Constitution was never changed to legalize this power.

History has shown time and again how corrupting the influence of power can be. Edmund Burke said: "The greater the power the more dangerous the abuse." In 1888 John Fiske, a Harvard historian, said: "If the day should ever arrive when the people of the different parts of our country shall allow their local affairs to be administered by prefects sent from Washington...on that day the progressive political career of the American people will have come to an end, and the hopes that have been built upon it for the future happiness and prosperity of mankind will be wrecked forever."

Passage of the Seventeenth Amendment in 1913 meant that senators were chosen in a general election instead of being elected by state legislatures. On a practical level, state legislators were much more able to see that senators protected state rights than is the case with voters involved in many varied activities. Federal programs like unfunded mandates would never have passed if senators were still elected by state legislators. The removal of this important protection established by the Founders played a major role in weakening state sovereignty. It is not by chance that the federal government grew so large in the years after this amendment was passed.

It has been increasingly accepted that the federal government has a right and duty to exercise greater and greater power. This view represents "the first principle of totalitarianism: that the state is competent to do all things and is limited in what it actually does only by the will of those who control the state."[8] The New Deal made people think that government was the source of our happiness. The federal government is supposed to be the agent of the states, but today it is the other way around. The federal government has gone from being a servant with few powers to a master with virtually unlimited power. The Constitution is ignored, the principle of limited government is forgotten, and great power has been transferred to fewer people. "Like so many other nations before us, we may succumb through internal weakness rather than fall before a foreign foe."[9]

The bureaucracy and executive branch have become much more powerful, while the legislature has conceded many of its powers, such as the power of the purse and declaration of war. Constitutional government has been replaced by bureaucratic decrees. There is a growing conflict between the people and the experts who make policy. These experts rarely reflect the real values and concerns of the American people. Yankelovich calls this "creeping expertism" and says "it undermines the country's ability to reach consensus on how to resolve important issues."[10] Think tanks have narrowed the political debate using statistics to support any position.

Administration has replaced electoral politics, and policy is decided in the executive bureaucracy. The bureaucracy is used by those who distrust the people as another layer to separate the ruling elite from the people. Alexis de Tocqueville called this "administrative despotism." Bureaucracy is undemocratic, because it rests on the belief that an expert's opinion has more value than a nonexpert's. Eugene McCarthy warned: "The only thing that saves us from bureaucracy is inefficiency. An efficient bureaucracy is the greatest threat to liberty." Too often local and state officials are overruled by federal bureaucrats who often think they are above the law. If constitutional government is restored, there must also be a serious debate about the role of bureaucracy and administrative law in our Republic. This is long overdue. Administrative agencies are not even described in the Constitution.

Rep. J.D. Hayworth has introduced H.R. 2727, requiring that regulatory rulings would not take effect unless Congress voted for them. For too long legislative power has unconstitutionally shifted to administrative agencies.[11] The public must become more involved and educated, while the bureaucrats must be more willing to listen and let people become involved in decisions. The experts and technocrats have encroached on the people's territory. This problem is one more reason why fewer people vote. Whoever wins, few promises are kept and little changes. People increasingly understand that the bureaucrats and ruling elite make the decisions with little input from the people or regard for what they want.

That people have wanted greater federal involvement in their lives weakened state rights. Only since the 1994 election has state rights again become a national priority. There has yet to be much discussion of the fact that the federalization of so many government functions has also greatly weakened the basic rights of the individual. People should understand that as they demand more aid from the federal government, it increasingly comes at a very heavy price—the loss of our freedoms. As a consequence of so many functions being federalized, we as a people have become far too dependent on the federal bureaucracy. We are being bribed into slavery! Fortunately people are awakening to this reality, and bringing federal projects to your district no longer guarantees reelection.[12]

A key part of the problem is that lobbyists represent millions of Americans, not just a few special interests. The entitlement programs represent about one-sixth of all personal income. The federal government has gotten too big partly because most people love entitlement programs. "The ultimate problem with all process reforms is that lobbies are us, and you cannot isolate a democratic government from its own society."[13] People must be willing to make fewer demands on government. That people think federal programs are free is a distorted view. Money for federal programs ultimately comes from the people, and an increase in federal programs promotes an increase in federal control over our lives.

Reviving state rights is solidly grounded in our constitutional history. Under the Constitution the federal government doesn't have the authority to set up many of the programs that it has instituted in this century. It is remarkable that the federal government owns or controls one-third of all land in America. There are many federal programs that should be cancelled, consolidated, or transferred to the states. These programs include welfare, housing, energy, commerce, agriculture, education, environment, public power, and most forms of crime prevention.

Limiting areas the federal government could regulate worked for 150 years, partly because the power of Congress to regulate interstate commerce was narrowly interpreted. In 1895 the Supreme Court stopped federal regulation of sugar in *U.S. v. E.C. Knight Co.* because interstate commerce was narrowly affected. In 1937, under pressure from Roosevelt, the Supreme Court used the commerce and general welfare clauses in Article 1, Section 8, of the Constitution to expand the power of the federal government into many areas always reserved to the states. The general welfare clause was meant to limit federal spending; instead, especially since the New Deal, it has been used in just the opposite manner. It was meant to benefit the nation and people as a whole, such as in national defense, not to benefit individuals or special interest groups. In 1798 Thomas Jefferson said: "Congress has not unlimited powers to provide for the general welfare, but only those specifically enumerated."[14]

The first Agriculture Adjustment Act passed in 1933 under the general welfare clause of the Constitution was declared unconstitutional by the Supreme Court in *U.S. v. Butler* (1936). Congress responded by passing similar legislation under the guise of interstate commerce, and the Supreme Court declared this similar law constitutional in *Wickard v. Filburn* (1942). Filburn grew crops only for his family. The court said if a farmer had not used his own feed, he might have bought someone else's wheat, which might affect the price of wheat which was transported in interstate commerce. Henceforth the commerce clause was extended to cover what wasn't interstate or even commerce. Through such machinations our Constitution has been subverted by the courts and politicians. Previously, intrastate commerce only conducted within a state was left to the states to regulate. The Supreme Court had said that production is inherently local.

Alexander Hamilton warned in *The Federalist Papers*, number 17: "Supervision of agriculture and of other concerns of a similar nature...which are proper to be provided for by local legislation, can never be desirable cares of a general jurisdiction. It is therefore improbable that there should exist a disposition in the Federal councils to usurp the powers with which they are connected; because the attempt to exercise those powers would be as troublesome as it would be nugatory."

In recent years many federal environment, welfare, civil rights, and crime laws have passed using the commerce and general welfare clauses. In *Heart of Atlanta Motel v. U.S.* the 1964 Civil Rights Act was upheld under the interstate commerce clause. Since 1965 the federal government has been using preemption statutes transferring entire areas of authority from the states to the federal authorities, with national standards being established. While I strongly support the civil rights revolution, to continuously increase federal authority will ultimately cause our demise as a free people. As *Time* magazine noted, despite what the federal government likes us to believe, areas such as crime prevention and education are reserved to the states under the Constitution.[15]

After the Civil War, Congress gradually expanded federal criminal jurisdiction regarding federal agencies, such as activities involving interstate commerce. The Post Office Code of 1872 made it a crime to promote obscenity, fraud, or lotteries. In 1896 Congress provided funds to build the first federal prison. Only in this century have we seen a vast increase in federal crimes and the establishment of federal police such as the FBI. In 1910 it became a federal offense to take a woman across state lines for immoral purposes, and in 1919 transporting a stolen car across state lines became a federal crime. The 1994 crime bill placed under federal jurisdiction numerous acts involving drugs, guns, and juveniles that have traditionally been controlled by state and local governments. Even car-jacking and child support are now federal concerns.

Despite Clinton's "Mandate for Change" describing crime as an area in which "no federal role is justified," we got the Brady Handgun Violence Prevention Act of 1993 and the Violent Crime and Law Enforcement Act of 1994. Senator D'Amato and other Republicans call for more federal involvement in crime prevention while at the same time proclaiming that they are cutting the federal government. Senator Biden said on August 22, 1994, that under the Violence Against Women Act, which is part of the 1994 federal crime law, if officers do not make arrests in domestic violence cases, police department can lose federal funds; yet on the same day Senator Biden said Washington wasn't exerting control over local police. Senator Feingold voted against the 1994 crime bill saying "The architects of our nation purposely did not establish a national police force and largely left law enforcement as a state and local responsibility....Some members of this body are no longer committed to this aspect of federalism and local control. They apparently would have us federalize almost every crime that has made a headline anywhere in our nation."

Wilson Nicholas, a delegate to the Virginia convention that ratified the Constitution, said: "Congress has power to define and punish piracies, counterfeiting, and felonies committed on the high seas, and offenses against the laws of nations; but they cannot define or prescribe the punishment of any other crime whatsoever without violating the Constitution." In *Brown v. Maryland* (1827) Chief Justice Marshall said: "The police power, unquestionably remains, and ought to remain, with the States." Until this century federal courts upheld the view that the federal government could only deal with crimes specifically mentioned in the Constitution. In 1911 the Supreme Court said: "Among the powers of the State not surrendered—which powers therefore remain with the State—is the power to so regulate the relative rights and duties of all within its jurisdiction as to guard the public morals, the public safety, and the public health, as well as to promote the public convenience and the common good." At the founding of this Republic, there were only four federal crimes: treason, counterfeiting, piracy, and crimes against the laws of nations. Now there are 3,000 federal crimes, 300,000 federal administrative regulations, and about 85,000 local governments with 513,200 elected officials, or one in every 500 people. Our Republic is being destroyed by thousands of laws and enforcers.

While conservatives in Congress attack social-welfare spending programs as wasteful, no one in Congress proclaims that there is no authority under the Constitution to spend the people's money on the welfare state. Such spending is unconstitutional because the Constitution does not grant the federal government the authority to spend such money. In 1794 James Madison criticized aid to French refugees: "I cannot undertake to lay my finger on that article of the Constitution which granted a right to Congress of expending, on objects of benevolence, the money of their constituents." In 1854 President Franklin Pierce vetoed a bill for the mentally ill saying: "I cannot find any authority in the Constitution for public charity." To provide such financing would be "subversive to the whole theory upon which the Union of the States is founded." In the late 1800s Congress increasingly appropriated money for veterans' pensions and public charity based on the "general welfare." President Grover Cleveland rejected hundreds of these bills saying, "I can find no warrant for such an appropriation in the Constitution." I happen to support providing some public support for people in need, but it should only be done by the states. The federal government has no constitutional basis to provide such aid.[16]

Since the New Deal, states have had to rely on the federal government for money to run many programs. With most tax dollars going to the federal government, the states don't have the fiscal independence to serve their constituents and preserve their sovereignty. The power of taxation has been largely transferred to the federal government, with the important policies of the day established by Washington. By the 1960s states and cities generally received 25 percent of their funding from the federal government, which made it much easier for the federal government to dictate policy. If federal taxes were lowered, state taxes could be increased proportionally, per the wishes of the people so that people paid about the same taxes each year, depending on what programs the states established. The states would then have the funds to pay for many programs now being run by the federal government. For instance, if the U.S. Education Department was closed, it would be possible to calculate what that department was spending each year and then lower federal taxes based on that rate. Time should be allotted before these federal programs are closed, so people in each state could decide what federal programs they might want to establish and how much funding would be needed.

Returning government to the states would ease the growing sense of alienation and loss of control over their lives that millions now feel. Thomas Hobbes said: "Freedom is government divided into small fragments." This shift back to the states would also be an effective means to restore the Constitution and prevent tyranny yet still assist people as they gradually get over the addiction of government aid. A weakened federal government would have less power to blackmail states into accepting more federal control or lose federal money.

States are much better able to handle programs partly because they are closer to the people and are thus more efficient and responsive. Local authorities get faster feedback to improve programs. Local problems are better handled by local governments than by a distant federal bureaucracy, and states cannot create money so their potential for abusive powers is limited. Already many states have reformed their welfare rules with many improvements, and people are gradually being weaned off welfare. With such poor results from the huge sums spent for the war on poverty, it is time for a change.[17]

Returning many federal government activities to the states would weaken the power of the lobby groups. They would have to divide their resources for 50 states. Various states could test different solutions and programs to see what worked best, and there would be more competition and variety. If one state becomes too rigid, people and businesses can move to other states. New York and California, with high taxes, have made it difficult for businesses, so many companies have moved.

Transferring certain federal powers back to the states is not a new idea. Presidents Eisenhower and Nixon formed commissions to study this. Eisenhower warned in the 1950s: "Those who would be free must stand eternal watch against concentration of power in government." He appointed the Kestenbaum Commission to study ways federal programs and powers could be transferred to the states, but nothing was accomplished. When the Advisory Committee on Intergovernmental Relations made a few proposals in 1969, again nothing was done.

More recently this same committee suggested a three-part pragmatic test to determine which government should be involved in various programs. First, the federal government should not be involved in programs where there is a strong history of local involvement. Education and police enforcement exemplify this. Little of value is accomplished by federal intrusion in these areas. Second, what is the relative amount of federal financing in relation to total government spending? For instance, highway construction, law enforcement, and education receive far less money from the federal government than does welfare aid. Third, would ending federal aid cause destructive competition among the states? Should there be federal equalization of standards in some areas such as with environment or welfare laws, so that states with strict standards will not be punished when other states have lax standards? A fourth criterion is whether a particular program is really of national concern. Bruce Babbitt, currently Clinton's Secretary of the Interior, said in 1981, as governor of Arizona, "Congress ought to be worrying about arms control and defense instead of potholes in the street."[18]

When Senator Kerry ran for president in 1992 he promised to reduce the number of cabinet posts by half and to reduce nonentitlement domestic spending by a quarter. Shortly before the 1994 elections, Utah governor Mike Leavitt said

"The common citizen may not use the term 'unfunded mandate,' but they know intuitively that the federal government is reaching beyond what was intended." In 1992 the Brookings Institution published a book, *Reviving the American Dream*, by Alice M. Rivlin, who became deputy director of the Clinton Administration's Office of Management and Budget. She said "The federal government has taken on too much responsibility and should return some of its functions to the states. A clearer division of responsibilities between the states and the federal government could make both levels operate more effectively." The Republicans trounced the Democrats in the 1994 election partly because of a promise to diminish government.

On November 6, 1994 CBS released a poll in which 63 percent of the public felt the federal government should be doing less for us and 30 percent felt that it should be doing more. We have to dismantle much of the federal government because it has gotten too large, out of control, and distant from the people which it no longer represents. Not only would this be in accord with the Constitution, it would provide more effective government for individuals and many businesses and lessen the power of lobbyists. Americans must give up the idea that the federal government can solve all problems.

When the *Wall Street Journal* reviewed the book, *Lost Rights*, the heading was "Fix Washington Before It Enslaves Us All."[19] Even this bastion of the establishment is getting the picture. A sad example of how ridiculous things have become was shown on the evening news in early December, 1994. Federal legislation will require cities to change most of their street signs so they are more legible to the Washington bureaucrats. Denver, for example, will have to spend $2 million to satisfy this requirement. Allowing the federal government to interfere this much in our daily lives was never the intent of the Founders. If they understood that the federal government would one day control the shape of street signs there would never have been a federal government.

There has been a move to restore more responsible representation by establishing new local governments. In 1992 Staten Island voted overwhelmingly to secede from New York City. Nine counties in Kansas and parts of Texas, Colorado, and Oklahoma are trying to become a new state in Western Kansas. People in several regions of Washington state are trying to establish new counties, as that state's Constitution allows, and there is a move to divide California into three states for better representation.[20]

State, local, and federal authorities should privatize and deregulate many government functions as many other countries have done in recent years. Private businesses can collect garbage more efficiently than the government, and tens of billions of dollars could be saved and earned by selling various federal agencies, such as Amtrak and low income housing.[21] Only recently did Congress agree to sell the helium reserve from the 1920s, although special interests assure us this reserve remains vital to national security. Deregulation of the trucking industry is expected to save up to $20 billion a year as the shipping industry is freed from the clutches of the ICC.[22]

There are often problems in distributing federal grant money. When the Justice Department recently awarded money to local communities to ease crime, Indianapolis lost to a suburb with a much lower crime rate. Politics, not local need and efficiency, too often decide federal grant money. This issue would remain a problem if states took over many federal programs, but state and local grants would receive closer scrutiny, and local officials would have a better understanding of local problems.

In *Demosclerosis*, Jonathan Rauch describes how democracy is being weakened by an inability of government to act and make things work. "In principle, the U.S. government's situation is like the Soviet economy's....In both, the method of trial and error reached the point of critical failure. In Washington, old programs and policies cannot be gotten rid of, and yet they continue to suck up money and energy. As a result, there is less and less money or energy for new programs and policies."[23]

Every federal program takes on a life of its own, so it will be extremely difficult to transfer power from the federal government to the states. It is difficult to change, much less kill or transfer, a federal program once it has been established, even after it has served its usefulness. We will only reverse the trend towards greater federal power when we elect people who want to rid themselves of the power they have been given. The New Deal view of an all-powerful, beneficient central government must be replaced with a return to federalism and a separation of powers.

Gradually states are taking more aggressive action to curtail the federal government. California and 21 other states passed a resolution asserting state sovereign rights under the Tenth Amendment. The California joint resolution 44 said: "Whereas, the scope of power defined by the 10th Amendment means that the federal government was created by the States specifically to be an agent of the States; and Whereas, In the year 1994 the States are demonstrably treated as agents of the federal government; and...whereas, Many federal mandates are directly in violation of the 10th Amendment to the Constitution of the U.S." The resolution also demanded that the federal government immediately stop mandates that are beyond the scope of its constitutionally delegated powers. Similar resolutions have been introduced in most other states.

A more radical solution has been proposed by the Committee of 50 states which is chaired by former Utah governor J. Bracken Lee. The goal is to get 38 states to pass the Ultimate Resolution so if Congress allows the national debt to reach six trillion dollars, or if Congress or the president by any means including by Executive Order (EO) ever attempt to abolish or suspend the Constitution, then the Union will automatically be dissolved back to 50 sovereign states. By 1996 the national debt had reached over five trillion dollars.

The objective is not to actually dissolve the Union but to establish the legal principle that this power will automatically exist to be exercised if the federal government goes too far in removing our rights. For instance, if the president signed an Executive Order declaring martial law and removing all guns from the people or restricting travel, this resolution would automatically take hold, if approved and the federal government would be dissolved. In such a situation this solution would be far more effective and necessary than nullification. By March, 1994 this resolution had been introduced in nine states; it missed passing in the Arizona House by a 27-26 vote. There have already been two sanctioned instances of secession—West Virginia was formed out of Virginia, and Vermont from New Hampshire.[24]

The Sovereignty Resolution calls for Congress to use its constitutional mandate (Article 1, Section 8, Clause 5) to provide interest free loans of up to $360 billion over four years to local tax-supported bodies to pay current debts and to finance capital projects. This would create many jobs, help local businesses, improve the economy, and restore the deteriorating infrastructure. By January 1, 1996 this had been endorsed by 3,295 local governments including the U.S. Conference of Mayors and the Michigan legislature. As usual the corporate-controlled press won't discuss this resolution despite its growing popularity. Banks would earn no interest under this plan.[25]

After the large corporations, the greatest factor causing the end of constitutional government in America has been judicial tyranny by federal judges. Thomas Jefferson said: "It is a very dangerous doctrine to consider the judges as the ultimate arbiters of all constitutional questions. It is one which would place us under the despotism of an oligarchy." Federal judges will inevitably increase federal power. The Supreme Court has gone from being an arbitrator of constitutional questions to protecting the power of the corporations and the federal government, especially the executive branch. In *Dyett v. Turner* (1967) the Utah Supreme Court said: "The U.S. Supreme Court...has departed from the Constitution as it has been interpreted from its inception and has followed the urgings of social reformers....It has amended the Constitution in a manner unknown to the document itself....The federal courts have arrogated unto themselves the powers and duties which rightfully belong to the state courts."

Increasingly in the last 100 years, powerful corporate interests have deliberately subverted the intent of the Founders by appointing judges who would enhance corporate and federal power and weaken the constitutional system of checks and balances. While many today attack the New Deal as representing the demise of constitutional government in America, this attack really began in the late 1800s, when the federal courts led by the Supreme Court started destroying state sovereignty and allowed the federal government to take over numerous duties and responsibilities that under the Constitution had been left to the people and the states. States did not turn to the Supreme Court to leave the Union before the Civil War partly because the Constitution does not grant federal courts the right to control state sovereignty. The Constitution did not create judicial supremacy, and there is extensive evidence that the Founders never granted the Supreme Court the power to rule over the president, Congress, or the states.[26]

Congress should reaffirm the Tenth Amendment, and courts should be instructed to not preempt state or local authority unless specifically permitted by the Constitution. Congress, as it did after the Civil War per the Constitution, Article III, Section 2, should specifically limit the jurisdiction of courts to act in ways that limit state sovereignty.[27] On September 6, 1995 Rep. John Shadegg introduced H.R. 2270, while Senator Spencer Abraham introduced a similar bill in the Senate, requiring Congress to identify the constitutional authority for all bills.

In *U.S. v. Cortner* the court found invalid the Anti Car Theft Act of 1992 because the Feds had no authority under the interstate commerce clause to extend its authority here. This decision was reversed by the Sixth Circuit Court of Appeals. In 1988 Congress passed the Indian Gambling Regulation Act to regulate gambling on Indian reservations. Three courts found this violated the Tenth Amendment, but they were reversed by the Tenth Circuit Court of Appeals.[28] These appeals judges should be impeached and fired.

Several recent Supreme Court decisions offer some hope, but it is too early to tell if the court is determined to enforce the Tenth Amendment and support state sovereignty. The Supreme Court in *New York v. U.S.* (1992) supported New

York, which refused to accept radioactive waste, because New York was a sovereign state protected under the Tenth Amendment. The court said "Congress cannot commandeer the legislative or regulatory processes of the states" and the "Constitution divides authority between federal and state governments for the protection of individuals."

In *U.S. v. Lopez* (1995) the Supreme Court ruled that the federal Gun-Free School Zones Act was unconstitutional. Congress had no right to decide that it was illegal for schools to allow guns in or near schools. This was a clear misuse of the commerce clause and a gross overextension of federal powers. In the decision Justice Thomas wisely warned: "The substantial effects test suffers from the further flaw that it appears to grant Congress a police power over the nation." The government told the court it could not even list any limits to federal government power under the commerce clause. An observer in *Forbes* magazine warned, if there are no limits to the power of the federal government then "we have a totalitarian state."[29] Amazingly, the dissenting justices said the court cannot go against the main views of public opinion. Apparently they haven't yet seen the 1994 election results. Clinton was horrified at this decision saying: "I am determined to keep guns out of our schools." He instructed the attorney general to find a way around this court ruling, again showing his contempt for the Constitution. Forty states already have laws preventing guns near schools.

Many want to maintain federal authority. The *New York Times* said, in response to this decision, to weaken congressional power would be a return "to the misguided rulings of earlier times." One member of Congress said this ruling could invalidate hundreds of federal laws. That is just the point! The commerce and general welfare clauses have been misused since 1937 to break with 150 years of constitutional government. Before 1937 the Tenth Amendment curtailed federal power. The Supreme Court has played a major role in severely damaging our system of constitutional checks and balances. Hopefully, this will now be reversed. Federal judges in 1994 told Congress it was improper to federalize many crimes.

Instead of the states deciding what powers will be delegated to the Feds, the federal government and courts have taken many powers from the people and states, which completely violates the Constitution and the stated wishes of the Founding Fathers. Yet the Washington politicians wonder why they are held in such contempt by the people. Tocqueville warned against the habit of centralization and the survival of a free people. He said: "I am of the opinion that a centralized administration is fit only to enervate the nations in which it exists, by incessantly diminishing their local spirit."[30]

None of the original 13 States would have ratified the U.S. Constitution if the people understood that the federal government would someday have such tremendous power. We must encourage competition among the sovereign states and protect the rights of individuals to limit government and prevent tyranny and monopoly power. This will also weaken the influence of interest group politics.[31] If the federal government cannot be significantly disbanded, we should start over with 50 sovereign states keeping the Constitution, making some slight adjustments as the people desire and try for a fourth time to establish a federation among the states—being more careful to control a new federal government and to protect the rights of the people and the sovereign states.

# Chapter VII

# Early Signs of Treason

"Who controls the past controls the future: who controls the present controls the past."

George Orwell

"The pretense of objectivity conceals the fact that all history, while recalling the past, serves some present interest."

Howard Zinn

There are numerous incidents in the 20th century that show how dangerous the bankers and corporate elite are. Carroll Quigley described how international financiers worked behind the scenes in many conflicts influencing governments and making deals. The Laurence Boothe Papers at the Hoover Institution document how, in return for economic concessions, Wall Street assisted the 1912 rebellion of Sun Yat-sen in China. The corporate elite have fomented many rebellions and wars. To the ruling elite war is just another means to increase power and profits.

During and after World War I numerous bankers, corporate leaders, and government officials provided assistance and millions of dollars to place the communists, and later Hitler and Mussolini, into power. Some apologists have claimed that money was only given to the communists to keep Russia in the war against Germany during the first world war, but the evidence clearly refutes this view. These financiers also supported the anti-communists, like Admiral Kolchak in Siberia. It was important to support both sides to insure future profits. Some of the financiers supporting the communists, like Thomas Lamont head of the Morgan banking group, also supported the fascists.

While various authorities such as Gary Allen have discussed this interaction, Antony Sutton from the Hoover Institution at Stanford University has provided the most irrefutable and detailed evidence of this alliance in several books, especially in *Wall Street and the Rise of Hitler* and *Wall Street and the Bolshevik Revolution*, using U.S. State Department documents, congressional reports, released archives such as from the Nuremberg trials, and newspaper reports. Sutton spoke before the Republican platform committee in 1972, but his news conference was cancelled, and when he returned to the Hoover Institute he was ordered to not make any public statements and his contract with the Hoover Institute was not renewed.

The Rockefeller-controlled Chase Bank (later Chase Manhattan Bank) helped finance the Bolsheviks as did Lord Milner, head of the London Round Table, a member of the British cabinet, and director of a London bank. The *Washington Post* on February 2, 1918 said William B. Thompson, a director of the Federal

Reserve Bank of New York, gave the Bolsheviks one million dollars to spread their doctrine. On October 17, 1918 William L. Saunders, deputy chairman of the Federal Reserve Bank of New York, wrote to President Wilson "I am in sympathy with the Soviet form of government as that best suited for the Russian people...." John Reed, a communist, worked for the *Metropolitan* magazine which was controlled by Morgan. Jacob Schiff, head of the New York bank Kuhn, Loeb & Company, heavily financed President Wilson's 1912 election. On February 3, 1949 the *New York Journal-American* said: "Today it is estimated, even by Jacob's grandson, John Schiff, a prominent member of New York society, that the old man sank about $20 million for the final triumph of Bolshevism in Russia. Other New York banking firms also contributed." Jacob Schiff helped found the Council on Foreign Relations.

Much of this nefarious activity took place from 120 Broadway in New York City. A few of the parties based at this address included: the New York Federal Reserve, GE, Guaranty Trust Co., Franklin Roosevelt, and the first Soviet ambassador to the U.S. The first Soviet bank was controlled by Morgan with its Guaranty Trust Company the U.S. agent. American International Corporation, founded in 1915 by Morgan interests and located at 120 Broadway, played a key role in supporting the Bolshevik revolution, and later some of its directors such as Arthur Lehman and Pierre Du Pont supported Roosevelt.

On March 24, 1917 the *New York Times* revealed that Schiff had financed the distribution of revolutionary literature to 50,000 Russian military prisoners captured during the Russian-Japanese war. The *Times* article quoted a later telegram from Schiff in which he said: Trotsky was "what we had hoped and striven for these long years." In January, 1916 Schiff arranged to bring Trotsky to the U.S. Trotsky entered the U.S. without a passport and was then given a U.S. passport to get back to Russia.[1] There was an international warrant for his arrest, and when he was detained in Canada, U.S. authorities got him released. In the June, 1919 issue of *MacLean's*, J.B.MacLean said Trotsky was released "at the request of the British Embassy at Washington...and that the Embassy acted on the request of the U.S. State Department, who was acting for someone else."[2] In *The Road to Safety*, Arthur Willert, Washington correspondent for the *London Times*, said Colonel House, chief aide to President Wilson, told him President Wilson wanted Trotsky released. He conveyed this request to the British government. Because Canada and England wanted to keep Russia in the war, it was not in their interest to allow Trotsky to get back to Russia to help end the war. When Trotsky returned to Russia, he learned that Max Warburg, the Hamburg banker, had granted him funds in a Swedish bank. This credit helped finance the Russian revolution.[3] De Witt C. Poole, the American charge d'affaires in Archangel, Russia, quit because Wilson continued supporting the Bolsheviks. With American troops in Russia supposedly to stop communism those who understood what was really happening were quite angry.

In *The Intimate Papers of Colonel House*, Charles Seymour said House was able "to prevent the formulation of a policy, demanded by certain groups among the French and British, of assisting the anti-Bolshevik factions in Russia." The U.S. illegally gave loans to the Soviet Union partly through the Federal Reserve bank. Individuals like Averell Harriman and companies like Standard Oil of New Jersey actively negotiated trade arrangements with the communists, while banks like the Chase National gave loans to the Soviet Union.[4] Sutton spent 10 years researching *Technology and Soviet Economic Development*. He also wrote *National Suicide: Military Aid to the Soviet Union* and *The Best Enemy Money Can Buy* documenting how certain Western corporations and financiers built the economy of the Soviet empire. In June, 1944 Averell Harriman, then ambassador to the Soviet Union, in a report to the State Department, quoted Stalin as saying that about two-thirds of all large enterprises built in the Soviet Union had been built with U.S. aid. This pattern continues today, as a vast amount of advanced technology is being quietly transferred to China, partly through Secretary of Defense William Perry's business ties and the U.S. Patent Office.[5]

Early this century the corporate elite infiltrated the right and left in America. The Guaranty Trust Company helped found the anti-Soviet United Americans. On March 28, 1920 the *New York Times*, quoting the United Americans, warned of a Soviet invasion of America within two years. Before World War I the Morgan bank also infiltrated domestic left-wing political groups.[6] "It must be recognized that the power that these energetic Left-wingers exercised was never their own power or Communist power but was ultimately the power of the international financial coterie...."[7] Oswald Spengler said, in *Decline of the West*: "There is no proletarian, not even a Communist movement, that has not operated in the interests of money, in the direction indicated by money, and for the time being permitted by money...." It was easy to exercise this control because these groups needed money and wanted to influence the people. The purpose was to keep informed as to the thinking of radical groups, provide a mouthpiece so they could blow off steam, and be in a position to veto their actions especially if they became too radical. Morgan money established *The New Republic*. Walter Lippmann, an early recruit of the London Round Table Group, became a widely influential reporter who was used to direct American public opinion.

Although much of this history has been cleansed, as suggested by the accompanying cartoon, early in this century many Americans understood this corporate communist interaction. This was done, not because of a belief in these ideologies, but to gain monopolistic control over foreign markets, to create wars for more profits, and to progress towards a one world government. Sutton said: "Revolution and international finance are not at all inconsistent if the result of revolution is to establish more centralized authority."[8] The radical left, especially the communists, supported greater government control which was in alignment with the corporate elites move towards a one world government. The view that capitalists and communists are enemies is a fraud perpetuated to hide the fact that both groups have long worked together. When Trotsky died, *Foreign Affairs* said: "He gave us, in a time when our race is woefully in need of such restoratives, the vision of a man. Of that there is no more doubt than of his great place in history."[9] In an 11-page salute, the lords of Wall Street bid farewell to comrade Trotsky. International communism was created by the bankers to enslave the masses. Few scholars acknowledge, this partly because universities and think tanks often get money from the banks and corporations that committed this treason. C.B. Dall in *FDR, My Exploited Father-in-Law* is one of the few sources to discuss this interaction.

James and Suzanne Pool, in *Who Financed Hitler*, describes how wealthy businessmen from the U.S. and various European countries financed Hitler's rise to power. Many of the German firms that supported Hitler were linked to U.S. and other foreign corporations. Most of the directors of U.S. subsidiaries in Germany strongly supported Hitler. In the 1920s and 1930s, Wall Street and firms like GE

## "DEE-LIGHTED!"

Cartoon by **Robert Minor** in *St. Louis Post-Dispatch* (1911). **Karl Marx** surrounded by an appreciative audience of Wall Street financiers: John D. Rockefeller, J. P. Morgan, John D. Ryan of National City Bank, and Morgan partner George W. Perkins. Immediately behind Karl Marx is Teddy Roosevelt, leader of the Progressive Party.

Cartoon used: by Robert Minor in 1911 for *St. Louis Post-Dispatch* and Ford provided money and technical aid to develop German and Italian industry. New York bankers like J. P. Morgan and Kuhn, Loeb and Co. helped Mussolini solidify power. German munitions firms like I.G. Farben could not have developed their extensive war capacity without this foreign aid. On the board of directors of I.G. Farben, which produced the gas used in the death camps, were Henry Ford, Paul Warburg, a New York banker, and Charles E. Mitchell of the Federal Reserve Bank of New York. William Dodd, U.S. Ambassador to Germany, reported on the interaction of U.S. industrialists with the Nazis in *Ambassador Dodd's Diary, 1933-1938*. This aid was planned and deliberate. The scholar Gabriel Kolko said: "The business press (in the U.S.) was aware from 1935 on, that German prosperity was based on war preparations. More important, it was conscious of the fact that German industry was under the control of the Nazis and was being directed to serve Germany's rearmament...."[10] This interaction was part of the deliberate plan to establish a financial system of world control that Carroll Quigley described in *Tragedy and Hope*.

In the 1930s many Wall Street and media interests, such as the Hearst newspapers, supported fascism. The July, 1934 issue of *Fortune* was devoted to glorifying Italian fascism saying: "Fascism is achieving in a few years or decades such a conquest of the spirit of man as Christianity achieved only in ten centuries....The good journalist must recognize in Fascism certain ancient virtues of the race....Among these are Discipline, Duty, Courage, Glory, Sacrifice." Prominent newspapers like the *Chicago Tribune, New York Times*, and the *Wall Street Journal* praised Mussolini for bringing stability and prosperity to Italy.[11] In January, 1933 the *New York Times* editorialized under the banner "The Tamed Hitler" that there would soon be a "transformation" in Hitler as he started "softening down or abandoning...the more violent parts of his alleged program." For years numerous scare stories attacked the communist threat, but the press saw fascism as a stabilizing factor. In 1983 the *Boston Globe* described how the American press supported Hitler.[12]

The corporate elite saw fascism and the supposed reforms of Hitler and Mussolini as a way to preserve capitalism and increase their wealth and control over society. They created the conditions that led to the New Deal to limit competition and enhance economic and political control. In 1936 in *I'm For Roosevelt* Joseph Kennedy said "an organized functioning society requires a planned economy....Otherwise, there results a haphazard and inefficient method of social control." There were many similarities between the New Deal and Hitler's four year plan, and both were supported by the same industrialists. People like Putzi served as intermediaries between Wall Street, Washington, and the Nazis to coordinate and promote their common policies.[13]

Sutton studied many sources, including archives from the Roosevelt library, and has documented in *Wall Street and FDR* many of Roosevelt's activities. While history tells use FDR was a man of the people, he was actually a creature of Wall Street. Since the late 1700s the Roosevelt family has been involved in banking. In the 1920s FDR held 11 corporate directorships, two law partnerships, and was president of a major trade association. During this period he often used questionable politics for economic gain; yet few historians have discussed his extensive business activities. He worked closely with many unsavory elements on Wall Street who supported the Nazis and communists, and many of these corporate interests also helped Roosevelt. This nefarious interaction with the Council on

Foreign Relations (CFR) and one-worlders is often discussed by C.B. Dall in *FDR, My Exploited Father-in-Law*. Walter Teagle of the Federal Reserve Bank of New York helped the Nazis and worked in Roosevelt's National Recovery Administration (NRA). Roosevelt supporters Bernard Baruch and his aide, NRA head Hugh Johnson, were based at 120 Broadway. GE, a financial backer of the communists and Nazis, actively promoted the New Deal.

The NRA originated with the Swope Plan which was developed by Gerald Swope, president of GE. It also had its origins with Bernard Baruch and the 1915 U.S. War Industries Board.[14] The NRA established centralized corporate and government control over industry. Henry Harriman, president of the Chamber of Commerce, called the NRA a "Magna Charta of industry and labor" and said there must be a "planned national economy." The large corporations wanted government intervention to prevent competition. Hoover refused to support the Swope Plan because of it fascist nature, so Wall Street turned against him. People like Senators Wagner, Borah, and Gore were not fooled, and they attacked the plan as a scam to give the large corporations control of the nation's wealth.[15] Historians will one day understand that Hoover was right when he called the New Deal a "fascist measure." Fortunately, the NRA was a failure and was found unconstitutional by the Supreme Court in 1935.

When the NRA floundered, the corporate elite turned to a second plan to establish a dictatorship. They were aware that Hitler and Mussolini had used veterans' groups to take power. In the early 1930s General Butler was the most popular general in the U.S., especially among the veterans, because he was tireless in his efforts on their behalf. Butler had the gift to speak without notes and keep an audience spellbound. He had served in the Marine Corps for 33 years, being posted overseas on 12 expeditions, and had received the Congressional Medal of Honor twice, one of only four men to be so honored. He retired in 1930 as a major general in the Marines. In 1933 a Wall Street bond trader, Gerald MacGuire, approached General Butler gradually revealing plans to make him head of the American Legion (AL) and create an army of 500,000 veterans to take control of the government. Van Zandt head of the Veterans of Foreign Wars said he was also approached by the plotters. The Du Ponts controlled the Remington Arms Company which was to supply arms to the veterans' army. Butler was perhaps the one officer in the U.S. who could have recruited thousands of veterans, which is why the corporate elite tried to use him. The AL was established in 1919 by rich officers including Grayson Murphy, the boss of MacGuire. Into the 1930s it was controlled and used by big business especially to control the unions.

Butler was pressured to lead a new organization which appeared in September, 1934 called the American Liberty League. Officials in the league included John W. Davis, Democratic presidential candidate in 1924, and Al Smith former, governor of New York and Democratic presidential candidate in 1928. In the early 1930s, Davis was chief attorney for the Morgan Bank, while Smith worked for the Du Pont family. Smith attacked the Roosevelt reforms, even stating in 1936 that the New Deal was guiding the nation into communism. Other members of the league included the Mellon group, Rockefeller group, and the Pitcairn family. According to the Scripps-Howard press and its UPI wire service, one of the few pro-Roosevelt organs of the national press, leaders of the league were also executives with U.S. Steel, GM, Standard Oil (now Exxon), Chase National Bank, Goodyear Tire, and Mutual Life Insurance. Several groups openly associated with the league were fascist, anti-labor, and anti-Semitic.[16] The Du Ponts financed various American fascist groups such as the American Liberty League, Clark's Crusaders, and the Black Legion, which was fanatically against blacks and Jews.

Butler remained completely loyal to the Constitution, listening to the treasonous plot to gather evidence and learn who was behind it. After the charges of a plot were made public, Congress held an investigation, although only three people testified. Paul French, a reporter for the *Philadelphia Record* and *New York Evening Post*, had gained MacGuire's confidence and he supported Butler's testimony. French even quoted MacGuire as reporting that someone on Wall Street with $700 million planned to create an army in the Civilian Conservation Corps. This was a third back-up plan to seize the country. MacGuire also testified but was caught in numerous lies. Butler implicated people with J.P. Morgan, the Rockefellers, GM, E.F. Hutton, and General MacArthur, who was a son-in-law to a Morgan partner.[17] It is not certain if MacArthur was involved in the plot although some of his aides like George Van Horn Moseley and Charles Willoughby attacked the Jewish influence and had strong fascist leanings.[18] MacArthur called the plot "the best laugh story of the year."

After French published stories about the plot, there was public concern partly because powerful people named in the plot were not even called before Congress to testify. When Thomas Lamont of the Morgan Bank returned from Europe he told reporters "Perfect moonshine! Too utterly ridiculous to comment upon!" This was the typical way the plotters responded. Remember this point. In the future if prominent politicians and respected businessman are accused of treason, however detailed and reliable the charges, it will be denied.

Although Congress did a poor investigation, the investigating committee on February 15, 1935 said it found evidence "verifying completely the testimony of General Butler....There is no question that these attempts were discussed, were planned, and might have been placed in execution when and if the financial backers deemed it expedient."[19] Unfortunately, Congress took no action against the plotters because it was too late. The large corporations already controlled all the levers of power. Not only did Congress refuse to get testimony from various corporate leaders involved in the plot, some of General Butler's and Paul French's testimony, especially concerning the involvement of corporate leaders, was suppressed in the released reports. Along with Congress, the White House also suppressed corporate involvement in the plot.[20] Despite the concern of many, the mass media belittled the plot. "The largely anti-Roosevelt press of the New Deal era scotched the story as expeditiously as possible by outright suppression, distortion, and attempts to ridicule General Butler's testimony as capricious fantasy."[21] On Dec 3, 1934 *Time* magazine in an article entitled "Plot Without Plotters" ridiculed the plot.[22] *The Nation* and the *New Republic* said fascism comes from pseudoradical mass movements so Butler's revelations of a Wall Street plot was not a worry.

Fortunately, Butler's full testimony was published by a reporter, John Spivak, and by George Seldes when the investigating committee accidently gave Spivak the complete version. In 1967 Spivak wrote *A Man in His Time*. He said: "What was behind the plot was shrouded in a silence which has not been broken to this day. Even a generation later, those who are still alive and know all the facts have kept their silence so well that the conspiracy is not even a footnote in American histories." He was also concerned that the committee refused to call the wealthy conspirators before it and was angry that nothing was done after Congress confirmed this treason. Spivak said the plot failed because "though those involved had astonishing talents for making breathtaking millions of dollars, they lacked an elementary understanding of people and the moral forces that activated them."[23]

George Seldes discussed the plot in *Facts and Fascism*, in his newsletter *In fact*, and in *One Thousand Americans,* he said: "There was one of the most reprehensible conspiracies of silence in the long history of American journalism." About these events in the 1930s House speaker McCormack said: "The (*New York) Times* is the most slanting newspaper in the world....They brainwash the American people."[24] The national media cannot be trusted to educate and protect the rights of the people. Jules Archer in *The Plot to Seize the White House* has preserved the records of this plot, and many of these events from the 1930s are also discussed in *The Revolt of the Conservatives* by George Wolfskill.

General Butler strongly attacked the role of big business in national affairs. On August 21, 1931 he said: "I spent 33 years...being a high-class muscle man for big business, for Wall Street and the bankers....I helped make Mexico...safe for American oil interests in 1916....I helped make Haiti and Cuba a decent place for the national City (Bank) boys to collect revenue in....I helped in the rape of half a dozen Central American republics for the benefit of Wall Street....Looking back on it, I might have given Al Capone a few hints." He accused big business of causing U.S. entry into the first world war and said, on WCAU radio in Philadelphia, that his military expeditions overseas were "the raping of little nations to collect money for big industries" that had large foreign investments. Butler wrote *War Is A Racket* declaring that war "is conducted for the benefit of the very few at the expense of the masses. Out of war a few people make huge fortunes....Newly acquired territory promptly is exploited by the...self-same few who wring dollars out of blood in the war. The general public shoulders the bill." Butler told Spivak "War is a racket to protect economic interests, not our country, and our soldiers are sent to die on foreign soil to protect investments by big business." If General Butler were alive today, the recent invasion of Haiti and Mexican loan guarantee would have shown him that nothing has changed.

Roosevelt did not have the plotters arrested partly because of his intimate ties with these people. Certain plotters supported Roosevelt and many of them, such as the Du Ponts and Remington Arms had offices at 120 Broadway, which was described above. That Davis and Smith, two of the conspirators, had been democratic presidential candidates in the 1920s also did not encourage Roosevelt to expose the plot. "There is strong evidence to suggest that the conspirators may have been too important politically, socially, and economically to be brought to justice after their scheme had been exposed...."[25] While Roosevelt's exact role in the plot has never been delineated, that he refused to investigate the plot, even after Congress concluded that it was real, means that he violated his oath of office to defend the Constitution.

That no action was taken against any of the plotters was an extremely dangerous precedent. They should have been arrested and tried for treason and sedition and received long prison sentences if found guilty. Instead they were allowed to continue their treasonous acts, which helped cause World War II and the present dangerous situation that we now have in America. This could have been stopped in the 1930s. Corporate influence in our society today makes it impossible to find this plot discussed in any school history books, although in 1977 Hollywood did a movie *The November Plan* on the plot. General Butler is one of the great unsung heroes of our Republic.

Butler's charges against big business were strengthened when the Nye Committee investigated the influence of the armament industry and bankers to draw the U.S. into World War I. Between 1934 and 1936 this committee held numerous hearing that described the great profits the munitions industries and financiers made from the war.[26] Wall Street helped finance most U.S. trade with the allies from 1915 to 1917. Bankers like J.P. Morgan testified and Senator Nye said: "The record of facts makes it altogether fair to say that these bankers were in the heart and center of a system that made our going to war inevitable." The committee issued seven reports in 1935 and 1936 declaring that while evidence did "not show that wars have been started solely because of the activities of munitions makers and their agents" it was "against the peace of the world for selfishly interested organizations to be left free to goad and frighten nations into military activity."[27]

Andre Tardieu, Ambassador to the U.S. and later French Prime Minister, wrote *France and America* and said American loans to the allies made a U.S. victory essential for America.[28] New York Mayor Fiorello H. La Guardia said: "Wars are directed by bankers." Antibusiness sentiment was extremely strong, and these hearings were hugely popular, making headlines around the world. News analyst Raymond Swing expressed the view of most Americans when he said "It is almost a truism that the U.S. went into the World War in part to save from ruin the bankers who had strained themselves to the utmost to supply Great Britain and France with munitions and credits."[29] Today these hearings are almost totally forgotten because they have been removed from our history.

General Butler was not the only individual who attacked the bankers. After Governor Huey Long became a senator, he called for a redistribute of wealth in America. In various congressional speeches Long attacked the power of Morgan and Rockefeller and this secret ruling class.[30] In April, 1932 he said the supposed plan by the government to soak the rich was really "a campaign to save the rich....Unless we provide for the redistribution of wealth in this country, the country is doomed; there is going to be no country left here very long." On May 26, 1933 Long called for an investigation of the influence of the J.P. Morgan banking empire on the Roosevelt administration. He also said our involvement in the Spanish-American War and World War I were murderous frauds perpetrated to support Wall Street, which hated and feared him.

In February, 1934 on national radio Long inaugurated a Share Our Wealth Society to redistribute wealth in America. In the midst of the depression this program was hugely popular. By 1935 there were 27,431 Share Our Wealth clubs existing in every state with at least 4,684,000 members. Long was extremely popular, with a powerful political base in the South. As many were aware, he had decided to run for president in 1936, establishing a third party, since he expected Roosevelt to get the Democratic nomination. He might have won or perhaps have thrown the election to the Republicans. A secret poll revealed that Long, as a third party candidate would get three to four million votes and that he would seriously weaken the Democratic party in many states.[31] Long represented a direct political threat to the corporate elite which had to be dealt with. On August 9, 1935 Long, in Washington, discussed a plot to kill him. He was shot September 8, 1935 and died a few days later. There were charges of a conspiracy but solid proof was never provided.[32] In 1939 two critics of Long said Washington knew about the assassination in advance.[33]

On November 23, 1937 GM and Du Pont representatives met with Nazi leaders in Boston and signed an agreement aligning GM and Du Pont with Germany. The goals were to defeat Roosevelt in the next election, remove Jewish influence in America, and place an American fuhrer in the White House. A secretary at the meeting sent a copy of the secret agreement to George Seldes, and he published it in his newsletter *In fact*. On August 20, 1942 Rep. John M. Coffee read the agreement into the *Congressional Record*, demanding that action be taken against the Du Ponts and officials at GM, but nothing was done. During the 1930s the Du Pont family controlled GM through stock ownership.[34]

Before and during World War II, there was considerable Nazi support in the U.S., which is rarely discussed today. Groups like the Christian Front and Silver Shirts had hundreds of thousands of followers including people in the military, police, and National Guard. They planned to provoke a communist uprising and use that excuse to establish a fascist state. There was a serious concern about a coup d'etat; these groups were extremely violent with many blacks and Jews attacked in various cities. Hundreds disappeared. Leaders like William Bishop were arrested and brought to trial. While some were convicted, others were freed. The FBI and certain members of the cabinet actively worked to negate this influence, but the large corporations and certain members of Congress supported these factions, so prosecutors like Bill Maloney and O. John Rogge were ultimately fired or forced to resign from the government. These fascists were protected by powerful people in the government. By the late 1930s, seven senators and 13 representatives were using their free mail privileges to distribute Nazi literature. Some of this activity continued throughout the war.

A good example of the fascist influence during the war was the case of Martin Monti. While stationed in the U.S. Army in Italy, he stole a plane and flew to enemy territory. Brought to Berlin he broadcast via radio Nazi propaganda to American troops. As a reward he was made a lieutenant in the SS. After the war, for this treason, he was given a 15 year suspended sentence and allowed to reenlist. Good Nazis were needed to fight communism.

Considering the association of Wall Street and the newer American fascist groups with the European fascists, there was probably a close alignment with these two American groups which represented a fourth attempt by the corporate elite to establish a fascist state in America. However, this has not yet been clarified by historians. One prominent American Nazi, Lawrence Dennis, formerly of the State Department, worked for E.A. Pierce and Co., a Wall Street firm. Many of these groups supported retired General Moseley, past aide to General MacArthur, to be their leader. In a 1939 speech before the New York Board of Trade, Moseley praised Hitler and Mussolini and attacked the Jews, Roosevelt, and communism.[35] Arthur L. Derounian, under the pseudonym John Roy Carlson, spent five years studying American fascists and, in *Under Cover*, reported that one leader, Merwin K. Hart, had considerable support from many business leaders including Lamont Du Pont and officials at GM, Remington-Rand and Otis Elevator Company.[36]

In 1940 opinion polls showed that over 80 percent of the people did not want to get into a European war, and the America First Committee (AFC) had 850,000 members and millions of sympathizers. Although it refused to work with Nazi organizations and had many Jewish members, it was attacked as being pro-fascist and anti-Semitic in a manner similar to today's attack on the militias. Isolationism was equated with racism. This was typical government and media propaganda. Except for infiltration by fascists and anti-Semites in a few places, this populist movement simply believed in peace. It supported the Bill of Rights and attacked excessive federal government power and secrecy. Members included future presidents John F. Kennedy and Gerald Ford. John Flynn, a leader of the AFC, became a strict constitutionalist when he realized that Roosevelt, with the New Deal, was paving the way for a future dictator. Flynn became a major critic of the New Deal partly because Roosevelt brought so many Wall Streeters into the government.[37] He investigated how Roosevelt, Wall Street, and the British conspired to use film, radio, and the press to promote war and to slander groups like the AFC for wanting peace. Flynn discovered that Carlson, who wrote *Under Cover*, also wrote for the communists and his attack on the AFC was partly Wall Street propaganda to weaken legitimate American patriotism.[38]

*Trading With the Enemy*, by Charles Higham, is a remarkable book that presents in great detail the financial transactions of American corporations with the Nazis before and during World War II. Much of this information was obtained through the Freedom of Information Act in the late 1970s, before that act was weakened. Industrialists especially from American, England, and German met in 1920s and 1930s to divide up the world through secret agreements. Published in 1983, Barnes & Noble reprinted it in 1995.

Planning another war, various bankers established the Bank for International Settlements (BIS) in 1930 in Switzerland, so bills between countries could be more easily paid during a war. Owned by the world's central banks and Morgan Bank, it was also used to send millions of dollars to Germany to build its war machine. Throughout World War II, BIS was used to pay bills between the U.S. and Germany, and BIS remained a correspondent bank for the Federal Reserve Bank in Washington. World War II was planned in the board rooms of Berlin, New York, and London. Various corporate/banker groups like the CFR blocked the U.S. and England from interfering with Hitler's aggressive moves before the war. A world war meant great profits and offered another chance to establish a second League of Nations and world government.

The Chase Bank, Standard Oil of N.J., Morgan Bank group, ITT, RCA, Ford, GM, and many other American companies provided the Nazis with crucial war supplies during World War II, while thousands of Americans died fighting the Axis powers. These companies and people were called the Fraternity. Nazi corporate assets in the U.S. were also protected during the war. The U.S. war effort never benefited from this trade, and it was sometimes hindered because certain supplies America needed were instead diverted to the Nazis. Some U.S. corporations distributed pro-Nazi literature in the U.S. before and during World War II because they wanted the Nazis to win the war. Then it would have been easier to establish a similar fascist state in the U.S. President Roosevelt supported this trade by signing E.O. 8389 on December 13, 1941 which legalized trading with the enemy. Just as with the collapse of the Soviet empire, when the power of the secret government is broken, many of our heroes will be exposed and forgotten. "The auto industry, the oil industry, the aluminum industry, the steel industry and many great corporations sabotaged America before and after Pearl harbor...."

## CHAPTER X—GENERAL LICENSES

### GENERAL LICENSE UNDER SECTION 3 (a) OF THE TRADING WITH THE ENEMY ACT

By virtue of and pursuant to the authority vested in me by sections 3 and 5 of the Trading with the enemy Act, as amended, and by virtue of all other authority vested in me, I, FRANKLIN D. ROOSEVELT, PRESIDENT of the UNITED STATES OF AMERICA, do prescribe the following:

A general license is hereby granted licensing any transaction or act prohibited by section 3 (a) of the Trading with the enemy Act, as amended, provided, however, that such transaction or act is authorized by the Secretary of the Treasury by means of regulations, rulings, instructions, licenses or otherwise, pursuant to Executive Order No. 8389, as amended.

FRANKLIN D ROOSEVELT

THE WHITE HOUSE

*December 13, 1941.*

H. MORGENTHAU, Jr.
*Secretary of the Treasury*

FRANCIS BIDDLE
*Attorney General of the United States*

Various congressional investigations and the Assistant Attorney General of the U.S., Thurman Arnold, "have produced incontrovertible evidence that some of our biggest monopolies entered into secret agreements with the Nazi cartels and divided the world among them."[39] The U.S. auto and aviation industries constantly delayed converting to tank, plane, and military vehicle production, so there was talk of their production facilities being taken over by the government.[40] I.F. Stone discussed this treason in *Business As Usual*. Arnold warned that war production was being crippled by the machinations of certain large corporations. He complained about their international agreements. On June 26, 1941 Secretary of Interior Ickes said "If America loses the war it can thank the Aluminum Corporation of America." Alcoa had a cartel agreement with I.G. Farben, so Germany had sufficient aluminum for war production while the U.S. lacked enough aluminum before and during the war.[41] *The Milwaukee Journal* suggested the death penalty for corporate leaders who sabotaged the war effort. However, most large newspapers took ads from these corporations and defended their actions.

In 1939 with the U.S. very short of rubber, Standard Oil of N.J., the largest oil company in the world, in the Jasco accord agreed that I.G. Farben would control the production of synthetic oil, with Standard Oil producing it in the U.S. only if and when I.G. Farben allowed this. This deal blocked American development of synthetic rubber. Senator Truman on March 26, 1942 called this treason.

Even with a war, this serious charge by a prominent senator was largely ignored by the press and only two important newspapers reported this charge. The Truman, Bone, and Kilgore Committees said Standard Oil had "seriously imperiled the war preparations of the U.S."

Standard Oil of N.J. sent oil and oil parts to Germany through South America, Spain, and Switzerland throughout the war and at lower prices than the U.S. paid. It even refueled German U boats on the open seas. The Germans were constantly short of oil, so this aid probably prolonged the war by many months. Only Standard Oil, Du Pont, and GM had the rights to tetraethyl lead, a key additive used in gasoline.[42] In 1992 the *Village Voice* reported that the Wall Street investment firm Brown Brothers Harriman arranged for the Nazis to get and be trained in using tetraethyl lead in 1938. A senior partner of this firm was Prescott Bush, father of George Bush. This supply was critical to conduct modern warfare. In 1939 the Germans were short of this fuel, so they purchased $20 million of it from Standard Oil to invade Poland.

On March 26, 1942 Rep. Jerry Voohis entered a resolution in the House to investigate the BIS to learn why an American remained president of a bank which was aiding the Axis powers. During World War II, R. Buckminster Fuller served as head mechanical engineer of the U.S.A. Board of Economic Warfare. In this position he saw government transcripts of intercepted phone conversations, letters, and cables. "As a student of patents I asked for and received all the intercept information relating to strategic patents held by both our enemies and our own big corporations, and I found the same money was often operative on both sides in World War II."[43]

ITT provided telephones, air raid warning devices, radar equipment, and 30,000 fuses per month for artillery shells to better kill allied troops. This rose to 50,000 fuses a month by 1944. ITT also supplied ingredients for the rocket bombs that hit England. During the war two of the largest tank producers in Germany were Adam-Opel and Ford of Cologne. Both were wholly owned subsidiaries of GM and Ford.[44] Ford trucks were built for the German army while the Chase Bank kept its branch open in Paris throughout the war, with the agreement of the New York office, to provide financial services to the Nazis. "On January 6, 1944, the U.S. Government had indicted the Du Ponts and Imperial Chemicals Industries of Britain for forming a cartel with I.G. Farben of Germany and Mitsui of Japan....The Du Ponts secretly helped in the armament of Germany, and especially aided Hitler," even betraying military secrets to Germany.[45] During the war U.S. owned factories in Germany were often deliberately not bombed by the allies. Several sources claim that after the war the U.S. government paid firms like GM millions of dollars because some of their factories did sustain damage from allied bombings.

Throughout the war, a Philadelphia company controlled by the Sweden-SKF company supplied the Nazis with large quantities of ball bearings via South America, although the U.S. was short of these items. Without ball bearings, planes and trucks could not operate properly. Some of the employees and executives at the Philadelphia plant protested what was occurring but the Fraternity was too powerful for the U.S. government to do anything. One partner running this firm was William Batt of the U.S. War Production Board, while another partner, Hugo von Rosen, was cousin to Hermann Goring, head of the Nazi air force.

During the war many American insurance companies reinsured their business through Swiss insurance companies which further insured the polices through German companies. Because of this these foreign insurance companies knew in advance the sailing date, location, and cargo contents of U.S. ships going to Europe. This is why so many ships were sunk. Even after the Justice Department told U.S. insurance companies to stop forwarding such information, the practice continued for at least one and a half years into the war. The Germans also obtained the blueprints of many insured U.S. installations, like the White House, which made it easy to identify and blow up key buildings. In 1945 so much of this information was found in the files of German intelligence that they had a good understanding of U.S. military production.[46]

While these corporations did this trade for profit, they also believed in fascism. Like Hitler they considered democracy and communism inherently subversive. Many business leaders were also extremely anti-Semitic. Henry Ford wrote *The International Jew* in 1927 and attacked the Jews in various newspapers such as the *New York World*. Many in Germany, including Hitler, were very influenced by this book, and Ford was one of the few people praised in *Mein Kampf*. Ford's book also helped make respectable the bizarre ideas of the Nazis. The *New York Times* on December 20, 1922 reported that Ford was funding Hitler, then an obscure fanatic.

Based on government documents and interviews with many retired U.S. and British intelligence agents and diplomats, the book *The Secret War Against the Jews*, described much corporate treason before, during, and after World War II. The authors confirmed much information provided in *Trading With the Enemy* while adding many new insights. Allen Dulles was called one of the worst traitors this Republic has ever had. The British established a wiretap network in Manhattan to learn who was aiding the Nazis. Then they brought in a hit squad that secretly killed American businessmen, bankers, lawyers, and dockworkers involved in this trade. Reportedly this was done with the agreement of Roosevelt. The British operation was led by William Stevenson, who later wrote *A Man Called Intrepid*, in which he described some of these activities.[47] In 1989 the *Washington Post* published an article on British operations in America during the war. A reporter was allowed a brief look at a 423-page document the British wrote in 1945 describing these activities.[48]

Throughout World War II American diplomats in Switzerland included prominent Wall Streeters like Allen Dulles. Head of U.S. intelligence in Switzerland during the war, Dulles for years had worked for German firms and he conducted secret meetings with the Nazis that Roosevelt was not aware of.[49] He wanted an allied/Nazi alliance against the Soviets, and he reportedly gave the Nazis the allied war plans for Europe. When Dulles went to Switzerland, a law partner, De Lano Andrews, replaced him to continue representing various German firms in New York. Lada Mocarski, director of the New York branch of Schroeder Bank, became U.S. Vice Counsel in Zurich. Leland Harrison, U.S. minister in Berne, Switzerland, helped Standard Oil ship the Nazis oil. These diplomats protected American business interests in Germany, and if German firms needed supplies like oil or munitions they provided assistance.

Allen Dulles was legal advisor to the Anglo-German Schroeder Bank. This was the German bank for I.G. Farben, and Quigley, in *Tragedy and Hope*, said this bank helped bring Hitler to power. The Dulles brothers attended the meeting, which was sponsored by the Schroeder Bank, of leading industrialists in Berlin on January 4, 1933, in which the commitment was made to support Hitler. A Cologne branch of this bank, the Stein Bank, was the main financier to Himmler and the SS leadership. When Hitler took control in 1933, Kurt von Schroeder became the German representative to BIS. Schroeder was arrested after the war, but he was not prosecuted.

John Foster Dulles, later Secretary of State, along with his brother Allen Dulles, was a partner at Sullivan and Cromwell, the New York law firm that handled loans to Germany during the 1920s and 1930s, and they handled all I.G. Farben legal work in the U.S. In 1936 a Schroeder investment group merged with a Rockefeller group to form the Schroeder Rockefeller Company. The alliances of these corporate elitists would take hundreds of pages to describe.[50]

Only one American went to jail for this treasonous trade with the enemy during World War II. Throughout the war, senior government officials like Treasury Secretary Henry Morgenthau, Jr. tried to stop this treason, while others such as Dean Acheson, a former Standard Oil lawyer and later Secretary of State, blocked efforts to stop this trade. Several times there were threats to stop oil supplies to the allies if pressure against this corporate treason didn't end. For protecting Nazi industrialists, one British officer was court martialed and jailed for two years, while several American officials were dismissed. It is understandable why many now promoting the new world order have such contempt for the American people. Their treason was promoted and protected by the federal government, and the guilty were rarely punished. Some senior American officials who tried to stop this treason were after the war called communists and forced to retire.

During World War II James Martin headed the Economic Warfare Section of the Justice Department. This group studied German international business agreements. After the war Martin spent several years in Germany leading efforts to end Nazi influence and break up their cartels. In 1950 he wrote *All Honorable Men*. In great detail this book depicts the secret alliances between German, U.S., and British companies through secret treaties, foreign subsidiaries, patent restrictions, and interlocking directorates. Directors of Standard Oil, GE, and ITT, through German subsidiaries and personal contacts, contributed money to Himmler's Circle of Friends until 1944.[51] For these contributions the companies were protected by the SS, and they got first pick of slave labor for their factories. If there were any problems, certain U.S. government officials made sure the money flow continued. After the war U.S. Army Colonel Bogdan tried to hide this money transfer from investigators.

Martin explained how, after the war, attempts to end Nazi influence, break up the large German cartels, and seize Nazi assets in various countries were deliberately blocked, supposedly to assist German recovery. He called the group that successfully went against official U.S. government policy towards Germany the international brotherhood or the international fraternity. Documents seized after the war showed how companies like Ford and Chase Bank conducted business as usual with their European subsidiaries during the war. The U.S. Treasury wanted to investigate numerous banks including Chase, Morgan, National City, Bankers Trust, and American Express but this was blocked.

Key American representatives in Germany after the war came from large corporations like Rufus Wysor from Republic Steel Corporation, Frederick Devereux from AT&T, and Louis Douglas from GM. The First Director of the U.S. Economics Division in Germany, Colonel Graeme Howard from GM, wrote a book in 1940 *America and a New World Order*. The next head, General William Craper was Secretary-Treasurer of Dillion, Read & Co. an investment banking firm that played a major role in lending money to Germany after World War I. These people and many aides they brought to Germany deliberately blocked Washington's anti-Nazi policies after World War II. Martin said: "In the end we were caught between businessmen representing private interests and others of the same persuasion holding official positions, where they had power to change the orders under which we operated." Many of these people, like General Clay, were members of the CFR.[52]

In 1948 after many complaints about U.S. policy not being carried out in Germany, Congress held an investigation. The Ferguson Committee report was released April 15, 1949, but the Army still refused to carry out U.S. policies. Alexander Sacks an American official trying to carry out these policies said: "The policies of the Roosevelt and Truman Administrations have been flagrantly disregarded by the very individuals who were charged with the highest responsibility for carrying them out." For his honesty he was promptly fired, although he was reinstated.[53] U.S. corporations were afraid that if the Nazis were prosecuted, their own involvement would be revealed.

Martin warned about the dangerous power of the large corporations that governments needed to control. He complained that our government had not stood up to this great economic power partly because of a belief that corporations do not need to be governed. "We cannot allow the lack of social responsibility characteristic of the international behavior of private corporations during the last quarter-century to become a pattern for government." He understood that economic power must be brought under some kind of responsible control. "Since power is a public trust, the first job of a government is to see that power is used in the public interest and not against it. This is where a government must be different from a corporation....National governments in all parts of the world have granted power over segments of their national economies to various corporations...." to "build a private 'world government.' This new order, stretching far beyond the boundaries of any one nation, has operated under no law except the private law of the agreements themselves....It is time to view the results of this abdication by constitutional governments in favor of private governments." Martin warned that just as the large corporations brought Hitler to power, unless something was done to limit corporate power, something similar could happen in the U.S.[54]

Certain influential Nazis realized they would lose the war so they gradually moved large sums of money, people, and corporate structures overseas, with the help of people like the Dulles brothers. Called "The Odessa" a 1945 U.S. Treasury Department report said the Nazis had established at least 750 businesses overseas capable of bringing in $30 million a year to support Nazi operations. Nazis helped create South Africa's racist laws and South American death squads, they trained the Arabs to fight Israel, and the many Nazis allowed into the U.S. subverted our institutions and culture.[55]

U.S. investigators after the war deliberately changed, ignored, or concealed evidence of war crimes against Nazi scientists and officials. Our laws were violated and many Nazi scientists moved to the U.S. under Project Paperclip.[56] For years the immigration of Nazi war criminals into the U.S. was kept out of the press, or there was biased reporting. U.S. intelligence agents changed the records of many Nazi war criminals, so that by 1955 about 800 Nazi scientists were working in the

U.S. As described in some National Security Council directives in the late 1940s and 1950s, this was official U.S. policy. As civilian High Commissioner in Germany in 1949, John J McCloy, a leader of the CFR, helped direct Project Paperclip.

For years after the war, a Nazi General Gehlen was the main source for U.S. intelligence regarding the communist nations. Later it became clear that he deliberately provided false information or exaggerated the capabilities of the Soviet Union and its allies, which caused the West great harm. General Karl Wolff, an SS officer and aide to General Gehlen, said: "We'll get our Reich back again. The others will begin to fight among themselves eventually and then we'll be in the middle and can play one off against the other." Gehlen deliberately brought his intelligence organization to the U.S. so he could secretly help the Odessa operations and create East West tensions.[57]

U.S. officials and the corporate controllers loved Gehlen's lies because his information justified the cold war and the spending of billions of dollars for the national security state. And certain fascists in the U.S. quietly supported preserving Nazi influence. These Nazi war criminals were also used by our government to promote ideals of freedom and democracy in the communist nations. Often Nazi-like propaganda was filtered into the messages received by the communist nations.[58]

After 1950 the Displaced Persons Commission openly allowed fascists into the U.S. The CIA-inspired Crusade for Freedom used various fascist groups to support the cold war in the U.S. These individuals joined right wing groups and an Eastern European emigre fascist network linked to former Nazi collaborators entered the Republican party through its ethnic programs such as the Heritage Groups Council.[59] In 1971 the *Washington Post* did an article on the fascist background of some elements of the Republican party.[60] In September, 1988 the racist and anti-Semitic leanings of certain Republican ethnic leaders was revealed and eight officials were forced to resign from the Bush campaign.

Many of the banks and corporations conducting these treasonous activities are the same groups today plotting to establish a one world government. While there may today be no individuals in these businesses who committed treason before and during World War II, few would argue that international corporations today are much less loyal to America than was true 50 years ago. Millions of jobs have been lost as corporations shift manufacturing jobs overseas for more profits. The devastating impact this has on the U.S. is not relevant to these corporations. While this certainly does not mean every international corporation would commit treason, it does suggest that the treason conducted in World War II would not be foreign to many present day conglomerates.

Setting up antagonistic forces to create a war is a normal business practice that doesn't get discussed in history books. Bankers are almost always the one group guaranteed to profit from a war, and when they prolong a war, profits are higher. On December 9, 1950 the *Chicago Tribune* said: "The members of the council (CFR)...have used the prestige that their wealth, their social position, and their education have given them to lead their country toward bankruptcy and military debacle. They should look at their hands. There is blood on them—the dried blood of the last war and the fresh blood of the present one (Korean War)." To this we can add the Vietnam and Gulf Wars.

Frederick C. Howe acknowledged in, *Confessions of a Monopolist* in 1906, that a monopoly was essential to acquire great wealth and the best way to establish this was through politics, making society work for the large corporations under the guise of public interest. The welfare state, fascism, communism, and socialism are really similar means used by the corporate elite to gather wealth and control the people. Those who reject the view that there is a secret government in control and that these groups intend to remove the Constitution and establish a police state should carefully reflect on our history early this century. The corporate elite attempted to establish a dictatorship then so it should not surprise the objective observer that these forces are now attempting to do the same thing. As politicians demonstrate every day, the rule of law has been replaced by the rule of money in America.

# Chapter VIII

# Rise of the Corporate State

"The 20th century has been characterized by three developments of great political importance: the growth of democracy, the growth of corporate power, and the growth of corporate propaganda as a means of protecting corporate power against democracy."

Alex Carey[1]

"To erect and concentrate and perpetuate a large moneyed interest...must in the course of human events produce one or other of two evils, the prostration of agriculture at the feet of commerce, or a change in the present form of federal government, fatal to the existence of American liberty."

Patrick Henry

While it has been suppressed from our history, in *Liggett v. Lee* (1933) Supreme Court Justice Brandeis described how, in the early years of our Republic, states either wouldn't allow or sharply restricted the formation of corporations because they limited freedom and opportunity for the people. The people kept the power to charter corporations strictly in the hands of the legislature. Corporations were chartered to serve the public good, corporate privileges were often conferred for a fixed terms of years, and strict limits were placed on the allowed indebtedness. Previously corporations could only be established for specific activities; permission to incorporate for any lawful purpose was not common until 1875. At times the corporate privilege was revoked, when the state felt this was best for the community. For years there were strict limits on the amount of authorized capital that could be used when a business incorporated. Until 1918 mining companies could incorporate in Maryland with only up to $3 million.

Many forget that corporations have no inherent right to exist. This is a power granted by the state. Gradually limits on corporate charters were removed through corporate influence, money, and lawyers, as judges issued rulings to support corporations. States competed with each other to raise money by chartering corporations with few requirements. That many corporations today are registered in Delaware is a vestige of that competition. The movement of large corporations into thousands of small towns gradually shifted economic and political power from Main Street to Wall Street, which created a disparity of income and concentrated wealth. Brandeis said big business limited self-government by eroding the civic and moral capacities of the people and by controlling democratic institutions.[2]

Until the late 19th century the law primarily focused on the rights of individuals. After the Civil War the role and rights of corporations were gradually established. The Supreme Court, in *Santa Clara County v. Southern Pacific Railroad* (1886), said corporations would now be considered "persons" for purposes of the Fourteenth Amendment. A corporation became a legal fiction granted legitimacy by judicial and legislative degree. The revolutionary trends of the 18th century that began in America and France and promoted individual liberty were weakened with the introduction of corporate rights.

Increased concentration of wealth and power in the hands of fewer people developed after the Civil War. Before the 1880s society was mostly agrarian and most businesses were directly managed by the owners. Most people were self-employed; they owned their own land, produced their own food, and there was little manufacturing. Gradually people had to work for others to earn money. There developed an economically powerful elite, and most people worked for others as laborers. Around the turn of the century, 90 percent of the population was still self-employed. By 1992 only four percent of the people were self-employed. We are no longer a nation of shopkeepers, farmers, and independent craftsman. This change helped make money foremost in people's lives. The new corporate order meant less democracy and increased concentration of economic power, with business controlling all means of production. The old mercantile aristocracy became the new corporate elite. With mechanization fewer workers were needed on farms, so people moved to the cities. The loss of small farmers to the cities meant the loss of many independent thinkers, which weakened the democratic fabric of our Republic. Large businesses now dominate agriculture. Aided by the railroad the frontier disappeared and a truly national economy developed.

The rise of and preoccupation with mass-market consumerism and indulgence gradually developed after the Civil War, especially in the 1890s. "In the decades following the Civil War, American capitalism began to produce a distinct culture, unconnected to traditional family or community values, to religion in any conventional sense, or to political democracy. It was a secular business and market -oriented culture, with the exchange and circulation of money and goods at the foundation of its aesthetic life....The cardinal features of this culture were acquisition and consumption as the means of achieving happiness; the cult of the new; the democratization of desire; and money value as the predominant measure of all value in society."[3] The psychoanalyst Erich Fromm said: "In contrast to the nineteenth century, in which saving was a virtue, the twentieth century has made consumption into the main virtue." The age of mass consumption also brought with it the dawn of the advertising industry, and people's habits were changed to consume more. And people were socialized to accept the harsh conditions of mass production in factories which many workers rebelled against.[4]

God was replaced by gain. Caring relationships were too often replaced with a desire to succeed in business. Instead of having a close relationship with one's family, a career became more important. Corporate values replaced family values. One result, of course, is the much higher divorce rate today. One's standard of living became the primary focus and objective in life. Our ideal of freedom became the ability to purchase and consume. We were no longer proud citizens of a Republic; we became consumers in a market economy. World War I "had not been fought for democracy or for nationalism but for industrialism" to ensure that "the power of production would never again be endangered...."[5]

"From the 1890s on, American corporate business, in league with key institutions, began the transformation of American society into a society preoccupied with consumption, with comfort and bodily well-being, with luxury, spending, and acquisition....American consumer capitalism produced a culture almost violently hostile to the past and to tradition, a future-oriented culture of desire that confused the good life with goods. It was a culture that first appeared as an alternative culture...and then unfolded to become the reigning culture of the U.S."[6] Aided by the industrial mobilization of World War I, corporations attained an increasingly dominant role in America.

This new culture was promoted by commercial groups allied with other elites attempting to accumulate ever greater amounts of capital. Other conceptions of the good life were pushed aside. Business leaders cooperated with educators, politicians, social-reformers, entertainers, artists, and religious leaders to create a new economy and culture. American public life was diminished as democratic traditions and institutions were pushed aside to make way for the new culture. New institutions like the Harvard Business School and the Metropolitan Museum of Art were recruited to shape the new America. At the turn of the century during the age of the muckrakers, magazines attacked monopolies and private economic power. By the 1920s magazines had gone from exposing corporate corruption to praising business success and the consumer society. The corporate way become the American way partly because big business gained control of the media. Socialism never succeeded in America because the goals of socialism such as a classless society and liberty for all already occurred in America, or at least this is what the media told us.

Inspired by growing incomes and a rising standard of living, many capitalists and progressive reformers promoted a new form of democracy at once more inclusive and more confining than before. Self-pleasure and self-fulfillment over community or civic well-being became the norm. Comfort and prosperity became the cornerstone of life in America. The influential economist, John Bates Clark, said that despite the growing inequality of life in America, democracy could be ensured through the free market and the ever growing supply of goods and services.

This new thinking was discussed in *The New Democracy* by Walter Weyl in 1912. Weyl said: "Democracy means material goods and the moral goods based thereon....To socialize our consumption we must therefore depend upon the direct or indirect action of the state...."[7] A new and improved morality, a new ethics of pleasure would be derived from a new economic order in conjunction with political democracy. Weyl and other prominent thinkers like Simon Patton, an economist and professor at the Wharton School of Economics, felt that modern corporations were moral institutions, and there was nothing wrong with the new emphasis on money and consumption.

A powerful populist movement arose with many farmers, independent merchants, religious leaders, social-reformers, socialists, intellectuals, economists, and unionists attacking this new way of life. Previously, democracy was thought to be partly based on ownership of property and control of one's production. In 1879 the economist Henry Carter Adams warned: "Either you must establish a more equitable division of property and produce or the fatal end of democracy will be despotism and decadence." Part of the broad appeal of the prairie populist, Rep. William Jennings Bryan of Nebraska in the 1890s, was a rejection of the new value system offered by the corporate culture and a call to restore Jeffersonian grass-roots democracy. Large corporations were often hated and considered undemocratic. The "patriotic role" that corporations supposedly played during World War I changed this attitude. According to the press, the corporations helped preserve democracy. Intense antibusiness sentiment eased during the war because business produced the goods needed to win the war.

Many religious people at the turn of the century criticized the new values of the corporate culture. Today many religious groups have closely aligned themselves with the corporate culture. Most people don't realize that millions of Americans have been captivated and transformed by a corporate culture that was once considered quite foreign and alien to traditional American political, economic, and spiritual values.

Citizen involvement that had spawned the progressive movement changed to citizen apathy. One commentator in the 1920s said "The private life became the all in all." The disgust that many now feel towards public office and politicians was quite common in the 1920s.[8] Apathy and cynicism ruled the day. The public was too busy trying to get rich to notice or care what the politicians were doing.

In 1924 Samuel Strauss, a political scientist and journalist, wrote an article about the changes in America that is even more relevant today. "Something new has come to confront American democracy. The fathers of the Nation did not foresee it....That which has stolen across the path of American democracy and is already altering Americanism was not in their calculations" and would have been considered abnormal to them.[9] The Founders could not have foreseen, nor would they have necessarily agreed with the importance of manufacturing and money in America.

Consumptionism produced remarkable changes in America. People stopped attacking the very wealthy as luxury, comfort, and security became the essential elements of the good life. Strauss said "The new kind of man sees, not human beings, but things at the centre of life." The new man "had no interest in keeping us free...except as we must be free to consume goods."[10] Television insures that we continue to equate consumerism with democracy. President Woodrow Wilson said: The truth is we are all caught in a great economic system, which is heartless."

It was felt all people had an equal right to consumer goods. The revolution in mass production and growth of consumer capitalism filled stores with goods to satisfy needs not yet understood to even exist. The present focus in society is how to develop enough interest in goods that are produced, i.e., how to produce consumers. Good government has come to mean that the government provides the people with the means to buy more goods. The progressive Senator Robert LaFollette, Sr. said: "The welfare of all the people as consumers should be the supreme consideration of government."

We have gone from being a nation of citizens, with rights and responsibilities, to being consumers addicted to more and more goods that the corporations produce for us to buy even when there is no need. Consumerism had replaced citizenship. G.K. Chesterton, an English author, made many trips to the U.S. in the 1920s and 30s. He said: "Americans are good neighbors rather than good citizens. That pure and positive public spirit has faded from their life more than from that of any people in the world. What is the matter with America is that every American has been tacitly or loudly taught that his job is not only more vital than his vote, but more vital than that virtue of public spirit which the vote represents."[11]

Critical of anti-democratic business corporations, Chesterton said: "Industrial capitalism and ideal democracy are everywhere in controversy; but perhaps only (in

America) are they in conflict." Only in America was "industrial progress...the most undemocratic....The reality of modern capitalism is menacing the (democratic) ideal with terrors and even splendors that might well stagger the wavering and impressionable modern spirit. Upon the issue of that struggle depends the question of whether this great civilization continues to exist...." When defining our Republic, Chesterton compared the collapse into capitalism to the collapse into barbarism and the fall of the Republic. He said capitalism is like feudalism, with people employed and guarded by large corporations much like the feudal lords cared for and controlled the serfs.[12]

The power of the federal government expanded enormously during and after the Civil War, as a vast bureaucracy developed and the government intervened more in political, social, and economic matters. The traditional government role of regulating business gradually included serving business. In the 1890s government intervened to absorb commercial banks' losses, and after 1910 the U.S. Commerce Department expanded its activities. Business gradually depended on government guarantees of bank deposits and farm loans. These trends prepared the way for the New Deal. Led by the press and Washington, people allowed the federal government in league with business to play a more prominent role in their lives. The New Deal economic reforms represented the political application of economic and social trends that had been taking place for some years.

There was a nationalization of the political system during the New Deal as political power shifted from local and state government to the federal government. In the federal government the executive branch and bureaucracy were strengthened and freed of party control, while the legislature was weakened as was the people's sense that they were actually represented by government. Corporations and the two political parties developed together, each promoting the other, with individual citizens increasingly removed from the political process.

There was also a shift in constitutional law along with a change in how we perceived the role of government. Instead of having a government of limited powers, with a federal government that could only act in certain areas per the Constitution, a new federal government was born with unlimited powers to tax and rule in whatever fashion it deemed appropriate. Experts henceforth decided how we were ruled, as the people learned to follow orders. Supposedly experts who were above partisan politics would make technical decisions. The controlled media made sure the people didn't understand what had happened. The corporate culture became so strong that in 1939 the House Un-American Activities Committee called Consumers Union, which produces *Consumer Reports*, un-American.

President Roosevelt said the task of modern government was "to assist the development of an economic declaration of rights, an economic constitutional order." The traditional reliance on individual self-reliance was replaced by a new understanding of individualism, with government regulating the economy and guaranteeing people protection from the uncertainties of the marketplace. Thus was the welfare state born. Increasingly, our liberties were defined by the freedoms the state granted; they were no longer God given as described in the Declaration of Independence.

Instead of a Constitution that protects our liberties as described in the Bill of Rights, economic rights became the primary focus. This is another historical basis for the weakening of our liberties. People have minimum wages and the welfare state but in the process we also have asset forfeiture laws, no knock warrants, and rule by executive degree. A person can often work at a decent wage but they may have all their assets seized. We are trading a false sense of economic security for the loss of our rights.

President Reagan once said: "What I want to see above all is that this remains a country where someone can always get rich." The desire and wish for wealth has replaced the desire and wish for freedom and the preservation of our rights. A much better goal is that this remain a Republic where everyone always has the God-given rights and freedoms that the Founders fought so hard to establish. There is today in America a new tyranny, with a state religion called the market economy. The market has succeeded and we are unhappy, materialist, and increasingly no longer free.

Instead of people relating to each other as individuals something outside ourselves, money, constantly intervenes. Previously money had value because it represented objects. Now money controls people because it has such a powerful influence over our lives. Objects are now valuable only in that they represent money. "W.H. Auden thought that the most striking difference between Americans and Europeans was to be found in their different attitudes toward money. No European associates wealth with personal merit or poverty with personal failure. But to the American what is important is not so much the possession of money but the power to earn it as a proof of one's manhood!"[13] We are valued for the money we control not for integrity of character. With the corrupting influence of money and monetarization of feeling we should not be surprised that cheating in school and rampant crime have become the norm.

Politicians during elections ask if people are better off economically. "The question is only and always about money, never about the spirit of the laws or the cherished ideals that embody the history of the people....To the extent that the wish to be cared for replaces the will to act, the commercial definition of democracy prompts the politicians to conceive of and advertise the Republic as if it were a resort hotel. They promise the voters the rights and comforts owed to them by virtue of their status as America's guests....The government...preserves its measure of trust in the exact degree that it satisfies the whims of its patrons and meets the public expectation of convenience and style at a fair price."[14] When spiritual considerations are active in life one inevitably strives to assist others. When money becomes the all in all, it is survival of the fittest, and a society deteriorates.

Increasingly corporate speech has gained First Amendment protection.[15] Corporations are using the Bill of Rights to protect themselves from state and federal laws especially with the expansion of environmental, health, and safety regulations. In California a public utility company used the First Amendment to overturn state regulations that lowered utility rates. Business has long attempted to gain for corporations the same constitutional rights that a citizen has except for voting. However, the more corporations have rights like citizens, the less rights citizens have. Citizens do not have the funds that corporations have, and a corporation can continue indefinitely and in many places. If you sue a corporation, long distance travel may be required. We are all second class citizens before the power, wealth, and influence of corporations. When corporations commit crimes, they wish to be considered as artificial legal entities that cannot be held legally liable for their offenses. When convicted of crimes they still have all their political rights, unlike an individual who may lose his right to vote and even his freedom.

Corporations should lose their rights of citizenship, or the responsibilities of citizenship that apply to individuals should be vehemently applied to corporations.

During the 20th century there has been a shift from direct financial control to management control of corporations, with the banking community increasingly exerting its influence quietly and in the background. Stockholders rarely have a decisive say in how large corporations are managed, despite what is sometimes claimed. And the large corporations are generally closely associated with each other through joint advisory groups and various social, political, and trade associations. Members of the CFR and TC usually come from the corporate elite.

Large management-run corporations usually operate in an authoritarian, hierarchical, and bureaucratic manner. They are not conducive to democratic thinking. They act increasingly like governments, and increasingly the federal government acts like these large corporations. While there are established checks and balances against unbridled government tyranny, however weakened these limitations have become, there are few real checks on unlimited corporate tyranny. The Republic has gradually been replaced by the corporate totalitarian model, with most people taking orders and having few rights. The Bill of Rights rarely applies in the work place. "Today's rhetorical attacks on 'big government' for interfering with business have largely succeeded in obscuring the fact that it is big business, not big government, that primarily regulates the lives of ordinary Americans."[16]

Today corporate officials play an increasingly dominant role in government. Senior government leaders come from banker/corporate financed think tanks and foundations with an occasional representative from labor. Economic and political power is controlled by the corporate elite, supported by an out-of-control intelligence apparatus. U.S. government economic policy is dominated by the Federal Reserve Bank, a private corporation. Government supposedly provides a sound infrastructure, stable society, and educated workers while business provides modern technology, a growing economy, and assistance during emergencies such as in a war. This alliance of government and the corporate elite is especially relevant in international affairs, as NAFTA and GATT have demonstrated. Increasingly this alliance means the exclusion of all other groups. Labor unions and universities provide fewer and fewer leaders in the federal government.

Russell Mokhiber, in *Corporate Crime and Violence*, presented 36 serious cases of corporate crime. In many of these cases numerous people were injured or killed. Fifty suggestions are offered to curb corporate crimes. In *U.S. v. Dotterweich* and *U.S. v. Park*, the Supreme Court held that business executives can be held criminally liable for violating the Food and Drug Act. This liability should exist whenever a business violates the law, and there should be stricter laws preventing the destruction of documents when corporations are involved in litigation. As in Australia and England, U.S. prosecutors should be allowed to entrap corporations. State and local prosecutors should become more aggressive against corporate crime because federal laws are so weak and poorly enforced. In 1990 California passed the Corporate Criminal Liability Act which includes possible criminal prosecution of managers if they don't report health and safety problems within 15 days of discovering such problems.[17] Corporate managers should take responsibility for their actions as the law requires of private citizens. Too often, corporate executives are above the law.

A limit should be placed on consent decrees when corporations are sued by the government allowing corporations to not acknowledge violating the law. A court approved consent degree can leave no trace of liability or culpability. This often makes it easier for corporations to hide felonious conduct, and individuals have more difficulty obtaining relief in civil litigation. Convicted corporations should more often be required to repay their victims. There should be better protection for whistleblowers, heavy fines, and forced retirement of an executive from a business upon conviction of serious criminal activity. Lawyers can lose their license when convicted of a felony; the same standard should apply to business executives.

Ralph Nader suggested, repeatedly offending corporations should be fined, lose government contracts, and lose the right to take part in public debate, such as appearing before Congress or lobbying bills. Currently, FBI reports ignore corporate crimes, such as financial fraud and occupational homicide. According to the FBI, about 24,000 people are murdered each year, but 56,000 people die from work-related diseases and accidents. Repeat offenders should be targeted to create more corporate accountability. Such corporations should be forced to sell a unit that continues to violate the law, lose the right to hold certain licenses as in the media, or lose their charter to exist. However, prosecutors often won't prosecute corporations.[18]

The law today is used to force compliance to the values of the corporate elite. Corporations often dominate legislatures, preventing laws that would hold businesses accountable or improve safety precautions. When new bills are presented intense lobbying by businesses weakens them. Politicians are afraid to antagonize businesses because of a need for campaign donations, and there is a cultural homogeneity among legislators, judges, and administrators with businessmen. Lax standards towards corporations also exist partly because of biased news coverage. Corporations now define what is right and wrong in our society because they control the media. The norm has become the morality of corporate manufactured news.

People convicted of minor crimes like using marijuana often receive harsh sentences while corporate felons that kill people get no prison time. The public is less resentful towards corporate crimes then direct violent crimes. There are today two justice systems in America—one for individuals and another for corporations. Jail for corporate executives would be a strong deterrent to criminal activities. Just as the group Mothers Against Drunk Driving awakened the public conscience to punish drunk driving, we need to take a much more serious look at corporate criminal activity especially when people are seriously injured and killed.

A classic example of how the federal government bends to the will of business today is the regulation of the meat and poultry industries. Each year at least 6.5 million Americans, and possibly many more, get ill from eating chickens. At least 1,000 people die, with children and the elderly especially at risk. The figure is much higher when you add the illnesses from eating diseased meat. Yet government inspection of the meat and poultry industries has changed little in this century, despite the fact that there now exists more sophisticated methods to inspect food that a few businesses and some European countries now use. The problem is that American meat and poultry industries did not want tighter inspection standards and they are powerfully connected politically. In the fall of 1994 Agriculture Secretary Mike Espry was forced to resign because of "gifts" he had accepted from the poultry industry, and only in early 1995 did the Clinton regime finally agree to establish improved standards of meat and poultry inspection.[19]

On October 27, 1994 after three years of denial Prudential Securities finally admitted that it had broken the law by selling limited partnerships in the 1980s. Over 120,000 people suffered losses in this criminal operation. Prudential Securities paid a $330 million fine to conclude criminal charges, and last year it paid $371 million in fines to federal and state regulators to settle civil charges. Although many people suffered and the fines were quite high, no one involved in this scam went to prison. Corporations can do just about anything, yet they are above the law when it comes to serving time in jail.[20]

Businesses complain about federal legislation, but they often hide behind the federal government to block state laws they dislike. Business groups want to keep decision making focused at the federal level, where they have a better opportunity to control the outcome. While corporations now control both national political parties, some state governments have become more responsive to the people. From Baltimoreans United in Leadership Development to Industrial Areas Foundation in Texas, many community groups have formed.

The Republican party is trying to federalize laws dealing with negligence and product liability. Again businesses will be able to hide behind the federal government. This needed reform should be done by the states. Federal laws now prevent state and local authorities from taking legal action against deceptive advertising by the airline industry. Only the U.S. Department of Transportation can regulate this area. The result is that the airlines are among the worst abusers of false advertising in the nation, and the federal government will do almost nothing about this. The airlines hide behind the federal government, while the people are cheated.

Typically industry agrees to weaker federal standards if that frees them from stricter state rules. In 1994 banks got new interstate banking laws that overrode state limits on bank branches. Automobile manufacturers have fought to have federal laws replace stricter state standards on issues like auto emissions. When Vermont passed a law requiring credit reporting firms to automatically provide free annual credit reports, banks and consumer lenders worked to get a weaker federal law that would preempt this state law. Under the Constitution, the laws of Congress take precedent over state law, but traditionally Congress usually acted when the states hadn't acted, not to supersede state law. In recent years, this has changed. By 1988, 350 federal preemption laws had passed with 225 of them passed in the last 30 years. Powerful corporate lobbying groups are negating the wishes of people expressed on the state and local levels. Large corporations also turn to the government to avoid the risks of the market, as in defense procurement or public utility regulation.

There is growing anger at the federal government for protecting corporations with preemption laws. New York is trying to enforce its strict lemon car laws without federal interference as car manufacturers would like. The National Conference of Commissioners on Uniform State Laws has established a Uniform Commercial Code to have consistent laws for interstate commerce with less federal interference.[21] If state laws offer consumers more protection, such laws should not be preempted. Federal preemption laws should be used only to protect individual rights.

Billions of tax dollars go to farm subsidies, defense contractors, and mining companies each year. The Cato Institute found that almost every Fortune 500 company gets some form of corporate welfare from the federal government. McDonalds has received $1 million and Tyson Foods $11 million for foreign advertising. The Progressive Policy Institute listed corporate tax breaks over five years including $5.9 billion for expanding intangible drilling costs for oil and gas, $5.7 billion tax credits for non-conventional fuels, $5.3 billion tax-exempt, private-purpose revenue bonds, and a $1.7 billion exemption for credit-union income. In the past 10 years up to 1994, $149 billion in farm subsidies was paid out. In Kansas the average farmer received $20,000 to $40,000 a year. In a recent period 50 percent of farmers' aid went to the wealthiest one percent of the farmers. Over $55 billion a year is spent on corporate welfare. Many of these businesses are highly profitable. The Democratic Leadership Council and the conservative Heritage Foundation came up with a long list of corporate welfare programs that could save hundreds of billions of dollars. People are increasingly contemptuous of the federal government, partly because it created a welfare state for corporations while giving people the bill.[22]

The classic example of how nothing has really changed is the passage of the Federal Agricultural Improvement and Reform Act by Congress in 1996. According to the press this would finally cut farm subsidies, but this is a lie. Under the just-ended formula, because farm prices are so high, government welfare to farms would have dropped sharply. Instead, with aid separated from crop prices, farm aid will increase. Read James Bovard's article in *Barrons* to appreciate how this bill protects the corporations.[23]

While reducing government welfare payments to people, the 10 point Republican Contract With America did little to reduce corporate welfare. Despite many promises, Congress barely cut corporate welfare.[24] Much corporate welfare originated with the Democratic party, especially during the New Deal and the Great Society. When the Republicans made some proposals to cut corporate welfare, Clinton rejected such efforts. Perhaps one day the labor unions will wake up and realize that neither party represents their interests. Despite all the rhetoric, some corporate welfare has actually increased. The Agriculture Department is spending $110 million to advertise U.S. products overseas which is 30 percent over 1995. Clinton recommended increasing corporate aid by four percent.[25] Important consumer protections are being gutted, such as consumer protections against fraudulent financial advisors, while New Deal bank protections and the 1991 Truth in Savings Act may soon end.[26]

The book, *America: Who Really Pays the Taxes*, shows how unfair our tax structure has become. Taxes on corporations have dropped sharply, while taxes on the middle class have risen precipitously. Before, the government taxed the rich. Now, it borrows money from them and pays interest. A General Accounting Office (GAO) study in 1993 said that 40 percent of the corporations doing business in the U.S. with assets of $250 million or more paid income taxes under $100,000 or paid no income tax at all. Another GOA study revealed that 34 percent of all corporations in the U.S. with assets over $100 million paid no income tax in 1989. During the 1950s, corporations in the U.S. paid 23 percent of all federal income taxes. By 1991 this had dropped to 9.2 percent, while the corporate share of state and local taxes stayed about what it was in 1965.[27] In 1945 corporations paid 50 percent of all federal tax revenue; now they pay about seven percent.

The concentration of corporate power in the hands of fewer people has led not only to great economic inequality in income but also to increased control over the work place. It is now harder for workers to organize unions; the company can close and move overseas. The social safety net has been weakened, and it is much harder to attain a good job, food, and housing. There is also more employer surveillance and regulation of employees. Workers, like the serfs of old, are expected to be devoted to a company. Requiring employers to provide benefits like health insurance also increases the protector-dependent relationship. Workers are pressured to be more servile and to snitch on coworkers. Management at the Mazda plant in Flat Rock, Michigan said the workers belong to the company, they don't work for the firm. Workers were pressured to wear Mazda caps.[28]

In recent years companies have sued people who publicly opposed corporate projects. Litigation is an effective means to keep citizens from complaining.[29] Peter Montague, an environmental reporter, alleged that a report on dioxin filed by a Monsanto Chemical Co. scientist was fraudulent in methodology and use of data. That scientist is now suing Montague. Once the suit was initiated, press coverage of this alleged corporate fraud ceased.[30]

Corporations are increasingly suing or threatening to sue the media. Philip Morris Co. sued ABC for a story on *Day One* about nicotine in cigarettes. In July, 1994 the Health Care Reform Project, a group of organizations supporting Clinton's health-care reforms, held a news conference and stated that Pizza Hut paid for health insurance for its Japanese and German workers but not for its U.S. workers. Pizza Hut said this was libelous, so four television stations in Washington, D.C. refused to air the story. In early 1994 a reporter for KMOL-TV in San Antonio refused to retract a story that a local business objected to. He was fired.[31] As a result of these suits, California and New York passed laws blocking such corporate suits, and these corporate suits were ruled illegal by the Colorado Supreme Court.[32]

Another way in which millions of Americans are suffering from the power of Wall Street is in the derivatives boom. The bankruptcy of Orange County is hardly unique. Many governments and thousands of individuals lost huge sums of money to Wall Street, because the investment banks were allowed to present these complex investment instruments without explaining what was being sold.

Corporations today finance a counterrevolution of ideas to replace political parties and vigilant citizens as the key source of ideas. Corporate-sponsored think tanks increasingly provide expert opinion for government officials and the national media. Dissenting voices rarely speak in the national media.[33] Progressives, like Noam Chomsky and Gore Vidal, have generally been banned from the national media for years, and now, except for a brief period after the Oklahoma bombing, members of the Patriot movement are also denied access to the national media.

Workers are being pressured to support a company's political goals. In mid-August, 1994 IBM used E mail to 'advise' its employees about how to vote on health care reform. Citizens should be able to vote as they want without corporate pressure. Hundreds of corporate political organizations now organize the agenda and provide the financing that overwhelms the voice of the people. Business political-action committees replaced labor as the largest source of campaign money by the early 1980s. In 1974, labor unions accounted for half of all PAC money; by 1980, they accounted for under one fourth. Corporations have the money to pass laws and follow the regulatory agencies, while private citizens and labor groups cannot match this funding. Corporations have the financial resources needed in our new economic democracy.

Despite the fact that the 1992 election represented the first time since 1981 that the Democrats controlled both Congress and the White House, labor achieved none of its goals. Yet many pro-business goals were achieved such as NAFTA and the blocking of health reform. According to the National Library of Politics and Money, in the 1992 election, business groups donated $50.7 million of the $88 million that went to Democratic candidates. Today, the Democratic party represents business interests much more than it does labor.[34]

Today, corporations also dominate our culture. "Much of the nation's physical space, outdoors and indoors, is now a private preserve, carrying the messages and culture of the corporations that dominate economic and political life."[35] The book, *Market Madness*, provides suggestions to overcome the incessant marketing ads that we constantly face. Ads promote cigarettes, alcoholic beverages, and junk food which damage our health, while violence on TV promotes crime and a value system alien to our heritage. Sporting events are surrounded by corporate images. Shopping addiction is a 20th century disease.

"Not only through propaganda and socialization but also through 'good works,' or the appearance of such, do capitalists achieve hegemonic legitimacy. The ruthless industrialist becomes the generous philanthropist....The primary goal of capitalist cultural dominance is not to provide us with nice concerts and museums but to give capitalism's exploitative reality a providential appearance, so that people learn not only to accept, but to admire and appreciate, the leadership and stewardship of the owning class...."[36] People in television and artists in many fields often cannot promote their views or artistic creations if it goes against the corporate view. Libraries, theaters, and performing arts centers are increasingly under corporate control because of the need for money. Our culture and entertainment are increasingly determined by a small number of network executives and distributors. Museums have become "public relations agents for the interests of big business and its ideological allies."[37]

Corporate amusement parks like Disneyland and Sea World and the shopping mall culture are now the norm of society. The town square, as a center for gathering and shopping, has been replaced by the corporate-owned mall. Various court decisions support mall owners' right to prevent distribution of material. Political expression is often banned. In 1985 a New York Appeals Court held that a mall owner could ban political leaflets saying the state's Bill of Rights "governed the rights of citizens with respect to their government and not the rights of private individuals against private individuals." To this court, a corporation can violate any of our civil rights and the law offers no protection. A dissenting judge protested: "In the past, those who had ideas they wished to communicate to the public had the unquestioned right to disseminate those ideas in the open marketplace. Now that the marketplace has a roof over it, and is called a mall, we should not abridge that right."[38] New Jersey and several other states have given limited rights to protest in privately owned malls.[39]

Corporate propaganda has for decades infiltrated the schools which need money. Schools put ads on buses and broadcast music with commercials, while businesses provide free supplies with ads. Teachers have lost control over the curriculum, and it is hard for students to differentiate between education and advertising. Channel One television with corporate ads now reaches 350,000 classrooms.[40] Corporations and foundations "have altered academic priorities, reduced the importance of teaching, degraded the integrity of academic journals, and determined what research is conducted at universities. The social costs of this influence have been lower-quality education, a reduction in academic freedom, and a covert transfer of resources from the public to the private sector."[41] Universities and nonprofit organizations provide special services and trained personnel for the corporations. *Covert Action* said scientific research is for sale to corporate money.[42] Corporate controlled science is confusing the public and influencing the politicians.[43] The cost of higher education rose 170 percent in the past decade, but this is being used to subsidize corporate influence in the universities. Corporate research is more important than teaching as corporate-funded think tanks, endowed chairs, consulting jobs, and research grants become the norm at universities.

Children have become addicted to TV, junk food, and pop music while family interaction and control is increasingly subverted by corporate entertainment. Children are taught to become good corporate citizens by learning to consume, while both parents are forced to work away from the home because incomes keep falling. As wages dropped in the early 1970s, women went to work and the size of families shrank. The deliberate weakening of the family and the sense of community has made it easier to gradually introduce a new system of values that moves our society away from traditional values to suit the needs of corporate America and the new world order.

Even our religious and patriotic holidays have been desecrated by the corporations. Corporations have methodically worked for decades to influence the churches.[44] Christmas has become a contest to see who can buy and sell the most. The love of Christ has become incidental. Lincoln and Washington's birthdays have become Presidents Day, which has become a contest to find the best furniture deals. The Statute of Liberty is now used in a TV ad to sell cars. None of our cultural heritage is safe from the corporate onslaught.

More recently, corporate greed has infected medicine as HMOs interfere with the rights and judgments of doctors and patients. Doctors often have to get permission from accountants before they can recommend expensive treatments. A patient's health is determined by the all-powerful dollar.[45]

"The diminution of public expression and influence that can be found is not the consequence of a decline in national creativity or some other organic disability. It is the result of deliberate and successful efforts to reduce, even eliminate, the public realm in favor of the corporate sector....The corporate envelopment of public expression and creativity has been a direct outgrowth of the enormous expansion of corporate wealth and power in the postwar decades....The phenomenal growth of American capitalism in the years after 1945 helps to explain the deep penetration of corporate values and influence in American politics, law, education, culture, and life overall." The corporations also led the way into international alliances which were never a part of our history.[46]

"The drive to privatize and bring under corporate management as many elements of economic and social activity as possible in the last half century has tipped the balance of democratic existence to an uncomfortable precariousness ....There is no assurance that the corporate governors in America are inoculated against the fascist (strong state) solution to a politically threatening crisis." There has been "the erosion of democratic principle and practice in the informational-cultural sphere. Given this weakening of the national democratic fabric, the advent of the coercive state is hardly precluded."[47]

Various political commentators have warned that unlimited and unaccountable corporate power is not compatible with our traditions of constitutional government. The Founders understood that each class would press for too much power, so institutional checks were necessary to balance the various segments of society. Madison said the diffusion of power among a multiplicity of factions helped guarantee that no one special interest group could ever gain control of the federal government to control the rest of society. Different groups counterbalanced each other. Madison and Hamilton were especially influenced by Montesquieu's and Aquinas' notion of separating and dividing powers throughout society. The Founders feared concentrated economic power, so only 40 corporations were charted when our Republic was established. Just as the shared power between the states and federal government has been broken by the dangerous growth of federal power, the corporate elite have now gained so much power that the counterbalancing power of other interest groups is not sufficient. Pluralism, the interaction of conflicting interest groups, no longer works. You cannot have a free society when one segment of society becomes so dominant, and we cannot depend on the federal government to be a balancing arbitrator. This is the heart of our predicament.

The traditional pluralist model of many different groups and citizens actively involved in politics presenting a counterbalance to each other is no longer valid in corporate-controlled America. "A substantial part of government in the U.S. has come under the influence or control of narrowly based and largely autonomous elites....The distinction between the public and the private...has been compromised far more deeply than we like to acknowledge....The very idea of constitutionalism sometimes seems to be placed in question."[48]

"Today's emerging tyranny emanates from a New King, from a nonliving power center composed at its core of monolithic corporate entities encased and protected by endless layers of government bureaucracies....The New King's principal means of control is the media that sells us the myths of freedom....A New King was crowned when we capitulated to a regime that was no longer sensitive to people but to non-people—to corporations, to money, and to power."[49]

"The growth of corporate...enterprise has produced a social milieu in which individual liberties or freedoms are not highly valued...." There has taken place "a constitutional change of the greatest magnitude—the fusion of economic and political power into the corporate state, American style....In the corporate state, control by the citizenry is not possible. Nor...is control of the apparatus of the state by legislative organs....Legislators act less as a check on the bureaucracy than as a part of the decisional process. In so doing, they do not represent the citizens of the nation." They represent various interest groups. "The elite has never been reluctant to use violence when considered necessary to stamp out threats, internal or external." Attacks on the labor movement have certainly demonstrated this. If full repression takes hold in America, it will be announced under the banner of freedom. Huey Long once said if fascism is ever introduced into America it will be used in the name of anti-fascism.[50]

"The new partnership (between government and business) is emerging at the same time that a vast conglomerate merger movement concentrates a larger portion of our national wealth in the hands of a smaller group of corporations. The two forces accentuate each other, producing a unique brand of corporate state in which the government and private sectors threaten to coalesce in a way that could be antithetical to democracy itself. Countervailing forces—in industry, government, and even in organized labor—are meshing in power alliances that can signify the formation of an elitist group with the power to determine the course it wishes to follow quite independent of the customary processes of popular democratic participation."[51] Calvin Coolidge once said: "The business of government is business."

Many large corporations have laid off thousands of workers despite the growth of profits and sales.[52] High unemployment is now accepted as the norm because the corporate controlled press tells us this is acceptable. Millions of Americans have been forced to accept low-paying jobs. The percent of Americans working for Fortune 500 companies has dropped from over 20 percent of non-farm employees in 1973 to half that in 1994. It remains to be seen if the political influence of these corporations will also drop as they abandon America.

There is too much centralized and unchecked corporate power today for any Republic to survive, especially if the people are to have a voice in government. Every modern industrial society must learn to control the power of the large corporations and still protect the rights of its workers. During the New Deal many felt that a large federal government would resolve this problem. Recently Arthur Schlesingler, Jr. warned that to weaken the federal government will not return power to the people, but will instead transfer power to the large corporations.[53] Liberals such as John Kenneth Galbraith, in *American Capitalism: The Theory of Countervailing Power*, said competing corporations balanced each other. In past years many felt the labor unions were a counterbalance to big business, but that clearly is also not true.

To restore competition many large banks and conglomerates should be broken up with stronger regulation and antitrust laws; otherwise, political intrigue against our government and way of life will continue. Tighter rules should be established to limit the ability of ex-government officials to work for corporations, especially as lobbyists, while government regulations that weaken labor unions should be removed. Restoring state sovereignty and having the states work together would weaken corporate power, because the corporations would then have to work with 51 governments instead of one central government which they now dominate. The federal government must not be allowed to continue as a vehicle to expand corporate control over our lives.

Investor activism and boycotts to influence corporate policy are constructive. People from labor, environment, minorities, and local communities should be on the boards of large corporations, and employee ownership, as with United Airlines, is helpful. By the 1970s, seven European countries required employees to be on corporate boards. This has resulted in less labor trouble, improved productivity, and generally has not limited corporate profits. Such a policy should be required by law in the U.S. Corporations must be made accountable to the community and workers and not just to stockholders. The huge sums of money in pension funds should be used to support the infrastructure and community investment and should not be used for leveraged corporate buyouts and mergers. Some stockholder rights and profits should be transferred to workers, and society should insist that corporations remain out of the political arena.

As long as there was not too much government interference in people's daily lives and living standards continued to rise, people believed, as the media assured us, that the corporate elite believed in the political values that have been the basis of our constitutional government. Except during the populist era and the great depression, people weren't too concerned about growing corporate power. Today, this has changed and more people are very concerned about how the corporations and banks dominate politics and all aspects of society. The goal of corporations is to make money not to enrich the ethical, cultural, and social fabric of society.

Recently various groups have formed to curtail corporate power. Some want to require federal corporate charters to have minimum standards of corporate conduct. That path would further enhance federal and corporate power. Instead the Constitution's commerce clause should be used to require minimum standards that states must meet when they charter a corporation involved in interstate commerce. The Boston-based Program on Corporations, Law and Democracy wants to again require limited corporate charters, reestablish the people's control over corporations, and remove corporate constitutional rights. In extreme cases, when a corporation repeatedly violates the law, as recently happened with a Japanese bank in New York, its right to exist should be revoked as was often done in the past. Once again corporations must prove that they exist to serve the public welfare.[54]

C. Wright Mills spent many years studying the "power elite" in America concluding that the corporate elite make the key political decisions while political parties occupy a secondary middle level.[55] The corporate elite represent a private economic and political power that is unaccountable to the people. Since the 1994 election it has been understood that the American people want less federal government control. In time it will be equally understood that the people are also tired of being controlled by large corporations, as is increasingly happening in the new world order.

# Chapter IX

# Rise of the Transnational Corporations

"There can be no effective control of corporations while their political activity remains."

Theodore Roosevelt

"The corporations...have successfully leveraged economic power into political power that undercuts the Constitution."

Charles Reich

The growth of modern transnational or multinational corporations has created many problems for our constitutional form of government. These changes have come upon us almost unannounced and with little recognition by the general public, although in recent years more people are examining the implications of this development. From trade and banking to tourism, human rights, and environmental concerns many activities are now global in outlook and influence. These cross-border economic, social, cultural, and political interactions are increasingly being directed and controlled by large corporations not by governments. Especially with the end of the cold war, economic not military competition rules supreme. Globalization represents the radical transformation of the global economy to benefit large corporations.

Nations have lost the power to control their economies, and financial markets often determine the success or failure of government programs. The *Boston Globe*, on April 11, 1994, said: "Corporate taxes are crumbling in many industrial countries as companies move their booked profits from one locale to another, telling different stories to different tax collectors." In 1993, the General Accounting Office told Congress that 40 percent of corporations with assets of at least $250 million paid under $100,000 in U.S. income taxes. *Dateline*, on August 18, 1995, said the U.S. government isn't properly taxing foreign corporations in the U.S., because U.S. corporations would then be forced to pay higher taxes overseas. About 75 percent of foreign corporations with U.S. operations pay no U.S. taxes.

Large corporations now can compete on equal terms with governments. They are accountable to no one, as the BCCI scandal demonstrated. Multinational corporations can move their production to countries where wage and production costs are much lower. Until recently, this could not be done easily because of political considerations and a lack of capital and technology. However, there has been an increased fusion of economic and political power because of increased capital flows and technological advances. There is now one global work force, with labor far cheaper in third world nations. National interest is determined by what industry, not the people, wants. In 1973 George Ball told the House Committee on Foreign Affairs: "The multinational corporation not only promises the most efficient use of world resources, but as an institution, it poses the greatest challenge to the power of a nation-state since the temporal position of the Roman Church began to decline in the 15th century."

The rise of the corporate state has given transnational corporations the power to threaten the very existence of democratic institutions throughout the world. Local political movements and regulations have been weakened, while international organizations like the World Bank are beyond democratic control. Steve Solomon, in *The Confidence Game*, said many governments are transferring power to central banks. Institutions and agreements like the World Bank, GATT, NAFTA International Monetary Fund (IMF), UN, Inter-American Development Bank, World Economic Forum, Ford and Rockefeller Foundations were established by the corporate elite "to create a new, highly undemocratic governing structure for the global economy. These institutions are imposing a global corporate agenda designed to extract wealth and resources from poorer countries and communities and concentrate them among the global elite."[1] Representing the corporate elite, the World Bank supports programs that increase trade at the expense of social stability, the environment, and worker welfare.[2] Under the guise of free trade, corporate control over our lives increases while national sovereignty is weakened. The goal is global economic union to create political union and a one world government. Henry Kissinger, on July 18, 1993 in the *Los Angeles Times*, said: "What Congress will have before it is not a conventional trade agreement but the architecture of a new international system...a first step toward a new world order." NAFTA represents "the vital first step for a new kind of community of nations."

As economic power grew and expanded overseas, the multinational corporations received government assistance to manage their economic empires. Greater corporate involvement and interaction with the government required greater secrecy to maintain the myth of democracy to keep the people quiet. Meanwhile corporate control over the people grows, labor unions continue to weaken, disillusionment with government grows, and free market ideology rules. With little accountability to workers or the public, multinational corporations now have tremendous political power in the U.S.[3] Accompanying this transformation has been a growing transfer of bad corporate debt to the government.

James Morgan, in the London *Financial Times*, described the "de facto world government" now forming in the "new imperial age." This world government will represent and serve the multinational corporations, preferably with the consent of the ignorant masses, but, if necessary, force and terror have and will continue to be used. The military arm of the coming one world government, for now, is money and capital flows. In the immediate years ahead, the growing UN army, its armed agent NATO, and the disarmament of individual nations will make countries powerless to protect their rights and sovereignty.

The West has used international institutions, military power, and economic resources to maintain political and economic dominance over third world nations. Democracy through a manipulation of market forces is being used as a weapon to promote the profits of transnational corporations. Foreign aid increasingly represents the corporate agenda. The goal of U.S. foreign policy is to promote capitalism, not democracy. Especially in China, Africa, and Latin America political reform is cosmetic because of the growing influence of multinational corporations.[4] Trade with China is no longer limited because of human rights, but a trade war almost developed when China illegally reproduced patented goods. Charles

Lane, in *The New Republic*, recently said he might be denied some lunches at the CFR because he supported what many Republicans and the people demand: sharp cuts in foreign aid. Lane even called the arguments of those defending foreign aid acts of desperation. Foreign aid has often been an extension of the national security state and part of the vast corporate welfare programs of the federal government. It has for too many years been used to promote dictators who have nothing to do with our moral values. Foreign aid should end or be sharply reduced and be used primarily where the people actually benefit.[5]

U.S. government agencies, such as the U.S. Information Agency and the Agency for International Development, promote false or "low intensity democracy" around the world.[6] It costs the U.S. less to do this than to support an open and often unstable dictatorship, and social stability is more important in the global economy. The Trilateral Commission called for flexible methods to increase social control with less coercive methods.[7] A small group of elites legitimatize their rule with carefully controlled elections. The goal is stability, preferably through persuasion, for economic gain.[8] These ideas were promoted by Joseph Schumpeter, who said democracy only means that people have the opportunity to accept or refuse the men who rule them.[9]

Third world governments are usually controlled by a ruling elite who may terrorize or kill those who interfere with official policy. Multinational corporations are relatively free to operate in these countries with favorable terms that included cheap labor, low taxes, and limited social programs, while local poverty grows as income distribution becomes more unequal. Local elites are bribed to control the people and prevent unions and dangerous popular movements. The welfare of the people is irrelevant. Democratic dialogue interferes with corporate efficiency. Examining how transnational corporations act in third world countries offers a clue to what is planned for the U.S., Europe, Canada, Japan, and Australia. In a one world government, transnational corporations wouldn't have to worry about inconveniences like strong labor unions, grass root revolts, or environmental issues. People who raised these issues will simply disappear.

Different countries strive to bring new corporations into their region by offering numerous benefits in bidding wars. Nations are forced to compete with each other for foreign investment and aid, which lowers the business costs of the multinational corporations but also lowers incomes and weakens the social and economic fabric of many nations. The result is increased unemployment, lower wages, more debt, weakened infrastructure, and slower economic growth. "The world is being moved by state-corporate policy towards a kind of third world model, with sectors of great wealth, a huge mass of misery, and a large superfluous population, lacking any rights because they contribute nothing to profit-making for the rich."[10]

Consumers in third world countries are sold inferior products by the multinationals through sophisticated marketing techniques that include Western logos and brand names.[11] More expensive Western medical drugs replace native folk medicines that are much cheaper and often more effective. Providing large scale food aid to third world nations has damaged their agriculture base and made them dependent on western bankers and corporations to survive. We spend billions to provide food aid, yet for decades far less aid was provided to make these nations self sufficient in food production. This dependency made it easier to control and exploit the natural resources of third world nations.

There is growing resistance to the expanding power of the corporate elite and Western cultural dominance of globalization, as the world's living standards drop. In Bangalore, India, 500,000 farmers protested GATT provisions that allowed corporations to limited their freedom to use certain seeds. Hundreds of thousands of farmers protested against GATT in the Philippines. The urban slums of third world nations, like Brazil, were made much worse during the Green Revolution. Overly efficient farming drove people off the land into the cities weakening families, destroying social stability, and leaving people unable to support themselves. Over 3.1 billion people live off the land. If farming productivity in the third world matches Western nations, at least two billion people will become unproductive.

Between 1980 and 1992, Mexican manufacturing productivity rose 41 percent, and real wages fell 32 percent as Mexico entered the international market place. The result was a revolt in Chiapas, Mexico partly because NAFTA helped the ruling elite but not the people. The Mexican rebels called NAFTA "the death certificate for the indigenous people of Mexico." In Mexico perhaps 800,000 small farmers will be forced off their land and have to move into the cities unemployed. Hundreds of U.S. corporations have established factories along the U.S./Mexican border. People trying to unionize are fired or assaulted, environmental conditions are among the poorest in the world, and wages remain low with the active support of the Mexican government.

The Mexican economic collapse shows how our government continues to represent the bankers, not the American people. William Seidman, past chairman of the FDIC and of the RTC, said Wall Street stood to lose $10-15 billion from the Mexico collapse, so it naturally turned to Washington to be saved. Desperate to protect Wall Street and stop people from saying NAFTA was a disaster, Clinton, without congressional approval, violated the Constitution by committing $9 billion and then a further $20 billion credit line to help Mexico. Over 90 percent of the funds available in the Exchange Stabilization Fund, an emergency agency established in 1934 only to defend the dollar, was illegally used. In July, 1995, the House voted 245 to 183 to halt further disbursement of the remaining $8.5 billion in the Clinton loan, but the House leadership blocked implementing this vote. Numerous domestic projects are slashed or cancelled yet, at least $29 billion was available to rescue Wall Street, and *The Nation* said Mexico had secretly receive $12 billion in credits from the U.S., Japan, and Europe in the months before the late 1994 debt crisis. While these loans were meant to support Mexico and the peso, much of the money actually went to Mexican and foreign elites.[12]

As the weakened dollar demonstrates, there is no way paying such large sums of money could be justified as being in America's national interests. Patrick Buchanan said: "The looting of America on behalf of the new world order has begun." According to *The Economist*, by June, 1994 U.S. banks had Latin American loans totaling $50 billion. *Time* magazine said that 380,000 jobs will be lost in the next four years from NAFTA, and there will be between $13-28 billion in lost output.[13] Now that NAFTA has passed many corporations have broken their promises and moved more jobs outside the U.S. Current laws often provide tax incentives to corporations when they close plants and export jobs.

The Mexico crisis also exemplifies how our news is managed. The "experts" the national media used to speak about Mexico often came from financial firms with large investments in Mexico. Between 1992 and 1994 the largest holder of Mexican stocks and bonds was Goldman Sachs, which is the firm Secretary of the

Treasury Robert Rubin worked for. He played a major role in arranging the Mexican bailout. Ralph Nader said Rubin should have recused himself from the Mexico loan because of his obvious conflict of interest. Goldman Sachs has also been a major financial supporter of Clinton. When the Mexican president visited the U.S. in October, 1995 the press praised Mexico for repaying $700 million due on the loan; however, the press ignored the fact that $2 billion was then due, but Mexico lacked the money to repay that on time. Today Mexico's debt is $153 billion, which is much more than in 1982.

Dr. Felipe Arismendi, a UN economist, and certain Mexican officials, such as Hugo del Valle, who work for the UN in New York, said Wall Street firms were warned in advance by the Federal Reserve Bank about the collapsing Mexico economy, so they withdrew about $30 billion. *Newsday* headlined: "Surprise Profits for Top N.Y. Banks." The Mexican bailout was a bank relief act. Citibank, Chase Manhattan, and Chemical Bank all made considerable profits, despite having large holdings in Mexico. Mexico spent most of its foreign reserves throughout 1994, and the Federal Reserve was aware of what was happening.

In late 1993 the director of the Ethos Capital Management Inc. in New York said: "There are things that would disturb any investor when you talk about re-defining income distribution." Wall Street does not want the Mexican people to increase their wealth. A leaked Chase Manhattan memo on January 13, 1995 warned that the Chiapas uprising should be crushed to calm the international investment community, and the ruling party should consider committing electoral fraud to maintain control and stability. According to the memo it would be frivolous to have social and economic reforms and improve people's lives, because it was more important to repay international investors. This memo was sent to 100 major investment groups. John Sweeney, of the Heritage Foundation, in a January 25, 1995 report also called for stopping the Chiapas rebellion to restore investor confidence. On February 9, 1995 the Mexican government responded by conducting military operations against the rebels.[14]

In the future, how many hundreds of billions of dollars will U.S. taxpayers have to pay to bailout Wall Street in other failed business ventures. Other nations with unsound fiscal policies will figure they can also be rescued by American taxpayers. Already the *Wall Street Journal* reported May 4, 1995 that the previous week the U.S. Treasury Department had made a loan to Argentina via the Exchange Stabilization Fund.[15] Walker Todd, ex-attorney for the Federal Reserve, reported in the *Sacramento Bee* that U.S. officials were planning to rescue Japanese banks by having the Federal Reserve, supported by the Treasury Department, purchase up to $50 billion worth of U.S. securities from Japanese banks. Details of this scam were leaked to Todd by government officials. Since Japanese voters are unwilling to pay for the mistakes of their banks the U.S. will help. Part of this scam was discussed by Rep. Leach on October 16, 1995.[16]

The IMF said 10 nations could have trouble similar to Mexico's. For markets to work, investors must also suffer for their mistakes partly to prevent worst mistakes from occurring. Risk and reward must be preserved. On the same day the $40 billion Mexican loan was proposed by Clinton, the Democrats said the party needed to get back to its roots with labor and the minorities. How stupid they think the people are!

Despite the Mexican fiasco, Clinton is proceeding to expand NAFTA throughout Latin America.[17] The book, *Western Hemisphere Economic Integra-*

*tion*, which is dedicated to David Rockefeller, explains why the Western Hemisphere should be joined in an economic union. Negotiations are underway for the entrance of Chile into NAFTA, although attempts to fast track such legislation in Congress failed. Newt Gingrich, Henry Kissinger, and others want a North American and European union called a North Atlantic Free Trade Area (FTA), and said it should merge with NAFTA.[18] Naturally *The Economist*[19] and Secretary of State Warren Christopher[20] support this next step towards a one world government. On March 3, 1996 Christopher was in Brazil urging adaptation of the FTA. The May/June, 1996 issue of *Foreign Affairs* contained an article by Charles A. Kupchan promoting a "transatlantic union" between Europe and the U.S, and *Forbes* on July 1, 1996 had an article promoting a transatlantic union, partly because this would limit American protectionism.

Plans to create one European currency by January 1, 1999 are part of the one world agenda to have a united Europe. At a 1983 economic summit, Ronald Reagan said: "An integrated world economy needs a common monetary standard....But, no national currency will do—only a world currency will work." In 1984 *Foreign Affairs* called for creating a single common world currency and "a pooling of monetary sovereignty."[21] In an editorial, *The Economist* said creating one European currency was part of the "broader designs for Europe's political future" that included plans for one police force and one foreign policy.[22] Bernard Connolly, a 17-year career Eurocrat, wrote *The Rotten Heart of Europe*, harshly attacking the single currency and the hidden political objectives to promote the corporate elite at the expense of the people. Promoters of one European currency will attempt to establish one central bank, which will damage each nation's sovereignty.

Sir James Goldsmith said GATT will be a disaster for the industrial nations because unemployment will greatly increase and wages will drop sharply.[23] On November 15, 1994 Goldsmith spoke before the Senate Committee on Commerce. He said: "What we are witnessing is the divorce of the interests of the major corporations and the interests of society as a whole....We have a system ...being proposed...which will result in massive unemployment, massive hemorrhaging of jobs and capital, but which will increase corporate profits....There is absolutely no doubt whatsoever that the World Trade Organization (WTO) is a major diminution of sovereignty....GATT, the global free trade, is the replacement utopia for Marxism. It is another one of these mad utopias."[24]

On June 10, 1994 Rep. Gingrich testified before the House Committee on Ways and Means about GATT. He said: "We need to be honest about the fact that we are transferring from the U.S. at a practical level significant authority to a new organization. This is a transformational moment. I would feel better if the people who favor this would just be honest about the scale of the change....This is not just another trade agreement....We have to be very careful, because it is a very big transfer of power....(and) We are not likely to take (our authority) back."[25] Just before Gatt was ratified, Senator Hollings said: "This Gatt agreement is being pushed by David Rockefeller and the Trilateral Commission."

The *New York Times* on May 23, 1992 included an article entitled "The End of Sovereignty" promoting the new European system. However, after 20 years, the Common Market has been a disaster for social stability and the economic well-being of many Europeans. In the last 20 years, the GNP of France has grown by 80 percent while unemployment has grown from 400,000 to over five million. Over four million are jobless in Germany. This is what awaits the industrial world with GATT.[26] Goldsmith called for replacing global free trade with regional free trade. Instead of specialized economies, there should be diversified economies with the free movement of capital and managed trade to protect jobs, social stability, and small businesses. Too often experts rely on Wall Street, forgetting about the rest of the nation. Wall Street and Main Street are not the same.

Sharply increased long-term unemployment and slowed growth in Europe developed partly because jobs were exported as tariffs came down with international trade agreements. Corporations say the solution is to reduce the role of government in business, cut taxes, and privatization to make businesses more efficient. However, expanded trade can benefit all only if it also protects labor rights and wage standards. Working closer with workers and having better relations in the work place can enhance productivity. Economic growth should be used to increase social stability and the happiness of the people.

In America wages have been dropping for over 20 years, while corporate profits continue to grow as globalization expands. The traditional tie between corporate profits and better wages for workers no longer exists in the U.S. or Europe. The manufacturing base is being exported with millions of jobs lost. M.I.T. economist Lester Thurow said: "No country without a revolution or a military defeat has ever experienced such a sharp shift in the distribution of earnings as America in the last generation." Using the media the large corporations have engineered a silent revolution.

Many highly trained and educated people cannot find work, or they are forced to take low paying service jobs. Once unemployment benefits end, after about six months, these people are removed from the unemployment statistics. Many more people are unemployed than what the government and press admit. This is partly why so many people are nervous about their jobs, despite claims that the economy is booming. Workers increasingly have no value except to increase corporate profits and power. The third worldization of the U.S. is making many people poor with a small elite in control. The better off the people are, the harder it is to control them. When people are kept poor and are forced to work harder for less money, they have less time and energy for politics. Even *Time* admitted that the middle class is shrinking while the poor and very rich increase.[27] In October 24, 1994 *Time* said the U.S. has the largest gap between the rich and poor of any major industrial nation. Upward mobility for U.S. workers is no longer assured.[28]

Since 1992 Congress has permitted U.S. corporations to hire over one million foreigners in two programs. The Permanent Alien Certification and H-1B visa programs allows companies to replace U.S. employees with cheap foreign workers. The companies are supposed to first try to hire capable U.S. workers but this is usually a farce, and many high-tech jobs go to foreign workers. It is easier and cheaper for the corporations to import trained foreigners, instead of educating Americans. Taxpayers pay $60 million a year to administer this corporate welfare. Even the White House and other government agencies hire foreign workers. The *New York Times* admitted that tens of thousands of highly skilled professionals have been laid off so the large corporations can import this cheap labor supply.[29] Senator Simpson's recent attempt to limit this influx of foreign workers was defeated by the corporate onslaught.

Charles Lasch, in *The Revolt of the Elites and the Betrayal of Democracy*, described the contempt, arrogance, and scorn the corporate elite feel towards the American people. They no longer believe in the Constitution, so the elite act irresponsibly. We are heading towards a two-class society, with the ruling elite feeling little loyalty or responsibility towards the U.S. The new patriotism is corporate profits and self-aggrandizement. Civic responsibility is sacrificed for profits in the global market. Traditional public institutions like political parties are used to increase power and control over the people. United to an "international culture of work and leisure" our elite rulers feel "indifferent to the prospect of national decline."[30] The ruling elite have more in common with their counterparts in Hong Kong and Frankfurt than with the American people.

Leaders of multinational corporations represent their businesses; they do not act in the best interests of the U.S. or of other nations within which they reside. The U.S. has for years contributed tens of billions of dollars to the IMF, so banks could collect on their loans to third world nations. Robert B. Reich said that, increasingly, U.S. owned corporations have no special relationship with Americans, so it makes no sense to trust these corporations with our national competitiveness. "The interests of American-owned corporations may or may not coincide with those of the American people."[31] A vice-president of Colgate-Palmolive said: "The U.S. does not have an automatic call on our resources. There is no mindset that puts this country first."[32] The U.S. Bureau of Economic Statistics said 20 percent of all U.S. imports come from foreign subsidiaries or affiliates of U.S. firms. Many large U.S. corporations like Citicorp (51 percent), Chevron (55 percent), and Gillette (66 percent) have shifted much of their assets overseas. In the past, wealth was usually concentrated in a region or nation and a particular industry. Today, wealth is more purely financial and easily shifts between nations.

The ability of money to move quickly between nations has created job insecurity, falling incomes, rising debt, and a weakened middle class. Lasch, in describing the collapse of the middle class in third world nations, said this same fate may await the U.S. The existence of a trading and manufacturing class has been crucial to establishing a stable nation state for hundreds of years. Aristotle said a large middle class "has a great steadying influence and checks the opposing extremes" of the rich and poor. Once a large and stable middle class develops, there is always a demand for self-government. Unrestrained market forces destroy communities and traditional family and spiritual values, which ultimately weakens national sovereignty. "The revolt of the elites against time-honored traditions of locality, obligation, and restraint may yet unleash a war of all against all."[33]

There is a need for more community action to mobilize people to counteract corporate power. Ralph Nader said: "Societies rot from the top down. They reconstruct from the bottom up." We should help people mobilize at the community level, not ask what Washington will do for the people. The U.S. should promptly leave GATT and NAFTA. H.R. 499 to withdraw from NAFTA should be supported. Committing $29 billion or more to save Wall Street in Mexico and defend a poorly constructed trade agreement is ridiculous. We should protect our sovereignty, workers jobs, and use trade to improve our standard of living.

All parties can benefit from international trade agreements but only if they are properly structured. NAFTA and GATT represent attempts to use trade as a weapon to destroy national sovereignty to establish the one world government. In 1974 *Foreign Affairs*, the voice of the CFR, published an article stating: "The 'house of world order' will have to be built from the bottom up rather than the top down....An end run around sovereignty, eroding it piece by piece, will accomplish much more than the old-fashioned frontal assault." Richard Gardner, a CFR member and past assistant deputy secretary of state, called for world government, surrender of U.S. sovereignty, strengthening the central role of the UN, increased use of UN troops, and changing "the ground rules for the conduct of international trade" such as with GATT. Strengthening international agencies such as the World Bank and UN Development Programs was seen as strengthening international agencies and weakening the influence of individual nations in world affairs. These new policies "will subject countries to an unprecedented degree of international surveillance over up to now sacrosanct 'domestic' policies." Gardner believes this approach "can produce some remarkable concessions of sovereignty that could not be achieved on an across-the-board basis."[34]

The GATT agreement regulates governments much more than businesses; governments must adjust their policies so corporations can grow. Under GATT, the WTO is creating panels to review and reject the laws of member states that interfere with international trade. Nations must comply or face sanctions. Before GATT passed, 42 state attorney generals told Clinton GATT was unconstitutional and it would cancel many state laws. Already Europe, Japan, and Canada have issued reports attacking U.S. federal and local laws as unfair barriers to free trade. Pesticide regulations, nutritional food labels, nuclear licensing, the Marine Mammal Protection Act involving tuna and dolphins, and court agreements allowing native Americans to protect their natural resources are called unfair non-tariff trade barriers. Based on U.S. ratification of the International Covenant on Civil and Political Rights, British lawyers tried to stop Texas from executing a convicted rapist-killer. Under NAFTA, Mexico has filed a complaint over a labor dispute with Sprint in San Francisco. This type of intervention in our internal affairs will become normal under GATT and NAFTA. Even small nations can now challenge and change U.S. laws.

On January 17, 1996 the WTO supported a claim by Venezuela and Brazil that the U.S. Clean Air Act discriminates against foreign oil refiners and this decision was upheld on appeal. Hundreds of consumer protection laws will be lost in this manner, which will also increase corporate profits. The corporations will say it is the fault of a foreign body, and the people will have no real recourse as they have already been sold out by their representatives. Phony politicians like Dole who voted for GATT complained about this decision but many similar decisions are now inevitable.

Nations should join together and demand an international corporate code of conduct, with labor, health, and environmental rights and enforcement procedures. Unions should be allowed to organize. International organizations like the World Bank should be closed. Groups from different nations should work together to counterbalance the actions of the multinational corporations. Governments should adapt monetary policies that raise the people's economic standards and lessen the gap between the rich and poor.[35] When a corporation closes U.S. factories to move jobs overseas, it should face a special tariff to import their products into the U.S.

Drastic steps must be taken to restore balance to our trade with China and Japan. For too long we have been played like fools by these nations, especially since certain corporations benefit from this sharp trade imbalance. Secret stock ownership of many Japanese corporations by Wall Street is one reason why nothing has been accomplished to end the huge balance of trade deficit with Japan. "American Big Business was found at the time of the first World War to be linked to Japanese Big Business through the Harvey cartel...." Companies with investments in Japanese firms from early this century included GM, GE, Standard Oil, Westinghouse, Eastman Kodak, and Singer Sewing Machine. After World War II, Rockefeller agents bought into more Japanese companies at a sharp discount. This quiet interaction between Japanese and American corporations continues today.[36]

With Japan, free trade means unfair trade. Now that GATT has passed, Japan refuses to even negotiate with the U.S. about the huge trade imbalance. Instead they have turned to GATT mechanisms for protection. After 27 years, it is time to recognize that we must have managed trade with Japan. Even some commentators said the recent auto agreement with Japan was managed trade. We should sit down with Japan and China and develop a program over several years to restore an almost equal balance of trade. It is time to end the vast transfer of our economic wealth to other nations. The huge trade imbalance is more evidence that the Washington politicians represent economic interests not the American people.

Historically Holland, England, and now America have shown that free trade causes serious problems for developed nations as wages are lowered and the manufacturing base is exported. The working classes benefited when foreign competition was controlled, as in early nineteenth century England and in the U.S. after World War II. Open immigration into the U.S. weakens U.S. sovereignty, keeps wages low, and limits the ability of unions to grow. This is partly why the national media supports immigration and attacks as racists those who want it limited. With open borders, corporate profits raise while U.S. wages drop. U.S. corporations go overseas for cheap labor while foreigners immigrate to the U.S. seeking higher wages.

From the time of George Washington until World War II, except during the first world war, we had a policy of isolationism. However, while this policy kept us from foreign political alliances it also included managed trade, usually done to benefit America. As Benjamin Franklin said: "No nation was ever ruined by trade." Our economy and manufacturing base developed with economic treaties between various nations. In recent decades the corporate controlled press falsely claimed that the choice is only for free trade or isolationism and strict limits on trade. This is disinformation used to increase corporate profits and surrender U.S. sovereignty to the planned world government. Rep. Duncan Hunter, in a letter published in the March 18, 1996 *Business Week*, noted that free trade is a recent policy with a poor track record. We should return to our historical policy of managed trade which means that American jobs and sovereignty will again be protected.

New Zealand has shown how populist policies and free-market reforms can benefit an entire nation, including the people and large corporations. After 10 years of reforms, New Zealand has a government surplus, low unemployment, and 59 percent of all government employees have been fired.[37] American corporations must be forced, through tax incentives and penalties, to bring manufacturing jobs back to the U.S. This would make it easier to remove more people from public welfare and unemployment compensation, which would also bring down taxes. There would also be improved social stability and less crime as more people worked. If the manufacturing base of the nation is destroyed, the middle class will be severely weakened. It is time to remind American multinational corporations that they have responsibilities to America.

# Chapter X

# Rise of the National Security State:
# The Cold War and Democracy

"No truly sophisticated proponent of repression would be stupid enough to shatter the facade of democratic institutions."

Murray B. Levin

"The cause of liberty becomes a mockery if the price to be paid is the wholesale destruction of those who are to enjoy liberty."

Gandhi

Part of the strategy to increase federal power and destroy state authority has been to shift from a Republic to a nation state with increased nationalism and an aggressive foreign policy. When is the last time you heard a politician refer to America as a Republic. The shift from a Republic to a nation state with an empire is part of the age-old battle of the few to control the many. Emotional appeals, however irrational, have historically been used to increase loyalty to the government. Appeals to nationalism and war provide a rationale to direct and control the people, to justify and promote the goals of the ruling elite. War discourages dissent and encourages conformity. External threats of communism provided an excuse for huge military expenditures and increased control of the people.

The seeds of the national security state and our moral decline started with the Spanish American War in 1898. That war allowed both political parties to control rampaging populism, as people were diverted from criticizing the corporate elite and urged to rally around the flag. There had been a recent depression, the frontier was filling up, and as America's manufacturing base increased, the ruling elite felt foreign bases were needed to increase foreign exports. The people paid to develop an empire, while the ruling elite reaped the economic rewards from these foreign adventures.

War was a logical continuation of America's imperialistic manifest destiny as the continental U.S. was fully occupied. In 1895 an editorial in the New York *Journal of Commerce*, then one of Americas main newspapers, criticized "the artificial patriotism being worked up at the present time" including "the fashion of hanging the flag from every schoolhouse and giving the boys military drill." The first time the pledge of allegiance to the flag took place in a schoolroom was in 1892. The original pledge of allegiance was formulated by a socialist, Francis Bellamy. Today only the U.S. and the Philippines have an oath to their flag.[1] Only gradually was it thought proper to hang flags at every school. While I am not criticizing saluting the flag, surely no one will challenge the patriotism of our forefathers, who for over a hundred years, did not feel it necessary or proper to pledge allegiance to the American flag as an emblem of their patriotism.

Development of the national security state intensified during and after World War I, as the policy of isolation from involvement in foreign conflicts ended. Before the U.S. entered World War I, some agitated for entry into the war to "forge a national soul" for the country. They felt war would give rise to "a new religion of vital patriotism...of consecration to the State," and that a foreign war would fill people with "a strong sense of international duty." Instead of protecting our rights and freedoms with as little government as possible, the emphasis in the new America was to have more respect for a strong national government that we were indebted to.

The new religion of the market economy was joined with the new religion of nationalism. We were no longer a Republic, with a strong independent people who relied on themselves with as little government as possible. Reverence for the Constitution was gradually replaced by a cult of the nation.[2] Some understood that the interventionalists wanted to replace the Republic with a feared nation state that would destroy the Republic. Senator William J. Stone said if we entered the European war "We will never again have this same old Republic."

Indeed, this period was filled with mass arrests with protest equated with disloyalty. Publications with unpatriotic ideas were banned from the mail, and there was little freedom of the press. The two political parties worked together, and people deemed radical were brutally suppressed. In 1917 the Attorney General said he had several hundred thousand citizens watching others to protect us from radical elements. Various immigrants, especially if they were union organizers, were deported as threats to the state. The red menace was equated with labor unrest, especially after Russia turned communist. The threat of communism was a convenient excuse to attack the labor movement. By 1920 the government had files on two million people.

America has been in a continuous state of war since 1941. Historically wars have played a key role in increasing the state's power, size, and fiscal spending, and that has certainly been true in America. We have been at war during 20 percent of our history, yet all but five of the federal government cabinet posts and most federal agencies were established during a war.[3] James Madison said: "Of all the enemies to public liberty, war is, perhaps, the most to be dreaded....War is the parent of armies, from these proceed debts and taxes; and armies and debts, and taxes are the known instruments for bringing the many under the domination of the few....No nation could preserve its freedom in the midst of continual warfare."[4] At the constitutional convention Madison also said: "A standing military force with an overgrown executive will not long be safe companions to liberty. The means of defense against foreign danger have been always the instruments of tyranny at home." Tocqueville warned that "All those who seek to destroy the liberties of a democratic nation ought to know that war is the surest and the shortest means to accomplish it."[5] Centralized power is essential to establish a dictatorship, and power is most easily centralized by war or by the expectation of war. "This centralizing tendency of war has made the rise of the state throughout much of history a disaster for human liberty and rights."[6]

Many people called it a coup d'etat when President Kennedy was assassinated. It is more accurate to say the coup d'etat took place when the national security state was established in the late 1940s. "The cynicism of this coup d'etat was breath-taking. Officially we were doing nothing but trying to preserve freedom for ourselves and our allies from a ruthless enemy that was everywhere monolithic and all-powerful. Actually, the real enemy were those national security statesmen who had so dexterously hijacked the country, establishing military conscription in peacetime, overthrowing governments that did not please them, and finally keeping all but the very rich docile and jittery by imposing income taxes that theoretically went as high as 90 percent. That is quite an achievement in a country at peace."[7]

While the cold war often did not involved actual fighting, this period has had a major negative impact on basic American beliefs and institutions. The cold war was partly manufactured by the U.S. to maintain control over the people. The American people were lied to to create a vicious enemy, the Soviet Empire, to justify the cold war and arms race. According to R. Buckminster Fuller, during 1947-1950 the invisible government decided to start the cold war to keep capitalism in business and to prevent the Soviet Union from producing a higher standard of living then that which existed in the U.S.[8] In 1950 Einstein said: "The men who possess real power in this country have no intention of ending the cold war."

The view that the Soviets caused the cold war is wearing thin. In 1967 Arthur Schlesinger, Jr. claimed in *Foreign Affairs* that the West had to act against the Soviet Union because Stalin was paranoid. Although many non-therapists believe this, the historian William A. Williams demonstrated the fallacy of this view. For instance, there is no evidence that U.S. policy was ever based on such an opinion of Stalin. Instead, as Schlesinger acknowledged, Stalin took many actions hostile to the West only after the U.S. intervened in Eastern Europe and throughout the world.[9]

Especially since the 1960s, people like Walter La Feber and Walter Karp have increasingly said the U.S., not the Soviet Union, mainly initiated the cold war. Truman reneged on various Yalta agreements. The U.S. exaggerated the Soviet threat, calling most Soviet moves an attempt at world conquest, and unnecessarily spent the nation almost into bankruptcy by creating a permanent war economy. H. W. Brands said: "The cold war had resulted largely from the efforts of the U.S. to export capitalism across the globe. American leaders, concerned that a repetition of the depression of the 1930s would trigger the collapse of the American way of life, and convinced that preventing a repetition required opening foreign markets to American products, sallied forth to bring as much of the world as possible into the American economic sphere."[10] Barton J. Bernstein said there is evidence that "American policy was neither so innocent nor so nonideological....By overextending policy and power and refusing to accept Soviet interests, American policy-makers contributed to the Cold War....There is evidence that Russian policies were reasonably cautious and conservative, and that there was at least a basis for accommodation."[11]

One of the best documented books on the cause of the cold war is *Harry S. Truman and the War Scare of 1948* by Frank Kofsky. Immediately after World War II, the corporate elite and many intellectuals were very concerned that a depression with mass unemployment would develop without an arms race. The trauma of the 1930s was still fresh in the minds of many. I don't suggest that communism wasn't a serious threat. Godless communism was and is completely anathema to values we as a people hold dear, but it could have been confronted without the cold war and might have been, except that the bankers wanted to enhance their power, profits, and control over the people.

The aircraft industry would have collapsed without large government procurement orders after the war. *Business Week* said: "The aircraft builders, even with tax carrybacks, are near disaster....Right now the government is their only possible savior—with orders, subsidies, or loans."[12] GE, Westinghouse, GM, the Du Pont family, Chase Bank, and the Rockefellers were heavily invested in the aircraft industry. They used their influence to promote the war scare and rearm America to protect their investments and increase profits.

Truman's war scare was supported by press propaganda. After the war there was a massive campaign to promote capitalism to counteract the communist menace and damage the unions. In 1950, *U.S. News & World Report* said: "Government planners figure they have found the magic formula for almost endless good times....Cold War is the catalyst. Cold War is an automatic pump-primer. Turn the spigot and the public clamors for more arms spending." Threats of war were good for business.

According to *Business Week*, sharply increased military spending was a strong prop for business, there would be less unemployment, and increased war spending would limit the growth of welfare spending. While military spending doesn't alter the economy, growing "welfare and public-works spending," in contrast "does alter the economy." Welfare programs "create new institutions" and, even worse, they "redistribute income."[13] Better to spend the country into bankruptcy and have tens of thousands of Americans die in needless foreign wars than risk the people gaining more economic and political power. With an arms race and a permanent war economy, it was much easier to control the people and to further enrich the corporate elite. Self aggrandizement of the ruling class and ideological concerns replaced practical considerations of America's national interest.

The reality was that, while Stalin and the Soviet Union were not easy to deal with, it was in the national interest of the East and West to maintain peace to recover from the devastation of the recent war. The actions of the Soviet Union after the war gave cause for alarm, but there were better ways to deal with that threat. It would have been possible to develop a policy of mutual tolerance without massive rearmament, but even the possibility of this was rejected. "Regardless of how outlandish or nonsensical most 'conspiracy theories' may be, the fact of the matter is that members of the ruling class and the power elite in the late 1940s showed themselves ready to resort to conspiratorial machinations whenever they deemed it necessary."[14] The ruling elite in America found it in their interests to create a permanent war economy and the cold war.

In 1948 the historian Thomas Bailey wrote: "Because the masses are notoriously shortsighted and generally cannot see danger until it is at their throats, our statesmen are forced to deceive them into an awareness of their long-run interests." Of course lying to the American people was hardly new. It was just that the stakes were higher, but then so were the profits. In 1978 Carl Bernstein interviewed Clark Clifford, who as a close aide, saw Truman every day. Clifford said: "The President didn't attach fundamental importance to the so-called Communist scare. He thought it was a lot of baloney....It was a political problem. We did not believe there was a real problem. A problem was being manufactured. There was a certain element of hysteria."[15]

It is difficult for us now to look back and appreciate the climate of hysteria, fear, and panic that our government created. Washington created an impression that the Soviets were imminently going to start a war by invading Western Europe.

There was a constant barrage of concern about the Soviet threat and the need to spend billions of dollars to stop the communist menace. Truman used deceit and manipulation with baseless claims of an imminent Soviet military threat. By deliberately misrepresenting Soviet intentions and using highly inflammatory language, the Truman administration manipulated Congress and the people creating an atmosphere of crisis. "We are compelled to conclude that, more often than not, there was no real connection between the military and foreign policy programs the Truman administration urged on Congress on the one hand and the dangers to which the administration claimed to be responding on the other. Instead, expediency and improvisation ruled the day: the administration first decided what it wished to extract from Congress and the electorate, and then, as events during the spring of 1948 illustrate, reached for the nearest available pretexts to justify its demands."[16]

Not everyone accepted this analysis. In February, 1948 General Eisenhower in a speech before the National Press Club expressed strong doubts that the Soviet Union intended to start a global war with the West. "The Soviet Union is in no position to support a global war," he said.[17] The *Wall Street Journal* in an editorial complained about this emotional and factless government policy. "Yet we have not been told precisely what this crisis is, what form of danger we are to prepare against. Nevertheless we are told, it is a tremendous crisis and Congress ought to do all the things the President asks without stopping to debate them....To get these programs approved Congress is bombarded with alarums and excursions ....We have a right to expect more than that from our leaders."[18]

The most difficult problem that Truman faced during the 1948 war scare was that the Soviets tried to improve relations. The Soviets desperately wanted to avoid serious conflict with the West, and they initiated aggressive actions as a defensive measure after being sharply rebuffed in their attempts at reconciliation. There is evidence suggesting that the Soviets blockaded Berlin to force the West into serious negotiations to avoid an arms race they could ill afford. On May 10 in a letter to the U.S. ambassador and on May 17 in a letter to Henry Wallace, Stalin attempted to negotiate with the U.S. At the very least you can negotiate with another state to see if there is any basis for improved relations. Instead Washington promptly rejected these peace feelers referring to the dangerous Soviet threat. When Stalin died in 1953 the Soviets again put out feelers to improve relations. Although even Winston Churchill asked the U.S. to at least attempt to negotiate with the Soviets, our response was no. The cold war was too good for business.

The U.S. was so bellicose towards the Soviet Union in the late 1940s partly because only the West had nuclear weapons, and it realized the Soviet Union had sustained so much damage in World War II that it had no interest in a prolonged fight with the West. Kofsky spent considerable time studying the archives of the Truman administration and found no evidence of a serious fear that the Soviets intended to attack the West. Instead evidence suggested that Stalin feared being invaded by the West. After World War II intelligence estimates of the Soviet Union almost universally supported the view that, while the Soviet Union was hostile towards the West and in the long term hostilities might be initiated, there was no immediate intent to start a war. This analysis did not change during the 1948 war scare.

Little consideration has been given to the effect on the captured nations after the cold war began. The leaders of the U.S. military government in Germany,

Lucius Clay and Robert Murphy, initially opposed German partition partly because of the effect it would have on the East Germans. While Soviet rule had been established, many noncommunist elements were allowed to remain in society and the real terror of the police state only began with the start of the Marshall Plan, as Melvyn P. Leffler in *A Preponderance of Power: National Security, the Truman Administration and the Cold War* noted. Stalin constantly ordered communist parties in the West to work within the system and not to initiate revolutionary actions. Except in Greece and Czechoslovakia this policy was followed.

Even when a communist insurgency started in Greece in 1946, Soviet aid was non-existent and U.S. officials were well aware of this. Our Secretary of State acknowledged "the present Soviet and satellite attitude in withholding a firm commitment" to the Greek communists. In 1947 when the Soviet Union established a new international organization, the Communist Information Bureau, Greek delegates were kept out. And no communist nation ever recognized the communist government established in northern Greece.

The Czechoslovakian communists were quite popular, partly because of the traditional relations and trade between Russia and Czechoslovakia and the great fear Czechoslovakia had of a resurgent Germany. The communists already controlled much of the government including the police, and it was obvious that there would be little serious internal opposition to a full take-over. Internal documents showed that the CIA at the time found no evidence that the Czechoslovakian takeover was part of a grand design to conquer all of Europe, as Truman proclaimed in support of rearmament.

The National Security Act of 1947 was more fully implemented in 1950, with edict NSC-68 outlining the policies of the U.S. in the cold war. This document was declassified in 1975 during the post-Nixon attempt to clean up government. It demonstrates how we never really intended to negotiate with the Soviet Union. The objective was to greatly increase conventional forces and nuclear power, develop foreign alliances, sharply increase taxes, and mobilize the entire American society through fear and terror to stop communism. This radical new policy was never openly debated. Our original Constitution was secretly replaced with the national security state, and few noticed.

There was one other reason why the elite wanted to create the cold war. Except for a few years during World War I, the U.S. had followed George Washington's advice to avoid foreign political entanglements. George Washington said: "It is our true policy to steer clear of permanent alliances." Thomas Jefferson declared we should have "peace, commerce, and honest friendship with all nations, entangling alliances with none." A strong isolationist movement kept the U.S. out of the League of Nations, and most of the country was very isolationist during the 1930s. The corporate elite feared that after the war the country would once again turn inward, so the cold war was needed to create a need for foreign political alliances.

An active external threat kept Americans involved in world affairs. The State Department was very concerned that Americans would not persist in being interested in international relations. In September 1945 an aide warned Secretary Forrestal that Americans would not support a "complete realignment of government organizations...to serve our national security in the light of our new world power and position." Yet active participation in world affairs was crucial to support the long term goals of the corporate elite to destroy national sovereignty and through international trade and foreign alignments, to establish a one world government.

Accompanying the new cold war was the signing of the NATO alliance in 1949, which represented a sharp break with our past. Senator Robert Taft, a leading politician in the late 1940s, recognized what a change it was for us to enter the NATO alliance. He criticized our being tied to the actions of 11 other nations. "The history of these obligations has been that once begun, they cannot easily be brought to an end....There is no limit to the burden of such a program or its dangerous implications." How right he was![19] Taft said he was "More than a bit tired of having the Russian menace invoked as a reason for doing any—and every—thing that might or might not be desirable or necessary on its own merits." Ex-Secretary of State Dean Acheson said the government overcame rising isolationist sentiment to internationalism because the Korean War "came along and saved us."

In 1950, in *National Security and Individual Freedom*, Harold Lasswell warned that continuing war may create "garrison states," political systems obsessed with national security, where perpetual war or the perceived threat of war leads to the concentration of all political power in the hands of an elite devoted to violence. Ultimately this condition leads to a totalitarian state. "Overzealousness in the cause of national defense weakens rather than strengthens total security....To the extent that intimidation is threatened or applied at home, we have a police state."[20] "Here in truth, lay the supreme merit of the new Cold War gospel. It allowed America's leaders to wage unceasing war against the American people."[21]

To maintain our external involvement supposedly meant there was a strong need for stability in the U.S. which a strong security state would ensure. Liberties had to be sacrificed because of dangerous external menaces. Threats of a communist menace served the purpose of our corporate masters. "It creates a climate of opinion and a political atmosphere that makes it easier to discredit and repress labor militancy and progressive and anti-capitalist viewpoints at home and abroad."[22] In 1953 I. F. Stone said: "The young were taught to distrust ideas which had been the gospel of the Founding Fathers."

Repressive activities of the federal government continued throughout the cold war. Many artists were blacklisted, and background checks on federal employees, uniformed service personnel, and people in industries connected to national defense became the norm. By 1958, 9.8 million Americans had been investigated and millions had taken a loyalty oath. The easiest way to justify increased federal authority was by appealing to national security.

In response to the cold war, our government was altered so the country would be protected against communism. Congress created a separate national security state within the executive branch of the federal government. This included the Central Intelligence Agency (CIA), Atomic Energy Commission (AEC), and the National Security Council (NSC) There was no peacetime precedent for the powers conferred on these organizations. They had the power to classify and to determine who would be told what was being done, and they were authorized to function with little real oversight from the elected officials. The cold war allowed the president and executive branch to assume increased unilateral powers. The president had almost unlimited power to define national security.

Especially towards the end of his administration, Eisenhower became more concerned about the nuclear arms race. He realized that even he had no real knowledge of what was being done and it might not be possible to stop the wild growth of nuclear arms. Eisenhower was deeply shocked when he saw how the Pentagon planned to conduct a nuclear war. It is partly for this reason that he said at his farewell address, "Until the latest of our world conflicts, the U.S. had no armaments industry. American makers of plowshares could, with time and as required make swords as well. But now...we have been compelled to create a permanent armaments industry of vast proportions. This conjunction of an immense military establishment and a large arms industry is new in the American experience....We must guard against the acquisition of unwarranted influence, whether sought or unsought, by the military-industrial complex. The potential for the disastrous rise of misplaced power exists and will persist. We must never let the weight of this combination endanger our liberties or democratic processes. We should take nothing for granted."

Over the years many respected commentators have warned how the cold war has negatively altered our form of government. Stewart Udall, former Secretary of Interior for JFK and congressman, said: "During President Truman's administration, obsessions about national security altered the relationship of the American people to their government by constricting the openness that had been a hallmark of American democracy....My experiences and observations told me that the cold warriors contempt for restraint had poisoned our politics....I was dismayed when, although the contest with Communism ended without violence, Cold War attitudes and values continued to dominate American policies and policy making." Udall concluded: "As I look back in the 1980s, it was painfully evident that ...we...paid a heavy moral and political price by ignoring the open-government commands of our Constitution....We must dismantle the national security state we created to combat Communism and return to the constitutional principles and ethical values that animated our democracy's evolution....If our society is to regain the resilience and openness that once made our democracy a model for other countries, we must reaffirm our cherished political ideals and institutions...."[23]

In 1973 Senator Fulbright said: "War and conditions of war are incompatible and inconsistent with our system of democracy. Our democratic system is bound to be eroded, and an authoritarian system is bound to take its place. We are in that process now...." Senator Mike Gravel said the cold war created a new culture in America "a national security culture, protected from the influences of American life by the shield of secrecy."

According to Lewis Lapham, "Under the pretext of rescuing people from incalculable peril, the government over the last fifty years has claimed for itself enormously enhanced powers of repression and control. The obsession with security in all its forms...national, personal, and municipal—has shifted the balance of the American equation....Without the operatic stage set of the cold war, the American national security state was hard pressed to define its purpose, and the American people were beginning to understand how much money and poetic imagination had been invested in the making of the Communist menace."[24]

Bill Moyers said: "I find it stunning, looking back, how easily the cold war enticed us into surrendering popular control of government to the national security state....For 40 years a secret government has been growing behind...stately tributes to American ideals, growing like a cancer on the Constitution....The secret government has no Constitution. The rules it follows are the rules it makes up....How does it happen that to be anti-communist we become undemocratic, as if we have to subvert our society in order to save it. In the name of national security much is kept secret and the president can do whatever he wants in secret to preserve national security while destroying our civil rights....Government was supposed to protect society against lawlessness; now it became a lawbreaker, violating the Constitution in effect, in order to save it.

"The people who wrote this Constitution lived in a world more dangerous than ours. Yet they understood that even in perilous times, the strength of self-government was public debate and public consensus....They left us safeguards against men whose appetites for power might exceed their moral wisdom. To forget this—to ignore the safeguards, to put aside our basic values out of fear, to imitate the foe in order to defeat him—is to shred the distinction that makes us different....An open society cannot survive a secret government. Constitutional democracy is no romantic notion. It's our defense against ourselves, the one foe who might defeat us....The principle of accountable power is now...repeatedly violated in the name of national security."[25]

According to Gore Vidal: "The unloved American empire is now drifting into history on a sea of red ink....Thanks to money wasted in support of the national religion (corporate national security state), our quality of life is dire, and although our political institutions work smoothly for the few, the many hate them...." This is why politicians now run against the federal government although they continue to support it. During the years of the national security state "corporate America not only collected most of the federal revenue for 'defense' but, in the process," greatly reduced its share of federal taxes.[26]

William Greider asked: "How can the nation begin to restore a peaceable economic balance and evolve toward a society that is not so relentlessly organized around the machinery of war?....After four decades in place, the national-security state is not going to go away any time soon....If nothing much changes, there will be a continuing political imperative to seek out new conflicts that justify the existence of the national-security state. The CIA, if it remains independent and secretive, will keep churning out its inflated assessments of new 'threats.'"[27]

The cold war kept Americans united by fear, but now that the cold war is over the government still remains on a war footing. "The permanent mobilization has altered the democratic relationships profoundly, concentrating power in remote and unaccountable places, institutionalizing secrecy, fostering gross public deception and hypocrisy. It violated the law in ways that have become habitual. It assigned great questions of national purpose to a militarized policy elite. It centralized political power in the presidency at the expense of every other democratic institution. The question is: Now that the enemy has vanished, is it possible that democratic order can be restored?"[28]

Along with the development of a vast national security establishment came an unchecked intelligence bureaucracy. The system of classifying thousands of documents only really started during and after World War II. Before World War II there was never such widespread use of security with dozens of bureaucratic agencies classifying millions of documents. This unprecedented process is a dangerous abuse of power to control information and mislead the public. Truman issued Executive Order (EO) 10290 extending the secrecy system to civilian departments on September 24, 1951. Congress never approved this classification system. While it is reasonable to keep some documents secret, few would accept the need to keep so many documents classified and for so many years.

In a free society, real national security depends on an informed electorate. Secrecy in government represents a loss of democratic participation in government. Millions of people are disgusted with the political process partly because government has become one big secret. We can no longer openly and freely debate important issues. The key issues of our time are decided behind closed doors by a few people who often aren't even elected to office. Article I, Section 5 of the Constitution allows each House to keep certain items secret, but it was never the intent of the Founders to have secrecy become the norm in running the government. James Madison said: "A popular government without popular information or the means of acquiring it is but a prologue to a farce or a tragedy, or perhaps both." Excessive government secrecy shows how the government distrusts the people.

David Wise in *The Politics of Lying* said: "The government has increasingly gained control over channels of information about military, diplomatic, and intelligence events. Frequently the press and public, unable to check the events independently, can only await the appearance of the President on the television screen to announce the official version of reality....Because of official secrecy on a scale unprecedented in our history, the government's capacity to distort information in order to preserve its own political power is almost limitless."[29] Secrecy often covers up fraud, waste, and mismanagement.

Secrecy and crisis enhanced executive power and increased the role of law enforcement agencies. Instead of Congress and the public having a say in policies, we are presented with completed events done because of the superior information the president has. Examples include the Vietnam War and the Bay of Pigs invasion of Cuba. Even many in the executive branch do not get important information to do their jobs because of the insane drive to keep documents secret. "Secrecy is one of the President's most important tools of power for it permits him to control information about crucial foreign policy decisions and events, and to filter the truth before it reaches Congress and the voters.[30]

"The excuse for secrecy and deception most frequently given by those in power is that the American people must sometimes be misled in order to mislead the enemy. This justification is unacceptable on moral and philosophic grounds, and often it simply isn't true....The elitists who make national security policy ...feel that they alone possess the necessary information and competence to deal with foreign policy crises and problems. Government deception, supported by a pervasive system of official secrecy and an enormous public relations machine, has reaped a harvest of massive public distrust."[31]

CBS *Evening News* on June 15, 1994 said in 1993 Congress finally discovered that it costs over $16 billion to keep documents secret, with about 32,400 people employed. Congress couldn't find out the CIA costs because that was considered a secret The total annual bill in the same period to run the State and Justice Departments was 16.5 billion dollars. Even the Department of Education paid for secure phone lines.

The present classification system is very influenced by President Reagan's EO 12356 issued April 6, 1982. It states that "Information may not be classified under this Order unless its disclosure reasonably could be expected to cause damage to the national security," and that government agencies should err on the side of secrecy. The result has been that more officials have the authority to classify documents and more documents are now classified. The organized declassification of documents started by President Eisenhower in 1953 stopped. History is a menace to national security.

When the Freedom of Information Act (FOIA) was set up in 1966 the intent was to allow anyone to see any government document except for specific exemptions, like military secrets or sensitive financial data. It was supposed to take 10 days to get a response for a FOIA request. Since the early 1980s the FOIA has been considerably weakened, and government agencies became quite resistant to FOIA requests after EO 12356 was signed. Documents already released under the FOIA could again be classified under EO 12356. When in doubt, classify a document or withhold it on any technicality. The will of Congress in passing the FOIA law was partially negated by this presidential edict which violates the Constitution. Also, a 1985 presidential directive ordered the transfer of government information to private industry. Then these companies charged whatever they wanted, which is one more technique used to keep information from the people.

A 1986 amendment to the FOIA was supposed to ease the costs involved in making an FOIA request, but instead that act has been used to force people to show that FOIA requests are in the public interest. It is now often necessary to sue the government to get information released through the FOIA, and documents are often withheld because of political embarrassment. Different agencies use different strategies to prevent the release of documents, and the entire process has become very capricious. It now often takes two years or more, to get information released under the FOIA, which makes it hard for reporters with a deadline. Some agencies respond quickly to FOIA requests, while it is very difficult to get documents from military and intelligence agencies. In 1990 the FBI closed 78 percent of the FOIA requests by saying the requests were flawed or the records requested weren't available.[32]

Former U.S. ambassador to Germany Kenneth Rush held secret meetings with the Soviet Union in 1971. After retiring he gave his notes to the State Department. Later when he tried to get the notes back while writing his memoirs he was turned down because they were classified. A historian wrote a study on why a Pentagon project failed. The Pentagon later said the study was so secret that the author couldn't read it. At his Senate confirmation hearing future head of the CIA Woolsey was asked how the CIA could be less secretive. He said that he'd rather discuss that in a secret hearing.

The courts usually support government attempts to make it harder to get documents from the FOIA.[33] This is especially true with the Washington, D.C. Circuit Court of Appeals which reviews most FOIA cases. When national security is claimed to withhold documents, the courts usually agree with the government. The CIA won one case when it refused to release documents concerning the use of mind-control drugs on unwitting subjects. In *Washington Post v. U.S. Department of Defense* (1991) the court, citing national security concerns, withheld information based on "little more than a showing that the agency's (CIA) rationale is logical."[34]

In 1990 the Congressional Research Service concluded that by the year 2,000 75 percent of all federal government transactions will be handled electronically. The Clinton Justice Department supported the Bush view that it wasn't necessary to preserve electronic records as is required with paper documents. Fortunately, on August 13, 1993 a court ruled against the federal government. Clinton also fought legal attempts to publish the records of secret meetings over health care under the

Federal Advisory Committee Act. And the administration claims it has broad authority to keep records from being released under the FOIA by labeling records presidential instead of agency records.

Today, even though the cold war is supposedly over, there are now more documents then ever kept classified. Clinton pledged to have a more open policy, but the government was classifying more papers than under Bush. In April, 1993 Clinton set up a task force to review ways to reduce excessive overclassification of documents with a new EO. Part of the problem is that the head of this task force, Steven Garfinkel, headed the Information Security Oversight Office for Reagan and Bush. Many key players in the national security state have been kept in place by Clinton. Garfinkel was quoted in several publications as stating that he feels most Americans don't care about excessive secrecy in government and that a new EO would "put a fresh coat of paint on" the order he would have given George Bush.[35]

On November 10, 1994 Clinton released EO 12937[36] which declassifies 43.9 million pages of classified files including 22.9 million pages from after 1945. EOs have been proposed to automatically declassify documents after 25 years and to release much material obtained from satellite intelligence. People who want to study this field should read the *Secrecy and Government Bulletin* put out by the Federation of American Scientists.[37] On April 17, 1995 Clinton released EO 12958 which replaced EO 12356. This furthers the process of declassifying more government documents.

While these EOs are an improvement, little will change as long as the Democratic/Republican party controls the government. EO 12937 only releases one percent of all classified cold war documents. A new system is needed so that far fewer documents get classified, and over the years most documents are automatically declassified. Congress should establish strict standards as to what can be classified, and when the executive bureaucracy tries to subvert the will of Congress, there should be strict civil and criminal fines. Congress should also establish an agency with the authority to look at any government documents to see that its will is being fulfilled.

Archibald MacLeish, the Librarian of Congress between 1939 to 1945 and former Assistant Secretary of State, understood how far we had diverged from the teachings of the Founding Fathers. The dignity of the individual with God given rights has been overwhelmed by a "faithless materialism." In the 20th century we have gone from being a free society that protects individual rights to having massive state intervention in our lives. In fighting communism we copied it, as the power of the state grew and the rights of the individual weakened. "By putting the hatred and fear of Russia first we opened the sacred center of our lives...the freedom of mind and thought—to those among us who have always hated those freedoms and who know well how to use our fear of Russia as a mask to cover their disguised attacks. The spread of legalized thought control...across the country is not the work of chance. It is the work of freedom-hating men....What has been happening to the people of the U.S. in the last few years is something that can destroy the inward vitality of the nation if we let it go on."[38] If we continue to separate ourselves from the teachings of the Founding Fathers, we as a people will be lost. MacLeish said that terms like revolution and freedom had developed new limited meanings. Today terms like militia and patriot are also vilified, although such people established our Republic. We must find the moral courage to restore the dignity of the individual by restoring constitutional government in America.

We sacrificed the ideals of the Republic, human decency, and the rule of law in the war against communism. Many foreigners turned against America because we turned against the principles that led to the founding of this Republic. In the name of stopping communism, anything was acceptable. President Eisenhower said in 1954: "If the U.S. is to survive, long-standing American concepts of 'fair play' must be reconsidered." Cold war myths and misconceptions have warped our national ethos. In the process of winning the cold war, we lost our moral integrity as a nation.[39]

John Le Carre said: "The fight against Communism diminished us....It left us in a state of false and corrosive orthodoxy. It licensed our excesses and we didn't like ourselves the better for them. It dulled our love of dissent and our sense of life's adventures." According to Felix Morley, former editor of the *Washington Post,* "The underlying issue for Americans is whether we shall continue the controlled central government that was designed, or slip unconsciously into one of the forms of dictatorship encouraged by the profound upheavals of two world wars."[40]

An edited book, *National Security and the U.S. Constitution,* constantly attacked the problems of maintaining national security in a democracy. Some of the authors said national security can be better maintained without a democracy. It is difficult reaching a consensus, especially when speed is essential with so many participants in national policies. "The U.S. constitutional system so constrains the executive that the nation is now unable to respond to international threats and challenges....Covert action and democratic accountability are incompatible....The pluralism of the American political process has impeded rationalized intelligence organization."[41] Patrick Kennon, a CIA agent for many years, said "The police state became the ideal if not the norm" as more complex societies develop. Kennon sees a "credible threat of force" as necessary for the modern nation state.[42]

Both the U.S. and the Soviet Union lost the cold war. Along with the loss of civil rights, the economics of each nation were seriously damaged. The arms race increased the national debt and weakened most social service programs. While we fought the cold war, our allies modernized their economies to their competitive advantage. The military budget provided important benefits for scientific research and development which created many jobs, but military priorities have weakened our economic development, with the cold war economy actually displacing more jobs than it created. Much of the national debt is from the defense spending in the 1980s.[43] If our defense budget was cut to around $150 billion it would still be larger than what Western Europe and Japan spend on defense.[44] Paul Kennedy, in *The Rise and Fall of the Great Powers,* demonstrated that typically nations become leading states through war and then decline when they become overextended.

More money should be spent on conversion of industry from military to nonmilitary production. Most jobs in the defense industry could be preserved if there was a major shift to environmental protection and clean-up and a major investment in renewable energy development. Such a move would also provide ample opportunities for research and development companies, while the jobs created in these new industries would generally be higher paying skilled labor. New jobs in solar energy, fuel cells, electric cars, and high energy appliances would employ many people in high paying jobs. Such an approach would also lessen industry concerns that environmental issues are hurting jobs and business growth while greatly improving our quality of life. The benefits of such a policy are obvious, but it won't happen while the Democrats and Republicans control

Congress and the White House. The invisible government will not allow the security state to be dismantled. And "the political and economic elite will support deficits that finance the military and enrich the wealthy, but not deficits that support social spending, full employment and downward income distribution."[45]

Many large defense contractors are not interested in conversion to nonmilitary production and research. They feel that new threats will develop that will expand military procurement. While Clinton as a candidate spoke glowingly of cutting the defense budget after he was in office there were limited cuts and recently the defense budget has grown.[46] We should restore the rights protected in the Constitution and also rebuild our infrastructure and improve Americas competitive position in world markets. Our national security has been threatened by our weakened economic position, which developed partly because the government concentrated on security and defense issues.

One of the best kept secrets of the 20th century is that World War II is over. We should today declare World War II and the cold war over, close our overseas military bases, and bring the troops home. There is no longer any serious military threat to Europe, and it is completely unnatural for the U.S. to remain the dominant European military power. Not only does having thousands of our troops overseas weaken America's economy, but leaving thousands of American troops overseas will ultimately turn our allies against us. Many times while in Europe, I watched the controlled anger of Germans looking at American troops in German restaurants and gas stations. If large numbers of foreign troops were stationed in America for 50 years there would be deep resentment. American troops remain overseas today because our power hungry leaders refuse to end the national security state not because of any vital American interest. The overemphasis on national security has been counterproductive on all levels. We must not allow the secret government to use propaganda to create numerous new enemies to justify the continued existence of the national security state.

## Chapter XI

## The CIA and the
## Intelligence Community

"The principles of a free Constitution are irrevocably lost when the legislative power is dominated by the executive."

Edward Gibbon

"During the Bolshevik revolution in Russia, Lenin created the Cheka (later the KGB), a secret organization...filled with zealots who terrorized opponents. They made up their own rules, they chose their own missions, and they judged their own operations. You say it can't happen here? Well, before deciding for sure, let's look at the history of our secret government."

Bill Moyers

In August, 1994 there was a brief uproar in Congress because it was discovered that the National Reconnaissance Office (NRO), which runs the spy satellites was building a huge new headquarters in Virginia. The cost was going to be $350 million. To hide the true purpose of the building, millions of dollars in taxes were paid by the construction company, although the federal government would not normally pay such taxes. People in Congress were upset because they weren't informed of this project as is required.[1] When the oversight committees in Congress cannot even keep track of such a massive building just outside Washington, D.C., it is obvious that the intelligence community is involved in many activities that the American public and its representatives have no idea about. During this uproar one representative on the oversight committee said that, while they don't learn about various internal activities of the CIA, they are supposed to approve building projects. What about everything else?

Clinton agreed to an open congressional hearing on the NRO building project according to his press secretary because "the American public deserves a full accounting of how their tax dollars are being spent." Yet during the hearing the NRO head refused to answer questions about the agency such as the number of buildings it owns and the related costs. It was also revealed that the building was deliberately hidden from the oversight committees, but this was just called negligence. The incident shows the contempt the intelligence community has for Congress.

There was also a rare admission that information on this building was considered above top secret. One of the first public discussions that there were various security classifications above top secret was in *The Politics of Lying*, by David Wise in 1973. Senator Gore and most or perhaps all of Congress were not even aware of these higher classifications. Information that is above top secret will rarely be discussed in Congress, because it includes secret plans to remove the

Constitution and establish a dictatorship. There is also the ongoing surveillance of Americans which is why the NRO is so secret. It uses advanced technology, much of which has never been discussed, to spy on thousands of Americans.

According to news reports President Clinton also wasn't aware of this building project and this may well be true. There are about 10 classifications of security above top secret and Clinton, only being the president, has a very low security clearance barely above top secret, so he is not allowed access to most security matters. It is partly for this reason that newspapers have stated that Clinton usually leaves security matters to others. I wrote to the House and Senate committees that have oversight for the intelligence community and asked who had access to information above top secret. One committee refused to answer and the other just sent a list of their members. Perhaps no one in Congress has security clearance to access information above top secret. If this is so, how can Congress fulfill its constitutional mandate to provide funds and keep track of such spending?

On September 29, 1994 the ABC News show, *Primetime Live*, suggested that the NRO was completely beyond the control of Congress. The NRO had recently signed a $10 billion contract even though Congress had ordered it to not do that without first receiving congressional approval which had not been given. Congress, weeks later, accidently learned that this contract had been signed. Congress doesn't understand that it is increasingly irrelevant to the national security state. In the 1970s Senator Church warned about the ability of the National Security Agency (NSA) to monitor all forms of communication and if this isn't stopped "There would be no place to hide. If this government ever becomes a tyranny, if a dictator ever took charge in this country, the technological capacity that the intelligence community has given the government could enable it to impose total tyranny, and there would be no way to fight back....I know the capacity that is there to make tyranny total in America and we must see to it that (the intelligence agencies) that possess this technology operate within the law and under proper supervision, so that we never cross over that abyss. That is the abyss from which there is no return."

In July, 1994 $30 billion was voted for the intelligence community. In July, 1994 an attempt to declassify the full intelligence budget was defeated in the House, and Clinton claimed it would damage national security. Tim Weiner in *Blank Check* "found hundreds of programs camouflaged under code names, their costs deleted, their totals disguised. Code words and blank spaces stood where facts and figures should have been."[2] On September 24, 1995 the *Washington Post* said the NRO had secretly hoarded over $1 billion without telling the CIA, Pentagon, or Congress. Then in late January, 1996 the *New York Times* said the total "lost" by the NRO was over $2 billion.[3] Next, on May 16, 1996 the *New York Times* said the total money "lost" was $4 billion and there was "a complete collapse of accountability" by the NRO.

Under the Constitution Article 1, Section 9, Clause 7, only Congress can appropriate funds and there shall be a regular accounting of how funds are spent. James Madison said: "This power over the purse" is "the most complete and effectual weapon with which any Constitution can arm the immediate representatives of the people."[4] Thomas Jefferson said controlling the purse was "one effectual check to the dog of war by transferring the power of letting him loose...from those who are to spend to those who have to pay." The Founders rejected secrecy in government and felt the people should have full knowledge of what the government was doing to keep government honest, open, and accountable to the people. Patrick Henry said a free people must never "allow the national wealth...to be disposed of under the veil of secrecy." James Madison also said: "Knowledge will forever govern ignorance. And a people who mean to be their own Governors, must arm themselves with the power which knowledge gives."[5]

Government agencies must submit their budgets at regular intervals to Congress for review. Yet the CIA and most of the intelligence community violates this constitutional requirement especially with the secret or black budget. Weiner found that most members of Congress including members of the House Armed Services Committee had never even heard of the black budget. With a black budget money flows in from various sources with no one to check on what is happening. The black budget funds programs the president, head of the CIA, and the Secretary of Defense want kept hidden from the public. Many of these programs are also kept secret from the president, with the secret government in charge.

In April, 1976 the Church Committee said the black budget was unconstitutional. "The budget procedures which presently govern the CIA and other agencies of the Intelligence Community prevent most members of Congress from knowing how much money is spent by any of these agencies or even how much money is spent on intelligence as a whole....The failure to provide this information to the public and to the Congress prevents either from effectively ordering priorities and violates Article I, Section 9, Clause 7 of the Constitution...." A few months earlier Senator Church said: "If we are to preserve freedom and keep constitutional government alive in America, it cannot be left to a President and his agents alone to decide what must be kept secret....Congress cannot now in secret matters exercise its constitutional responsibilities in an orderly way."

"The black budget is a creature of the cold war. The policy of secret spending began as an emergency measure at the dawn of the postwar world. It was conceived as a shield to conceal the secret wars of the CIA....Soviet secrecy fed American fears. Lacking facts, the U.S. assumed the worst....Fear begat funds....The obsession with secret operations spread throughout the great machinery of the American presidency. Soon the CIA and its sister agencies were reading Americans' mail, poring over their telegrams and tax returns, tapping their telephones, infiltrating church groups and college organizations, penetrating the press and manipulating the news....The secret forces created to fight communism abroad evolved into a power that threatened constitutional government at home."[6]

The part of the secret government that involves the intelligence community really began with the Manhattan Project, the secret program to build an atomic bomb. Until World War II the focus of American intelligence was to gather useful information not to conduct covert operations to change foreign governments. However, the Office of Strategic Services, led by General William Donovan, shifted to not only gathering intelligence but also to changing events. In 1944 Donovan sent a proposal to President Roosevelt to establish a permanent intelligence agency after the war. The plan was leaked to a reporter for the *Chicago Tribune* who called it a "super-gestapo agency" while some in Congress compared it to the Soviet secret police.

When the CIA was established in 1947 many felt it would be dangerous because it was unaccountable. A few conservatives said the CIA, with its secret budget and cloaked activities, would give the chief executive too much new power to conduct foreign affairs, including wars, in secret without there even first being an open debate, approval, and appropriation. The very purpose of the CIA was to get around the democratic processes, empowering the president in the process. Secretary of State Dean Acheson had "the gravest forebodings" about the CIA warning that once it was established neither the president "nor anyone else would be in a position to know what it was doing or to control it."

Despite the objection of a few people between 1947 and 1974 there was an attitude of benign neglect because of a cold war consensus that people in the CIA were men of honor who would do what was required to protect the nation against communism. The power of the security state increased partly because, although a few people in Congress were supposed to keep track of the intelligence agencies, this never occurred. From the earliest days, the intelligence community was out of control with no real congressional oversight.

In the mid-1950s oversight committees under the Armed Services and Appropriations Committees were established to bring more structure to congressional oversight of the intelligence community. However, there was only occasional oversight by senior members of Congress, like Senator Richard Russell and Rep. Carl Vinson. Most in Congress found this sufficient, believing that the executive branch should be in charge. In 1954 Senator Mike Mansfield warned that "Secrecy now beclouds everything about the CIA—its cost, its efficiency, its successes, and its failure....Once secrecy becomes sacrosanct, it invites abuse." But this was a lone voice. During this period the CIA provided little information to Congress, and often years went by with the congressional subcommittees on intelligence never meeting.

Former Rep. Stewart Udall said in the 1950s his mentor was Senator Carl Hayden, chairman of the Appropriations Committee. For years Hayden was an important watch dog of the intelligence agencies. One morning after a courier dropped off a CIA summary, the senator told Udall that he didn't follow what the CIA was doing because then he would also be responsible. Udall later said: "It was obvious that republican self-government was losing out as citizens and their elected representatives were kept in the dark concerning crucial facts. How could any democracy properly function...If a 'cleared' elite was given power to frame the action options, and members of Congress were not allowed to debate policy options or to participate in the making of decisions that affected the nation's security?"[7]

Senator Allen Ellender, chairman of the Senate Intelligence Subcommittee of the Senate Appropriations Committee, also said he didn't want to know what the CIA was doing. In 1955 Senator Leverett Saltonstall, an influential member of the Armed Services Committee, said: "It is a question of our reluctance...to seek information and knowledge on subjects which I personally...would rather not have." In 1954 Lt. General James Doolittle headed a commission to justify the ongoing intelligence activities. He said: "Hitherto acceptable norms of human conduct do not apply. If the U.S. is to survive, long-standing American concepts of 'fair play' must be reconsidered." The dirty business of spying was kept secret, with the executive branch providing cover in the name of national security, however criminal or unconstitutional the conduct.

President Kennedy said, after the Bay of Pigs disaster, that he planned to shatter the CIA into a thousand pieces and scatter it to the winds. In 1963 Truman attacked the CIA as a danger to democracy. "Those fellows in the CIA don't just report on wars and the like, they go out and make their own, and there's nobody to keep track of what they're up to. They spend billions of dollars on stirring up trouble so they'll have something to report on....It's become a government all of its own and all secret. They don't have to account to anybody. That's a very dangerous thing in a democratic society, and it's got to be put a stop to."[8] Senator Symington, while on the Committee for CIA Oversight, said "There is no federal agency of our government whose activities receive less scrutiny and control than the CIA."

In the winter of 1970-1971 the press published stories that the CIA had formed an army of 36,000 in Laos to fight communism. No one in Congress was aware of this, although a few members were aware of a Laos operation. Congress learned that the CIA was spending large sums of money buried in the Pentagon's inventory of weapons. The National Security Act of 1947 did not grant the CIA power to conduct secret wars, and there is no evidence that Congress intended to grant such power to the CIA. However, in the spring of 1948 a presidential edict secretly established a covert action section in the CIA with the president secretly in charge of these activities. The CIA Act of 1949 was approved by Congress but no one understood what was being approved because it involved secrets that Congress could not be told. This law allowed the Office of Management and Budget to freely transfer funds from any agency to the CIA without regard to any laws limiting or prohibiting transfers between appropriations. The CIA did not have to explain how the money was being used.

The CIA has always been more interested in covert operations including foreign wars, assassinations, and overthrowing foreign governments, than in traditional intelligence gathering and analysis. This is a key reason why it has often failed to provide accurate intelligence. The CIA has engaged in hundreds of covert operations, like overthrowing the Salvador Allende Marxist government in Chile. Few in Congress had any knowledge of these operations. Covert operations caused sharp disagreements between Congress and the executive branch, and they have been conducted because of a loose interpretation of existing laws and secret presidential edicts. Congress sometimes gave partial approval by secretly funding these operations, often not even realizing what it was funding. The Intelligence Oversight Act of 1980 required the CIA to keep Congress informed of covert operations, but this act gave covert operations a degree of legitimacy for the first time by permitting them, in special circumstances, with no Congress consent being required.[9]

Our foreign policy has increasingly become a military policy. The National Security Council (NSC) was established in 1947 to be a civilian advisory group to the president, but it "has become a command post for covert operations run by the military. Far removed from public view and congressional oversight, they are accountable only to the one man they serve. The framers of the Constitution feared this permanent state of war, with the commander in chief served by an elite private corps that put the claims of the sovereign (president) above the Constitution."[10]

With the establishment of the Church and Pike Committees in the 1970s, the period of benign neglect of what the CIA was doing ended and Congress tried to control the CIA. During this period it was discovered that the CIA had a Domestic Operations Division which spied on Americans. This was illegal under the CIA's charter. Operation CHAOS kept tabs on thousands of Americans for over 15 years, especially Vietnam War protesters. The CIA shared information with other law enforcement groups on 300,000 Americans and had files on over 1,000 U.S. groups.[11] Supposedly, the object of spying on Americans is to control people in the name of freedom. Yet in the process of saving the country, you destroy the democratic fabric of the nation.

Senator Church called the CIA "a rogue elephant on a rampage." The Church Committee found that over "$10 billion was being spent by a handful of people, with little independent supervision, with inadequate controls, even less auditing, and an overabundance of secrecy." The GAO was not allowed proper access to study the books of the CIA, yet private accounting firms were allowed to audit its books. The CIA also secretly infiltrated its personnel into various areas of the executive branch. It was found that covert actions "are irregularly approved, sloppily implemented, and at times have been forced on a reluctant CIA by the President and his National Security Advisor."[12]

When the Church Committee asked James Jesus Angleton, a senior CIA official, why he disobeyed a direct order from the White House to destroy the CIAs stockpile of poisons he responded: "It is inconceivable that a secret arm of the government has to comply with all the overt orders of the government." When leaders of the CIA refuse to follow orders from Congress or the executive branch, whose orders are they following? The CIA has for years been a law unto itself doing what the secret government wants. This is an extremely dangerous situation for any country.

After the late 1970s false records were again used to fool Congress and once again Congress ignored the CIA. When Reagan appointed Casey head of the CIA, covert operations and the black budget greatly increased.[13] In 1984 it was revealed that the CIA had mined Nicaragua's harbor without first telling Congress as required. When an American and Chilean were killed by a car bomb in Washington, DC in 1986, Bush pressured the Justice Department to not investigate thoroughly because of national security concerns. CIA operatives worked with Chilean agents in this plot. That an American citizen was killed in the nation's capital didn't matter.

During the Iran-contra affair, a CIA station chief Joseph Fernandez faced four counts of perjury and obstruction of justice, but the Justice Department brought no charges. Special prosecutor Lawrence Walsh said national security could be used to cover-up the crimes of intelligence officers, making them a special class above the law. Senator Kerry said: "They were willing to literally put the Constitution at risk because they believed somehow there was a higher order of things. That's the most Marxist, totalitarian doctrine I've ever hear of in my life....You've done the very thing that James Madison and others feared the most when they were struggling to put the Constitution together, which was to create an accountable system which didn't have runaway power, which didn't concentrate power in one hand so that you could have one person making a decision and running off against the will of the American people."

The intelligence community has infiltrated all walks of life in America. The fight to publish *The CIA and the Cult of Intelligence* exemplifies how the CIA uses pressure and threats to keep newspapers and book publishers from releasing negative information about it. The CIA has gotten professors to manipulate student groups and to build files on students who may be targeted for future activities. It has paid professors and journalists to write over 1,200 books.[14] The Church Committee couldn't force the CIA to reveal the names of these people. In

1980 when Harvard passed an internal regulation requiring professors to report any relationships with the CIA, the CIA sued Harvard and won claiming its First Amendment rights were being violated. The Intelligence Authorization Act for 1992 contained the National Security Education Act with the goal of using the higher education system to train and recruit intelligence agents especially with foreign language and area training skills. CIA recruiters remain quite active on many college campuses.

The intelligence community has also long had a close relationship with the banking and financial communities and their federal regulators. The CIA can usually violate banking regulations with little or no consequence. There is a constant pattern of intelligence operatives using national security claims to avoid public scrutiny and criminal prosecution. The courts usually allow this sham. In 1988 Robert Maxwell sued the First National Bank of Maryland and later agents of the CIA, FBI, and Justice Department. This Baltimore banker in 1986 told Treasury Department officials that the bank had violated the law by laundering money. Maxwell was forced to quit as manager of international letters of credit when he questioned the legality of transactions for an account, Associated Traders Corporation, which he claimed was a CIA front for illegal operations.

Maxwell has been unable to get another job in banking and he suffered a mental breakdown. The CIA threatened to have his lawyer disbarred and to have Maxwell indicted for releasing classified information, and it filed a motion asking that the information not be released because of national security. Naturally, the court agreed. National security should mean the protection of a citizens' rights, but this ruling meant that Maxwell lost his chance for justice. This ruling also extended government secrecy to private businesses, which would give immunity to CIA's contractors.[15]

U.S. intelligence agencies used BCCI extensively for covert operations.[16] According to *Newsweek* there is even evidence that the CIA helped establish BCCI. The key players in establishing this bank were all connected with U.S. intelligence.[17] The CIA worked very closely with BCCI and had accounts in the bank throughout the world. The secret arms deal with Iran, which violated the Arms Export Control Act, was financed by BCCI, and there is evidence that BCCI helped transfer Saudi money to the Contras.[18] During the BCCI investigation, people close to the intelligence community advised the bank on how to mislead congressional investigators.

That the CIA is a law unto itself was also demonstrated in the S&L scandal. Pete Brewton, in *The Mafia CIA and George Bush*, described how this fiasco was a scam operation carried out by the bankers, big business, mafia, and the CIA often under the protection of certain Washington politicians. Loose alliances were formed by these groups to raid the same banks. Sometimes they worked together and sometimes they were just aware of each other's activities. The taxpayer was left with the bill. There were instances, during an FBI investigation, when the CIA said the person was working for the CIA so he was released. "The S&L crimes and debacles illustrate the servile quality of Presidents and Congresses, who view themselves primarily as agents of business, serving up a costly feast of corporate socialism for which powerless taxpayers get the check."[19]

Crucial bank documents such as loan records, title company disbursement sheets, and federal and state examination reports were not available to reporters, but Congress had the authority to obtain and make these documents public. This was never done. Few people in Congress, the FBI, or the Justice Department ever asked where the money went and what could be done to get it back, because this was an inside job with many allies of Congress and the bureaucracy involved in the theft. The public can pay for all the losses, but we have no right to see where the money went! Colleagues involved in the S&L scam were let off easily by the rest of Congress.

"In fact, the Justice Department itself has become a major layer of protection for the main beneficiaries of the savings-and-loan crisis."[20] Yet the Justice Department managed to trace some of the Medellin Cartel's drug money in more difficult circumstances. The organized strike force that conducted successful S&L prosecutions in several states was closed during the S&L crisis. This was an inside operation and the government didn't want to arrest its own supporters. Instead law firms were hired to track the money, but they accomplished almost nothing because they were generally allied with the Washington politicians and the people they were supposedly investigating. During the 1988 elections the S&L scandal was kept out of the news and it only broke months later. Congress, the Justice Department, and the press focused on flamboyant crooks in the S&L industry, while the main recipients of the money escaped untouched. Poor business judgment was used as an excuse, but this was rarely the case.

In one $200 million transaction involving 21,000 acres in Florida, the borrowed money went to St Joe, a paper company owned by the Du Pont empire. This was learned because of a dedicated federal regulator Kenneth Cureton, but when he tried to obtain records of the bank on the Isle of Jersey, England where the money went, the Department of Justice's International Division, which approves subpoenas to offshore banks, blocked him. Several banks lost huge sums of money in this transaction.[21]

In February, 1990 Rep. Frank Annunzio ask CIA Director William Webster to appear before his Financial Institutions Subcommittee, just after the *Houston Post* reported alleged CIA involvement in the S&L scandal. Webster refused saying he should instead appear before the intelligence committee. Webster lied, saying that CIA officials were in touch with the Assistant U.S. Attorney in Houston mentioned in the article. As usual the House Intelligence Committee refused to conduct a full investigation. It made no real attempt to track the money or explore allegations of CIA and mafia collusion. The *Houston Post* article named six CIA people tied to financial institutions and the CIA admitted to Congress that it had a relationship with five people connected to failed S&Ls and it had done business with four banks that failed. There are also indications that failed S&L money went to operations controlled by the CIA, such as the Iran-contra affair. The CIA said this was classified information, and the committee refused to pursue the matter further.

The director of the intelligence committee's staff was Dan Childs, a 26 year veteran of the CIA. Placing such people at the disposal of key congressional oversight committees is one way the CIA effectively makes such oversight ineffective. In January, 1991, just after the House Intelligence Committee released its CIA/S&L report, Childs went back to work for the CIA.

Part of the reason this fraud succeeded and little money was ever returned was because the press refused to do its job. While several good books were written, few newspapers tried to discover where the money went and fewer explored the CIA and mafia involvement in the scam that Pete Brewton and later Stephen Pizzo, in

*Inside Job The Looting of America's Savings and Loans*, had discussed. Pizzo also asked if some of the stolen billions had gone into illegal covert operations.[22] In 1995 Rep. Spencer Bachus, head of a committee studying government efforts to recover $2 billion stolen from a Texas S&L, said the Treasury Department repeatedly refused to cooperate and provide records for their investigation.

"All government bureaucracies perpetuate a certain exclusivity. But shrouded in secrecy, the CIA—like other spy agencies—is culturally more insular than most agencies....In the CIA the natural bureaucratic impulse to protect the institution is compounded by the bond of secrecy. And a culture is spawned that shields the agency from FBI investigations, congressional busybodies, and citizens...."[23] William Colby, former head of the CIA, said many employees of the CIA separated themselves from involvement in normal activities and became exclusively involved in intelligence activities. This created a distorted outlook on life. There developed "an inbred distorted elitist view of intelligence that held it to be above the normal processes of society with its own rationale and justification, beyond the restraints of the Constitution, which applied to everything and everyone else."

To the CIA Congress is the enemy, and when investigated, the CIA's usual response is to lie or deceive with disinformation. This is why Congress has never understood what the CIA was doing. Ralph McGehee, a former CIA agent, said, in *Deadly Deceits*, in 25 years he had never seen the CIA tell Congress the truth. The only thing guaranteed is that the CIA will lie, and no one in Congress will do anything. The CIA encourages perjury before Congress, such as when the Church Committee investigated the CIA's involvement in Allende's removal as president of Chile.[24] In November, 1980 John Gentry, a CIA analyst resigned, charging that the agency had lied to support executive branch policies. Later the CIA lied several times before the Senate Select Committee on Intelligence about when it had stopped transferring intelligence information to Iraq.[25]

When Congress questions the intelligence community about suspicious activities, intelligence agents often refuse to release information. During the BCCI investigation, the CIA refused to discuss the activities of Abdul-Raouf Khalil, Saudi Arabia's liaison to the CIA. The State Department even refused to help locate this person to serve legal papers, until regulators learned he often visited the CIA station chief in Saudia Arabia. The manager of the BCCI branch in Panama testified that the bank laundered drug profits for Noriega. When Senator Kerry requested records on Noriega the CIA, NSC, and other intelligence agencies refused to comply. Several people admitted that the Federal Reserve destroyed files revealing the relationship between BCCI and the CIA and NSC.

John Stockwell, a former CIA field agent in Angola in the late 1970s, headed the CIA's Angola desk in Washington. In *The Praetorian Guard*, he described how a lawyer entered his office and purged his files of incriminating evidence of illegal CIA activities in Angola. George Bush, then head of the CIA, who had previous testified that no illegal activities had taken place in Angola, returned to Congress and reaffirmed that he could find no files involving CIA misconduct in Angola. Congress dropped its investigation.[26] After Stockwell resigned from the CIA in 1977, he provided five days of detailed testimony to a closed congressional committee about illegal CIA activities in Angola. Congress listened and did nothing. With Watergate so recent, Congress didn't have the stomach for another big scandal, so the problem of an out-of-control intelligence agency got worse.

Early in 1995 the House Intelligence Committee threatened to subpoena a former top CIA official after he refused to discuss the agency's attempts to hide the loss of Soviet-bloc agents in recent years. According to the *Washington Post*, this committee found evidence that there was "a plan to restrict telling Congress about what was going on" so the CIA could "keep it under wraps."

In March, 1995 there was another uproar when Rep. Robert Torricelli revealed that one or more Americans, including Michale DeVine, had been killed by CIA informants in Guatemala. Torricelli received information from Clinton officials angry with the CIA actions. This link was covered up for some time by the CIA, which upset many people. The CIA reportedly paid $44,000 to Guatemalan Colonel Alpirez after learning that he had killed DeVine. According to former DEA agent Celerino Castillo, DeVine was killed because he learned of Guatemalan military drug trafficking.[27] Rep. Torricelli even received a report allegedly from someone in the NSA that internal documents were being destroyed to remove evidence. The FBI conducted an investigation but naturally found nothing.

Since 1976 twenty U.S. citizens have been attacked or killed in Guatemala. We may never know how many of them were attacked by CIA informants. Rep. Torricelli is to be congratulated for speaking up. Newt Gingrich attacked Torricelli saying he violated his oath of secrecy as a member of the House Intelligence Committee. However, the information Torricelli released was not received during any Intelligence Committee meetings, and Toricelli said "Under circumstances where the issue is criminal conduct, I believe that oath is in direct conflict with the oath that every member takes to adhere to the Constitution and the laws of the U.S." When one learns of a criminal act, one must speak up or become an accomplice to that crime. People should ask Gingrich how many Americans have to be murdered before it is acceptable to criticize the CIA for its criminal activities. Gingrich and his crowd will do anything to protect the secret government.[28]

On December 3, 1995 CBS's *60 Minutes* interviewed Toto Constant. For several years, while a paid CIA informant and senior Haitian official, he actively worked to defeat U.S. policy towards Haiti. On October 3, 1993 Constant led a protest demonstration against the landing of 400 U.S. and Canadian troops in Haiti. Then at a White House meeting the CIA said there would be considerable violence if the troops landed, although others disputed this. During this period the CIA leaked information to Congress challenging Aristide's mental stability, when Clinton wanted to restore Aristide to power in Haiti. The U.S. government has its policies, but so does the CIA. When there is a conflict, the CIA will sometimes disrupt administration policies. In this instance the CIA was probably protecting its drug supply lines through Haiti. The only thing unusual about this case was that part of the CIA's disinformation efforts surfaced.

In recent years seven or more CIA station chiefs have been removed from their posts because of illegal or unsavory activities. A station chief in Cyprus stole at least one valuable religious icon from a church. Instead of being arrested, these officials were transferred and then sometimes allowed to resign. The arrest of Richard Ames for spying is not the only instance of an intelligence agent gone bad.

According to Ames, "the espionage business as carried out by the CIA and a few other American agencies, was and is a self-serving sham, carried out by careerist bureaucrats who have managed to deceive several generations of American policymakers and the public about both the necessity and value of their work. The information our vast espionage network acquires at considerable human and ethical costs is generally insignificant or irrelevant to our policymakers' needs. Our espionage establishment differs hardly at all from many other federal bureaucracies, having transformed itself into a self-serving interest group immeasurably aided by secrecy."

Some in Congress have acknowledged that this traitor has accurately describe the sham that is the CIA. Little of value is really accomplished, but you always had to look busy. Ames exposed almost every important CIA operation and agent in the Soviet Union and Eastern Europe in the mid-1980s, but the CIA ignored evidence that he was a spy. The FBI even saw Ames improperly meeting secretly with the Soviets in 1986, but the CIA did nothing. By 1989 the CIA knew that Ames had paid $540,000 cash for a home; yet he only earned $69,000 a year. In 1991 Ames failed a lie detector test, but was passed anyway. The CIA took two years to investigate a report that Ames was living well beyond his means.[29]

Ames was once found drunk in a Rome gutter while working for the CIA. It was also fairly common for him to fall asleep at his desk in the afternoon after his drinking binge during lunch. According to the *Los Angeles Times*, the Dominion Bank of Virginia told the IRS that Ames was depositing large sums of money but no action was taken.[30] A child could have identified Ames as a high security risk, yet people on the Senate oversight committee were amazed at all this, because they have no understanding of what takes place in the CIA. Naturally CIA director Woolsey fired no one over the Ames affair.

There is more to this fiasco than we have been told. On the day Ames was arrested the *New York Times* reported that he worked in the CIAs "narcotics intelligence operation."[31] In a detailed article on Ames' involvement in the drug war, The *Wall Street Journal* said Ames was "a key figure" in stopping drug trafficking, and asked if he was somehow involved with the KGB in the drug trade?[32] Another suspicious fact is that Ames often visited Columbia where his wife is from. Part of the money paid to Ames by the KGB came from U.S. taxpayers out of western aid money sent to Russia.[33] However, did the money he received come only from the KGB or also from Columbian drug gangs?

Reportedly Ames was paid several million dollars by the KGB which he spent lavishly. We are told he was quite careless or stupid in not hiding such wealth. It is one thing to believe that Ames was careless or stupid, but it goes beyond belief to agree with the press that several regulatory agencies were also so negligent. Many regulatory agencies are well aware that the CIA has been heavily involved in illegal drug trafficking for many years, and that especially when national security is proclaimed, the CIA is left alone. As a kingpin in the CIA's drug operations, Ames would be justified in believing that he was protected. As one more drug dealer in the CIA no one would touch him. Many in the CIA have large sums of money from their illegal drug operations.

Peter Maas, in *Killer Spy*, said after some months of investigating Ames, enough evidence had been gathered so that the FBI wanted him arrested. They needed permission from the Justice Department which initially refused, supposedly because if Ames and his wife were arrested, there would be no one to take care of their young son, and the press would be very upset. Remember Ames had caused the arrest and death of many CIA agents in the Soviet Union, and he was suspected of being one of the worst spies in our nation's history. Aside from the fact that a grandmother was available to care for the son, we are supposed to believe that the Justice Department suddenly became a social welfare department. Certain people in the Justice Department and CIA were very nervous that Ames' arrest would reveal illegal drug trafficking operations.

In late 1995 it was revealed that Ames helped the Russians plant double agents, who for years fed false information to the CIA. The CIA realized in 1991 these agents were providing disinformation but 95 reports were provided to policy makers including two presidents, usually without even a warning that the information provided might be false. These reports overestimated Soviet economic and military strength, probably causing the U.S. to needlessly spend billions of dollars for defense. The *New York Times*, in an editorial, said when an intelligence agency willingly misleads the government with disinformation from the communists this "is as out of control as it gets."[34] Senator Specter interviewed a Russian expert in the CIA for 42 years. The retired agent said providing information from suspected double agents was proper and it was the role of the CIA not higher officials to make this decision. Not understanding that Congress is irrelevant to the intelligence community, Senator Specter was shocked.[35]

The last president who tried to curtail the CIA was President Kennedy. This is one reason he was killed. In the name of national security, the mantra of the intelligence community, any act is acceptable even if it destroys the democratic fabric of our Republic. Many in the intelligence community feel their experience enables them to understand the security needs of the U.S. better than America's elected officials. The dangerous fanatics who have perpetuated so many atrocities upon the American people in the name of national security are far more dangerous to the survival of this Republic as a free society than was ever the case with communism. People in the security state felt international communism needed to be stopped even if America was turned into a police state in the process.

A good example of what a career in the CIA does to people is the book, *The Twilight of Democracy*, by Patrick E. Kennon. He worked in the CIA for 25 years and concluded that instead of a democracy run by the people we need a society run by skilled technocrats. Efficiency is more important than free will and freedom. Run by "faceless but expert bureaucrats" democracy has triumphed as an ideology but not as a system of government. He said democracy "has become marginal as a system of government" so we should turn to bureaucratic experts in the "relentless march of specialization." Specialization demands bureaucracy.

George McGovern said: "If it is acceptable for the CIA to break the law in the name of national security, why shouldn't others place national security above and beyond the reach of the Constitution?" The Founding Fathers "would have been appalled by the secretive, unchecked unilateral operations that have been carried on by the Presidents and their staffs in recent decades....Unfortunately, many of our Presidents since the end of World War II have violated the law and the Constitution. From Korea, the Bay of Pigs and Vietnam to Watergate, Iran and the covert war in Nicaragua, Presidents have weakened the nation and their own credibility by dishonoring the Constitution. Most of these violations have been made in the name of national security...."[36] At what point does the incessant paranoia over national security, which is so often just an excuse for illegal criminal activities, become treason. Thousands of American citizens have lost their constitutional rights, sometimes being killed, in the name of national security.

Many Americans think congressional oversight committees are actually keeping track of the intelligence community, but this has always been a complete myth. How can the oversight committees do their job when for years they have no idea what programs the money is being spent on? Congress is told the magic words, national security, and an inquiry ends. In 1987 the National Academy of Public Administration concluded that congressional oversight is "more geared to garnering media attention than making government work better...." In 1991 *Common Cause Magazine* published a review of the congressional oversight committees. They concluded that "Congress on the whole is failing to carry out its government oversight responsibility." Oversight is a key role of Congress to see where money is spent and how programs are carried out, but our representatives are more interested in raising money to be reelected.

In the 1970s Congress changed the federal budget-writing process so that budget power was concentrated on new budget committees. Other committees lost control over the federal budget. During the 1980s many committees rewrote their rules removing the power to issue subpoenas or launch investigations. Today, oversight committees rarely conduct serious investigations. Constitutional checks and balances no longer apply. Experienced investigators like Thomas Trimboli get fired from oversight committees, because they take their job seriously. Few whistleblowers are now willing to come to Congress because nothing is done.

Many have provided evidence to Congress that the CIA and other government agencies are flooding the country with illegal drugs, but Congress does nothing. Congress had evidence of the S&L scam long before anything was done. By the time action was taken the cost was far higher than it needed to have been. There was evidence that the Reagan administration was illegally supporting the Nicaraguan contras at least two years before the Iran-contra hearings. Congress refused to investigate the charges by Knight Ridder that there were detailed plans to remove the Constitution and establish a police state with FEMA arresting over 100,000 people. And no one in Congress is willing to find out where the $28-30 billion annual black budget goes in the intelligence community.[37]

Congress is worried about leaks of classified information when it should focus on the abuses of power by the intelligence agencies. Ralph McGhee said in *Deadly Deceits:* "There is a little bit of fear that if you go after the intelligence community your career is threatened." Stich in *Defrauding America*, said the CIA has the power to destroy any politician who threatens it.[38] The CIA is getting increasingly involved in domestic politics, which is illegal. When Rep. Henry Gonzalez attacked the Bush regime for helping arm Iraq before the Gulf War, Bush used the CIA to block this investigation and had the CIA investigate Gonzalez for revealing supposedly top secret information.[39] It is extremely dangerous in a free society to use the CIA to attack one's political foes.

The November, 1993 issue of *Criminal Politics* reported that NAFTA passed by a much higher vote than had been expected partly because the CIA lobbied intensely, even threatening to expose illegal activities by certain members of Congress if they didn't approve NAFTA. *Worth* magazine also reported on this lobbying, although the discussion was toned down in this widely read financial magazine.[40] Close monitoring including electronic surveillance of Congress by the intelligence community has gone on for decades. Evidence is gathered to blackmail people. The CIA reportedly threatened to reveal the pedophile activity of a senator in 1991 to force him to vote a certain way. His vote was switched. The CIA has long provided children to certain members of Congress and other influential people partly to blackmail them. Along with the CIA and FBI, the mob and foreign intelligence agencies also have prostitute rings in Washington to gather information.[41] Hoover kept detailed files on many people in Congress and this information was used at times. This was discussed in various books such as *From the Secret Files of J. Edgar Hoover* by Athan Theoharis. Members of Congress may be investigated by federal agencies or as with Senator Church after his investigation of the CIA, the opposition may be funded to defeat someone.[42] The president and key people in Congress must support the intelligence community or they will be black mailed, defeated in office, or even be executed by a heart attack or an accident.

Former Nebraska state representative John W. DeCamp wrote *The Franklin Cover-Up: Child Abuse, Satanism, and Murder in Nebraska* describing how young children were kidnapped and used for sex. Some were taken to Washington parties and the 1992 Republican convention for sex. Some were also killed in satanic activity. State and federal prosecutors took part in the cover-up, and various public officials identified in the book threatened to sue DeCamp, but no one ever did. Perhaps fifteen people were murdered, including the chief investigator for the Nebraska legislature in this cover-up.

The CIA is an extremely dangerous organization that is anathema to the survival of America as a free society. Its continued existence is a disaster waiting to happen. In 1991 and again in 1993 Senator Daniel Moynihan introduced the End of the Cold War Act, proposing to abolish the CIA and transfer its activities to the State Department and Pentagon, where there could be more political oversight. Moynihan said: "We have become a national-security state, a country mobilized for war on a permanent basis, and we got into the business of saying everything is secret. Can we recover the memory of what we were before we became what we are now? Can we recover a sense of proportion in the national-security state? The task of purging the Cold War from our institutions is enormous."

Former CIA agent McGehee feels that the CIA should be abolished and that it isn't salvageable. It is too much under the political control of presidents and the NSC to produce accurate intelligence. The CIA is only one of 13 intelligence-gathering agencies. While it analyzes foreign economies, many think tanks and universities do the same. There is vast duplication and waste of spending with the $28-30 billion intelligence budget that would be lessened if the CIA was closed. The Ames fiasco was only one example of bureaucratic sclerosis. Many intelligence reports produced by the CIA have been extremely inaccurate. The CIA also often blocked military intelligence from deploying officers who spoke foreign languages and who could mix with the local population.[43]

I. F. Stone said: "The biggest menace to American freedom is the intelligence community." Presidential edicts that place the intelligence community above the law should be cancelled. No one should be above the law. National security should never be a valid excuse to prevent someone from defending themself. Most forms of covert operations should be criminalized. This would help shift the intelligence community to intelligence gathering and analysis. And the intelligence community should be required to submit its budget for a full review each year as required by all branches of the government under Article I, Section 9 of the Constitution.

There should be a new monitoring agency carefully directed by Congress with the job of closely monitoring all intelligence agencies. This organization should have the power to, at any time, without advanced notice, review any files and at any installation throughout the country. The members of this agency should have the highest security clearance and be carefully chosen because of their belief and loyalty to the Constitution and Bill of Rights. There are many retired CIA agents who are disgusted by the illegal activities of that organization. Some of these people would be excellent leaders of this new agency. The government already has similar agencies with agents to monitor, for example, banks and stock brokers, so this proposal is not unique. This is the only way a Republic can survive with an intelligence community. It must be closely monitored.

Government wiretaps and searches should only be done with a court order that also fulfills the standards of the Bill of Rights. National security should never be used as an exception. Government bureaucrats who destroy or refuse to provide evidence as required by Congress should automatically be fired and then face civil and criminal charges including obstruction of justice. There is no room in government for people who deliberately hide information from the people's elected representatives. Congress with its investigative, subpoena, contempt, grant of immunity, and perjury powers already has the ability to control the bureaucracy. Unfortunately, this power is rarely exercised.

Despite the end of the cold war there have been few changes in the American intelligence community. Instead of working to dismantle the CIA and the intelligence community, the emphasis has been to develop new roles to maintain it. "The CIA of the 1990s is a vast global bureaucracy in search of a mission."[44] The Senate Select Committee on Intelligence proposed in February, 1992 that the CIA focus more on terrorism, environmental intelligence, and aiding transnational corporations with economic intelligence.[45] If the intelligence community expands into numerous areas not directly involving intelligence, we will inevitably suffer from the same pattern of abuses and criminality that has existed for so many years.

Already the CIA has shifted more to economic espionage. R. Buckminster Fuller said the CIA was "Capitalism's Invisible Army."[46] "The CIA, the FBI and other parts of the intelligence community are working hand in hand with the U.S. Fortune 500 and high-tech 'Third Wave' firms to spy on corporate and government officials overseas—and to thwart foreign economic espionage aimed at American companies." Many CIA agents now serve overseas, working undercover in businesses to gather intelligence, and people working in certain industries are recruited as spies.[47] Yet the CIA continued proclaiming that the Soviet Union was an economic giant until the fall of the Berlin wall. "And while the CIA uses our tax dollars to slavishly serve the interests of megacorporations, these same firms are busy exporting jobs and bilking the government on taxes and Pentagon contracts."[48]

Ever since World War II the military and secret police power of the U.S. has steadily increased, while our national security has decreased. The cold war against the Soviet Union is over and now the enemy is the American people. In the name of protecting the country our constitutional form of government is gradually disappearing. A security apparatus doesn't just close up shop. However devoid of reality, from the bomber and missile gap in the 1960s and the errors in estimating Soviet military spending, the CIA always came up with excuses to justify its budget and continued existence. To restore constitutional government the CIA must be disbanded with all its drug traffickers arrested.

# Chapter XII

# State and Federal Police

"If I told you what I really know it would be very dangerous to the country. Our whole political system could be disrupted."

J. Edgar Hoover

"He has erected a multitude of New Offices, and sent hither swarms of Officers to harass our people, and eat out their substance....In every stage of these Oppressions We have Petitioned for Redress in the most humble terms. Our repeated Petitions have been answered only by repeated injury. A Prince, whose character is thus marked by every act which may define a Tyrant, is unfit to be the ruler of a free people."

Declaration of Independence

Until the 20th century, law enforcement was generally a local and state responsibility as required by the Constitution. The FBI was established in July, 1908 as a branch of the Justice Department. Between 1917 and 1921 its agents compiled files on 200,000 people and organizations. Congressional critics of the government were monitored with break-ins of congressmen's offices.[1] Between 1917 and 1921 two thirds of the states enacted sedition laws that made certain speeches, writings, and associations illegal. These laws were used against many groups not advocating violence, and the corporate elite used them to block union activities. During the Palmer raids on January 2, 1920, almost 10,000 people were arrested in 30 cities, usually without warrants. Most of these people were released with all charges dropped, although some were deported. Ultimately these laws were declared a violation of the First Amendment.

Harassment of political protestors and minority groups has long existed and been well documented. On the rare occasion when Congress investigates these cases, the agencies often refuse to comply with requests for information or evidence is destroyed. Despite what people think, the Justice Department and FBI provided little help to the civil rights movement unless there was national attention. Mary King, closely involved in the struggle for civil rights in the South during the 1960s, said in the book, *Freedom Song:* "The FBI, supposed to be upholding the Constitution, was a major factor in the thwarting of constitutional rights for blacks in the South. Julian Bond and I made it a practice to report any incident or atrocity to the FBI, a formality we knew in advance would be futile, because of the frequent collusion between the FBI and local law officers....The FBI agents in the South tended to be segregationists...."[2]

COINTELPRO was a secret program established by the FBI "to expose, disrupt, misdirect, discredit, or otherwise neutralize" American citizens who were political dissidents. The existence of COINTELPRO was confirmed in March,

1971, when FBI files were burglarized in Media, Pennsylvania. Hoover supported COINTELPRO, recommending that political activist be arrested on drug charges and that disinformation be used to cause confusion and disrupt political activity.[3] In 1968 Hoover signed a directive to "expose, disrupt, and otherwise neutralize the activities of various new Left organizations."

People were fired, mail was opened, many were audited, phones were wire-tapped without warrants, propaganda and lies were fed to the media, and files were stolen. Peaceful groups were intimidated, and lawful political activities were disrupted. The FBI created violence in the ghettos and destroyed civil rights groups, discrediting them with forged documents. There were hundreds of illegal break-ins, theft of membership lists, encouragement of gang warfare, and infiltration of groups with agent provocateurs. M. Wesley Swearingen, an FBI agent for 25 years, confessed to participating in 238 break-ins. He said FBI agents had lied in many cities about their illegal activities.

In 1971 Robert Hardy was recruited and ordered by the FBI to lead a raid on the Camden Selective Service office. Everyone was arrested but the "Camden 28" were all acquitted because the FBI had engineered the crime. During Watergate it was revealed that the FBI had disrupted the activities of The Socialist Workers party for a decade. To seek social change meant you were the enemy. All this was done in the name of national security.

At a 1971 conference on the FBI held at Princeton University Thomas I. Emerson said: "The inescapable message of much of the material we have covered is that the FBI jeopardizes the whole system of freedom of expression which is the cornerstone of an open society....The Bureau's concept of its function, as dedicated guardian of the national security, to collect general political intelligence, to engage in preventive surveillance, to carry on warfare against potentially disruptive or dissenting groups is wholly inconsistent with a system that stipulates that the government may not discourage political dissent or efforts to achieve social change so long as the conduct does not involve the use of force, violence or similar illegal action....The government is so obsessed with its law-and-order function, so ridden with bureaucratic loyalties, so vulnerable to its own investigators that it cannot be trusted to curb its police force."

When the Senate Intelligence Committee investigated COINTELPRO it rejected excuses that the program was needed to protect national security. Instead it found that the real purpose was "maintaining the existing social and political order." Congressional investigations in the 1970s found that the CIA mail opening program contributed to a list of 1.5 million Americans in CIA computers.[4] The FBI created a list of over one million Americans from its surveillance activities, and it has a security index which lists up to 200,000 people to be arrested in a national emergency.[5] Senator Tunney in 1975 said the FBI maintained 15,000 names of people who would be arrested during an emergency. Over the years the FBI has several times ignored orders to stop keeping such lists.[6] The NSA monitored every cable sent overseas from 1947 to 1975. Army intelligence investigated over 100,000 Americans during the Vietnam War.[7] The House Un-American Activities Committee admitted that in its first 25 years it had gathered "300,000 card references to the activities and affiliations of individuals." It would be extremely naive to think that this vast criminality stopped in the 1970s just because Congress held some investigations.

COINTELPRO supposedly ended in the 1970s, but attacks on political activists continued with only the name changing. Ex-FBI agent M. Wesley Swearingen admitted in a 1980 interview, "Nothing else changed. We just kept right on using all the same illegal techniques for repressing political dissent we'd used all along. Only we began framing what we were doing in terms of 'combating terrorism' rather than neutralizing political extremists." The people and the press moved on to other issues, and the crimes continued in the name of protecting national security and the corporate elite. Various agents openly admitted lying before Congress.[8] "The lesson of Hoover's directorship—that a quasi-autonomous secret police agency can undermine democratic principles—has not been effectively addressed by Congress or the executive...."[9]

Federal authorities also killed people under COINTELPRO. On December 4, 1969 an apartment in Illinois was raided with Black Panther Party leaders Fred Hampton and Mark Clark killed. Others in the apartment were arrested and later accused of violent acts at press conferences. Then all charges were dropped. In November, 1982 after years of litigation, the government finally admitted that the FBI had violated the civil rights of the two murdered Black Panther leaders as well as others imprisoned that night, and $1.85 million was paid to the survivors of the deceased. In 1970 a car bomb killed student organizers Ralph Featherstone and Che Payne. The bomb was believed to have been planted by an FBI agent.[10] The FBI also worked with the Secret Army Organization, a right wing group that stored weapons, bombed radical groups, and tried to assassinate people targeted as radical political activists.

George and Joseph Stiner, believed to be FBI provocateurs, murdered L.A. Panther leaders Alprentice Carter and Jon Huggins on January 17, 1969. While they were convicted and sentenced to long prison terms, they somehow escaped from San Quentin in 1974. They have not been heard from since, and they may have entered the Federal Witness Protection Program. After Carter and Huggins were murdered, FBI agent Richard Held sent a memo to FBI headquarters describing the operation as a success. On May 23, 1969 another Black Panther, John Savage, was killed, as was Black Panther Slyvester Bell in San Diego on August 14, 1969. In July, 1970 in Houston, Texas police killed Carl Hampton, black leader of the People's Party. According to released information, FBI operatives probably killed at least six to nine Black Panthers.

Labor activists like Karen Silkwood were also harassed or killed. Silkwood died in a bizarre car accident in 1974 while trying to give Kerr-McGee documents to a *New York Times* reporter. The FBI, ignoring the evidence, quickly closed the case. It sabotaged congressional inquiries and attacked Silkwood as a drug addict. In the 1970s FBI penetration of the American Indian Movement (AIM) resulted in the murders of Mae Aquash and Jancita Eagle Deer in 1976.[11] In 1978 two members of the Puerto Rican independence movement were killed by a special local police unit the FBI managed. The Puerto Rican intelligence bureau acknowledged in court that files were kept on 74,000 people.[12]

During a 1976 lawsuit against the Chicago Police, it was discovered that the department's security section kept files on 800 groups including the League of Women Voters and the NAACP. Hundreds of agents were assigned to infiltrate these groups. The Feds helped a militant group, the Legion of Justice, to physically attack dissidents. In 1982 the ACLU filed a suit against the L. A. police red squad for similar activities. In 1992 Mike Rothmiller, in *L.A. Secret Police:*

*Inside the LAPD Elite Spy Network*, revealed much about the L.A. secret police.[13] Illegal surveillance was common, and no suspicion of criminal activity was necessary.

Almost no one in the government was punished for these illegal activities. Citizens should have an efficient method to complain when abused by the police, beyond the cumbersome, corrupt, and expensive judiciary. Many people who attempt to change the status quo by pointing out the problems of society are labeled terrorists. When Reagan took office he pardoned the only two jailed FBI officials convicted of authorizing illegal break-ins in the 1970s. What was the high principle that Reagan spoke of when he pardoned these people? Is there a principle above the Constitution and the rule of law?

In the 1980s the FBI spied on various peace groups including the Physicians for Social Responsibility. In 1988 it was learned that the FBI had kept a file on former Rep. Phillip Burton for 18 years.[14] Ross Gelbspan, in *Break-Ins, Death Threats and the FBI*, described extensive illegal FBI activities against critics of U.S. policy in Central America. According to the Center for Constitutional Rights in New York, since 1984 there have been over 300 suspicious incidents with 150 unexplained break-ins. In 1987 Peter Dale Scott was researching a book on drugs, weapons, death squads, and the contras, with support from the International Center for Development Policy in Washington. Someone entered the center's offices and stole certain relevant files.[15]

In the summer of 1989 Congress announced that 1,600 groups had been improperly targeted and harassed. A list of these groups was never published. "Organizations that are targeted and penetrated by secret federal agents are seriously disrupted. The public record is replete with exposes of agents encouraging illegal activity, including murder, to discredit the organization in question."[16] Then the Justice Department goes after them, and the public sees them as criminals. If individuals or groups aren't in the quiet middle class, as defined by our corporate masters, they get demonized by the press and are harassed by government agents.

The past illegal activities of the FBI against American citizens has been well documented in many books.[17] What is less well known is that these activities continue today. In recent years environmentalists, people who want to legalize drugs like marijuana, third party movements, supporters of jury nullification, and the Patriot movement and militias are targets of government harassment.

In the fall of 1993 the Associated Press (AP) reviewed 17 complaints of brutality by the Bureau of Indian Affairs Police on six reservations. After a six month investigation, the AP concluded that excessive force was used with little discipline. In 1992 and 1993 America's Watch issued two reports on the brutality of the Immigration and Naturalization Service. Homeschoolers are harassed in many states. Postal inspectors visit corporations to review company records in search of violations, and then says it is being lenient with its fines because violators could be sentenced to 30 days in jail.

The FDA conducts numerous raids throughout the U.S. using local police. For instance, the clinic of Jonathan Wright, MD. was raided on May 6, 1992. With guns drawn police broke down the door and ordered people to raise their hands. This was a medical clinic that looked like any in America; the only "crime" here was that natural remedies were being used. In a 14 hour search dangerous items like U.S. postage stamps were seized along with $100,000 in medical supplies. An editorial in the main local newspaper, the *Seattle Post Intelligencer*, demanded an explanation for "the Gestapo-like tactics used in" this raid.[18] In 1995 all charges were dropped, but the medical supplies weren't returned.

The FBI office in San Francisco has over 600 pages of documents on Earth First. It has been watching this group since it was founded in 1980.[19] In 1982 the FBI tried to get an extortion indictment against an Earth Firster who gave Interior Secretary James Watt a letter threatening civil disobedience if he continued to push policies that damaged the environment. Prosecutors said there was no case. The Federal Law Enforcement Training Center in Glynco, Georgia trains all federal agents except the FBI and DEA. It has a domestic terrorism course that includes Earth First and the Animal Liberation Front. They also watch other supposed terrorist groups like Greenpeace.[20]

Four Earth Firsters, including the founder Dave Foreman, were arrested in Arizona in 1989 on conspiracy charges for attempting to bomb power lines. A government agent, Michael Fain, had infiltrated Earth First and urged the activists to break the law, even providing acetylene tanks to cause the destruction. Defense evidence at the trial included an FBI tape that they wanted to "pop" Foreman "to send a message." The government spent $2 million over two years to infiltrate Earth First. A star witness for the government had a serious drug problem and was paid by the FBI in cash to avoid an IRS tax lien.

On May 24, 1990 Earth First Activists Darryl Cherney and Judi Bari were injured, Bari very seriously, when a bomb exploded in the car they were driving. Within minutes of the explosion, the FBI Terrorist Squad arrived and according to court testimony said "these were the types of people who would be involved in carrying a bomb....These people, in fact, qualified as terrorists." According to the FBI and Oakland police, the bomb was planted behind the driver's seat, which allegedly proved that the two saw it and knowingly transported a bomb. However, photos taken at the scene definitely proved that the bomb was placed *under* the driver's seat. Photos showed the back seat was barely damaged, while the front seat was extensively damaged. Also, the bomb was wrapped in nails and triggered to explode from motion. It would be suicide to knowingly drive with such a device.

Bari and Cherney were immediately arrested after the bombing, Bari during surgery, and charged with illegal possession of explosives. To support this false charge, Cherney's house and van were searched without a warrant. The head of the FBI office in San Francisco at this period was Richard W. Held, who had directed many COINTELPRO programs. The prosecutor three times delayed the proceeding claiming there were no other suspects. During this period the national press slandered the two victims calling them eco-terrorists per the FBI line. As in a police state, the government announces the guilty and the controlled press follows the party line. On July 17, 1990 all charges were dropped from a lack of evidence, but for over two years the FBI continued looking for evidence to use against Bari and Cherney.

Fifty environmental groups demanded a congressional investigation, but when Rep. Don Edward's subcommittee demanded information the FBI refused. In May, 1991 Bari and Cherney sued the FBI and Oakland police for false arrest, illegal search, and civil rights violations. They claimed that the FBI and Oakland police plotted to frame them. Held, also named as a defendant in the suit, failed to settle the case, so at 52 he retired from the FBI. The courts three times found there was sufficient evidence to proceed to trial, but the FBI continued to withhold evidence from Bari and Cherney.

Gradually the court forced the FBI to release its files to the plaintiffs. The car bombing occurred just before the start of the 1990 Redwood Summer Earth First campaign to save the redwood forest, and Earth Firsters, including Bari, had received death threats. Bari obtained 5,000 pages of FBI documents of the investigation showing there was no attempt to search for the real bomber. When the FBI finally closed its official investigation on October, 1992, it had never even investigated the death threats against the environmentalists. Death threat letters were never even sent to a lab for analysis.[21]

Even more remarkable, evidence released showed that two weeks before the bombing, the FBI held a bomb school in the redwood forest. Four Oakland police officers and two FBI teachers, including Frank Doyle, Jr., attended the school and then appeared at the car bombing just after it occurred. Doyle directed the investigation and said the bomb was behind not under the driver's seat. Evidence surrendered by the FBI in the lawsuit included a tape with one agent laughing and saying: "This is it. This was the final exam." No one has explained why the FBI was teaching police how to plant car bombs! During the bomb school, a bomb with the same solder, tape, glue, and other components as the Bari car bomb exploded at a local timber mill. Environmentalists were blamed for this act.

The bombing was used as an excuse to harass and establish closer surveillance over environmentalists throughout the U.S. To investigate the bombing, the FBI obtained letters-to-the editor files from North Coast California newspapers. Only the *Santa Rosa Press Democrat* refused to comply with this demand. Mike Geniella, a reporter for this newspaper, wrote an article criticizing the bombing investigation and the FBI's targeting of Earth First in various states. Two weeks later the *Press Democratic*, which is owned by the *New York Times*, removed this award winning reporter from the timber beat. In the new world order the definition of a free press will change dramatically.

The FBI also gathered the names of local environmentalists from the police to build its file of names. However, the FBI did not seek the names of those harassing and assaulting environmentalists. The FBI even compiled a list of 634 people nationally who had spoken by phone with Earth First, and it gathered detailed information on these people. Here we get a peek at how the FBI quietly continues to monitor thousands of people.[22]

On August 4, 1995 a van belonging to someone in the U.S. Forest Service was destroyed by a bomb. The media uniformly described this as the work of government protestors. With the FBI teaching the police how to set car bombs and the ATF conducting exercises in setting car bombs (see Chapter XVI), did the government blow up this car so certain groups could be criticized?

Local police also often violate people's rights. In *Blood Carnage and the Agent Provocateur*, Alex Constantine presented evidence that outside provocateurs were involved in the 1965 and 1992 L.A. riots. In the 1992 riot a former police dog trainer admitted that the L.A. Police Department (LAPD) sent him into Koreatown to ignite flares at Korean-owned shops, especially when blacks drove by. The LAPD has for years worked closely with the CIA and other intelligence agencies. Residents in parts of L.A. saw outsiders deliberately setting fires. Police inaction obviously made the riots worse. The delayed deployment of the National Guard was also conveniently explained. Compton city councilwoman Patricia Moore said the police and government started the riot, and the panel appointed to investigate the riots included CFR members like Warren Christopher and former CIA head John McCone.

In 1993 New York state troopers were arrested for providing false evidence to get convictions. Now there is a police scandal in New Orleans and a massive scandal in Philadelphia with federal prosecutors subpoenaing 100,000 arrest records to identify who was falsely imprisoned. In Brunswick, Ohio on April 1, 1995, a social worker complained that John Lekan owned guns and, although no laws were broken, within an hour two police arrived. Lekan wouldn't let them in without a warrant and started singing the national anthem. When they broke down the door one was shot. Lekan and his nine year-old son were killed after a 45 hour siege involving 300 police and 200 firemen. During the assault a tank used tear gas. The police claim Lekan killed his son and himself, but no one believes this. Numerous shots were fired at the house and, once inside the home, the police removed the invalid wife and then two shots were fired. After this massacre, residents were warned to not repeat what they had witnessed, and more people joined militia units. The *Cleveland Plains Dealer*, one of the largest newspapers in Ohio, published a cartoon with the word "Brunswaco." When I asked permission to use that illustration for this book I was told "They didn't want to get involved." Perhaps it would irritate an advertiser or the government. The town hired ex-FBI agent William P. Callis to investigate the raid, and he concluded that the police were too eager to use force and an armored vehicle should not have been used.

On June 28, 1995 Mike Hill, a militia chaplain and former policeman, was killed by a state trooper while walking towards the trooper's car at 2:30 a.m. He had been stopped because of his license plate. Three other militia members who witnessed the killing confirmed that Hill wasn't touching the weapon by his belt, and the AP quoted the local sheriff Bernie Gibson as saying: "No officer's life had been threatened." Yet CBS *Evening News* on April 2, 1996 said Hill had pulled a gun.

In 1992 there was a standoff at Ruby Ridge, Idaho between Randy Weaver and his family and federal agents. Weaver, who had no criminal record and had served with valor in Vietnam, had failed to appear in court on a charge of possessing illegal firearms. He was deliberately entrapped by a federal informant who, for three years, solicited him to cut the barrels of several shotguns a quarter-inch below the legal limit. He never manufactured firearms and had not previously possessed an illegal firearm. The ATF incorrectly believed Weaver belonged to a Nazi group, so they entrapped him; and then they said he must infiltrate and spy on this group or be indicted. Weaver, arrested and indicted after refusing, became concerned for his life and property after court personnel gave conflicting statements about the case, including false statements that he might lose his property and children. One court official sent Weaver a notice to appear in court on the wrong day, so Weaver didn't appear in court on the correct date. A Justice Department attorney, aware of this error, still issued an arrest warrant.

The U.S. marshals made no attempt to meet with Weaver to serve the arrest warrant, but Weaver tried to negotiate a surrender if his safety was guaranteed. The marshals drafted a letter of acceptance, but the U.S. Attorney for Idaho suddenly ordered that negotiations end.[23] The marshals launched an 18 month surveillance and got military aerial reconnaissance photos taken by the Defense Mapping Agency. They even bought land next to the Weavers, intending to build a cabin and befriend him. The Weaver's mail was intercepted, psychological profiles were done, and $130,000 worth of spy cameras were installed.

Finally, six U.S. marshals came with no warrant, gave no warning, and never identified themselves. They deliberately upset the family dog and, when it started barking, they killed it. They fired at 14 year old Samuel Weaver and a friend, Kevin Harris. Not aware who these armed strangers were, they returned the fire. U.S. marshal Degan was killed, although no one is certain who killed him. As Samuel turned to run he was shot in the back and killed. The government immediately brought in from Washington, D.C. the FBI Hostage Rescue Team. While 400 federal agents were brought in, no attempt was initially made to contact Weaver and negotiate a surrender. Bo Gritz and at least one other source said the FBI almost dropped a gasoline fire bomb on the log cabin from a helicopter to end the siege. That would have killed most of the inhabitants as at Waco. When several family members and Harris returned to the shed where they had taken Samuel's body, they were fired on by government snipers, hitting Randy and Harris. Weaver's wife Vicki was shot through the head while holding her 10 month-old baby, blowing away half her face. Dick Rodgers, an FBI official, told Bo Gritz they deliberately targeted Vicki Weaver because a psychiatrist told them she would kill the kids before surrendering to the FBI.

These were trained marksmen. The FBI agent who killed Vicki Weaver from 200 yards testified at the trial that he could, at 200 yards, hit a target smaller than a dime. When Congress held hearings in September, 1995 this agent and others took the Fifth Amendment to avoid answering questions. However, several agents said that Randy Weaver had killed his son, a claim no one believed. Weaver's "paranoid fantasy" that the government was conspiring to get him was true, and the government constantly lied about the case. During congressional hearings, several federal agents said the responsibility for that atrocity resided only with Weaver because he sold illegal weapons.

The Justice Department's internal disciplinary, unit after a long delay, completed a 542-page report in April, 1994. The report concluded that the raid violated the Constitution and FBI internal procedures and recommended possible criminal prosecution of federal officials. Agents were ordered to shoot at any armed adult if they had a clear shot, which also violated Idaho law and the normal rules of engagement. Despite this report the Justice Department refused to prosecute any federal agents, saying the agents had reason to believe their lives were in danger so their actions were justified.[24] How a mother holding a baby in her arms can threaten FBI agents 200 yards away is not something that can only be explained in a free society. America should become a country where, if you blow out the brains of a mother just holding a baby in her arms, you should face criminal charges even if you are in the federal police, but this will not happen unless constitutional government is restored. No one should be above the law.

As a result of the critical report, Larry Potts the FBI agent who supervised the raid from Washington received a letter of censure in his file. Although this is the mildest of reprimands, Senator Hatch strangely said on national television on April 30, 1995 that being censured is a very serious matter. Potts also received a letter of censure when he lost a cellular phone. The life of an American citizen is worth a hell of a lot more than a telephone. Then Potts was promoted to second in command of the FBI. In a May 3, 1995 complaint to the Justice Department, FBI agent Eugene Glenn the on-scene commander of the Weaver assault, said Potts had issued the shoot-on-sight order and that the FBI's review of the operation was inaccurate and a cover-up to protect top officials of the bureau.[25] In July, 1995 Potts was demoted and then suspended, partly because FBI agent E. Michael Kahoe destroyed documents that would have clarified who issued the shoot-on-sight order. However, on March 1, 1996 the U.S. Marshal's Service presented its highest award for valor to its agents involved in this raid.

On April 19, 1993 an ATF assault on the Branch Davidian compound near Waco, Texas failed, and the FBI was brought in. It would have been easy to arrest the leader David Koresh outside the compound before the raid, and he had previously allowed searches of his home and peacefully surrendered in another legal case. However, the federal police wanted a show of force. Military helicopters were used during the Waco siege, because of a false report that illegal drugs were in the compound. The warrant also contained a charge of child abuse. Why did a federal warrant list what is strictly a matter for state authorities? Several FBI specialists strongly suggested not taking a very confrontational position with Koresh, but this advice was rejected.

During the final assault, as tanks attacked the compound, the FBI said "This is not an assault." What was it? For six hours CS gas was pumped into the compound, although this toxic chemical is illegal under the Chemical Weapons Convention signed January, 1993 by the U.S. and 100 nations. The government said this treaty banned using CS gas in international conflicts not domestically. Are we supposed to be comforted by this statement! This highly toxic gas is banned in war, but it is acceptable for the Feds to use it against Americans. CS gas is also highly flammable under certain circumstances, such as at Waco with a wooden structure, high winds, kerosene lanterns, bales of hay in the building, and very dry conditions. The evidence suggests that the fire started from the CS gas or the tank knocking over the kerosene lanterns. The FBI even blocked attempts to fight the fire, keeping the fire trucks away.[26]

Dr. Alan Stone, a Harvard professor of law and psychiatry asked by the government to investigate Waco, said medical literature, the CS gas manufacturer, and U.S. Army manuals declare CS gas dangerous especially in enclosed spaces and with children. Yet just after the Waco atrocity, Janet Reno said she believed CS gas was safe. Reno also said she ordered the raid because of concern that the children were being mistreated. Saving children by killing them is a logic that will become common in the new world order. The Justice Department report on Waco concluded: "Under the circumstances the FBI exhibited extraordinary restraint."

After the deaths Clinton said: "Janet Reno should not resign just because some religious fanatics murdered themselves." Clinton on *60 Minutes* said of the Davidians "Those people murdered a bunch of innocent law enforcement officials and when that raid occurred it was the people who ran that cult compound who murdered their own children, not federal officials. They made the decision to destroy the children that were there." Adolf Hitler couldn't have said it better. In court the 11 Davidians had already been found not guilty of such charges.

The Waco massacre expresses the contempt and fear that the secret government has against fundamental Christians, because they represent a threat to the success of the coming dictatorship. Partly because of certain Bible prophecies, such as in the Book of Revelations, the machinations of the one world government are better understood in the fundamental Christian community than by many other people. The *Los Angeles Times* described certain Christians as being dangerous extremists. It said the Michigan militia was led by a general who was a Baptist preacher.[27] Will the press next claim that all Baptists are extremists?

The FBI under Louis Freeh is determined to increase its power. Freeh pushed for expanded wiretap powers, yet there have been no wiretap requests against terrorists since 1988. The FBI has even gone international, setting up offices overseas. Crimes, like money laundering, are being used to justify establishing an international police force.[28] Senator John Kerry said "Organized crime is the new communism, the new monolithic threat."

In 1994 Peg Bargon, a middle-aged mother in Illinois, gave a native American "dream-catcher," a small hoop with feathers to Hillary Clinton. These were feathers gathered on the ground but this violated the Migratory Bird Treaty Act. A Fish and Wildlife Service agent learned of this "crime," so Bargon was prosecuted and fined about $12,000. Her neighbors now call the police to report feathers spotted on the ground.[29] One cannot be too careful. In the new world order, one must beware of the feather police.

There was a conflict about a large fossil found by the Black Hills Institute of Geological Research, Inc. (BHI) on private land owned by an American Indian, so the Feds got involved. On May 14, 1992 the Feds raided the BHI in Hill City, South Dakota. School children watching sang the *Star-Spangled Banner* and shouted "Shame, Shame." An FBI agent warned that "if any of those kids cause any trouble, they'll be taken down." Federal police can never be too sure about young patriots. That the South Dakota National Guard helped in the raid caused great anger. There were two other raids and the BHI and its officers faced 156 charges. The U.S. Attorney cited the 1906 Antiquities Act, although that act has been ruled unconstitutional and it specifically exempts fossils. This didn't matter to the federal fossil police! Before the trial the judge violated his oath of office by participating in plea negotiations that both sides had accepted. The Feds wanted to back down, but the judge felt the BHI was guilty! Although no one testified that they had been victimized by the BHI, the Feds used 92 witnesses during the seven week trial that cost almost $8 million tax dollars. Facing a biased judge, the defendants were found guilty on several counts, thus expanding federal power, which is why the suit was brought initially.[30] If the Feds weren't so concerned about bird feathers and fossils, perhaps they wouldn't need more agents to fight terrorism.

On October 7, 1994, 70 state and federal agents armed and in flak jackets raided the Green House Fine Herbs farm near San Diego. One Fed said the action began when they received a report about a rare bird nesting near the farm on the local river. During the raid workers were asked about their religious beliefs to see if they were in a religious cult. Some workers belonged to a yoga group. Certain employees were interrogated for three hours, and 30 boxes of records were seized. Reportedly, the authorities were looking for an excuse to seize the property. After a 1993 flood washed away over 20 acres, the farm group tried to get a permit to reclaim some land but was told by local officials and the U.S. Army Corps of Engineers that one wasn't needed because the work involved farmland. After 200 truckloads of soil were deposited, a state official said the land now belonged to the state, not the farm, because the river had changed course. The flood may have been caused by state action upriver.

A grand jury investigation of this case lasted over a year and probably cost $1 million. In August, 1995 two growers were indicted for conspiracy and pollution. They were charged with dumping illegal waste into the river and a landfill. The maximum penalty was 11 years in jail and millions in fines. The changing flow of a river can be quite expensive in the new world order. U.S. Attorney Alan Bersin said the pollution indictments were "a significant step in the government's commitment to improve the quality of life." In January, 1996 all charges were abruptly dropped. This ridiculous case angered many and, with an election coming, Clinton needs California.[31] With the extreme hostility of the FDA towards natural healing perhaps herbal terrorist bulletins will soon be issued by the Feds. Will this also improve our lives?

On January 8, 1994 at 7 p.m., about 139 agents from the FBI, ATF, DEA, IRS, along with state and local police blocked part of Amite, Louisiana and conducted a house-to-house search in a mainly black housing development. Was this a practice mission to conduct national house-to-house raids with state and federal police? The *Shreveport Times*, on September 20, 1994, described Operation Bottoms Up when 200 state, federal, and local police sealed off nine blocks of Ledbetter Heights and arrested 45 alleged members of a street gang. Reno praised the joint effort and said "the raid was the beginning of the joint federal, state, and local enforcement effort...."

Louis Katona III is a part-time police officer and gun collector. He loaned a grenade launcher to the ATF for a criminal trial, but it wasn't returned to him and Katona complained about this. The ATF felt Katona had obtained false signatures to purchase weapons, so his home was raided in May, 1992 with his firearms and car tires intentionally damaged. When his wife came home she was roughed up; she started bleeding hours later and had a miscarriage. In September, 1992 Katona was charged with 19 federal felonies for falsifying documents regarding the purchase of his guns. In April, 1994 the judge dismissed all charges before the defense even presented its case because the government's case was so weak. He ordered that the gun collection be returned, and Katona filed a suit against the government. ATF head Magaw agreed that agents could have first asked Katona about the signatures before the raid.

The home of Harry Lamplugh, a veteran, was raided by the ATF in May, 1994. He had no criminal record and had always carefully followed gun laws. When Lamplugh asked if they had a warrant a gun was put to his head and he was told to shut up. In eight hours they killed a kitten, opened the mail, damaged property, and seized cash, weapons, family medical records, and Lamplugh's membership list of 70,000. The warrant said "probable cause" with no other reason given for the entry. No one in the family was charged with a crime, but $18,000 of seized property was forfeited to the government. Lamplugh promotes 40 gun shows a year for groups like the American Legion and the Marine Corps League, and he openly criticizes Clinton and the ATF. The government wouldn't explain why this home was raided. It would be difficult to explain a campaign of terror against gun owners as part of the plan to remove guns from the people. In court the government said charges of harassment and brutality were "outrageous and utterly false." After Lamplugh appeared on the Gordon Liddy radio show, the family received death threats, his office was burglarized, and Lamplugh's wife was assaulted and threatened by federal agents who killed several kittens. The Feds are also terrorizing people to testify against Lamplugh.

At 4 a.m. on July 13, 1994 the ATF assaulted Monique Montgomery's home wearing Ninja outfits. Montgomery used a registered gun to protect herself against the unknown intruders, but of course the agents claimed that they identified themselves. Using high intensity lights the door was broken down and she was shot four times. No illegal guns or drugs were found.

On March 13, 1995 Dr. Jed Cserna was hospitalized in Ely, Nevada after a bad accident. Only semiconscious with a broken back, he was visited by a deputy and ask if he was armed because of a report that he owned some firearms. Although this physician is a member of the Idaho National Guard and a former member of the U.S. Forest Service, his home was raided in a search for weapons. The ATF got involved, not wanting to miss an opportunity to protect us from this doctor. Still in pain Cserna was later arrested and forced to ride 300 miles to be arraigned despite his condition. The *Ely Daily Times* said: "All their (ATF) methods accomplished was to convince some Ely citizens that maybe they are jack-booted government thugs." Recently Cserna was sentenced to jail for this minor weapons violation. Cserna was found guilty of not paying a transfer tax on one of the two pistols found at his home. For this "crime" he was sentenced to two years and nine months in federal prison, fined $10,000, and his medical license was suspended.

In one instance, several ATF agents wanted to enter a home without a warrant to look for guns. A local deputy got into a shouting argument with them, and told them they couldn't enter the home without a warrant. A backup deputy was sent to the scene with orders to disarm and arrest the ATF agents for burglary if they entered the home without a warrant, so they left.[32] The duty of police officers is to protect and serve the people. The Constitution is the highest law in the land, and if federal police commit unconstitutional acts, local police have a duty to the people to resist such unlawful intrusions to the fullest extent allowed by the law.

Sheriff Tim Nettleton of Owyhee County, Idaho announced on May 18, 1995 that federal law enforcement officials cannot act as armed peace officers in his county; if they try they will be arrested.[33] The sheriff of Catron County, N.M. has threatened to arrest the local head of the U.S. Forest Service for interfering with the right of citizens to graze cattle on public land. Okanogan County, Washington commissioners passed a resolution that federal police need the written permission of their sheriff to enter the county on official business. Rep. Chenoweth may introduced legislation requiring federal agents to get permission from the local sheriff to enter a county on official business. An ex-sheriff in the Indiana legislature has introduced a bill requiring federal agents to first notify sheriffs before taking local legal action or face criminal and civil charges.

In January, 1994 and again in 1995 the ACLU, NRA, and other organizations petitioned Clinton to establish a national commission to investigate misconduct by federal police agencies and to take action "to reduce constitutional and human rights violations" by these agencies. Problems include improper use of deadly force, physical and verbal abuse, improper use of no-knock warrants, inadequate investigation of misconduct allegations, entrapment and improper inducement of criminal activity, use of unreliable informants, and asset forfeiture laws. Guns seized by federal agents are rarely returned, even after a person is found not guilty. So far Clinton has not responded. Attorney Robert Sanders, the former head of criminal enforcement at the ATF, said: "Instead of focusing on selected criminals, there is an indiscriminate focus on anyone who owns guns." Some in the ATF consider Sanders a traitor which shows how dangerous the ATF is.[34]

Complaints against the ATF have continued for many years. After the 1968 Gun Control Act was passed the ATF, which was given responsibility to enforce it, took aggressive action against gun owners partly because there was little need to do its traditional work of stopping moonshining. The ATF used the vague language of the 1968 law to entrap and arrest many gun owners. In 1971 Ken Ballew suffered permanent brain damage and paralysis in one such raid. In July, 1995 he died from his injury. As it does today the ATF had focused on seizing guns not on stopping crime, and they harassed people who criticized them. The First Amendment may exist but so does the ATF, and one must be aware of this.[35] In the early 1980s Congress held hearings on the ATF. In January, 1982 the Senate Constitutional Rights Subcommittee report said "It is apparent that enforcement tactics made possible by current federal firearms laws are constitutionally, legally, and practically reprehensible...." ATF violations of the Second, Fourth, and Fifth Amendments were described. It said that about 75 percent of ATF gun prosecutions involved ordinary citizens with no criminal intent or knowledge, who were entrapped by technical violations. In some cases people were prosecuted for interpretations of the law which the ATF had not even published in the Federal Registrar. Someone was prosecuted for an act the AFT acting head said was perfectly legal. Misconduct by agents and supervisors was gathered, yet little changed as we see today.

There are many reports that federal police, especially the ATF, are collecting records of who owns guns as a prelude to the registration and ultimate seizure of all guns. In the Fresno, California police department, an ATF agent used a computer to track firearms owners and fed that information into a national computer. During the militia hearings, Senator Spector openly asked for the names and addresses of militia members. Why does the government want such information? Are these people going to be arrested during a national emergency? The Feds are specifically raiding the headquarters of various organizations to collect names and addresses of members.

Using a questionable search warrant federal police raided the national headquarters of the North American Freedom Council on October 19, 1994. Similar raids have taken place in numerous branches of this group which provides information on the IRS. Names and addresses are always seized.[36] On November 12, 1994 the FBI raided the home and headquarters of a national militia group, United States Special Field Forces (USSF) in Woodbridge, Virginia. The reason for the raid was that the back of an I.D. card said Property of United States Government instead of Property of United States Special Field Forces. The card correctly listed the name and address of the organization, and this improper identification was not associated with any crime. Based on this error a warrant was obtained to search for USSF documents "of its members." In a free society making a slight error on an identification card would hardly justify raiding someone's home, especially with such a broadly based warrant. Everything concerning the USSF was seized.

While there are many problems with the police, as the anger grows, we should remember that many police would be aghast at the new world order if they understood the planned dictatorship. Anger should be directed more to the behind-the-scenes corporate controllers than at government officials conveniently available, who are usually merely carrying out order. There are many decent police who believe in the Constitution and who are extremely angry at the vast criminality taking place in Washington. Michael Levine, author and former decorated DEA agent, often receives calls from frustrated agents who describe phony busts and important drug cases cancelled by politicians. The author of *The Clinton Chroni-*

*cles* receives many calls from frustrated federal authorities. The Michigan militia reportedly has established safe houses to protect people in government coming forward with information.

In early 1995 an issue of *The Agent*, the magazine of treasury agents including the FBI, ATF, and IRS, criticized management problems in the treasury bureaucracy, and said senior officials in the ATF and FBI should be indicted over Waco. ABC's *Day One* on September 14, 1995 described an FBI sting operation of NASA that was stopped before senior officials could be arrested for corruption. Various FBI agents were very upset and one quit the bureau. In August, 1995 FBI agent Frederic Whitehurst said the famed FBI crime lab has been fabricating evidence for years in hundreds of cases to get convictions. Holding a doctorate in chemistry he has complained for years, but there was no publicity until his statements affected the World Trade Center and O.J. cases. Refusing to comply with false lab results, he was demoted and transferred.[37] The Justice Department found serious problems with the FBI lab in the Ruby Ridge case; the FBI lab had authenticated Foster's suicide note which other experts have discounted. There have been five internal investigations against this whistleblower.

When whistleblowers go to Congress, the press, or the Justice Department little occurs. Rodney Stich in *Defrauding America* named dozens of Americans, such as Gunther Russbacher and Michael Riconosciuto, who were killed or imprisoned by the government when they tried to reveal government criminal activities. Not only are people murdered, but "It is standard practice for Justice Department prosecutors to silence or discredit whistleblowers and informants, especially intelligence agency personnel, by charging them with federal offenses for carrying out what they were ordered to do by their handlers." When someone becomes a threat the government will have them arrested on false charges, seize their assets, pay people to lie under oath against them, pressure and bribe judges, and have all evidence sealed because of national security, preventing public access to it.[38]

A typical example of how the FBI threatens agents who reveal corruption involves the 28 page confession of William R. Stringer in a deposition before a judge in 1994. Stringer had been an FBI agent in the South for many years and was 67 and dying when he gave the confession. He explained how the FBI planted evidence to set up Byron De La Beckwith to be jailed for a murder he never committed. And on orders from the FBI the local police killed someone and accidently also killed a female FBI informant. Stringer first disclosed these activities to the Justice Department in 1976, when the Attorney General called for agents to step forward and reveal illegal activities. When the FBI learned of this they sent agents from Washington who threatened Stringer and warned him to retract his story. Even in the 1970s with the many hearings and investigations little really changed.[39] The *Jackson Advocate* in its December 14-20, 1995 issue reported that, with this confession and new evidence uncovered by ex-judge W.O. Dillard, De La Beckwith may get a new trial. Dillard has filed a Friend of the Court petition to free Beckwith.

In January, 1993 the *Washington Post* did a six part series on persecutory abuse. Evidence is withheld from the defense, grand juries are manipulated, and witnesses are intimidated. Federal agents who terrorize or kill citizens are never punished, as in the Waco, Randy Weaver, and Judi Bari cases. Over the years people like Rep. Brooks, Senator Moynihan, and Rep. Wise, Jr. tried to learn what steps were being taken to correct such abuses, but the Justice Department refused to cooperate. This situation shows why there should be laws in place forcing government bureaucrats to provide information Congress requires. If an agency refuses to respond, give them seven days and then fire, fine, and arrest people in that department until the people's representatives can learn exactly what is going on. In a free society bureaucrats should not be allowed to withhold information from Congress. Of course one also needs representatives who will protect the people's rights.

Another dangerous trend is the gradual federalization and militarization of state and local police into a unified national police force. The Founding Fathers warned against this. J. Edgar Hoover in 1964 opposed a national police force. Supreme Court Justice Robert H. Jackson said: "I cannot say that our country could have no central police without becoming totalitarian, but I can say with great conviction that it cannot become totalitarian without a centralized national police....A national police...will have enough on enough people, even if it does not elect to prosecute them, so that it will find no opposition to its policies." On June 16, 1936 Hitler established a unified police force throughout Germany.

Federal authorities are gaining control over state and local police through federal funding, growth of federal law enforcement agencies, and more federal crimes. The Law Enforcement Assistance Administration (LEAA) was created by the 1968 Omnibus Crime Control Act. A leader of LEAA, Clarence Coster, openly declared on March 3, 1971 that local police needed to be centralized to be governed better. This agency was abolished in 1981 because so many were against its programs.

With unfunded mandates and limited ability to tax citizens because of the overwhelming federal tax authority, states and localities are now being economically coerced to turn to federal authorities to financially support the police. State, local, and federal law authorities increasingly work together in multi-jurisdictional (MJTF) task forces conducting raids on people those in power deem to be a threat. The 1994 Omnibus Crime Bill established Rural Crime and Drug Task Forces in each federal judicial district to operate under the Attorney General. These federal rural task forces can work with local and state police to confiscate the property of citizens who are only under investigation.

Federal agencies like the Justice Department, FBI, DEA, and ATF are increasingly fight local crime. The DEA's REDRUM program pairs DEA agents with local police in 21 cities to solve drug-inspired murders. The ATF has formed 21 task forces to fight local crime.[40] While this enhances federal power, many experts feel that using federal agents to fight street crime is not very efficient.

There is also increased involvement of the military in law enforcement as the Posse Comitatus Act is weakened. This act is supposed to keep the Army and Air Force out of civilian affairs. Congress has allowed the state National Guard to participate in drug operations, if the troops are only under the state government. Congress passed 32 USC 112 (1990 and 1991) to provide federal money for state National Guard drug fighting.[41] Congress and the courts, especially since the 1980s, have increased military involvement in the war on drugs. In December, 1994 the House Committee on Foreign Affairs held a hearing on international narcotics control in which it listed a series of laws that now allow the U.S. military to stop narcotics in the U.S. *U.S. v. Bacon* (1988), *U.S. v. Brown* (1980), *People v. Wells* (1985), and *People v. Burder* (1979) have damaged the intent of the Posse Comitatus Act to separate the military from civilian policing.

During the Ruby Ridge hearings Senator Charles Grassley said "Law enforcement now cross-trains with the military's elite special operations forces. The military mission—to kill first—may have rubbed off on law enforcement....The FBI must stop thinking its the military and get back to being the FBI." Military facilities are now used to train law enforcement officials. In 1993 Washington, D.C. had its recruits undergo training at the U.S. Marine Corps base in Quantico, Virginia. Military surveillance equipment and helicopters are used in local police operations. *Black Helicopters Over America* by Jim Keith describes the continuous use of helicopters to harass citizens. Sarah McClendon interviewed armed forces spokesman Harvey Perrett, III, who admitted a $3 billion program helps fund a black helicopter base in Fort Campbell, Kentucky. The military and Justice Department have formulated a plan "Operations Other Than War" to use non-lethal weapons against civilians. This will further involve the military in civilian affairs. Lt. General J.H. Binford Peay, III, in the Army publication *Tomorrow's Missions*, said the military should be prepared to assist in domestic peace-keeping missions including anti-drug programs.[42]

Accompanying the growing federalization of crime is a massive increase in federal police agents. In 1967 the Federal Bureau of Narcotics had 300 agents. Recently the DEA, its replacement, had 3,400 agents. Federal police now make up 10 percent of the nation's total police forces. There are now 53 federal agencies that allow agents to carry arms, and about 140 federal agencies enforce compliance with federal laws.

Charles Meeks, executive director of the National Sheriffs Association said about increased federal intervention and influence over the local police: "By passing statutes in an effort to make (the crime problem) better we're getting closer to a federal police state." In 1993 under the reinventing government program, the National Performance Review report recommended "the designation of the Attorney General as the Director of Law Enforcement to coordinate federal law enforcement efforts." This is one more sign of a unified national police force.

There are many reports that federal agents have increased firepower. In May and August, 1994 the Georgia National Guard trained ATF members to use Bradley Infantry Fighting Vehicles. The September, 1993 issue of *Handguns* magazine said the EPA's Criminal Investigation Division (CID) has replaced revolvers with Glock 19 semi-automatic pistols. An official said the CID "decided to re-evaluate its firearms policy as it reorganized to undertake its expanded responsibilities under the Pollution Prosecution Act." In one state federal forest service officials purchased over 30,000 rounds of .45 calibre ammunition. The *Washington Times* reported on July 18, 1995, that the ATF had obtained 22 OV-10D aircraft. These planes were used by the Marines during the Vietnam War for gunfire and missile support of ground troops. Who in America are the federal police going to war against?

Groups targeted by the government, such as the Patriot movement and militias, should carefully study books like *War at Home* by Brian Glick to understand the harassment tactics used against them. Glick described four levels of illegal government harassment: infiltration by agents and informers, psychological warfare, harassment through the legal system, and extralegal force and violence, including murder. There may be intense surveillance, interviews to scare people into becoming informants, false arrests, political trials, or grand juries where you can be jailed for refusing to cooperate. The Feds publicly attack a group, infiltrate it, and inspire it to commit violence to discredit the entire group.

In the fall of 1994 the ATF's Intelligence Division sent a briefing paper to police departments across the nation with disinformation on the militias, and Janet Reno sent orders to 12 states to closely watch patriotic and militia groups, especially the leaders. If someone in a militia group is especially keen on promoting actual violence, that person may be an undercover agent. Already John Parsons, head of the Tri-State's Militia, an important militia for communications, admitted under oath at a trial that he was taking $1,775 weekly to report to the FBI and that he accepted $500 a week plus certain expenses to collect information for the FBI while on a trip to militia groups in New Mexico.[43] This group sent a fax threatening a civil war if the antiterrorism bill was passed. In other words, a militia lead by an FBI operative threatened violence against the government.[44] The result is that the press has another reason to attack the supposed extremist views of the militia. An official in a Washington militia started advocating violence. That group had access to fingerprint records, and they learned he was a federal agent. He was thrown out and weeks later turned up in a Kentucky militia.

The private security industry is another danger. It now employs over 2.5 million people, and in 1992 $52 billion was spent on private security while $30 billion was spent on the police. There are 1.5 million private security guards and only 554,000 state and local police. These private guards receive little training, and they participate in illegal activities such as union-busting and spying on people. Many criminals work in these agencies, and one guard made the FBI's 10 most wanted list. Some of these private security agencies work for the secret government. Often controlled by large corporations, this large security force could be used during a declared national emergency, although many of these people would not follow orders if they understood what was happening. The authorities feel it is safer to use private security companies, or foreign intelligence agencies such as from England, to commit illegal acts so the government has another level of deniability. This is one of the lessons from the 1970s congressional investigations.[45]

*Fortune* magazine presented a remarkable story of Allstate bringing in private investigators to harass its employees.[46] The House Committee on Interior and Insular Affairs said that after the *Exxon Valdez* oil spill, the oil industry hired Wackenhut, a large private security firm, to illegally spy on various people to identify whistleblowers. Targets of this campaign included Alaska state officials, and Rep. George Miller was almost added to the list. Wackenhut specializes in identifying whistleblowers and has long had a close relationship with the CIA and other federal police agencies. By 1966 Wackenhut had secret files on four million Americans, and it has branches in other countries.[47] The government supposedly needs a valid reason to spy on you, private corporations do not.

All law enforcement officials should be required to study the Constitution and Bill of Rights and be tested on them at times. The best way to restore constitutional government in criminal matters is to follow the advice of the Founding Fathers—disband most federal police agencies and restore crime fighting to state and local police. All federal police who have committed illegal acts against American citizens should face criminal charges before new independent oversight agencies with permanent special prosecutors established to prosecute such abuses.

A new code of honor in each agency should be established. In the military academies, if one learns of cheating by fellow cadets and doesn't report it, one may be expelled from the service. People in the military have an obligation to disobey unlawful orders. Why should we expect less from the police. If anyone in the police agencies is given an order that clearly violates the Constitution or the agencies mandate, they should refuse to follow such illegal orders, without fear of reprisal, and be required to report illegal orders to new oversight agencies to resolve such issues. People issuing illegal orders should be punished.

The rampant physical and verbal violence during police raids should be stopped. The Ku Klux Klan Act, forbidding the wearing of masks to terrorize the public, should be enforced to ban police from wearing masks. Increased use of volunteer police, as in the 1800s would lessen police criminality. Search warrants should be served within 30 days of being issued, and no hearsay or contradictory evidence should be used in issuing such warrants. Applications for a search warrant should include material on the reliability of witnesses.[48]

In 1924 Attorney General Harlan Stone, who appointed Hoover head of the FBI, warned "that a secret police may become a menace to free government and free institutions because it carries with it the possibility of abuses of power which are not always quickly apprehended or understood...." Today "An American police state has evolved, operating in the shadows side by side with the legitimate system of government....We have created a uniquely American police state, one that has managed to grow and operate within, or at least alongside, the democratic system ....It is unnerving to think that a kind of totalitarianism has taken root in America, but if we shrink from recognizing it, we shall not remove it."[49]

The Waco and Weaver massacres represent what the government may do in the future to seize guns. The Justice Department report on the Weaver raid shows that the government expected the assault "was not going to last long" because the Weavers would be "taken down hard and fast." These assaults were unique only in that so many died and there was so much publicity. Every year there are hundreds of improper raids, yet even when people are killed the police are rarely prosecuted. The Constitution is held in contempt and homes are assaulted with guns drawn, without warrants, and people and pets are often injured, tied up for hours, or killed while federal agents "protect the people." Yet the Washington crowd keeps wondering why people are increasingly angry at a tyrannical federal government when the economy is supposedly good.

The government attacks at Waco and Randy Weaver's home awakened many Americans to how dangerous the federal government has become. Since no one in law enforcement was really punished for these crimes, it only encouraged further atrocities against the people as we saw in Oklahoma. The police are above the law. Judges who issues vague search warrants often without probable cause bear great responsibility for damaging the Bill of Rights.

The FBI, CIA, and other organs of the secret government never stopped closely monitoring millions of Americans in the 1970s, because no one except Congress told them to stop. What was publicly proclaimed about respecting the rights of citizens were lies. I don't support left or right wing violence, but I also believe that people have a legal right to peaceful political dissent without the police conducting criminal acts against them. The increasingly aggressive stance that the police take shows how they often do not serve or respect the people. The objective is to force people to follow harsh rules and to face the consequences, including deadly force, if there is resistance.

## Chapter XIII

## Militias in American History

"Whenever the militia comes to an end, or is despised or neglected, I shall consider this union dissolved, and the liberties of North America lost forever."

President John Adams[1]

"No free man shall ever be de-barred the use of arms. The strongest reason for the people to retain their right to keep and bear arms is as a last resort to protect themselves against tyranny in government."

Thomas Jefferson

Traditionally the militia was used to defend the state and to maintain law and order. It was the firm intention of the Founders to allow states to maintain militias, partly to prevent tyranny and to protect the people's rights. The nature of the militia as a legal and political institution is at the heart of the role of the militia in our society.

Belief in an armed militia was firmly rooted in the experiences and political writings of many prominent authorities for hundreds of years before the founding of the U.S. In *The Art of War*, Machiavelli stressed that citizens should be armed. "It is certain that no subjects or citizens, when legally armed and kept in due order by their masters, ever did the least mischief to any State....Rome remained free for 400 years and Sparta for 800, although their citizens were armed all that time; but many other States that have been disarmed have lost their liberties in less than 40 years." James Harrington said: "Men accustomed unto their arms and liberties will never endure the yoke" of tyranny. Montesquieu criticized an Italian state that banned its citizens from bearing arms. William Blackstone, in *Commentaries*, defended the right to bear arms for self-defense as an auxiliary right belonging to the individual.[2] The English Puritans were typical in believing that bearing arms symbolized their freedom. Every colony had militias. Militias were seen as protecting the people against the excesses of British rule; indeed they played a role in several colonial revolts, such as in Virginia. The militia was described as a "school of political democracy."[3]

On March 23, 1775 the Continental Congress said: "That a well regulated Militia, composed of Gentlemen and Yeomen, is the natural strength and only security of a free Government." While there was criticism of the untrained militia during the Revolutionary War, they played a key role in the ultimate victory. The spark that incited the Revolutionary War involved the British trying to seize arsenals used by the minutemen, local militia units.

The excesses of British troops in America along with hundreds of years of similar experiences in England, had created a great fear of a standing army in the colonies. The view of many was expressed in the Virginia Declaration of Rights on June 12, 1776. "Standing armies, in time of peace, should be avoided, as dangerous to liberty...." Citizen militias were considered morally superior to regular standing armies. Anti-federalists attacked the new Constitution partly because standing armies would exist under the federal government. George Mason said: "When once a standing army is established in any country the people lose their liberty."

After the revolution this view changed and many felt a limited standing army was essential. The British controlled Canada, the French were in the West, the Spanish ruled Florida, and the Indians were a constant problem. Many agreed that a standing army was a necessary evil to protect the country but that it must be small and carefully controlled. People's rights could be effectively protected by a republican form of government that protected individual rights.

People like Alexander Hamilton defended the Constitution in 1787 by saying: "Nor can tyranny be introduced into this country by arms....The spirit of the country with arms in their hands and disciplined as a militia, would render it impossible." The state militias and the people's right to bear arms would protect the rights of the people and prevent the federal government from becoming too oppressive. Hamilton also said: "The best we can hope for concerning the people at large is that they be properly armed." George Mason said: "To disarm the people is the best and most effectual way to enslave them."

Patrick Henry said in 1787 during the Constitution debate: "The militia, sir, is our ultimate safety. We can have no security without it....My great objection to this Government is, that it does not leave us the means of defending our rights; or of waging war against tyrants." In 1788 Henry added: "The great object is that every man be armed." Henry was firmly against giving the federal government any control over state militias. James Madison said: "Americans need never fear their government because of the advantage of being armed, which Americans possess over the people of almost every other nation." Crime was another reason why many felt the people should bear arms. John Adams said: "Arms in the hands of individual citizens may be used at individual discretion...in private self defense."

In 1789 the *Philadelphia Federal Gazette*, a prominent newspaper, said "As civil rulers, not having their duty to the people duly before them, may attempt to tyrannize, and as the military forces, which must be occasionally raised to defend our country, might pervert their power to the injury of their fellow citizens, the people are confirmed in their right to keep and bear their private arms." It was widely accepted in the early days of the Republic that all people had a right to bear arms, and this right was not limited to the militia or the common good.[4] The Founding Fathers would have been horrified at how the federal government has taken control of the state militias.

Despite what is now sometimes falsely claimed in the heated gun control debate, a close review of original documents from the colonial period shows that no laws existed which prohibited free citizens from bearing arms. In every state the right of the individual to bear arms was accepted. "Legal articles and judicial opinions which deny that the right to keep and bear arms as a fundamental, personal right have no historical foundation, but rather are based on bare assertion to reach a preconceived result."[5] There was no serious dissent in adopting the Second Amendment.[6] To the Founders there was a close relation between the militia and the right to keep and bear arms. The idea that the Second Amendment guaranteed only a collective, not an individual, right originated in the 20th century.[7]

Most state Constitutions recognized the right to maintain a militia and the right of its citizens to bear arms. The North Carolina Constitution, Article I, Section 30 states: "A well regulated militia being necessary to the security of a free State, the right of the people to keep and bear arms shall not be infringed...." The Founders were absolutely determined that the people could bear arms and the states would maintain their own militias, with little control by the federal government over these militias in order to prevent government tyranny.

The militia clause in the Constitution was of great concern to the antifederalists because they felt greater federal control over the state militias would develop, so the Militia Act of 1792 became law. It was renewed in 1795, with some changes in 1807. The states were exclusively responsible for training and maintaining their militias. The federal government couldn't even offer advise. Except when in federal service, the militia was to be governed by the states.

During the War of 1812 New York, Massachusetts, and Connecticut refused to provide its militias to invade Canada. While a state court supported this position, the Supreme Court in *Martin v. Mott* (1827) ruled that the states should support the president as Commander-in-Chief. Except in a few large cities, there were rarely full-time police officers, so the militia was used at times to assist the sheriff. As Tocqueville said, the entire community often helped catch a criminal. We see a vestige of this today in the movies, when a posse of townspeople gather to catch a criminal.

In 1833 Supreme Court Justice Joseph Story wrote, in his famous book *Commentaries on the Constitution*: "The right of the citizens to keep and bear arms has justly been considered as the palladium of the liberties of a Republic; since it offers a strong moral check against the usurpation and arbitrary powers of rulers and will generally, even if these are successful in the first instance, enable the people to resist and triumph over them."[8] Even after the Civil War this was a common view. In 1894 Charles E. Stevens said, in *Sources of the Constitution of the United States*, the right to bear arms is "a right involving the latent power of resistance to tyrannical government."[9]

In 1861 the Militia Act of 1792 was further changed to make it easier to use federal troops to enforce federal edicts. Troops could now be used in their regular military capacity to resolve local issues. Before this time, troops were used like a posse with "the powers vested in the marshals." Troops were henceforth used like civilians under federal marshals. Of greater importance, federal troops could now be used by the president whenever it became impractical to enforce federal laws through normal judicial proceedings. Previously, under the 1792 Militia Act, military force was restricted to situations where resistance was "too powerful to be suppressed" by civilian authority. This act today stands as Title 10 U.S.C. 332. Engdahl said this broad authority has never been contested, but it could not survive a legal challenge.[10]

The Act of 1871 was even more extreme and may also be found unconstitutional if challenged. In this case, no distinction was made between "insurrection" and "violence, unlawful combination, or conspiracy." In any of these situations military intervention was acceptable, and now military force could be used *before* civilian enforcement of federal laws had been exhausted. This law is now 10 U.S.C. 333, and was used to justify federal use of force in the racial and urban disturbances of the 1960s.

After the Civil War many people criticized the domestic utilization of federal troops, especially with the continued federal occupation of the South. In 1878 the Posse Comitatus Act was passed as a rider to an Army appropriation bill and is today 18 U.S.C. 1385. It states that except, when authorized by Congress or the Constitution, the Army—with the Air Force later added—cannot be used as a posse comitatus to execute the laws. This law blocks U.S. marshals from using federal troops as a posse to enforce federal laws. Violation of this law calls for a fine of up to $10,000 and up to two years imprisonment. Because of congressional tactics used to pass this law, the Navy and Marines are not officially limited under this act, and there have been instances in the war on drugs when Navy personnel have been used domestically. Some feel our Navy functions under admiralty law.[11]

During the Spanish-American War, a state militia wouldn't fight in Cuba, believing the federal government didn't have the right to order it overseas. Some states believed that being sent overseas did not involve suppressing insurrections or repelling invasions, as described in the Constitution under Article I, Section 8, Clause 15.

After 1900 Congress and the courts greatly weakened the rights of the states and the people to maintain control over an armed militia. In 1901 the Army Reorganization Act reorganized the militia and enhanced the process of federalizing state militias. In the Dick Act of 1903 training by regular Army officers at regular Army schools with federal funding was introduced. In addition, the Militia Act of 1792 was repealed, and the militias were divided into the more professional National Guard and the "Reserve Militia," or unenrolled militia. From 1792 to 1903 states controlled the militias in peace, and there was dual state and federal control during war. After 1903 the militia was under dual control in peace and under federal control during a war. Gradually there were no limits to how long the National Guard could be federalized, and the guard could be sent anywhere in the U.S. or overseas. With the National Defense Act of 1916 each member of the National Guard took an oath of allegiance to the federal government as well as to his state. Members of the National Guard could be drafted into the federal military when needed. Under Roosevelt's emergency rule, the 1933 National Defense Act Amendments created the National Guard of the United States with dual enlistment in the state and federal National Guards. National Guard units were considered a reserve of the active military.

Before World War I federal courts rarely ruled on state militias, while the state courts issued some rulings that usually supported the right to bear arms and the right for the states to maintain a militia. In *State v. Kerner* (1921) the North Carolina Supreme Court said that the right to bear arms was "a sacred right based upon the experience of the ages in order that people may be accustomed to bear arms and be ready to use them for protection of their liberties or their country when occasion serves."

In the 1920s and 1930s Congress and the courts took steps to control the private ownership of certain guns to prevent criminal activity. *U.S. v. Warin* (1976) is especially interesting. Warin claimed that the Second Amendment should protect him from taxation because that interfered with his right to bear arms. The court rejected this position and said that only the preferred First Amendment rights were protected against license or taxes. This is a very important point that is rarely discussed. Today the government is increasing taxes in various areas of arms possession to limit the peoples right to possess arms. Ultimately an increasingly oppressive government could impose prohibitively expensive taxes on all our rights guaranteed in the Bill of Rights, so that these rights would become unusable. Government should not be allowed to impose a tax or fee on any of our rights. When this principle is violated with one right, as with the Second Amendment, all our rights are threatened.

In 1986 Maine refused to send its National Guard to an exercise in Honduras. In response, Congress passed the Montgomery Amendment, which removed a governor's right to refuse to allow the National Guard to be called up for training because of objections to location, purpose, schedule, or type of training. When Massachusetts and Minnesota separately challenged the constitutionality of this new law, lower federal courts supported the federal government, as did the Supreme Court. Initially the Eighth Circuit of Appeals found that the militia clause of the Constitution preserved state authority over the National Guard unless "there was some sort of exigency or extraordinary need to exert federal power." However, this court overturned itself. In the Massachusetts case, the lower court said: "The dual enlistment system makes the militia dependent upon Congress for its existence because, in a practical sense at least, the militia exists only when Congress does not want or need it as part of the army."

"The nation has completed a cycle, moving from a wholly state controlled militia system to a militia that, for all intents and purposes, belongs to the federal government, and is under its orders, whenever and however the national government wills and legislates."[12] Once again Congress and the courts have gone radically against the will of the Founders. State control over the militia, as desired by the Founders, has been greatly weakened while federal control has increased. Although normally the National Guard reports to the state governors, in wartime, resistance to federal law and federal court orders, or any declared emergency they are under the Defense Department and the president. Yet the Founding Fathers established the state militias, now the National Guard, to be independent military forces as a protection against government tyranny. Moreover, the militia was considered to include all citizens. Today, the National Guard is a select group separate from the people.

While the federalists and anti-federalist had different views as to the role of a standing army and state militias, none of them wanted the federal government to completely dominate state militias, as is now the case. That the states would control their own militias was understood to be one more protection against future government tyranny. The anti-federalists were quite right to be concerned that the Constitution gave the federal government too much power. If state sovereignty is to be restored, the original state control of the militias must be restored and federal authority over these units must end, except during serious foreign threats.

A good solution would be for the states to take back full control and training of the National Guard, establishing regional centers to provide professional training at lower costs. Equipment from the federal government could be loaned to these regional centers to help maintain training standards. These activities would be completely outside the control of the federal government unless there was a national emergency. There should be no National Guard of the United States, and members of the guard should only take an oath of office to their states according to the intentions of the Founders. Fortunately, while the National Guard is now dominated by the federal government, this is not true with the unenrolled militia.

An excellent recent book that explains the role of militias in American history is *Safeguarding Liberty: The Constitution & Citizen Militias*, edited by Larry Pratt.

## Chapter XIV

## Our Hidden Past:
## History of Martial Law in the U.S.

"I have no reason to suppose, that he, who would take away my Liberty, would not when he had me in his Power, take away every thing else."

John Locke

"A nation can survive its fools, and even the ambitious but it cannot survive treason from within. An enemy at the gates is less formidable, for he is known and he carries his banners openly. But the traitor moves among those within the gate freely."

Cicero

Martial law was declared in the U.S. 30 times between 1789 and 1975. When I scanned hundreds of American history books there was barely a mention of this fact. It is as if the slate has been wiped clean, although when one checks computer on-line services, it is possible to find some articles and books on the subject as suggested by the notes in this chapter. In the law journals there are also articles on martial law in the U.S., although this discussion has decreased in recent years.

Historically, there has been some confusion about the meaning of the term martial law.[1] Martial law is not military rule, which is the rule of a victorious army in an occupied country. Martial law is the use of military forces to control areas where civilian authorities have lost partial or full control, and there is a suppression of some civil agencies.[2] Nationally only the president should declare martial law, while most authorities agree that governors may declare martial law within their states. Our Constitution limits broad use of emergency powers or the suspension of constitutional protections even in emergencies.[3]

Usually only part of a state, such as a city, is placed under martial law. There have been times when troops were used to aid civilian authorities without martial law being declared. This was done partly for political reasons such as during the 1967 Detroit riots. Martial law has also been declared after natural disasters such as in Wilkes-Barre, Pennsylvania in June, 1972 after a flood following Hurricane Agnes.

During the War of 1812 Andrew Jackson declared martial law in New Orleans on December 18, 1814. After the British were defeated, martial law remained in effect despite the growing anger of local citizens until March 13, 1815, when the war ended.[4] In 1842 martial law was declared in Rhode Island during the Dorrs Rebellion. There was a popular movement involving a people's convention in 1841 which elected Thomas Dorr as governor. The incumbent governor called this an insurrection, imposed martial law, and called out the militia.

There was a broad repression of dissent during the Civil War. Lincoln withdrew the use of the mail for various newspapers that criticized the war. In the 1860s this meant that a newspaper couldn't survive. Prominent newspapers, like the *Journal of Commerce* and the *Daily News* in New York, were suppressed with U.S. marshals ordered to seize certain newspapers. Most newspapers reversed their policies and stopped criticizing the war or supported it.

Lincoln also suspended the writ of habeas corpus without congressional approval. On April 27, 1861 Lincoln called on the commanding general of the army to suspend the writ of habeas corpus on the rail corridor between Philadelphia and Washington, D.C. Later, this was extended to the rail corridor between Philadelphia and Maine, all of Kentucky, Maryland, and St. Louis.[5] Military authorities usually refused to free people who had been arrested when shown a writ of habeas corpus stating that no civilian court had authority over prisoners of war. When Congress asked for information about the arrests, Lincoln said it was not in the public interest to furnish the information. Constitutional safeguards to protect individual liberties were ignored.

Lincoln also sent troops into war without a congressional declaration of war saying it was a domestic insurrection so no congressional authority was necessary. While Lincoln saved the Union, the general public and many historians have largely forgotten or have forgiven his repressive measures. A more balanced approach to his presidency would bring more criticism of his emergency actions that were often not necessary or legal under the Constitution.

In *Ex parte Milligan* (1866) the Supreme Court held that in the absence of actual invasion, martial law and the military trial of civilians was illegal while civil processes were unobstructed and the courts in session. "The Constitution of the U.S. is a law for rulers and people, equally in war and in peace, and covers with the shield of its protection all classes of men, at all times, and under all circumstances....Martial law cannot arise from a threatened invasion. The necessity must be actual and present; the invasion real, such as effectually closes the courts and deposes the civil administration." However, the Supreme Court did not question the suspension of the writ of habeas corpus during the war or the arrest of civilians without charge.

Similar activities were executed in the South, but Jefferson Davis never declared martial law or suspended the writ of habeas corpus without his legislature's consent. Davis was less assertive of executive authority than Lincoln, and when he did exercise this power it was less obviously political and the order was less sweeping. Davis declared martial law in Norfolk and Portsmouth, Virginia on February 27, 1862. Three days later this was expanded to Richmond. Later martial law was declared by Davis or local military commanders in other parts of Virginia, east Tennessee, Memphis, Mobile, New Orleans, Atlanta, Salisbury, N.C., all of Texas and Arkansas, and parts of Louisiana and Mississippi.[6]

The North was especially aggressive in controlling the border states. On August 30, 1861 General Fremont declared martial law throughout Missouri.[7] Governor Morton declared martial law and acted with virtual dictatorship powers in Indiana between 1863 and 1865, after the Democratic-controlled state legislature refused to enact war measures.[8]

On September 24, 1862 Lincoln declared martial law and suspended the writ of habeas corpus throughout the nation. While the exact geographical territory of this proclamation was not outlined "the categories of offenses were vague enough,

## No. 51.

Dec. 1, 1865.
Preamble.

BY THE PRESIDENT OF THE UNITED STATES OF AMERICA:

# A PROCLAMATION.

*Ante,* p. 734.

WHEREAS, by the Proclamation of the President of the United States, of the fifteenth day of September, one thousand eight hundred and sixty-three, the privilege of the writ of habeas corpus was, in certain cases therein set forth, suspended throughout the United States;

And whereas the reasons for that suspension may be regarded as having ceased in some of the states and territories:

Suspension of the writ of habeas corpus, &c., revoked, except in certain states and territories, and the District of Columbia.

Now therefore be it known, that I, ANDREW JOHNSON, President of the United States, do hereby proclaim and declare, that the suspension aforesaid and all other proclamations and orders suspending the privilege of the writ of habeas corpus in the states and territories of the United States, are revoked and annulled, excepting as to the States of Virginia, Kentucky, Tennessee, North Carolina, South Carolina, Georgia, Florida, Alabama, Mississippi, Louisiana, Arkansas, and Texas, the District of Columbia, and the Territories of New Mexico and Arizona.

In witness whereof, I have hereunto set my hand, and caused the seal of the United States to be affixed.

Done at the city of Washington, this first day of December, in the year [L. S.] of our Lord one thousand eight hundred and sixty-five, and of the Independence of the United States of America the ninetieth.

ANDREW JOHNSON.

By the President:

WILLIAM H. SEWARD, *Secretary of State.*

in effect, to have placed the whole of the U.S. under martial law."[9] Later use of this proclamation confirms this. Throughout the North upwards of 38,000 people were arrested for treason and helping the enemy. People who discouraged enlistments or engaged in disloyal practices were arrested.

On December 1, 1865 President Andrew Johnson issued Proclamation number 51 ending the suspension of the writ of habeas corpus except in certain southern states, the District of Columbia, and the territories of New Mexico and Arizona. This proclamation did not even discuss martial law, and restoring the writ of habeas corpus did not end martial law. In the law libraries there are several systems and databases whereby you can check to see what changes took place over the years with various government edicts. There is no evidence that Lincoln's proclamation of martial law was ever lifted.

Charles Fairman said, in *The Law of Martial Law,* while there is a close relation between martial law and the writ of habeas corpus, there are also important differences.[10] Professor Joel Parker of Harvard Law School said: "The existence of martial law and the suspension of the habeas corpus have been said to be one and the same thing; but in fact the former includes the latter and much more." James G. Randall said regarding the actions of the government during the Civil War: "The suspension of the habeas corpus privilege did not, of itself, institute martial law."[11] Under martial law the loss of many rights such as assembly, curfew, and search and seizure of weapons typically takes place. These activities do not automatically have any relationship to the writ of habeas corpus. Suspension of habeas corpus during martial law may take place, but this is not automatic and loss of this right is but one manifestation of martial law. In addition, when the writ of habeas corpus is suspended this does not necessarily mean that martial law is established. The civil courts may still be in operation. There have, in fact, been instances when martial law was declared and upheld by the courts with habeas corpus not suspended.

*Black's Law Dictionary* clearly defines differences between habeas corpus and martial law.[12] It is unlikely that people would have just forgotten to remove the martial law that Lincoln established. I hope some group will take legal action to end the martial law of the Civil War, and people should demand action by Congress. If martial law from the Civil War is still in place, as appears to be the case, this is a dagger pointing at the heart of the people. People should not be fooled into thinking that the continued existence of martial law could not be used to violate the Constitution. Hitler was not alone in using existing laws to seize power. The continued state of martial law in the U.S. from the Civil War is one more tool the secret government could use to control the government, especially in a fabricated emergency.

The Feed and Forage Act of 1861, a Civil War emergency act, allowed the cavalry to purchase feed for its horses when Congress wasn't in session. *This act was used during the Vietnam War to spend millions of dollars without congressional approval.* An emergency law passed over 100 years ago was used to get around congressional spending authority. Here we see the dangers of emergency powers becoming law and remaining in place indefinitely.

Common use of the U.S. flag with yellow fringe around it in the courts is another sign that the U.S. is still under martial law. Such a flag is historically used by military troops. Army regulations 260-10 and 840-10 provide for using this flag. In a March 28, 1924 circular the Army Adjutant General said: "Ancient custom sanctions the use of fringe on the regimental colors and standards, but there seems to be no good reason or precedent for its use on other flags." Under 4 USC 1, the U.S. flag should include 13 horizontal stripes, alternating red and white with 50 white stars on a blue field. In *State of Minnesota v. Randolph C. Miller* (1995) when Miller filed a motion to replace the unconstitutional yellow-fringed U.S. flag the judge did this. Miller said this flag "signifies that tribunals conducted under such standards are under military law, and that the Constitution is suspended."

After the Civil War martial law was used fairly often especially in the West, including in parts of Idaho (1899), Pennsylvania (1902), and Colorado (1903-1904). Many of these situations involved labor and mining conflicts. Fairman said in the West "martial law has been proclaimed on so many occasions as to have become a household word."[13]

Martial law was declared by state governors for political purposes in Oklahoma (1935), South Carolina (1935), Arizona (1935), Rhode Island (1937), Tennessee (1939), and Georgia (1940). This was done based on *Moyer v. Peabody*

(1909) when the Supreme Court strongly supported the governors' right to declare martial law and limited the courts' right to challenge state governors. Rhode Island used martial law to stop horse racing. The governors often mobilized the National Guard although there was no violence or threat of violence. Weiner called these cases bogus martial law situations.[14] In *Sterling v. Constantin* (1932) the Supreme Court curbed the excessive use of martial law by state governors, limiting the application of *Moyer v. Peabody,* stating that governors could only declare martial law when there was actual violence. The Supreme Court also reaffirmed the Milligan rule that courts have the power to review martial law declarations.

Immediately after Pearl Harbor was attacked, the governor of Hawaii declared martial law, suspended the writ of habeas corpus, closed the civilian courts and invited the military authorities to take command, which they did. That was declared unconstitutional by the Supreme Court in *Duncan v. Kahanamo Ku* (1946). Here the court went beyond upholding the doctrine of judicial review for martial law and declared military trials of nonmilitary personnel as unlawful. Also, the court said the governor did not have the authority to close the civilian courts.

Martial law was declared 10 times between 1945 and 1969. Its most prominent use was to protect the civil rights of black Americans as in Little Rock, Arkansas (1957), Oxford, Mississippi (1962), and Selma, Alabama (1965). Often the state National Guard was federalized to enforce federal court orders. In 1968 martial law was also used to disperse marchers in Washington, D.C. Many were arrested, The courts ordered the government to pay large fines for this misuse of authority.

Some legal authorities have called for more carefully drafted emergency power legislation to protect people's civil rights.[15] While the courts have said that martial law can be declared during an emergency, exactly what would be an "emergency" and what steps can be taken have never been fully defined by the courts.[16] Present laws and cases concerning emergency executive powers do not provide the executive with standards to examine the legality of establishing martial law in domestic violence.

There are many other topics that can be discussed regarding martial law, but that would go beyond the scope of this book. An excellent booklet, published in 1982, is *The Use of Troops in Civil Disturbances in the United States*, by A. Kenneth Pye. This 42 page booklet has 154 footnotes which review the many debates and ramifications of martial law, as well as the important law journal articles and books on this topic up to 1982. Little has been published on this topic since then.

# Chapter XV

# Martial Law and Emergency Rule Today

"The essence of government is power, and power, lodged as it must be in human hands, will ever be liable to abuse."

James Madison

"Government is not reason; it's not eloquence; it is force. Like fire, it's a dangerous servant and a fearful master."

George Washington

The objective observer will appreciate that, if there are plans to establish martial law in the U.S., some preliminary work must be done to prepare for this. A few people cannot do the work and then expect thousands of people in law enforcement to carry out the plans. Certain people in government must learn something about these plans in advance, if these activities are ultimately to be activated. With the democratic traditions of our country there are many people in the government who do stand by the Constitution. It only takes a handful of such people to become horrified by these plans when they learn of them. This is partly why various plans for martial law in America have been leaked over the years.

According to documents released by the Freedom of Information Act (FOIA) martial law could be established during peace if there was "a complete breakdown in the exercise of government functions by local civilian authorities," reported the Defense Department. In 1971 David Packard, the Deputy Secretary of Defense, prepared a document "Employment of Military Resources in the Event of Civil Disturbances" that justified military control similar to martial law. This directive claims that Congress intended that there be two exceptions to the Posse Comitatus Act, which bars the Army and Air Force from engaging in domestic law enforcement. The exceptions are to restore public order when sudden and unexpected civil disturbances endanger life and property, disrupt normal governmental functions, and local officials cannot control the situation. Second, the military would step in when there is a need to protect federal property and federal government functions. Such loopholes make a farce of the Posse Comitatus Act. It was also claimed that for the military to step in a Presidential Executive Order would normally be needed, but this could be waived with "cases of sudden and unexpected emergencies which require that immediate military action be taken."[1]

In September, 1975 the Senate Subcommittee on Constitutional Rights was told by the director of the Federal Preparedness Agency (FPA), predecessor to the Federal Emergency Management Agency (FEMA), that he couldn't tell them about the activities at Mount Weather or any similar command/relocation centers. Congress didn't have a right to this information. *The Progressive* said this is "an actual government-in-waiting," and there were about 100 similar centers in the

1970s.[2] Mount Weather was established as the backup capital of the shadow government ready to take control in an emergency. Various federal agencies are represented here. In June, 1975 Senator John Tunney said the base held dossiers on at least 100,000 Americans and it was "out of control." The base reportedly has broad surveillance facilities in place. Senator James Abourezk said the entire operation lacked supervision from the courts or Congress, and there was no public mandate or charter for this base to operate under.

This emergency government was prepared to take over during the Vietnam War disturbances. Its internal reports recognize that during political unrest it may need to step in. This facility even published its own reports and recommendations on various national issues. In 1969 Nixon signed Executive Order (EO) 11490 allowing Mount Weather and the FPA to take over the country when the president proclaimed a national emergency. Exactly what such a national emergency would be is not defined, which is part of the danger. This EO was amended in 1979 to reflect the creation of FEMA. Little has changed today except that these secret bases are now part of FEMA.

In 1981 FEMA drafted emergency legislation called the Defense Resources Act, which was given to Congress in 1983. This act empowered FEMA to censor international communications, limit employment in areas of the national interest, condemn or seize property, and require loyalty oaths.[3] In a 1981 Defense Directive, Deputy Secretary of Defense Frank Carlucci said martial law would probably be declared by the president, but senior military commanders also have the power to invoke it in the absence of a presidential order.[4]

FEMA continues to gather data from other intelligence agencies and monitor political dissent, because peaceful protesters are considered potential terrorists. In 1983 the Senate Intelligence Committee heard that FEMA was conducting domestic intelligence operations but this was denied. However, FEMA has monitored the activities of many political groups, such as the Livermore Action Group in California.[5] In October, 1984 columnist Jack Anderson said FEMA had "standby legislation" that in a national emergency would "suspend the Constitution and the Bill of Rights, effectively eliminate private property, abolish free enterprise, and generally clamp Americans in a totalitarian vise."

Martial law might be declared during a nuclear emergency. On June 16, 1955 during exercise "Operation Alert 1955" President Eisenhower appears to have declared limited martial law. This exercise presupposed that the U.S. had been attacked by nuclear weapons. Hearings on this exercise were held by a House Subcommittee, although few people were aware of this. Reportedly "Unless the role and responsibility of State and local governments in both preattack and postattack civil defense functions is made clear...the entire burden of civil defense threatens to devolve by default to the Federal Government." In 1956 General Maxwell D. Taylor, Army Chief of Staff, told Congress the Army was ready to take control during an atomic attack if the president declared martial law, but "it has very little enthusiasm" for such a role.[6]

The Bay Area Lawyers Alliance for Nuclear Arms Control sued FEMA in the early 1980s to obtain plans concerning martial law and the government's response to nuclear war. One FEMA document titled "Martial Law" obtained through the FOIA described martial law as the suspension of "all prior existing laws, functions, systems and programs of civil government." There were no plans for lifting martial law once it was established. According to released documents FEMA has

22 secret EOs that the president may approve during a nuclear war. In addition, the National Security Council and the Emergency Mobilization Preparedness Board have many secret documents regarding how to respond to national emergencies. FEMA said many documents couldn't be released because of national security.[7] The public has no say in these matters.

In *Blank Check*, Tim Weiner said in DEFCON 1, the highest state of military alert when nuclear war is imminent or may have already begun, the nation is automatically placed under martial law.[8] Normally, U.S. forces are at DEFCON 4 or 5. Obviously nuclear war and modern warfare are extremely serious and require a rapid response, but the declaration of martial law in a high state of military alert perhaps without even a nuclear war actually starting has never been discussed openly in Congress, much less in the press so the people can reflect on these issues. Instead secret plans are made, and false excuses can be used to declare a national emergency and martial law, which could then be used as an excuse to disarm the people. In DEFCON 1 it would be difficult for soldiers and the people to start raising questions. Bruce G. Blair said in certain cases, local commanders have "independent authority" to take steps associated with DEFCON 1, 2 or 3 without first consulting the Joint Chiefs.[9]

Certain officials of the Reagan White House from the start of that regime ran a parallel secret government beyond the control or even knowledge of cabinet officials and federal agencies.[10] While some of these activities were discussed during the Iran-contra hearings, the activities of this secret government extended well beyond that arms deal. During the Iran-contra hearings, the head counsel for the Senate investigating committee, Arthur Liman, said there was a "secret government within a government." According to the *Miami Herald*, Oliver North and the National Security Council worked closely with FEMA to promote the secret government.[11] William Casey, head of the CIA, also conducted covert operations without proper congressional oversight.

In 1984 Knight Rider, a prominent news service, published information about RX 84, a plot to suspend the Constitution and put over 100,000 illegal immigrants and political prisoners into concentration camps. Some reports said over 400,000 people were going to be arrested with martial law declared during a national emergency which was not even clearly defined but which supposedly could include arresting dissidents during widespread political protests, nuclear war, or a foreign invasion. During this period the U.S. considered invading Nicaragua and there was concern about how people would react. The *Miami Herald* said the plot called for FEMA to take control of the nation and for military commanders to control state and local governments during a national emergency. According to papers obtained from the FOIA, FEMA conducted training exercise REX Alpha 84 and Night Train 84 on April 5-13, 1984, which called for detaining illegal aliens in military camps. President Reagan approved this exercise by signing National Security Decision Directive 52. The *Miami Herald* obtained a FEMA memo describing the exercise, which stated that the Alpha Two part of the exercise called for activating "emergency legislation, assumption of emergency powers...." Exactly what this emergency legislation is remains a secret.

According to congressional sources, the plot to declare martial law was part of a secret EO prepared by Reagan in May, 1984, that would be used during an emergency. Authority to declare martial law was also based on the Defense Resources Act which was to serve as standby legislation during a national emergency. If enacted this act would give a president broad powers equivalent to martial law.[12] In September, 1984 the *Washington Post* said Attorney General William French, in an August 2 letter to presidential aide Robert McFarlane, accused FEMA of trying to so increase its power that it would be an "emergency czar."[13] Perhaps French was also concerned about the plans for martial law.

The martial law part of the plot was described in a June 30, 1982 letter by John Brinkerhoff, a deputy to Louis O. Giuffrida, the director of FEMA under Reagan (1981-1985). The *Miami Herald* obtained a copy of this letter. The memo said that martial law means the suspension of all prior existing laws.[14] Louis O. Giuffrida had in 1970 prepared plans to place black radicals in detention camps.[15] He called for martial law if there was a national uprising of black militants with at least 21 million "American Negroes" being placed in "assembly centers or relocation camps."

We should all reflect on the number 21 million. Whenever a dictatorship is established, there are always various factions, and one can never be certain in advance exactly who will gain the upper hand. There are few blacks in the ruling elite, and it is very chilling that a fanatic like Giuffrida was placed in charge of FEMA, which would control the government during a national emergency. With the ruling elite having concluded that the world population must be radically diminished for life to survive on this planet, what would happen to many minorities if the one world dictatorship took hold?

In 1967 a novel *The Man Who Cried I Am*, was written by John Williams. The protagonist in the book discovered the King Alfred Plan which called for the arrest and extermination of all American blacks in a national emergency. Remember this was during many civil rights riots. Reportedly, Williams considered the plan real but could only get it published in a novel. As typically happens whenever horrific secret plans are released, many sources claimed they are false. Objectively there is no definite proof as to the validity or falsity of this plan. An almost identical version of this plan was leaked to various researchers after the book came out and a reliable source told Mae Brussel the plan was real. A plan by this name was in an Ohio prison system computer, and Dave Emory also believes this plan is probably true.

During the Iran-contra hearings, Oliver North was asked by Rep. Jack Brooks about plans for FEMA to suspend the Constitution and establish martial law. Senator Inouye, chairman of the Senate Iran-contra Committee quickly intervened, so North didn't have to publicly respond. What could be a worse threat to the survival of the Republic than to suppress information about a plot to remove the Constitution and establish a dictatorship. If ever there was news that should have been heard this was it. No one in government would investigate this plot and only a few in the press would even discuss it. Senator Inouye said this was "a secret government—a shadow government...(with) its own fund-raising mechanism, and the ability to pursue its own ideas of the national interest, free from all checks and balances and free from the law itself." Yet he refused to heed his own warning.

After this discussion Rep. Gonzalez gave an interview in which he said: "Tragically Rep. Brooks had been stopped by the chairman (Inouye). The truth of the matter is that you do have those standby provisions, and the statutory emergency plans are there whereby you could, in the name of stopping terrorism, apprehend, invoke the military, and arrest Americans and hold them in detention camps." The historian, Theodore Draper, said about the Iran-contra hearings: "If ever the constitutional democracy of the U.S. is overthrown, we now have a better idea of how this is likely to be done." People in the Patriot movement and militias understand this.

Much about FEMA remains secret. Even directors of FEMA aren't told about certain classified programs. Under Bush, when the House wanted to learn how certain FEMA funds were being spent, the director admitted he didn't know, and when Congress pushed the issue the political leadership declared national security and the budget was passed. It is remarkable how these two words keep Congress from fulfilling its constitutional duties.[16] According to one congressional report only 10 percent of FEMA employees are involved in disaster relief.

Several years ago, FEMA did such a poor job during many natural disasters because it exists to monitor people not to help during emergencies. For years FEMA refused to take some of its sophisticated communications equipment to disaster relief areas to keep its assets secret. According to the National Academy of Public Administration, 27 percent ($100 million) of FEMA's 1993 budget, without including the disaster-relief fund, went into a secret "black budget." On September 6, 1994 Clinton appointed George J. Opfer, a 25-year veteran of the Secret Service, inspector general of FEMA. If FEMA's main purpose is to assist in natural disasters, why is he from law enforcement? Clinton appointed James Witt as head of FEMA. He is described as the first head of FEMA with emergency management experience. Why is this the case if FEMA's main goal is to provide emergency relief?

In 1984 Secretary of State George Shultz lobbied vigorously for a preemptive strikes bill that would give him authority to list "known and suspected terrorists" within the U.S., who could be attacked and killed by government agents with impunity. Shultz admitted in a public address on October 25, 1984 that the strikes would take place based on information that would never stand up in court, and that innocent people would be killed in the process. He insisted, however, that people listed would not be permitted to sue in court to have their names taken off that list. Attorney General Meese said arrested people would be considered guilty until proven otherwise.[17] The *New York Times* said this bill was identical to Hitler's "Night and Fog" program.

In 1985 and 1987 the *San Francisco Bay Guardian* described the "Garden Plot," a secret plan developed in the 1960s to suspend the Constitution and declare martial law during an emergency. President Johnson had this plan developed after the Detroit riots to crush political dissent. Senator Sam Ervin discovered in the early 1970s that these plans included files on 18,000 Americans. Details of the plan were released under the FOIA by the Western States Legal Foundation.[18] On March 13, 1989 *Newsweek* said it may be time to have martial law because of crime and drugs. According to the article there are many calls for this, which was an obvious lie.[19] Was this article a trial balloon to see how people would respond?

On February 22, 1990 Rep. Newt Gingrich introduced H.R. 4079 that would have destroyed the Bill of Rights. This bill called for a declaration of a national drug and crime emergency with detention centers established in unused military facilities for violent criminals and drug offenders. Anyone even threatening to use force to protect himself or his property could be arrested. Under the broad language of the bill, thousands of political dissenters could have been arrested, because people could be arrested without clear evidence of criminal activity. The minimum sentence was to be five years and people's property could also have been seized.

The national press rarely discussed this bill and its implications. According to a 1994 *Time* article, Gingrich wanted to build stockades on military bases to house prisoners.[20] He hasn't given up yet.

In the Senate, Phil Gramm introduced S 2245, a similar bill. Read these bills and you will appreciate how dangerous Gramm and Gingrich are. Gramm speaks for the moneyed interests, which is why by early 1995, he had raised more money than anyone else ever had by that early date for a presidential campaign. Gramm showed his real nature when he single-handedly blocked a bill to tighten the law on becoming a registered financial adviser. The House unanimously passed the bill, and the Senate agreed to a weakened version to please Gramm. This bill would have made it easier to prevent convicted felons and incompetents from becoming financial advisers. The $16 million required to finance the bill would have only come from fees levied on financial advisers.[21] From illegally taking money from corporations in 1984 (151 contributions in all) to illegally using his staff for campaigning, Gramm is one of the most corrupt people in Washington.[22] Two hundred years ago, if congressmen proposed suspending the Constitution they would have been run out of town or would have been arrested for treason. Today we make one a speaker of the House and the other a presidential contender. When you control the media and money you can convince people of anything!

On July 9, 1990, six members of a U.S. Army intelligence unit went AWOL in West Germany. There was a worldwide high security alert to arrest them, and in mid-July they were arrested in Gulf Breeze. This small Florida town has for several years been the location of great UFO activity with some press coverage. The local police were told not to interrogate them, and they were allowed no outside contact. The national media completely distorted what they were doing and saying. For instance, few reported that they warned about an imminent war in the Middle East. Strangely, 21 days after being arrested, and after the Gulf War started, they were released with a general discharged.

Recently one of the six men, Vance Davis, has gone public, saying they fled the Army because, as members of an intelligence unit, they had been shown above top secret documents stating that covert elements within the military planned to establish a "Multi-Jurisdictional Task Force (MJTF)" that would restore law and order by changing the U.S. Constitution and replacing the FBI, National Guard, FDA, and IRS with a National Police Force called the Black Guard. They were also shown much information about UFOs, a high-level cover-up, and the arrival of aliens.

Starting in 1992 the National Guard, with the agreement of Governor Pedro Rossello, was used to stop crime and drug use in Puerto Rico. According to the Associated Press, "It is the first time American military units have been pressed into routine crime-fighting service with police." Rafael Albarran, a political scientist in Puerto Rico said: "The government is legitimizing military intervention within civil society." The guard were posted at 50 housing projects with barbed wire fences, and they monitored who entered and left these dwellings. These projects looked like war zones with heavily armed troops, helicopters, and armored personnel carriers. There have been numerous unlawful searches and seizures and many security cameras have been installed. In one incident a 14-year old girl was killed by a stray bullet, when residents thought undercover police were from a gang. Nothing like killing a child to protect her! The *Washington Post* reported on these events June 30, 1994, saying there have been many civil rights violations.[23]

There was little other national coverage of these events, which set a dangerous precedent. In 1993 the mayor of Washington, D.C. tried to use the National Guard to fight crime.

On May 10, 1994, 300 marines at the Twenty-nine Palms Marine Corps base were asked by a U.S. Navy officer to fill out a Combat Arms Survey, which in-cluded questions asking if they would swear allegiance to the UN and fire on Americans who resisted federal gun confiscation. Questions included: Number 39: "I feel the President of the U.S. has the authority to pass his responsibilities as Commander in Chief to the UN Secretary-General. I am a UN fighting person." Number 40: "I feel there is no conflict between my oath of office and serving as a UN soldier." Number 44: "I would like UN member countries, including the U.S., to give the UN all the soldiers necessary to maintain world peace." Number 45: I am a UN fighting person and am prepared "to give my life" to maintain "every nation's way of life." Number 46 states that the U.S. government bans all non-sporting firearms with a 30 day amnesty period. After 30 days, if U.S. citizens refuse to surrender their weapons the survey asks: "I would fire upon U.S. citizens who refuse or resist confiscation of firearms banned by the U.S. government."

Lt. Commander Guy Cunningham who gave this survey was interviewed in *Fishing and Hunting News*. He said: "The importance of my survey is going to have to be addressed on higher levels." This survey was reportedly conducted to see how Marines would act in non-traditional roles in military and civilian circum-stances. Are we supposedly to be comforted by the implication that if U.S. troops kill Americans who refuse to surrender their arms, it would be a non-traditional role!

The Department of Navy and Defense Department said this survey was part of a master's thesis and was not official government policy. They claimed it was only given to troops at one military base, but it was given to troops on many bases. *Modern Gun* magazine February, 1994 reported this survey or one very like it was given to elite Navy Seal units in September and October, 1993. About 80 percent of the soldiers are answering no to the question of killing American citi-zens who refuse to give up their guns. Reportedly, at least some of those who answered yes are receiving special treatment and reassignment. The March, 1994 Twenty-nine Palms base newspaper had a photo and report that members of the Council on Foreign Relations (CFR) visited the base and received a high-level tour. While I am not aware of evidence linking the CFR visit to this survey being given out a few months later, the timing is certainly suspicious because of CFR goals.

This survey created an uproar and actually backfired, in that it alerted thou-sands of troops and several million Americans to the fact that something very wrong is taking place. American troops should never under any circumstances be asked such outrageous questions. This survey has been widely discussed in certain publications such as the *American Legion Magazine* (November, 1994) and *Soldier of Fortune* (November, 1994 and August, 1995), on talk radio, and com-puter bulletin boards. Naturally, the national media won't discuss this. Despite what the military states it continues to ask soldiers strange questions. A 1996 Army Survey asks in question 30 if soldiers will agree to be part of a UN peace keeping/peace to be sent wherever needed?

Rep. Bob Dornan wanted to conduct a congressional investigation into the survey's origins and intentions, but the House leadership blocked this. In an

August 30, 1994 letter to Rep. Dornan, C.W. Hoffman, Jr., Staff Advocate for the Twenty-nine Palms Marine Corps base said the survey "did not in any way reflect official U.S. Marine Corps or U.S. Government policy" but that "the survey did consist of 46 questions regarding a variety of possible unconventional missions." This appears to be an admission that U.S. Marines may possibly be ordered to swear an oath of loyalty to the UN and to fire on American civilians who refuse to surrender their arms.

If you are in the military or law enforcement, carefully consider the implications of this survey. What will you do if you are ordered to kill Americans who refuse to give up their weapons? What will you do if ordered to kill peaceful Americans for any reason? What action will you take against those who would give such treasonous orders? Is your first duty and responsibility to the people and the Constitution, or to a corporate ruling elite that looks upon you with contempt. If you are in the military, you have a duty to not carry out unlawful or unconstitutional orders. Under the Manual For Courts-Martial (MCM) Paragraphs 169b, 171a, and 216d: "A general order or regulation is lawful unless it is contrary to the Constitution, the laws of the U.S...." Even though certain orders have an inference of legality, they must still be lawful to be enforceable. An act performed "pursuant to an order that a man of ordinary sense and understanding would know to be illegal" is unlawful. Robert S. Rivkin said in *The Rights of Servicemen* you should disobey certain orders, like committing war crimes. Duress is no defense unless it can be proved that you would have suffered immediate death or serious bodily harm if you refused to obey the order.[24] Anyone in law enforcement or the military who kills Americans under a phony martial law will also face the rage of the people.

The Navy admitted the idea for the questions in the survey came partly from Presidential Review Directives (PRD) 13 and 25 about creating "a U.S. military force structure whose command and control would include the UN." This is false in that PRD 13 and PRD 25 allow for U.S. forces to serve under, not alongside, the UN command. Under PRD 13 "U.S. commanders under UN command did not have to comply with orders which they believe are: (1) outside the mandate of the mission, (2) illegal under U.S. law, or (3) militarily imprudent or unsound." These limitations put into place by General Colin Powell, were removed with PRD 25, which was issued by Clinton May 3, 1994 after Powell had retired. Rep. Bob Dornan informed me that he and Rep. Doolittle introduced H.R. 3334 to strictly limit instances when U.S. forces could serve under foreign command. Rep. Jim Lightfoot and others tried to get PRD 25 fully declassified. Under the summary version of PRD 25 that was released, in certain circumstances including emergencies "the U.S. will agree to have a UN commander exercise overall operational control over U.S. forces." Clifford Bernath, Assistant to the Secretary of Defense, also said in responding to questions about reports of foreign troops in the U.S. "On a case by case basis, the president will consider placing appropriate U.S. forces under the operational control of a competent UN commander for specific UN operations authorized by the Security Council...." However, transferring control of the U.S. military to the UN is treason. On June 9, 1994 Rep. Mitchell tried to get this secret law declassified and reviewed by Congress. This was a rare instance when Congress tried and failed to get one of these secret edicts released. America is a country where secret laws are created by the president and Congress cannot even see them. This is not constitutional government.[25]

In August, 1995 Michael New, an Army medic stationed in Germany, refused an order to wear UN ensignias on his uniform when his unit was sent to Macedonia under the UN because it was not a lawful order. When New asked Army officers how his status would change if he wore UN insignias they refused to answer him. New said "I swore allegiance to my country not the UN," and he received thousands of letters of support. New's unit in Macedonia serves under a foreign officer and it surrendered their U.S. Army identification cards for UN identity cards. While the Geneva convention provides some protection to U.S. troops when taken prisoner this is not true for UN troops. Moreover, wearing UN emblems is not allowed under U.S. Army regulation 670-1.[26] New was court martialed in January, 1996 and found guilty of refusing to follow a lawful order to wear UN insignias and serve under the UN in Macadonia, but the case is under appeal in the U.S. District Court in Washington, D.C. Other soldiers have also publicly supported New. Army Sergeant First Class Edward Rasor held a news conference November 9, 1995 in Washington, D.C. and announced that he wouldn't serve under the UN or wear a UN uniform.

On October 6, 1995, Rep. David Funderburk sent a letter to Clinton with the support of over 20 other representatives complaining about placing U.S. troops under UN command and the persecution of New. As noted in this letter, placing U.S. troops under the UN violates the Constitution and a president has no authority to do this. Rep. Tom Delay has introduced H.R. 2540 with 70 co-sponsors, and Senator Craig has introduced S 1370 with 24 co-sponsors which amends title 10 and prohibits members of the armed forces from wearing UN insignias. While this is a good first step, Congress does not accept that the New case really involves a direct threat to U.S. sovereignty. U.S. troops should never serve under a foreign entity.

On October 5, 1994 the House passed H.R. 4922, the Digital Telephone and Privacy Improvement Act, also called the Wiretap Access Bill. On October 7, 1994 at 10:30 p.m. S. 2375 an identical bill passed by unanimous consent in the Senate. There was no floor debate in either House. By a unanimous consent vote, not one senator actually voted for the bill which gives them cover to deny responsibility for this un-Constitutional act. H.R. 4922 was introduced by Rep. Henry Hyde and S 2375 by Senator Patrick Leahy. Under Senate rules, one senator could have blocked the bill, but the few senators who expressed interest in doing this were visited by FBI Director Louis Freeh who convinced them to not stop the bill. Freeh said, "My real objective is to get access to the contents of telephone calls." A federal official expressed concern about "too much privacy in the wrong hands." The National Security Agency (NSA) also played a key role in promoting and getting this bill passed.[27]

Under this law remote-activated equipment is being used to instantly record phone conversations, faxes, and computer bulletin board messages. Even local phone companies have no idea whose phone calls are being recorded, because encryption is used. With this new law, the government will be able to tell instantly who you call and who is calling you. Supposedly this new law was needed because new technology such as fiber optics and digital switches made it harder to wiretap conversations. Some of the equipment required for this new law was reportedly installed in 1992, and the cost to taxpayers is $500 million, although it remains to be seen if Congress will actually grant this money. Phone company executives are upset because, if Congress refuses to allot the money to pay for the equipment needed to carry out this program, user fees will be increased and the public will get very angry. Hopefully, there will be legal challenges to this law. Since the equipment of private phone companies is being used, they may be liable.

Passage of the wiretap bill means there will be conspiracy trials based on conversations. People will be blackmailed by federal agents to stop legal political activities those in power don't like. As internal FBI documents revealed in the Earth First case, federal authorities are tapping thousands of conversations just because people called groups the Feds don't like. This bill was passed partly to give political cover to the national security state. It legalized what has continued for years. The massive electronic surveillance revealed in the 1970s never stopped. Aside from the activities of the FBI and CIA, NSA intercepts and monitors most forms of communication, and there are no public laws defining or limiting its authority. It has "spent a great deal of time and money spying on American citizens. For twenty-one years after its inception (1952) it tracked every telegram and telex in and out of the U.S., and monitored the telephone conversations of the politically suspect."[28] According to the Electronic Privacy Information Center there were 98,000 wiretaps in 1993.

The book, *The Secret War Against the Jews*, documents the massive wiretap program that has continued for years.[29] The authors said: "No citizen is safe anymore. Privacy is gone, search warrants are meaningless, the protections of the courts and constitutions have been overthrown entirely, without the knowledge or consent of our legislatures, presidents...." A second source revealing this criminality is *The Puzzle Palace*, by James Bamford. He said NSA has over the years wiretapped conversations of congressmen taking money from foreign governments and accepting bribes to sell their votes.[30] This enables the intelligence community to blackmail Congress.

During World War II the British were allowed to wiretap Americans, and to get around U.S. laws a sham was created so British officers at U.S. bases could ask for wiretap information on thousands of U.S. citizens. Thus supposedly, no U.S. agencies were doing the actual wiretap so no U.S. laws were broken. For instance, the 1978 Foreign Intelligence Surveillance Act limits U.S. intelligence agencies in domestic intelligence, but it places no limits on the activities of foreign intelligence activities in the U.S. Thus the massive U.S. wiretap program continued, supposedly under the leadership of British intelligence agents. Behind the scenes, British intelligence agents have been extremely active in America for much of this century. This farce continues today and is also used with Canada and Australia. Initially these wiretaps were conducted against Jews and Nazi sympathizers, but the program gradually extended to all Americans. This information was leaked by disgruntled agents partly because the wiretap program has gotten so ridiculous. Jewish children calling home from summer camps are wiretapped.

Grant Jeffrey, in the *Final Warning*, presents information that the government is monitoring all phone conversations in the U.S. with Cray super-computers. With certain people the conversations are targeted so that if specific words are used individuals then play back that discussion. The government can also download any computer as was done with the spy Richard Ames.

A clue to the vast wiretapping now taking place was revealed in October, 1995 when the FBI petitioned to wiretap up to one in every 100 phones. The objective was to simultaneously wiretap 1.5 million lines. The government could then intercept tens of thousands of calls at once. Phone company executives were shocked, because they have never seen the FBI monitor more than seven phones at once in the same office. Mark Rasch director of a security think tank said this suggests they're doing many more wiretaps than has been admitted.[31] CBS *Evening News* on November 30, 1995 said the phone company NYNEX admitted it had recorded thousands of phone conversations without permission. The *Wall Street Journal* said the telephone workers' union confirmed that 1 in 50 Mexican phone lines are wiretapped.[32] The Spanish war in the 1930s was a testing ground for the weapons used in World War II. In a similar fashion Mexico is a client state for various U.S. federal agencies and, from voting machines to surveillance technologies, what occurs in Mexico is also applied in the U.S.

Although the courts have at times blocked government wiretaps of Americans,[33] in more recent years a special court has readily complied with all government requests to wiretap conversations. On May 4, 1994 CBS *Evening News* said the Foreign Intelligence Surveillance Court (FISC) established in 1979 approved requests for electronic surveillance of Americans over 7,500 times. Meeting in secret in the Justice Department this court has granted all but one request. On February 9, 1995 Clinton signed EO 12949 greatly expanding the power of the FISC to allow the Justice Department to conduct physical or electronic surveillance without obtaining a search warrant in open court, without notifying the victim, and without needing to provide an inventory of what was seized. Evidence gathered under FISC jurisdiction can now be used in criminal trials. Previously such evidence was only used for intelligence. Many people have complained about the telephone bill, yet few are aware of this EO which provides even more authority to monitor people than that allowed under the telephone act. In 1972 *U.S. v. U.S. District Court*, the Supreme Court said warrantless surveillance violates the Fourth Amendment, warning that the "danger to political dissent is acute where the government attempts (acts) under so vague a concept as the power to protect 'domestic security.'"[34]

It is quite easy for the government to get people's phone records and there is no requirement for people to be notified of this. In 1978 the U.S. Court of Appeals for the D.C. Circuit said that phone records belong to the phone company not to customers. Typically, the government serves a subpoena to get phone records and the phone company automatically complies. In a recent year Pacific Bell received 14,765 subpoenas while Bell Atlantic received 7,098.

In 1991 Gregory Millman, a financial reporter, charged that billions of dollars in taxes owed by GM, Kellogg, and other large corporations were never collected by the IRS because of currency and interest-rate hedging techniques. Millman claimed that he used internal IRS documents to write the article. The IRS responded by getting his phone records and those of numerous other people in a broad sweep, which probably involved more work than the IRS exercised to collect these taxes. In 1991 Procter & Gamble got the Cincinnati police to examine over 35 million long-distance phone calls to find someone who was giving the *Wall Street Journal* critical information about the company.[35]

When I started making phone calls to gather material for this book, I soon started hearing clicking noises on both my phones. Once when I said what I thought of those listening on the other end, the noises promptly stopped. The wiretap comes and goes every so often, because a writer is rarely a high priority threat and the noises occur depending on whom I call. Once the noise was so loud and constant I called the local phone company repair department and told them there was a wiretap on my line using old equipment and asked them to get the government to switch to better equipment. The person wasn't surprised, and the noises soon stopped. Another time, while talking to a contact in Oklahoma, the line was cut twice in several minutes. I am aware of one person who has installed a device that lights up when a wiretap is activated on his line.

If you don't believe this, start calling various patriot or environmental groups expressing your interest in getting involved, and you will probably start hearing strange noises on your phone, although equipment is being gradually upgraded so before too long there will be no noises on the line when your phone is bugged. People with a high priority are already wiretapped with equipment that emits no noises. This is our tax dollars at work. While this is completely against the Constitution, I am not suggesting that there is any immediate physical threat to this surveillance. However, if one were to speak of committing violent acts, one might be arrested, disappear, or have an arranged suicide or accident, depending on how much of a threat one were perceived to be by the security state.

The main focus as in any tyrannical government is to remain in power by controlling the people, which means surveillance especially of those deemed to be a potential threat. Ex-head of the CIA James Woolsey told Congress that CIA spy satellites can hear almost any conversation. In late 1995 ABCs *Primetime Live* said since 1993 cameras have been used to record cars that go through red lights. This means cars can be located throughout the U.S., when this technology is applied nationally, as in inevitable. Of course, the people will be told the benefits of this tighter surveillance. Various federal agencies such as the IRS, DEA, FBI, Customs, EPA, and OSHA paid $97 million in 1993 to Americans who reported violations of laws. The *Washington Post* said the CIA has called on spouses of intelligence or military personnel to report any suspicious activities to the authorities. In the new world order, loyalty to the state will be more important than the family unit. Getting many people to spy on others is one more sign of a coming police state.

Increasingly, local police agencies use surveillance systems often with the support of the federal government. Military surveillance technology is now used in domestic police work.[36] Electronic surveillance is used to see who to arrest in the future. People are put into different categories, depending on their perceived threat to the government. This determines when they will be arrested in an emergency. After someone is initially categorized and put onto a certain list, surveillance generally takes place, with recording equipment which is occasionally listened to depending on what category you are in. If certain words are spoken, the recordings may be listened to more often.

In 1952 the World Association of Parliamentarians for World Government released a map positioning foreign troops in the U.S. as part of a world government. On September 21, 1992 Bush said at the UN: "The U.S. is prepared to make available our bases and facilities for multinational training and field exercises." Today there are growing reports of foreign troops and military equipment in the U.S. The NBC *Evening News* November 30, 1994 quoted the Pentagon as admitting there were currently 5,000 foreign troops in the U.S. undergoing training. While such training has continued for years, these troops are now coming to the U.S. in units instead of individually. NBC reported September 7, 1994 that 500 Russian troops would be in the U.S. in 1995 for training exercises. The *Washington Post* also reported on U.S. Soviet military maneuvers in the U.S. in

1995.[37] There are many reports of foreign troops at Fort Polk, Louisiana, Fort Riley, Kansas, and Holloman Air Force base in New Mexico CBS News on August 18, 1995 said 4,000 foreign troops from 14 East European nations were being trained at Fort Polk for UN peace keeping and civilian control operations. On May 2, 1996 the *New York Times* said a new agreement provided for training Mexican troops on U.S. bases.

In the summer and fall of 1994, U.S. troops were in Russia conducting maneuvers. There was an official admission that there were joint Russian/U.S. military exercises taking place in the U.S. and Russia but the announcement took place in Moscow. On September 5, 1994 General Pavel Grachev acknowledged that U.S. and Russian forces were conducting joint exercises in the U.S. as well as in Russia to deal with riots, terrorist attacks, and other emergencies.

*Spotlight* published evidence of UN/foreign troop movements in the U.S. and has produced many photos of Russian and UN military vehicles in America. Because of these reports, Congress was flooded with inquiries. Clifford Bernath, Assistant to the Secretary of Defense, sent people a letter on this topic declaring all is fine. He said some Russians may undergo training in the U.S. in 1995, and in March, 1994, 50 Russian soldiers participated in a joint exercise in Alaska. Bernath acknowledged that Canadian troops trained at Marine bases in southern California in early 1994. Their military vehicles reportedly moved on a 110-car train and some vehicles had UN markings. Senator Conrad Burns got a letter from the Department of the Army saying the railroad cars were loaded with Canadian army vehicles returning to Canada from Camp Pendleton, California where training had been conducted "under the umbrella of the UN."

While the Pentagon claims that reports of Soviet-bloc military equipment spotted in the U.S. are just old surplus, numerous photos show that the latest Russian equipment is showing up across the U.S. This includes the Russian Hind-E helicopter, SA-13 missile launcher, SA-13 Gopher surface-to-air missile system, BTR-60 armored personnel carrier, and T-72 and T-80 tanks. There are clearly too many Russian tanks and armor here to just be used in target practice and training exercises as the government claims, and none of this equipment is listed in the Pentagon inventory of military equipment.

According to the September 25, 1994 *Daily News*, in Alamogordo, New Mexico, there are "500 (foreign) operational tracked and wheeled vehicles" at the White Sands Missile Range in Alamogordo. The article included a photo of a long row of T-72 tanks which "stand at the ready." The article said there are similar "tank farms" with Russian military vehicles at military bases in Arizona, Florida, and Maryland. The Gulfport, Mississippi airport and Fort Irwin, California reportedly also have much Russian military equipment. The September 22, 1994 *San Diego Union Tribune* had a classified ad to hire someone to service Russian military equipment.

One citizen photographed a truck hauling a Russian T-72 tank along a highway north of San Antonio. When spotted taking the photos he was forced off the road. Two hours later when he returned home a car that had been behind the truck hauling the T-72 was parked in front of his home. This citizen got his shotgun and walked towards the car which promptly drove away. Since when is it a crime for an American to take photos of military vehicles on a public highway! And why should this be a secret? In 1994 a unit of German troops camped near Wickenburg, Arizona. No local authorities were told about this. A local resident told them to leave or he would come back with friends and drive them away using gunfire if necessary. They promptly left.

Will large numbers of third world troops be brought here supposedly for UN training, while the U.S. military is weakened and stationed overseas? The number of U.S. divisions has been sharply cut and thousands of U.S. troops are overseas. The people should demand that no foreign troops be allowed into the U.S. for UN related duties. We still have over 100,000 troops defending Europe from a Russian army that is collapsing, and in late 1995 Clinton committed 25,000 troops to Bosnia with many more providing support. From deployment in Somalia, Haiti, Kuwait, South Korea, and perhaps the Golan Heights, the federal government has an endless appetite to station troops overseas.

Many unsubstantiated rumors claim that hundreds of thousands of foreign troops are secretly stationed on U.S. soil. The *New American* did a 12-page report on foreign troops in the U.S., but it found evidence of no more than a limited number of foreign troops here.[38] While there may be over 5,000 foreign troops in the U.S., this has not yet been confirmed. The greater concern is what do these events mean? Today it is 5,000 or more foreign troops here. What will it be in the future? Are the military exercises in preparation for seizing all guns from the people? Are these foreign troops in the U.S. quietly getting familiar with the roads and terrain to provide guidance for large groups of UN troops that may later be brought in?

On November 5, 1993 Senator Roth introduced Amendment 1122 to the 1993 crime bill calling for the U.S. to hire Hong Kong police into the federal police. This was also discussed in Section 5108 of the same bill. Supposedly, they were needed to deal with Asian gangs in the U.S., and no limit was placed on the number to be hired. This amendment actually passed the Senate, but was removed in the House/Senate conference. With Hong Kong returning to China in 1997 this law would have provided a legal excuse to bring thousands of Chinese communist troops into the U.S.[39]

Another disturbing trend is that, in recent years, American troops have been conducting military exercises in our cities and suburbs, sometimes using live ammunition. Are these training exercises being conducted as a prelude to disarming Americans? The U.S. Army Office of Public Affairs said its urban warfare training is allowed under the Defense Department Authorization Act of 1987. While there has been heated discussion in some local newspapers about these exercises, the national media rarely discusses this topic. According to veteran reporter Sarah McClendon, in the *Washington Report*, August 26, 1994 "The U.S. Army admitted that it had been training local police and National Guard (units) in how to break and enter private property since 1987." The government has established a MJTF training facility in Belle Chasse, Louisiana to conduct anti-terrorist exercises. Increasingly, National Guard units are receiving training in urban warfare on U.S. military bases. Why is such training necessary?

A MJTF training exercise included the FBI and Marines in civilian clothes, with live ammunition used at the vacant Del Sol Hotel in Yuma, Arizona in the spring of 1994. Residents nearby were given no advance notice and some were scared by the gunfire. The Yuma raid was discussed on the front page of *The Yuma Daily Sun* on October 21, 1994. On June 12, 1995 residents of Des Plaines, Illinois were disturbed from their sleep by a MJTF training operation that involved low flying planes and live ammunition. Local police denied this was happening, but later admitted they were ordered not to talk about it. Key Largo, Florida residents were awakened by a similar military assault.

Plans to conduct a military exercise in the empty Book-Cadillac Hotel in Detroit were cancelled after news of the exercise was published in the *Detroit Free Press* July 23, 1994. The military wanted to place sharpshooters on the nearby Book Tower office building. However, a live ammunition exercise was conducted by a MJTF unit, including regular Army troops, in the Detroit suburb of Van Buren in late September and early October, 1994. Michigan State Rep. Deborah Whyman and some aides found live ammunition and an unused grenade at the scene, which was not even secured after the exercise. They were under constant surveillance while inspecting the buildings.

When the *The Olympian*, on July 5, 1994, published plans to parachute troops into downtown Rainer, Washington to fight a unit of the National Guard using blank ammunition, there was an uproar. Many citizens complained at a town meeting, and permission to hold the exercise was revoked. Citizens were scared when the Marines and FBI conducted a joint exercise, in late July, 1994, on Tybee Island, Georgia. Helicopters hovered over homes in the middle of the night. On July 18, 1994 a press release from Camp Pendleton announced that some Marines and Navy personnel would undergo urban training at "privately owned sites and military installations" near Sacramento from July 23 to August 3. According to the *Miami Herald*, Miami Beach gave permission for a military exercise to be held in early 1995 at the abandoned St. Hortiz Hotel. The Army wanted to use live ammunition in this hotel, which is in the heart of a busy district.

Several years ago the National Guard State Partnership Program was established to exchange American soldiers in guard units with personnel from the former Soviet Union, supposedly to promote democracy and human rights in these foreign countries. Arrangements have already been established between Alabama and Romania, Arizona and Kazakhstan, California and Ukraine, Colorado and Slovenia, Illinois and Poland, Indiana and Slovakia, Maryland and Estonia, Michigan and Latvia, Ohio and Hungary, Pennsylvania and Lithuania, Tennessee and Bulgaria, Texas and the Chech Republic, South Carolina and Albania, and Utah and Belarus. These 14 states reportedly volunteered to participate in this program. Have any citizens of these states even heard of this program? The Department of Defense is spending $33 million to promote this operation, and Russia will soon be a participant.

This is a program that could bring into the U.S. tens of thousands of soldiers from former communist countries, while our troops are sent overseas. These foreign troops would not defend our freedom, and if U.S. soldiers are out of the country it would be hard for them to protect the people. If such foreign troops were ordered to seize all arms here and kill those who resisted, they would probably follow such orders while most American soldiers would not. Moreover, federal authorities have been quietly removing tanks and other heavy equipment from certain armories.

The Defense Department wants to eliminate half the 110,000 Army National Guard combat troops. The remaining National Guard combat units would transfer to support activities like managing supplies. Supposedly this would be done to save money. Between 1989 and 1998 the active-duty Army is to be cut 36 percent, while the Army National Guard is to be reduced 20 percent.[40] There are also reports

In the News

## NBC & Me
Michael Moore skewers life in a summer TV series
**Accent, 1C**

## Paradise
Quaint Bay View is a little bit of Victorian heaven
**Homestyle, 16D**

In the Free Press

## Let's ride!
Cyclists pedal off today in Michigander III Backroads
**Local News, 3A**

## 10 under
Alfredsson beats weather and keeps U.S. Open lead
**Sports, 1B**

Chance of storms.
High 83, Low 65.

# The Detroit News AND Free Press

Metro Final

Saturday, July 23, 1994

35 cents, 50 cents outside metro Detroit

## Military may attack Book-Cadillac

BY JOHN GALLAGHER
Free Press Staff Writer

that Army reserve units would be placed under the command of FEMA during an emergency. An interview with a Jewish leader of the Texas Constitutional Militia in the December 4, 1994 issue of the *London Sunday Telegraph* helps explain why the National Guard is being weakened. Reserve guardsmen, police officers, and active duty military officers quietly work with militias across the country.

There are been unconfirmed reports that members of street gangs such as the Crips and Bloods are being recruited and trained to be used as shock troops to raid homes, seize guns, and arrest certain people. *Newsweek* had an article about gangs being in the military and the U.S. Justice Department working with them.[41] The *Washington Times* said the federal government allocated an initial $2.5 million to recruit street gangs into a neighborhood watch program in Washington, D.C. Will every city soon see this? In June, 1996 the press said the Justice Department was going to hold a conference with gang leaders from across the nation to discuss common problems. FEMA is involved in a secret program called the National Guard Civilian Opportunity Act which involves placing troubled youths in youth camps to give them military training and discipline. Gang members could be a vast resource to create terror. Just in the Chicago area, according to police reports, there are 100,000 gang members, and the White House on May 13, 1996 said there were 16,000 gangs with 500,000 members.

In 1979 William R. Pabst released a detailed report with the locations of various prison camps in the U.S. already established for civilians.[42] Reagan reportedly signed a national security directive activating 11 large prison camps. The U.S. Army field manual FM 41-10 titled Civil Affairs Operations, dated January, 1993, discusses methods for rounding up civilians and place them in detention centers. Included are FEMA chain of command information and diagrams of detention centers. Other U.S. Army documents state that it has plans for "regulation of civilian inmate labor utilization" and for "preparing requests to establishing civilian prison camps on (Army) installations." In 1994 C. Dean Rhody of the U.S. Army Training and Doctrine Command in Fort Monroe, Virginia sent a memo about a "Draft Army Regulation on Civilian Inmate Program" stating that "the new regulation will provide the following: (a) Policy for civilian inmate utilization on installations, (b) Procedures for preparing requests to establish civilian inmate labor programs on installations, and (c) Procedures for preparing requests to establish civilian prison camps on installations." When the researcher, Dennis Cuddy, called to confirm this memo, he was told the memo was "leaked" and was "premature" because it was a "draft regulation" that had not been finalized.[43] The U.S. Army War College report "The Revolution in Military Affairs and Conflict Short of War" states that the role of the military was changing from national defense to suppression and control of populations in the U.S. and under the UN.

According to the General Accounting Office, by 1994, 88 percent of the closed military bases had been taken over by other government agencies. Reportedly certain bases and FEMA installations are being turned into prison camps. The Seneca Army Depot by Seneca Falls, N.Y. is one Army base reportedly being closed and converted to a federal prison. Senator Alfonse D'Amato has confirmed that much heavy construction is taking place at this base which will be turned over to the National Guard. This and other closed bases usually ban the public, and barbed wire has been placed around many of these bases.

The Immigration Reduction Act of 1995 (H.R. 2162) calls for the Secretary of Defense to provide the Attorney General with a list of all closed military bases in the U.S. with facilities "suitable for detention and upon request of the Attorney General shall give assistance as the Attorney General may require to take possession of and operate such facilities." There remains an interest to provide facilities to imprison many people. RX 84, discussed above, calls for the arrest of 100,000 to 400,000 people, so the government must have facilities ready to suddenly imprison so many people. While I do not feel that conclusive evidence has been presented yet as to what is being done with the closed bases, this situation must be closely watched, especially because of our history of imprisoning or proprosing to imprison many people.

In the past, entire tribes of Native Americans were resettled or deliberately killed. Thousands of American Indian children were forceably taken from their families and placed in special schools or with non-Indian families to destroy their cultural roots. During World War I, governors from four western states asked the federal government to imprison members of the Industrial Workers of the World until the war was over. In 1939 the Hobbs "Concentration Camp" Bill passed the House by a large majority, calling for the detention of aliens. Over 110,000 Japanese-Americans were abruptly arrested and sent to concentration camps in harsh regions during World War II. None of these people had ever committed even one act against the U.S. Authorities were able to move fast because lists had been prepared in advance. The 1950 Internal Security Act had provisions to establish prison camps for subversives. Senator Paul Douglas helped draft this law without realizing he was on an FBI list to be arrested as a threat to national security. In 1968 the House Un-American Activities Committee advocated detention centers during the civil rights disturbances. It called for sealing ghettos, restricting entry, curfews, and the suspension of civil rights during a "guerrilla uprising." The full report reads like a gestapo tirade. Threatening or actually putting political dissidents into concentration camps is a well established tradition in America recognized by many people unless you are a politician or in the establishment press.

For a preview of the future, consider the tight control now in effect at U.S. airports. To board a plane a photo I.D. is required. If we one day wake up and discover that some excuse has been used to suspend the Constitution and establish martial law, would most of Congress in the name of national security not say a word? Would Congress be too busy taking money from special interests to enrich themselves to get reelected? What does it take for Congress to recognize and question treason and sedition when it takes place? Part of the problem is that many in Congress are closely allied with the corporate elite.

# Chapter XVI

# The Oklahoma Bombing

"All warfare is based on deception."

Sun Tzu Wu

"People who shut their eyes to reality simply invite their own destruction."

James Baldwin

There is ample evidence that the government is involved in a major cover-up in the Oklahoma bombing. Much about this atrocity have been revealed by various investigators including Dave Hall until recently owner of KPOC-TV in Ponca City, Oklahoma; Channel 4 KFOR-TV the NBC affiliate in Oklahoma City; Brig. General USAF (Ret.) Ben Partin; Ted Gunderson, an FBI agent for 27 years who retired as head of the FBI office in L.A.; John Rappoport author of *Oklahoma Bombing The Suppressed Truth*; J.D. Cash; and Pat Briley. One doesn't have to believe all the information these investigators have uncovered, but why is the national media keeping it from the American people? J.D. Cash, an Oklahoma reporter told me the local Associated Press (AP) branch wouldn't carrying his stories because the U.S. Justice Department wouldn't approve them. In a free society there would be outrage. Instead there is silence and news censorship.

As in any crime, one must examine who benefited to find a motive in the Oklahoma bombing. The secret government had seven objectives including: discredit the militias and Patriot movement, weaken the NRA which helped defeat many anti-gun congressmen in 1994, pass repressive bills in Congress, increase federal power to tighten control over the people, and destroying records about Waco and the Gulf War Syndrome which were reportedly stored in that federal building. The bombing also provide Clinton with another opportunity to call the Republicans extremists by linking them with the militias. The secret government wanted to slow the momentum of the new Republican members of Congress. In addition, on April 22, 1995, Hillary Clinton was questioned about Whitewater by independent counsel Kenneth W. Starr and three aides. You probably didn't hear about this because of the Oklahoma bombing.

If you are going to maintain a large national security state, there must be a threat to justify its continued existence. Otherwise too many people would realize that we don't really need to spend billions of dollars on a problem that barely exists. For the security state to continue, there must sometimes be large terrorist acts in the U.S. The last thing the national security state wants is peace and no enemies. For decades there was the communist threat. In recent years, with the declared end of the cold war, numerous "experts" have appeared in the media warning about the dire threat of terrorism. Meanwhile, terrorist incidents against Americans have dropped from 111 in 1977 to nine in 1987. In 1991 there were seven terrorist acts. Several years ago, the largest number of attacks on Americans overseas was in Chile against the Mormon church. People in the militias and Patriot movement strongly criticized the bombing, and they have nothing to gain and much to lose by committing terrorist acts. It is also strange that no groups claimed credit for the bombing, which is the norm with terrorist attacks.

We now have terrorism on demand when certain bills are before Congress. The FBI released a terrorist alert August 1, 1995 saying there might be a terrorist attack at the end of August to commemorate the Randy Weaver raid in 1992. On August 19, Clinton said "It's hard to imagine what more must happen to convince Congress to pass the bill." Then a terrorist alert for the airports was publicized in August, and right on schedule on August 28, three New York City area airports were closed for hours after a phone threat to an unlisted phone number at a key facility. The FBI suspected a disgruntled employee, because it would be very difficult for terrorists to get this unlisted number. These events occurred just as the House again considered passing the terrorist bill. The 1968 crime bill passed after King and Kennedy were assassinated, and another crime bill passed in 1994 after the World Trade Center (WTC) bombing.

Oklahoma may have been chosen partly because Governor Frank Keating had been an FBI agent, a senior official in the Justice Department, and Assistant Secretary of the Treasury in charge of the ATF. Instead of trying to answer questions about the bombing, Keating has criticized people in Oklahoma who question the government version of the attack and has said people should trust the government and the FBI. Keating has stymied efforts in the Oklahoma legislature, led by Rep. Charles Key, to get a state investigation of the bombing independent of the FBI. Also, in Oklahoma almost 45 percent of the jobs are government related so many people are afraid they will be fired and lose their pension if they complain about the investigation.

If you have difficulty believing the government was involved in the Oklahoma building consider what happened at the New York WTC. *The New Yorker* said the CIA funded and trained certain Afghan groups that trained some of the gang that bombed the WTC.[1] After the arrests, it was revealed on the front page of the *New York Times* October 28, 1993 that Emad A. Salem, a member of the gang and a retired Egyptian army officer, was an FBI informant who had secretly recorded his conversations with the FBI. Salem became a full-time FBI informant on November, 1991. The *Washington Post* said he stopped working for the FBI in 1992, supposedly because he failed a polygraph test. Despite these claims, after the bombing he again miraculously became qualified to be a government agent, and was paid one million dollars for his court testimony.[2] How convenient!

According to the transcripts, Salem targeted the WTC per FBI orders, and he wanted to use phony explosives to prevent damage to the WTC, but the FBI supervisor blocked this. The gang were amateurs, so Salem rented the garage and provided technical assistance to build the bomb. This was recorded on FBI surveillance tapes.[3] The FBI did just about everything to help the gang, but refused to arrest them. Salem told an FBI agent "Your supervisor is the main reason of bombing the WTC." The supervisor Salem complained about was probably brought in by higher authorities to make sure the terrorist attack occurred. FBI agent Frederic Whitehurst, who testified about improprieties with the FBI crime lab during the O.J. trial, also testified at the WTC trial. He was physically threatened and pressured to lie about questionable lab results.

Salem wanted to complain to FBI headquarters in Washington, D.C. about the local FBI's failure to stop the bombing, because he felt the FBI didn't listen to his warnings to stop the attack before it occurred. One agent agreed that the local FBI people "didn't want to get their butts chewed." Another agent said: "You cannot force people to do the right thing."[4] The FBI even tried to cover-up their actions to make Salem's claims unbelievable. Why didn't these revelations cause an uproar in Congress and the press? Instead there was silence and the Oklahoma City bombing. With over 1,000 people injured, it is amazing that no one has sued the federal government for negligence.

The Discovery TV channel, on April 28, 1996, said the arrests took place because of good police work and tracing the car axle code. Recently A & E TV presented a show on the WTC bombing and Mike Wallace referred to "a lucky break" in making the arrests. Then Salem's role as an FBI informant was noted, but no one explained why the bombing wasn't prevented. Perhaps one day James Fox, the ex-FBI agent in charge of the New York office during the bombing, will be forced to testify about these events. On May 19, 1996 *Parade magazine*, in a front page story that appeared in Sunday newspapers across the country, proudly and falsely declared that identifying the number on the rented van played a "crucial" role in arresting the gang. No mention was made of the crucial role the FBI played in setting up this bombing. Increasingly our society is built on lies.

McVeigh rented the truck used in the bombing in his own name, was arrested while speeding in a car without license plates, and he had no registration. It is also strange that McVeigh made no attempt to resist being arrested despite having a gun. He stayed in motels under his own name using the Nichol's Michigan farm as his home address. How could McVeigh have done such a sophisticated bombing and yet be so careless? That makes no sense unless he was deliberately set up to take the fall as Ted Gunderson and others have said. The same pattern occurred with Lee Harvey Oswald, James Earl Ray, and Sirhan Sirhan. McVeigh did not have the training, money, resources, or record of resourcefulness to do this bombing alone. *Time* was also told by investigators that McVeigh was not smart enough to pull off the operation alone. While McVeigh certainly seems to have been involved he was being used by others.

McVeigh had no reliable job yet he had lots of money. *Time* said he had $10,000 with no explanation of how he got this money.[5] McVeigh supposedly robbed Roger Moore, an Arkansas gun collector, November 5, 1994. Moore admitted being friends with McVeigh and said he was a guest at times. Reportedly, Moore has CIA and ATF contacts and ran a CIA front company. Linking McVeigh to this robbery may be disinformation to explain how McVeigh had so much money. When the *Detroit Free Press* filed an FOIA request to obtain information about this robbery, it learned that the FBI pressured the local sheriff to alter the robbery report. According to an affidavit given by FBI agent Arthur Baker, Moore did not even file an insurance claim for items stolen in the robbery.

Evidence suggests that McVeigh was known to the ATF and that he was possibly under surveillance for some time before the Oklahoma bombing. McVeigh was never even questioned about the Arkansas robbery, and he was at Waco, during and shortly after, the siege selling bumper stickers. The government used surveillance cameras to record such people. At a 1994 Arizona gun show, McVeigh was spotted by a government agent illegally selling an anti-helicopter weapon. No action was taken against him. NBC reported on August 1, 1995 that Glynn Tipton called the ATF because McVeigh was trying to buy large quantities of a fuel additive and a fuel used in auto racing which might be used in an explosive. The ATF did not act on this tip.[6]

John Doe 2 has still not been found. Just after the explosion the police released an All-Points Bulletin (APB) for a late model brown pickup driven by two Middle Eastern males. Within hours the FBI cancelled the APB, refusing to say why, and demanded that it not be rebroadcast. According to Dave Hall, the authorities had pictures of McVeigh and another person leaving the scene of the crime in this pickup. Yet weeks later, when Hall asked the authorities why they weren't still searching for this car along with John Doe 2, they denied having said there was such a car. When a tape of the admission was played the authorities had "no comment." J.D. Cash has interviewed almost 30 people who saw McVeigh with other people in Oklahoma and Kansas shortly before the bombing. Authorities have also not found the small trailer seen hitched to the Ryder truck that McVeigh rented in Junction City, Kansas.[7]

The *New York Times*[8] and *Newsweek*[9] interviewed various witnesses who saw John Doe 2 with McVeigh. However, the *New York Times* quoted authorities as saying they have turned up little evidence that John Doe 2 exists. *Time* also quoted investigators who now claim John Doe 2 doesn't exist.[10] An ex-FBI agent told *USA Today* "I'm starting to wonder if he exists if he wasn't a red herring." There was an announcement that John Doe 2 was identified as a U.S. soldier but this claim was quietly dropped. The people who rented the Ryder truck to McVeigh remain certain that a second person was with him and that John Doe 2 exists.

In Oklahoma City Channel 4 news director Melissa Kinzing confirmed the station has two witnesses who saw McVeigh and an Iraqi ex-soldier in a local bar, and a witness who saw an Iraqi driving away from the bombing in a brown pickup. Over the weeks, Channel 4 interviewed at least six people who saw McVeigh with several people including John Doe 2, and concluded that he is probably an Iraqi and a former member of the Republican Guard. In 1993 and 1994, Clinton brought thousands of Iraqi soldiers into the U.S. Many of them settled in Oklahoma. On October 18, 1993 the *Washington Times* said over 3,400 Iraqi soldiers and their dependents had settled in the U.S. with 4,600 more expected. On August 30, 1993 the *Salt Lake City Tribune* said 100 members of Congress wanted this program stopped. This is one more quiet operation that has brought thousands of foreign troops into the U.S.

Channel 4 KFOR-TV on June 7, 1995 presented a report on John Doe 2 claiming he was still in Oklahoma City, and eye-witnesses identified him with McVeigh. The FBI has refused to even interview this person. Although this Iraqi wasn't identified by Channel 4, two other local TV stations, Channels 5 and 9, interviewed this person and he denied involvement in the bombing. Channel 9 presented a time sheet supporting the person's claim that he was at work during the bombing, but Channel 4 found people at that business who confirmed that this firm doesn't use time sheets. On August 24, 1995 Al-Hussaini Hussain, an Oklahoma City resident and Iraqi who may have been in the Republican Guard, filed a suit against Channel 4 claiming they had falsely accused him of being involved in the bombing.

On August 17, 1995 Jayna Davis a Channel 4 reporter said: "These eye-witnesses show prime suspect McVeigh could not have acted alone....At least two more men, possibly three, were also there." NBC won't run the reports of these witnesses nationally, supposedly because Channel 4 won't give it the names of several of its witnesses who are terrified of being publicly identified. People remember the many deaths surrounding the Kennedy assassination.[11] Except in a few cities, like Seattle and New York, NBC stations have refused to carry the many reports by Channel 4 on the Oklahoma bombing because they don't support the government version.

Although aware who many of these witnesses are, the FBI refuses to interrogate them, others were told by the FBI to keep quiet, and none were brought before the grand jury or offered protection. On January 24, 1995 PBS radio interviewed several of the witnesses who saw McVeigh and John Doe 2. One said someone threatened to kill him if he didn't shut up. The independent investigator, Pat Briley, has received death threats and been harassed by the FBI. One witness not called to testify before the grand jury, Mike Moroz of Johnny's Tire in Oklahoma City, gave McVeigh and another person directions to the federal building at 8:40 a.m. on April 19. Private investigators believe John Doe 2 is a government agent or informant, which is why the government won't let these people testify before the grand jury.

There are at least five surveillance video tapes from buildings near the federal building that prosecutors have refused to release to the press or the defense. These videos show McVeigh with John Doe 2 just before the bombing, but the grand jurors were only shown video still photographs of the Ryder truck. The public release of a photo of John Doe 2 from a video would have made it easier to arrest him, which may be why this evidence is being suppressed. The FBI has admitted it is investigating two of its agents in the L.A. office for illegally attempting to sell a video for $1 million to two TV networks. These two agents did not even have the authority to possess these tapes. Oklahoma private investigator, Robert Jerlow, saw the video in L.A. and along with his attorney, Randy Shadid, got involved in negotiating with a TV network. Jerlow said John Doe 2 got out of the truck 2 to 5 minutes after McVeigh which means the defense might be able to claim that John Doe 2 not McVeigh set the bomb. Consider the many leaks about the Unabomber which upset the Justice Department. Increasingly federal police are leaking information and serving as media consultants.[12]

There is considerable evidence that it is absolutely impossible for a fertilizer bomb to have caused the resulting damage. Clinton appears to understand this. On June 12, 1995 the *Cape Cod Times* using an AP report quoted Clinton saying the bomb used in Oklahoma was "a miracle of technology." Retired Brigadier General Benton K. Partin is one of the world's foremost experts on explosives technology including precision-guided weapons and related target acquisition. He spent 25 years designing and testing weapons for the U.S. military. On July 13, 1995, Partin released a 23-page report on the Oklahoma bombing. It was put on the Internet and summarized in *The New American*.[13] The magnitude and pattern of damage made it impossible for the damage to have been caused by an explosion outside the building on the street. "The total incompatibility with a single truck bomb lies in the fact that either some of the columns collapsed that should not have collapsed or some of the columns are still standing that should have collapsed and did not." He said the pattern of damage suggested an implosion with explosives attached to the columns probably at the third floor because that is where the columns failed.

Authorities raised the bomb yield from 1,000 to 1,100, to 2,000, to 2,500, to 4,800 pounds. Using the official claim of 4,800 pounds of ammonium nitrate would yield on the high end 1/2 million pounds per square inch (psi) at the detonation site. It is a basic laws of physics that the destructive potential of an explosion dramatically falls off even a few feet from a blast. Traveling through the air the first column hit would drop to 375 psi and to 25-38 psi at more distant columns. Concrete yield strength is 3,500 psi and pressure in the hundreds of thousands of psi would be required to cause the resulting damage, especially to reduce concrete to powder as occurred at some columns. The general concluded: "This is a classic cover-up of immense proportions."

The WTC truck bomb with explosive power similar to the Oklahoma bombing destroyed no support beams although some were quite close to the truck. The truck bomb in Oklahoma supposedly destroyed 20 to 30 main support beams that were 30 to 75 feet away. This is simply not possible. If the blast came from one origin the pattern of damage to the surrounding buildings would have been rather circular. Instead, the pattern of destruction was more linear and directed mainly at the federal building suggesting a sophisticated explosion. Building debris including reinforced steel was blown outward towards the street, which indicated a blast from inside the building.

Ted Gunderson believes the main damage was caused by an electro-hydrodynamic gaseous fuel bomb developed by Michael Riconosciuto. The size of a pineapple it cost about $100,000 to build. It requires Q Clearance to build this secret device and only a few people in government have the technical ability to construct and use this devise. Riconosciuto's laboratory in Aberdeen, Washington was robbed in the late 1980s, and reportedly the signature from the Oklahoma bombing has been traced back to this laboratory. Gunderson prepared a report listing 15 reasons why an ammonium nitrate bomb couldn't have caused the resulting damage.[14] Damage to nearby structures was more extensive than what you would expect from just ammonium nitrate, which is not that efficient. It makes a loud noise but doesn't pulverize material unless packed into the area for direct contact. That much ammonium nitrate would have made the area dangerous with nitric acid in the air, but this did not occur. The explosion left no soot and only a small amount of unexploded fertilizer was present, which means an expert set off the blast. While the FBI said the axle from the Ryder truck was found three blocks away, why did it blow upwards when the bomb, which was above the axle, made a 30 foot crater, and a large ammonium nitrate truck bomb of this size would blow upwards and would not create a crater.

Further investigation is needed to clarify these two views, although it appears that General Partin is correct that demolition charges were placed on various columns. It would be difficult for anyone to place such charges in a secure federal building, and this is one more sign that this was an inside job. One witness claims she saw someone cutting into a column in the federal building several weeks before the explosion. When she walked over to the person, he covered his tools and said he was fixing up the building.

It is one thing to use a small ammonium nitrate bomb as farmers often do to remove trees, but to blow up one involving 4,800 pounds with about 20 containers linked together requires great technical ability. It is extremely difficult to build such a large device with numerous cannisters using home mixing equipment. The only way to have blast control with a 4,800 pound ammonium bomb would be with volumetric initiation which requires sophisticated electronic circuits. Very few people have the training to build such bombs. The *Albuquerque Journal* said the ATF in mid-August, 1994 conducted tests blowing up car bombs made of ammonium nitrate and fuel oil at White Sands, New Mexico. Was this a trial run in preparation for the Oklahoma operation?[15]

Two seismographs near the explosion clearly showed there were two or three explosions. Ray Brown, geologist for Oklahoma Geological Survey (OGS) at the University of Oklahoma in Norman, 16.25 miles from the explosion, initially said there were "two separate seismic events" and the simplest explanation is "two separate explosions." Dr. Brown believes that the second event could not be explained by surface wave velocity dispersion, air waves, or air-coupled Rayleigh waves.[16] ABC and other reporters visited the OSG, but this information was suppressed.

The second event could not have been the building collapsing. The April 19 blast had 60 million tons of concrete fall, while 200 million tons fell when the entire building was destroyed. Falling debris does not send the same high and low frequency waves as an explosion. Extensive seismograph equipment was used to record the demolition of the federal building. Equipment at Norman could barely record the demolition, unlike the clear record of the April 19 bombing, and the recording at the much closer Omniplex center was clearly different from the April 19 bombing.[17] Also, based on the laws of gravity the 11 seconds that separated the two blasts was too long a time period in a collapsing nine story building for the debris to have caused the second record on the seismograph. Steve Due, who operates one of the local seismographs, believes the second explosion was a "chain-reaction detonation of explosive materials."[18]

On June 1, 1995 the U.S. Geological Survey (USGS) claimed there was only one bomb explosion April 19 and wrongly said the scientists at OGS all agreed with this conclusion. Dr. Charles Mankin, head of the OGS, urged that the June 1 claim not be released until more evidence had been analyzed and, with other scientists, still feels the evidence suggests there were two blasts and that the USGS prematurely reached its conclusion.[19] The experts in Oklahoma also rejected the claim that the two events were one wave traveling at different speeds. Was the USGS pressured to help in the cover-up?

On November 20, 1995 at a meeting in Oklahoma City, Brown said he is now certain there were three explosions, and one of them was demolition charges, supporting General Partin's claims. Previously, Brown was not shown the complete seismograph record from the Omniplex center just 4.3 miles from the blast because it was seized by the FBI. In October, 1995 he obtained a better copy of the original seismograph, but the FBI still has the original and they won't release it to government geologists or to the defense attorneys who have been trying to obtain it. Brown and Tom Holzer, the government geologist at the meeting, agreed that they should see this original record to give a more complete analysis. Holzer said there may have been more than one explosion but this couldn't be proved. After the meeting, U.S. Prosecutor Ryan misquoted Holzer and said this conclusively confirms there was only one blast.[20]

An important factor in the bombing that has received little publicity is that the damage was much worse because munitions were illegally stored on the ninth floor of the federal building by DEA and ATF offices. The AP refused to carry stories published in the *McCurtain Gazette* about several illegal arsenal rooms in the Murrah building. Storing such material in office buildings violates state and federal laws. Munitions are only supposed to be stored in bunker-style arsenals. Information about the illegal arsenal rooms is being suppressed, partly because federal authorities are liable for huge damages in this criminal negligence.[21] The ATF is very worried about this, especially because in civil lawsuits broader discovery is allowed than in criminal lawsuits, and it would be much harder for federal authorities to withhold information. Already, local attorneys are exploring this; and Edye Smith, a mother who lost her two children in the blast, and her family have filed a wrongful death civil lawsuit against McVeigh. They plan to also sue the U.S. government. Of 462 federal employees affected by the bombing, all but Edye Smith and her mother-in-law were approved for workers compensation. This is how the government treats people who stand up to it.

Many believe the second explosion, which included the stored weapons, was more severe than the first. These munitions did not initially cause the blast but they made the resulting damage much worse and exemplify how the Feds have lied in this investigation. The arsenal room on the ninth floor collapsed onto the areas where the greatest number of casualties occurred, such as the day care center. The explosives included C-4 explosives, which will explode without a fuse under 3,500 pounds of pressure as occurred when the building collapsed. The authorities have generally denied storing any weapons in the building, although the regional head of the ATF in Dallas, Lester Martz, blamed the DEA for the arsenal room.[22] Cash believes there were four arsenal rooms in the Murrah building.

After the initial explosions, the media said work was stopped several times to dismantle unexploded bombs. Police radios said the bomb squad found "undetonated military bombs" in the building. Explosive experts and a bomb-disposal truck were brought in. Many people near the federal building heard and felt several explosions. Witnesses also saw several five gallon containers of mercury fulminate inside the building. This volatile material could have collapsed the entire building. Bill Martin, of the Oklahoma City police, told Phil O'Halloran, a local reporter, about this discovery and then the department wouldn't discuss this report. Dick Miller, Oklahoma City assistant fire marshal, said high explosives such as an intact container marked "High Explosives" were moved from the building right after the blast. One initial rescuer a veteran heard live ammunition going past him from inside the building.[23]

After the explosion, some unexploded munitions remained on the ninth floor although much had fallen to the ground, so munitions were removed from both areas. One civilian helping to remove munitions from the building weeks after the blast saw hundreds of guns, including a five-gallon bucket of hand-grenades, in the building. Witnesses even saw an ATF agent remove a TOW (anti-tank missile) from the destroyed federal building. Several times, FBI and ATF agents got into arguments as to when the munitions should be removed from the building.[24]

The *McCurtain Daily Gazette* obtained a film from the sheriff's department showing federal officials removing munitions from the federal building weeks after the explosion. On the film, the Feds yelled at the local police to leave the area. They did not want witnesses to see this evidence. This film confirms that there was an illegal arsenal room in the federal building. These munitions exploded in an area of the building where experts say the building could not have sustained so much damage from a truck bomb.[25]

Rick Sherrow, an ex-ATF agent, said this is not the first time federal agents illegally stored munitions in a public building. In 1987 Soviet rocket fuses exploded during a fire at FBI headquarters in Washington, D.C. After that, the ATF ordered federal officials across the U.S. to stop this illegal practice, but there have been other incidents.[26] The *Tulsa World* reported in April, 1990 that IRS headquarters in Tulsa was robbed. The loot included ordinance and thousands of rounds of ammunition.[27]

It is also suspicious that the government rushed to destroy the entire building as they did at Waco, before independent tests could be conducted by outside experts. The government wouldn't even allow McVeigh's lawyer to take scrapings from various areas of the building. The damaged columns had chemical traces which would identify the explosives used in the bombing. Various architects, including Jim Loftis who designed the building, said it was structurally sound and did not have to be demolished although he and others were pressured by the governor to support demolishing the building. Brig. General Partin and others tried to delay the building's destruction in order to conduct a thorough investigation. Partin wrote to various members of Congress saying "The damage pattern on the reinforced concrete superstructure could not possibly have been attained from a single truck bomb without supplementing demolition charges at some of the reinforced column bases....A careful examination of the collapsed column bases would readily reveal a failure mode produced by a demolition charge....A separate and independent assessment should be made before a building demolition team destroys the evidence forever." Instead, the rubble was removed and buried underground with a fence around it to keep people out, and people at the site were told to not let anyone in to examine the debris. Is there something to hide here? Reportedly, the new judge may allow the defense access to the destroyed building.

There is considerable evidence that the government had advance notice that a federal building, probably in the midwest, was going to be attacked. An informant told the U.S. Attorney in Denver, Henry Solano, that a federal building probably in Denver or the midwest was going to be attacked.[28] Conspirators included Americans and people with Arabic names. This person was transporting drugs between L.A. and Kingman, Arizona. McVeigh, Michael Fortier, and Terry Nichols spent time in Kingman. Although supposedly not credible this person got a letter of immunity September 14, 1994 from the Justice Department, which is not provided that easily. And the Feds spoke to him three times including as late as March, 1995. In early April he sent a letter to federal authorities in Denver warning that a federal building would be attacked within two weeks. Even after the bombing, the Feds still said this informant was considered unreliable, and he did not testify before the grand jury.

On March 22, 1995 *The Star-Ledger* in Newark, N.J. published a report from Eduardo Gonzalex, head of the U.S. Marshals Service. A reliable source said there was going to be a terrorist attack against a federal courthouse or government facility in the U.S. in conjunction with the WTC trial, with the intent to kill many innocent people to attract press attention. The threat was considered very serious, and security was being increased throughout the U.S. On April 20, 1995 the Israeli newspaper *Yediot Ahronot* headlined a story by Zadok Yehezkeli that, in recent days, U.S. intelligence officials received information originating in the Middle East about an imminent Islamic terrorist attack on U.S. soil.

The initial trial judge, Wayne Alley, admitted to *The Oregonian,* the largest newspaper in Oregon, on April 20, 1995 that he had been warned of a possible terrorist attack several weeks before the bombing. Because of this, the judge stayed away from the court and his grandchildren were kept out of the day care center. He was probably removed from the case by a higher court because it would have been rather bizarre for the trial judge to openly acknowledged he was warned in advance about a terrorist attack, while the authorities denied there was any such warning.[29] The defense had tried for months to disqualify Alley. Two days after it submitted the interview as evidence of his unsuitability he was removed by a higher court. The press refuses to discuss this interview and government prior knowledge of the bombing.

The FBI called the Oklahoma City fire department on Friday, April 14, and warned of a terrorist threat in the area possibly in the next week. When a local investigator asked Assistant Chief Charles Gaines about this he denied receiving any warning. Then Chief Dispatcher Harvey Weathers confirmed they had received a message from the FBI to be alert to a bombing. When told about Gaines' comment, Weathers said: "I'm not going to lie for anyone. A lot of people don't want to get involved in this." Two other dispatchers confirmed Weathers' story. The Oklahoma City fire and police departments have since been ordered to not speak about the bombing, and inquiries must go through the city attorney.

All Oklahoma City fire department communication tapes from that Friday until the bombing have been erased. This was called an error. When Channel 4 got the police log for the night before the bombing there were only two pages when normally it would be 12 to 15 pages. A public affairs official for the police department acknowledged to a local investigator that pages were missing and that a court order would be needed to release them. Under Oklahoma law such records and tapes from the police and fire departments should be readily available.

The media constantly refers to the *Turner Diaries* as the inspiration for right wing extremists to do the Oklahoma bombing. Yet the press ignores the fact that Martin Keating, brother of Oklahoma's governor Frank Keating, wrote a novel *The Final Jihad* in 1991, which much more accurately portrays the events of the Oklahoma bombing. This book described a federal building in Oklahoma being destroyed by someone named Tom McVay. The key suspect was stopped by an alert Oklahoma Highway Patrol officer. What are the odds of this novel's plot being just a coincidence when compared to the actual events? While writing the novel Frank Keating, then a senior official in the Justice Department, introduced his brother to some FBI officials, including ex-FBI agent Oliver Revell, who served as a consultant to provide ideas for the project.[30]

In addition, when Ted Kaczynski, the Unabomber, was arrested, a well-read copy of Al Gore's book *Earth In the Balance* was found in his cabin. This was generally kept out of the news. I don't think this incident should be used to attack the entire environmental movement, but the same standard should exist with the militias. Instead the press falsely claimes *The Turner Diaries* was the Bible of the right, to demonize the militias.

Various people report that ATF and DEA workers were told not to come to work that day because of a bomb threat. On September 12, 1995, KFOR TV interviewed three witnesses who spoke with an ATF agent on the street just after the explosion who admitted no ATF agents were in the building during the blast because they had been warned to not come to work that day. At least four independent witnesses saw the local bomb squad at a parking lot by the Murrah building between 7:30-8:30 a.m. shortly before the blast. Norma Smith told her relatives in Texas about this.[31] Attorney Daniel Adomitis told the *Fort Worth Star/Telegram* that he saw a bomb squad by the county courthouse at 7:30 a.m. the morning of the blast. Other witnesses saw a bomb squad by the IRS building that morning. The government denies all these reports.[32]

Pat Briley's wife works with the wives of two FBI agents, including Dan Vogel, and minutes after the bombing they called their husbands, and then said the FBI knew in advance about the bombing. Two days later they said they shouldn't have admitted this, and the conversation should not be repeated. In the days before the bombing, Dana Cooper, director of the day care center, who was killed in the blast, received numerous bomb threats, which she reported to several government agencies. At 9 a.m. sharp, some FBI agents normally brought their children to the day care center, while they conducted business in the building, but this wasn't done the day of the blast.

Although 15 to 17 ATF agents were assigned to the federal building in Oklahoma, none were in the building during the blast. Despite claims that some of them were injured or killed, no such victims were ever identified. The *U.S. News & World Report*, August 14, 1995, published the names of all the identified Oklahoma bombing victims with photos for most of them. No ATF, DEA, or FBI agents were listed here. Although there was massive media coverage of the Oklahoma bombing, few of the injured were interviewed. Victims like Judy Morse realized a bomb exploded inside the building, and the government didn't want the public to hear such reports. When Edye Smith asked, on CNN May 23, 1995, why no one from the ATF was in the building, a shocked announcer cut her off and the press didn't pursue this.

Lester Martz, regional head of the ATF in Dallas, on May 23, 1995 said ATF agent Alex McCauley and a DEA agent fell five stories in a free fall from the eighth to the third floor in an elevator during the explosion, and they managed to open the stuck door to escape. ATF head John Magaw repeated this story the next day on CNN. However, the company that inspects the elevators happened to have two inspectors across the street when the blast occurred. With a government inspector, they immediately examined the elevators, and they confirmed that the ATF story was not possible. Repairman Duane James called it pure fantasy. None of the doors were forced open and safety switches to prevent excessive speed remained in place. No elevator had a free fall which was impossible unless a cable was cut, which did not happen.[33]

This bombing is not the first instance of a terrorist attack in which the U.S. government had advance warning that was kept from the public. Previously it was reported that the U.S. knew in advance of a terrorist threat to Pan Am, and there was even a warning posted at an American Embassy. In the months after the destruction of Pan Am flight 103 over Lockerbie, many were angry at the government because this warning wasn't openly published. In July, 1995 the London *Guardian* said the State Department received a warning three weeks in advance that there would be an attack against Pan Am and U.S. military bases.

In late October, 1995, Hoppy Heidelberg a member of the grand jury that indicted McVeigh publicly complained that U.S. prosecutors were intimidating the grand jury refusing even to present witnesses who saw John Doe 2. About John Doe 2, in transcripts released by the defense, Heidelberg said: "I'm satisfied that I know the government knows who he is." Heidelberg said this person was a government agent or informant. "Either way...they had prior knowledge to the bombing, and that's what they cannot afford...to have come out." FBI agents went to Heidelberg's home and showing a gun confiscated his juror notes. When Heidelberg tried to get a copy of those notes, as allowed under the FOIA, the government refused to comply. When grand jurors wanted to directly question witnesses, prosecutors removed the witness from the room and after getting questions from the jurors asked such questions in their own words. This is quite unusual and represents serious misconduct by prosecutors. According to the federal grand jury handbook the government is supposed to assist, not block, a grand juror in a search for the truth. A grand jury is an independent body that serves as a check against an overzealous prosecutor.[34]

After complaining to the judge in early October, 1995, Heidelberg was removed from the grand jury and threatened with jail and a fine if he spoke up. His removal was partly based on an interview he had with an FBI agent. It is extremely rare for a grand juror to break the oath of secrecy, which is illegal, and publicly make such complaints. One expert said it only happens once every few decades. The government falsely claimed that Heidelberg was a militia radical. Just after Heidelberg was removed from the grand jury, Rep. Key on October 26, 1995 started gathering 1,000 signatures to have a county grand jury. He warned that "criminal obstruction of justice charges could be levied against any person or persons who have destroyed documents related" to the bombing. Although quite unusual, a judge has twice turned down the request for a grand jury and the decision has been appealed. In June, 1995 relatives of the bombing victims petitioned Congress to hold an investigation.

On November 3, 1995 The *Dallas Morning News* wrote an editorial that Heidelberg should be held in contempt. *USA Today* attacked Heidelberg in an article entitled "A 'Terrible' Turn in Bomb Case."[35] Is it more terrible that the government is covering up evidence about such a crime, or that one juror had the integrity to speak out? In November, 1995 U.S. prosecutor Patrick Ryan told the *Daily Oklahoman* anyone who disagreed with the government's version of the case was being unpatriotic. He said independent investigators were "extremists who want to somehow harm this country." The British couldn't have said it better over 200 years ago! As in a communist country, if you challenge the party line you are an enemy of the people. That a brave person speaks out in the name of truth is not acceptable to the government and our corporate controlled media.

The indictments, which didn't describe a motive, made it clear the Feds believe others are involved. "Others unknown to the grand jury" were described.[36] However, *Time* called the indictment "A Two-Bit Conspiracy" involving just two drifters with no broad conspiracy.[37] Nichol's lawyer, Michael Tigar, requested a hearing to explore government misconduct. There have been various leaks of information that are often false, federal authorities have prevented witnesses from speaking with defense attorneys, and they have provided information to the press while withholding it from the defense.

The *Rocky Mountain News* said on March 29, 1996 that FBI agent Whitehurst believes the FBI is illegally withholding evidence that is hurting the McVeigh defense. He wrote a letter last November saying: "I will consider it an obstruction of justice and will testify in court to that opinion...if that information is suppressed by the Department of Justice and/or the FBI." This evidence involves the testimony of another FBI agent that residue from the explosion had been found in McVeigh's shirt. At a pretrial evidentiary hearing on April 9, 1996, the U.S. prosecutor admitted that Whitehurst tested this shirt and found no chemical residue from the bombing. Reportedly, nine FBI agents have signed declarations supporting Whitehurst's statements about government misconduct in the Oklahoma bombing investigation. The judge in the case sealed these documents but they were leaked.

Witnesses have even been intimidated by the government. People who made statements different from the approved version have been so criticized that certain witnesses are afraid to come forward. Some witnesses are afraid to lose their pension. A safety officer in the federal building saw McVeigh in the building several weeks before the blast, and had information that could explain who owned the leg found in the rubble. He was told to shut up or his reputation would be ruined. After Heidelberg was dismissed from the grand jury, a reporter made an appointment by phone to see him. The Assistant U.S. Attorney for the case then reportedly called and told Heidelberg if he saw this person he'd be go to jail. This is another sign of widespread phone wiretaps. One person, seriously injured in the blast, has important information that sharply differs from the government story. An FBI agent came to her door and said an *L.A. Times* reporter was coming to her place and she would be in serious trouble if she spoke to him. Ten minutes later there was a knock at the door, which she refused to answer. Later by her door she saw a card from an *L.A. Times* reporter. By the spring of 1996, federal agents revisited certain witnesses to harass them into changing their stories.

McVeigh's lawyer, Stephen Jones, asked the court to force the CIA to release secret records about the Oklahoma bombing. Reportedly, he did this because the military secretly released records to him showing the involvement of the CIA and foreign nationals in causing the Oklahoma bombing. If this were obtained through the court it would probably be entered as evidence during the trial, but naturally the government cried national security to block this request. Jones appears to now understand that much is involved in this trial. He spoke of a broader conspiracy with McVeigh being only a foot soldier.[38] He has spoken of foreign nationals being involved in the plot, his investigators have spoken to people like Ted Gunderson, and there are signs Jones may mount a defense involving some of the evidence discussed here that is being covered up. In November, 1995 Jones told reporters when they know what he has learned about the government's role in the bombing, they would never again have the same view about the government and the way government intelligence works. McVeigh's sister in 1994 told a reporter at the *Spotlight* that her brother worked for the ATF. According to Heidelberg, during the grand jury proceedings, McVeigh's sister read a letter from her brother in which he claimed to be a member of a U.S. military Special Forces Group conducting criminal activity.[39] This important revelation has received little publicity.

However, it is difficult to believe the government will allow information on its involvement in the bombing to be presented in open court. The Feds will go to any extreme to continue the cover-up. Jones has complained about the location of the trial but it remains to be seen how serious he will be in challenging the government's case. Jones barely attempted to delay the federal building's destruction. Attorney John De Camp was prepared to file for a 30-day delay in the demolition as a lawyer for a victim. Jones contacted De Camp and asked him to back down because he would be in a better legal position to get this delay. De Camp agreed, also releasing his bomb expert, as Jones requested. Then Jones only asked for a 48-hour delay, he didn't use this bomb expert, and the defense agreed not to even take soil samples to investigate. De Camp was stunned. A defense lawyer in a criminal investigation has a right and duty to examine evidence at the scene of the crime. At the same time, in fairness to Jones, the rapid destruction of this evidence may provide grounds for an appeal.

Many similar cases in the past were settled before a trial took place, such as the killing of the Kennedys, Martin L King, and John Lennon. It is quite possible McVeigh and Nichols will be killed, an out-of-court settlement will be made, or the lawyers for the defendants will back off and not present certain evidence. During a trial, it would be a public relations disaster for the government if the truth came out. It remains to be seen what Jones will actually reveal in a trial. Gunderson said the security for McVeigh when he was initially moved was "very poor, sloppy, an open invitation for someone to kill him." Authorities refused to even give McVeigh a bullet-proof vest when he was initially moved, and no one knows how the crowd knew who he was and when he was being moved. In late August, 1995 the security chief where McVeigh and Nichols were jailed was removed after he attempted to increase security around them. Some investigators believe McVeigh was supposed to die in the blast, and this makes sense.

In a crime like the Oklahoma bombing with an on-going cover-up there are many loose ends. Why were thousands of elite Iraqi troops quietly moved to the U.S? Why did the government give immunity to the Denver informant and then, even after he was quite accurate, still ignore him? What is the relationship between the secret government and the foreign terrorists who may be involved in the bombing? The exact role of the U.S. government in this cover-up has not yet been clarified. When McVeigh was arrested, the officer's video recorded the license plate of a truck owned by Steve Colburn. He was arrested May 13, 1995 but nothing further has been heard about him. The unidentified leg found in the federal building was identified as belonging to a white male. Then the Feds said it belonged to a black woman. It is not that difficult for forensic experts to determine the sex and race of a victim.

A German friend of McVeigh's Andreas Strassmeir, may be involved in the bombing. Several witnesses claim Strassmeir was with McVeigh in Junction City, Kansas shortly before the bombing, and Strassmeir may soon be named in the Smith family's civil lawsuit. Coming from a prominent political family in Germany, he became a German officer with intelligence training in 1989 and then moved to the U.S. to visit KKK and neo-Nazis supporters. Phone records show that McVeigh and Strassmeir communicated including possibly on April 5 and 18, 1995, and Strassmeir admits meeting McVeigh. In December, 1993 the FBI said German and U.S. intelligence agencies would work together to limit the influence of Nazis in each country. This included surveillance of certain Americans. For years the government has used foreign agents to perform illegal acts in the U.S. to avoid being detected. Strassmeir admitted to the London *Sunday Telegraph* that he first lived in the U.S. in 1989 because he planned to work for the U.S. Justice Department on a special assignment.[40] The *McCurtain Daily Gazette* obtained an FBI memorandum dated April 26, 1995 that an imprisoned White Aryan Resistance (WAR) member had met McVeigh several years ago with John Doe 2 who was a German national.[41] On February 4, 1996 the *Sunday Times* of London said British and German extremists may be linked to the bombing.[42]

Strassmeir fled to Germany after the *McCurtain Daily Gazette* started writing about his possible involvement with McVeigh and the bombing and suggested he may be an undercover intelligence agent. His U.S. attorney Kirk Lyons confirmed that he returned to Germany through Mexico with the help of GSG-9, the German military counter-terrorist unit of which he is a member, reportedly because of death threats.[43] A warrant for Strassmeir's arrest for overstaying a tourist visa was never served, although the FBI received a copy of the warrant. In February, 1992, when Strassmeir's car was impounded, the State Department and governor's office called and said he had diplomatic immunity.

Cash received help in his investigation by someone from Interpol frustrated with the U.S. governments refusal to investigate various white supremists. In Tulsa, Cash visited Dennis Mahon, a leader of WAR, a former Ku Klux Klan leader, and a friend of Strassmeirs. Mahon and his brother own a sporty 1973 Chevrolet pickup similar to a vehicle the FBI was looking for immediately after the bombing. During the visit, Cash also spoke to Mark Thomas, leader of the Pennsylvania WAR, and he admitted being at Elohim City days before the bombing. Also discussed at the meeting was Mike Brescia, another WAR member and roommate of Strassmeirs at Elohim City. At least one witness has identified Mahon as driving with McVeigh the morning of the bombing. McVeigh's lawyer confirmed that, although it had questioned 11,000 people, the FBI had not questioned any of these people about their possible involvement in the bombing, although Mahon did give a deposition in Edye Smith's lawsuit. A member of the WAR, Richard Snell, was executed in prison by the government on April 19, 1995 hours after the bombing.[44] The *Denver Post* quoted Arkansas prison guard Alan Ablies as saying: "Snell repeatedly predicted that there would be a bombing or an explosion the day of his death."

On May 21, 1995 Reuters News Agency said *Newsweek* had information the government "pretty well knew who was involved in the April 19 blast, and that husbands and wives as well as children as young as 12, were going to be arrested at" Elohim City, a white supremist compound in Oklahoma. "The major players, already targeted by the FBI, were talking to investigators to get lighter sentences," and a government informant had provided information on the bombing. The government usually has informants in targeted groups. On May 21, 1995 WUSA in Boston profiled the *Newsweek* story, but this report was suspended and not widely disseminated. *Newsweek* only ran a watered-down story on May 29, 1995. McVeigh, Michael Fortier, and Terry Nichols visited Elohim City many times while Strassmeir lived there for some months, and no one could confirm Strassmeir's alibi during the bombing.[45] On October 12, 1993 McVeigh got a speeding ticket a few miles from Elohim City on the road to the village.

Reportedly, the extensive investigation by the Smith family, discussed above, has led them to conclude that Mike Brescia is John Doe 2. Eyewitnesses place Brescia with McVeigh in Junction City, Kansas shortly before the bombing. Just after the composite of John Doe 1 was released, before McVeigh was publically identified, a women in Kansas told the FBI John Doe 1 was McVeigh, who she had dated and John Doe 2 was Brescia, who a friend had dated. Amazingly, the FBI refused to even interrogate Brescia even though he remained at Elohim City for months after the bombing until the press started asking about him. Then he disappeared and no one is sure where he is today. Strassmeir is going to be named in the Smith lawsuit as a "U.S. federal informant with material knowledge of the bombing."

Lester Martz, regional head of the ATF, confirmed that there was a sting operation the night before the bombing, but he wouldn't confirm if the sting operation was related to the bombing.[46] Rep. Key also said someone involved in the sting operation confirmed its existence to him. Reportedly, there were ATF agents on a stake out of the Murrah building at 3:30 a.m., and they had a tracking device. At 4:30 a.m. these agents set up a road block two miles from the Murrah building, and other agents were probably watching another near by federal building. Some feel they were following McVeigh's car with a transmitter, and that McVeigh and his friends were going to be arrested before the blast, or the blast was supposed to occur early in the morning when no one was in the building. Others feel that because the sting operation failed, the Feds are trying to cover-up their advanced knowledge. Or the failed sting operation may have been a deliberate cover to carry out the actual bombing.

The WTC bombing involved an FBI informant working with terrorists possibly trained by the CIA. About the Oklahoma bombing Strassmeir said, "The ATF had an informant inside this operation. They had advance warning and they bungled it."[47] In the New York and Oklahoma, officials openly admit that they haven't yet found the masterminds of the crime and aren't sure how funds were obtained to support the bombing.[48] In each case, authorities claimed they were able to arrest people within a few days, because the vehicle ID number of the truck involved in the bombing was found, but this was false. The Feds already knew who they were looking for in New York. The vehicle identification number (VIN) of the Ryder truck supposedly led investigators to McVeigh, but GM said the VIN is not on the rear axle as claimed, and Ryder confirmed that it doesn't add VINs to its trucks. In each case, no one in Congress has demanded an explanation for the many discrepancies in these cases. Several congressional aides told one investigator that Congress would not permit hearings on the Oklahoma bombing, partly because they were afraid it would so undermine federal law enforcement that it might jeopardize passage of the Anti-Terrorism bill.

The many inconsistencies in the Oklahoma bombing raise serious questions about the integrity of the government's case. Why does the national media and progressive press refuse to discuss this government misconduct? If there was no federal involvement in the Oklahoma bombing, why are they covering up the facts? The government won't interview many witnesses because they would start talking about other people who they saw with McVeigh. Several private investigators believe the CIA was definitely involved with foreign nationals and American KKK/neo-Nazis members working together. During the Gulf War German Nazis openly supported Iraq, so it is quite possible Middle Eastern and German terrorists work together on certain operations. Hopefully, the rule of law will be reestablished in America so that the perpetrators of this atrocity can be arrested and brought to trial.

# Chapter XVII

# Recent Attacks on the
# Militias and Patriot Movement

"In the beginning of a change, the patriot is a scarce man, and brave and hated and scorned. When his cause succeeds, the timid join him, for then it costs nothing to be a patriot."

Mark Twain

"These are times that try men's souls. The summer soldier and the sunshine patriot will, in this crisis, shrink from the service of his country; but he that stands it now deserves the love and thanks of man and woman. Tyranny, like hell, is not easily conquered...."

Thomas Paine

As many are aware, in recent years thousands of Americans have joined unenrolled militias in many states. Militia units should be set up across the country to protect the people, as was the intent of the Founders. People should consider joining armed militia units to train, study, assist the people during emergencies, and to more effectively get involved in politics. If more raids like the Waco massacre take place, there will be an explosion of membership in the militias. Many state codes have laws allowing for general unorganized or unenrolled militias, but their role today is not well defined. In 1946 Virginia ordered its unenrolled militia to restore peace in a labor dispute. They are still regarded as a reserve source of manpower for the state National Guard and the Army. However, the National Guard, not the unenrolled state militias, are seen as the main source of manpower for the Army.

Many people joining militia units belong to the Patriot movement which exists in every state. People in this populist movement are often not armed. The movement includes constitutionalists, homeschoolers, tax protesters, progressives, New Agers, and Christian fundamentalists. Many would benefit by attending its meetings. While the Patriot movement is rather large, it has received little national media coverage even after the Oklahoma bombing. The militia movement is just the tip of the iceberg of a broad-based movement involving millions of people determined to restore constitutional government. Many people are joining the Patriot movement to stop the coming one world government, because so many things written about it for years are now actually happening.

The national media have continuously attacked the militias and patriots linking them to racism, anti-Semitism, and white supremacists like the Aryan Nation, although there is little evidence of this. The press often says the militias consist of angry white men; yet many Jews, blacks, and women belong to the movement.[1] The *San Francisco Chronicle* said, while groups that watch extremist organizations have claimed "the militia movement is linked to dangerous right-wing ideologies, they offer little supporting evidence." The article said militia members "engage in voter registration drives, assist local law enforcement agencies in flood relief efforts and other emergencies." This is what the Missouri militia did during recent flooding.[2]

Most people in the militias and Patriot movement have no prejudice against any race or color,[3] although there have been some generally unsuccessful attempts by racists to infiltrate militia units. In one incident, a militia unit in Fort Bragg, California was offered 1,500 acres for training. A check revealed that the man was a white supremacist, so the offer was rejected.[4] Sheriff Dupont said white supremacists in his Montana county initially tried to influence the local militia as it formed, but they were totally rejected.[5] According to the *U.S. News & World Report*, a few people from right wing groups have joined militia units, "but law enforcement officials believe most recruits are simply disenchanted with what they consider the growing intrusion of government into their lives."[6] When a few skinheads and neo-Nazis attended a Missouri militia meeting, they were thrown out, as was the person who said he could build landmines. This unit states in its manual that it will not tolerate racism or criminal behavior.[7]

*Time* said many militias throw out racists and some militias have minority members. James Aho, author of *The Politics of Righteousness* and a sociologist who has interviewed 368 people in the radical right, said "The vast majority of people in the militias are not violent or dangerous."[8] Most people in these groups are middle-class, law-abiding citizens who realize how dangerous the federal government has become. There is also a growing interaction between the Patriot movement and black nationalists. Many black Americans understand the danger of corporate domination and government abuses of power.[9]

While most people in the secret government are Christian, some are Jewish, and some claim there is a Jewish plot to control the world. The real religion of all these people is money and power. There is no Jewish conspiracy, just as there is no Christian conspiracy. To attack the religious views of a few bankers is morally reprehensible and provides no real insight into what is actually taking place. Attacking the secret government as a Jewish plot also falls into a trap, because then you are being anti-Semitic and that becomes the whole issue instead of actually analyzing the secret government. Even Jewish patriots who attack the secret government are called anti-Semitic. This is a classic example of attacking the messenger to avoid an intelligent discussion of the message. This strategy is another layer of protection the corporate elite use to keep the public from learning about their evil deeds. People like Henry Kissinger are promoted partly so people will see a Jewish conspiracy and be attacked on that basis, while the real work of the secret government is not even discussed. On February 2, 1995, the *New York Review of Books* reviewed Pat Robertson's book, *The New World Order*. While this book describes in great detail the history and plans of the corporate elite to establish the one world government, Robertson also mentioned certain Jewish individuals. The reviewer barely explored the theme of Robertson's book. Instead the review focused on the "question of whether Robertson was an anti-Semite."

Members of the secret government who claim to be Jewish are far less than a fraction of one percent of the millions of Jews throughout the world, most of whom have no interest or even knowledge of a secret government desiring world domination. It is morally wrong to slander an entire race because of the evil deeds of a few people. "A tragic canard, the Jewish conspiracy merits no further comment. Its existence, however, tends to unfairly discredit other conspiratorial interpretations of events that have nothing to do with making scapegoats of any ethnic or religious group."[10] While some people use anti-Semitic or racist remarks to attack the bankers, that is a minority view that offends most people in the militias and Patriot movement. One reason there is very little anti-Semitism in the Patriot movement and militias is because there are so many Jewish members. The 100-man militia unit in San Diego has a Jewish membership of 50 percent. Jews For the Preservation of Firearms has thousands of members, Nancy Lord, a Jewish attorney, represents members of the movement throughout the nation, and I am one more of thousands of Jewish members of the Patriot movement.

The national media often uses quotes from critics of the right, like Morris Dees and the Southern Poverty Law Center (SPLC), which calls the militias dangerous with ties to "hate-mongering groups," but they provide little evidence of this. The SPLC sent information to the U.S. Justice Department in October, 1994 about the supposedly dangerous militias, but the Justice Department until recently took no legal action because it received no evidence of illegal activity. The SPLC also wrote to many state attorney generals in May, 1995 asking that existing laws be applied to stop the militias. By April, 1996 no state had taken action against any militia, because most militia members follow the law. The Idaho Deputy Attorney General said people in the militias should not be cut off from the political process.

The SPLC is one of the wealthiest non-profit organizations in America. On April 25, 1986 *The Montgomery Advertiser* said Dees's entire staff of five lawyers and his top aide resigned because they were surprised to learn that the center's goal was to enrich Dees, not to help poor people. An ex-attorney for the center Deborah Ellis said: "I felt that Morris (Dees) was on a Klan kick because it was such an easy target—easy to beat in court, easy to raise big money on." Now it is the turn of the militias, so the SPLC can reach $100 million in assets. In 1993, the American Institute of Philanthropy, a watchdog over charities, gave the SPLC a low D grade because of its poor use of funds. Several times the SPLC has been accused of discrimination. On December 28, 1994 *The Montgomery Advertiser* reported that 12 former black employees experienced racial problems at the SPLC. In 1958 Dees supported George Wallace partly because he supported segregation. In the Joan Little case, Dees was dismissed by the judge after he was accused of trying to get a witness to commit perjury. Millard Farmer, a Georgia lawyer and ex-partner of Dees, sued and won after Dees cheated him out of $50,000.

Kenneth Stern, in *A Force Upon the Plain*, constantly claimed that arrested individuals had militia ties but usually no proof of this was offered. Guilt by innuendo is the mark of the government, the national press, and professional critics of the right. In *Loud Hawk*, published in 1994, Stern revealed that he was a lawyer for the militant American Indian Movement from 1975 to 1988. Harshly critical of the government, his phones were wiretapped and he was followed at times. Stern admitted that as a young lawyer he "would have thought bombing property was almost romantic, a sign of defiance...." Stern never denounced acts of violence by the left. In 1988 he established the National Organization Against Terrorism and, with the support of ex-CIA head George Bush and ex-intelligence officer Arthur Goldberg, he became a successful lawyer with many establishment connections. Who is the real Kenneth Stern?

Some phony experts now attacking the right are operatives working for the government or large corporations, others on their own or in conjunction with certain private groups, attack any action considered right wing, while some of these people are simply confused individuals making a living. Often these people make wildly exaggerated claims about the militias as a vehicle to raise money and enhance their importance. Morris Dees identified an 86-year-old woman in Colorado as a radical militia leader. His list of militia groups in Colorado and many other states was devoid of reality, but he has raised millions of dollars because of the supposed militia threat.

Professional critics of the right often name leaders of the Klan, neo-Nazis, and white supremacists as being leaders of the militias and Patriot movement. In January, 1996, the editor of *Media Bypass* rejected an ad from a Klan group and readers supported this. I listen to patriot talk radio for hours each day. It is extremely rare for someone to call such shows and promote white supremacist or racist views. About once a month, I do hear such a caller, and most programs cut them off. A popular patriot radio station, the USA Freedom Network, has a Jewish owner and several Jewish announcers. I have never once heard a radio announcer or guest promoting racist or anti-Semitic views. The objective observer can easily confirm this.

I am not saying that there are no racists in the militias and Patriot movement, but such involvement is minimal and it is a lie to claim otherwise. Attend a Preparedness Expo that takes place in various states, and you will not see any hate groups.[11] Even Chip Berlet, an extreme leftist who follows the movement, said that people in this movement are not especially racist or anti-Semitic but are part of a broader movement.[12] There are people in white supremacist groups who criticize the federal government and want the Constitution restored, just as members of these groups hold racial purity views. I am aware of one Christian Identity newspaper that presents patriotic themes. While some racist groups would probably like to bring in new members from the Patriot movement, they also harshly criticize the militias because militia members are not white supremacists. Jonathan Karl, author of *The Right to Bear Arms*, interviewed Aryan Nations' leader Richard Butler in the *New York Post*. Butler said the militias were traitors to the white race, and militias were a government-sponsored movement, maybe working with the CIA. As Karl told me, he is aware that the militias are not part of white supremacist, Klan, or neo-Nazi groups. Karl was on CNN, where he now works, just after the Freeman surrendered. He said only a small, small minority of militia members are white supremacists.

The hysterical media attack on the militias after the Oklahoma bombing was a propaganda barrage that had little to do with reality. People who think there is a free press in America are in a state of denial or are ignoring the evidence. In a free society, there would be at least some diverse opinion in the national press. The orders were given and there was a constant hysterical attack on the militias. How can you demonize the militias when the Nichols brothers attended one or two meetings of the Michigan Militia and were then thrown out because of their radical views! McVeigh denied being involved with the militias when interviewed and no one has ever presented proof to dispute this, yet to this day, critics of the right still blame the militias for the Oklahoma bombing, even though they provide no proof of this. The FBI has not arrested any militia member for the Oklahoma bombing.

In the gleeful rush to attack the right, proof of militia involvement in the Oklahoma attack was not necessary. James Ridgeway, in a April 25, 1995 *Village Voice* article, linked the militias to the Oklahoma bombing by using words like "It is probable" and "there is every reason to believe." Guess work and personal beliefs replaced professional journalism. It suddenly became politically correct to blame the militias for everything, from property rights issues to bombing abortion clinics. I went to one meeting where the speaker, a private investigator, spent 10 minutes blaming the militias for attacks on environmentalists and then acknowledged there was no proof of this. Over and over again, in the national media when the militias are discussed, there is typically one expert and one or more reporters who are extremely hostile to the militias. Only on occasion is there a rational discussion with opposing views presented.

In some instances, the media blatantly distorted the truth to attack the militias and Patriot movement. On April 27, 1995 ABC's *Day One* showed a headline of the *Resister* magazine describing the U.S. military's Combat Arms Survey which suggested U.S. soldiers might shoot citizens who refused to surrender their arms. The reporter called this right wing extremism instead of noting this was a U.S. government survey. The *Progressive, Harpers*, and several TV shows took Bo Gritz's words out of context and falsely claimed he supported the Oklahoma bombing, when the opposite was true. The press including *Time*, the *Wall Street Journal*,[13] the *Village Voice* on May 23, 1995, and many other publications quoted two local liberal reporter who falsely claimed that Sam Sherwood, head of the U.S. Militia Association in Idaho, had said a civil war may be coming and you may need to shoot legislators. Sherwood strongly denied stating this. He lived on a kibbutz in Israel, and the Idaho militia is extremely conservative in its actions. Unlike the ranting press, Mack Tanner, a retired U.S. diplomat, who wrote a detailed article on the militias in *Reason*, was at the meeting when Sherwood spoke. Tanner heard the opposite of what the press claimed. Sherwood asked that political action, not violence, be used to correct improper government policies.[14]

One result of the propaganda attack on the militias is that many people mistakenly look at the militias as a great danger, when the exact opposite is true. The militias exist in a defensive mode, formed in response to an increasingly oppressive government. Who is the real threat in America—people who call for a return to constitutional government, or a government that seizes property from hundreds of thousands of citizens and whose agents break into people's homes without due process even killing innocent citizens? If a militia threatens violence or is accused of violence, it may be an FBI operative, like John Parsons and the Tri-State Militia, when they threatened war with the federal government.

On July 30, 1995, Rep. Schumaker said regarding Clinton's involvement in the Waco raid: "Before you make some allegations...have some facts." This advice should apply to all Americans. Instead, opposition to government policies is called unpatriotic and racist. Amazingly Clinton said May 5, 1995: "You cannot be a patriot and despise your government." He would probably consider the Founders dangerous radicals. Clinton obviously has no understanding of our history. It has long been part of our heritage to be suspicious of state power. "Clinton has sought to intimidate critics of government policy by branding them as terrorists....Loud voices are not the same as violent deeds....Wide open debate is the best chance for restraining violent impulses....Information is the enemy both of out-of-control government and of paranoia. Vigorous, open dissent is a powerful check on government excesses—and an important, peaceful outlet for citizen grievances."[15]

*Clinical Psychiatry News* said government critics were suffering from "government-phobia." Supposedly, this recently discovered disorder has become an epidemic, with people becoming delusional and even psychotic. On May 3, 1996, NBC's *Unsolved Mysteries*, in a story on the Freemen, referred to a "pathological fear of the government." As in the Soviet Union, if you disagree with the government, you must be crazy. People like George Washington would be put in mental hospitals.[16] With tens of millions of people supporting the Patriot movement, the objective observer should consider whether there is mass hysteria, or are things happening in America that you should examine!

*USA Today* and CNN reported a Gallop poll on April 23-24, 1995, showing that 39 percent of the people felt immediately threatened by the federal government.[17] They were surprised at this high number, so they conducted another poll dropping the word "immediate" and were shocked to see the percent rise to 52 percent.[18] *The Los Angeles Times* conducted a similar poll and found that 45 percent felt threatened by the federal government. Thomas Jefferson said: "When people fear the government, you have tyranny, but when government fears the people, you have liberty." A *USA Today* reporter said the newspaper didn't understand what was happening, but the militias appeared to represent a political movement that had not previously been identified by the politicians and national media.[19]

On May 18, 1995 the *Washington Post*, in a poll conducted with ABC News, revealed that one in eight Americans (32 million) support the goals and activities of the militias and that six percent (15 million) of Americans consider the federal government the enemy.[20] The Patriot movement, which is much bigger than the militias, represents many more people, and this poll underestimated the true feelings of the country, because it was conducted just after the Oklahoma bombing during a massive campaign to demonize the militias.

You may be surprised to hear about these polls, because they received little publicity. These four polls involve five of the most prestigious news organizations in the U.S. That so many fear and distrust the government should make the objective observer explore what is really happening to our Republic. At what point do views held by tens of millions of people stop being called extremist or racist? At what point do supposedly extremist views become reasonable opinions when such views are held by millions of people? The anger and hostility that tens of millions of Americans feel towards the federal government is much broader and deeper than the Washington crowd and the national media will acknowledge, although many Republicans understand the popularity of the Patriot movement. The only Republican in Congress to harshly attack the militias was Rep. Peter King. He was shocked to be so criticized and his office was flooded with hundreds of angry letters and calls.[21]

Progressives joined in the rush to demonize the right after the Oklahoma bombing. For years, the left tried to rally the people to counteract the increasing power of the large corporations. Now that a powerful, populist, middle-class movement led by the right has developed that can threaten corporate power, many progressive leaders are quite upset. There is a tendency for progressives to automatically label anyone who has conspiracy views as a right wing fanatic. The error of this perspective is exemplified by the research of progressives like Noam Chomsky, Michael Parenti, Gore Vidal, and Holly Sklar, who often describe the same groups and problems as presented by the Patriot movement. When these people criticize the Council on Foreign Relations (CFR) and Trilateral Commission (TC), it is similar to concerns expressed on the right. The one world government that Noam Chomsky described in *World Orders Old and New* and in other writings[22] is similar to the new world order the right attacks. Holly Sklar's book, *Trilateralism*, described the TC and its plans for corporate influence but, perhaps as a leftist, she openly criticizes the right and its conspiracy theories.[23] The only difference between conspiracy theory and institutional analysis is that the former better describes a complex power structure whose machinations defy economic and institutional analysis.

After the Oklahoma bombing, David Helvarg blamed the militias and property rights groups for attacking environmentalists. Yet, in *War Against the Greens*, Helvarg identified three prime sources for attacks on environmentalists without naming the militias.[24] Alexander Cockburn was right to state that no one has provided any evidence that the militias are attacking environmentalists.[25] The call by progressives for more governmen power to suppress the right will only weaken the left. Inevitably, enhanced government power will be used to attack the left.[26] One progressive correctly said of the right: "These folks are absolutely correct that the fear generated by the Oklahoma bombing will be cynically manipulated by a state security apparatus desperate to further consolidate and extend its control in the name of antiterrorism."[27] However, hating the right and supporting big government the left, except for *Prevailing Winds*, has refused to discuss the government cover-up and many discrepancies in the Oklahoma bombing reports. Even with this atrocity, leaders in the left defend the government, which is one more reason why so many progressives have joined the Patriot movement.

People like Jerry Brown ask where all the progressives have gone. Noam Chomsky said people who joined the unions 60 years ago now join paramilitary groups. Recently the *New York Times* published an article about progressives forming a militia unit in Maine.[28] To publicize one more militia unit is unusual, but there is a potential threat to the corporate elite if the left and right join together. Recently, 125 members of this militia, including Earth Firsters and Buchanan supporters, lobbied the state legislature to weaken corporate power. This is the wave of the future. The progressive establishment should wake up before it becomes even more irrelevant. The Patriot movement is a genuine populist movement that includes many progressives. The right has grown so powerful in recent years, partly because it supports populist issues, the left has abandoned. For the left to be revitalized, it must understand that the foremost issue of our time is to restore constitutional government. After *The Nation* and *The Progressive* harshly attacked the militias, they published letters from upset readers correctly stating that the militias were not being accurately portrayed and the right was attacking the same forces these magazines often criticize.[29]

On May 10-12, 1996 leading progressives and environmental leaders met in Washington, D.C. at a conference presented by the International Forum on Globalization. The meeting was called to confront the threat of corporate dominance over democracy, traditional cultures and nationalities, human welfare, and the environment. The goal was to confront the problem of "unelected and unaccountable global elites who are seizing control of one-world governance." Internationalists and the TC were criticized. The World Trade Organization (WTO) was attacked because it was "designed to serve as a global governing body for transnational corporate interests."

Leading environmental groups like the Sierra Club attacked GATT and NAFTA. Carl Pope, director of the Sierra Club, said: "The global economy is not really inevitable (and) Pat Buchanan deserves a more serious look." Jean-Luc Jouvet of Greenpeace said: "We are staring catastrophe in the face." He acknowledged that statements from the World Bank about concern for the environment and the world's poor were false. "They were lies....There is no way any of us can ignore that reality now." Willard Smith of the Machinists and Aerospace Workers Union spoke for the AFL-CIO. He said that five years ago, "many of the people here were dreamy internationalists of one sort or another. But what we have seen of NAFTA, the WTO, and international financial speculation has been a rough wake-up call."

The press refused to discuss this conference because it did not suit the corporate model of what we are supposed to think. Most people in the militias and Patriot movement would agree with the conclusions reached at this conference about stopping the new world order. Except for a brief comment in the *San Francisco Bay Guardian*, the progressive press refused to even discuss this important conference. Wall Street has much more control over the progressive press than is generally understood.

The left and right have many similar goals and should work together to restore the Constitution and stop the large corporations from establishing the new world order dictatorship. Many in the left and right have already been working together to stop NAFTA, GATT and the anti-terrorist bill. The *Washington Monthly* correctly said the Patriot movement's constitutional views brought it closer to the ACLU and the New Left than to right wing conservatives.[30] The *New Yorker* described the merging of the left and right to fight the governing elite as "fusion paranoia." This is called paranoid because people who no longer accept the liberal mind-set of massive government control are considered crazy![31]

Most progressive critics of the militias and Patriot movement ignore the many constitutional issues that are at the heart of the movement; yet this concern is the key reason why so many progressives have joined the Patriot movement. Chip Berlet blames the rise of the militias and Patriot movement on economic problems and "anger over gains by oppressed groups" in the U.S. Scapegoating and wild conspiracy theories are to blame![32] Marc Cooper in the *Nation* said: "The constitutionalist rhetoric used by the 'patriot' militias merely cloaks the most bigoted of views."[33] These people are more concerned about citizens that criticize the government then about government abuses of power because they are blinded by their own ideology so they must attack anyone on the right.

Some voices on the left have acknowledged the constitutional concerns of the patriots. Alexander Cockburn attended a gun/militia rally of 2,500 and was pleasantly surprised to discover that the populist issues raised were similar to the concerns of the left. Martin Luther King, Jr. was cheered as was the imprisonment of a Detroit policemen for killing a black man. When given a copy of a speech just presented, Cockburn said: "Most of it could have been delivered by a leftist in the late sixties without changing a comma."[34] Cockburn asked why people who object to oppressive governments and economic regulations as in Mexico are hailed as heroes by progressives, but when Americans try to defend their rights over similar oppressive government policies progressives call these people right wing extremists and paranoid racists.[35]

Barbara Dority, in the leftist magazine *The Humanist*, said after the Oklahoma bombing, "This rush to judgment (of the militias) has been accompanied by a near-total avoidance of rational analysis, and much of the information attacking the militias is being distributed by anti-hate groups with their own agenda." Dority discussed the constitutional issues inspiring the Patriot movement and militias and agreed with many of these concerns.[36] *Reason* magazine had an excellent article on the militias by a retired U.S. diplomat. The author interviewed many militia members over several months and found that "culturally ignorant reporters" were telling "sensational stories" rather than looking for the truth. Instead of finding racists and anti-Semites, he found that most militia members were employed in middle class jobs and had a deep distrust of the government.[37]

The militias and Patriot movement follow the tradition of populism, not that of conservatives. The recent conservative attack on Buchanan, partly because he attacked the new world order and corporate dominance, exemplifies how conservatives and patriots differ.[38] Conservatives support free trade and an international outlook, while patriots support American sovereignty and managed trade. Populists attack the asset forfeiture and corporate-welfare laws that conservatives pass. Conservatives stress economic issues, while patriots defend constitutional rights. Conservatives pass numerous laws such as in welfare and education rarely acknowledging, as patriots do, that this violates the Constitution. Conservatives want more law and order, while patriots what to stop police tyranny. Conservatives like Newt Gingrich are considered enemies of the people by many patriots because he is a CFR member. Progressives attack patriots partly because they do not understand that patriots and conservatives are different, because when someone is perceived as an enemy, truth doesn't matter. The real fight is not between the left and right, it is between liberty and tyranny. Traditional liberals and traditional conservatives have sold out to the corporate elite and are destroying the Constitution.

Progressives who attack the right for wanting less government ignore our history. A massive federal government is not part of the Constitution. Charles A. Reich, in *Opposing the System*, described how the large corporations are quietly gaining total control. He said the constitutional system of checks and balances has been superceded by corporate control, yet he supports the New Deal social contract of big government helping the people. With the New Deal, liberals abandoned constitutional government and installed democratic centralism. Liberals claim that we need big government to help the people, yet they also claim to believe in the Constitution and the rule of law. This is the great liberal paradox. Most federal programs started in the New Deal are unconstitutional. Liberals ignore that the Founders did not trust government, so a central government with few powers was established with checks and balances installed. Along with restraining the corporations, many federal programs should be shifted to the states. Then constitutional government could be restored, and there would be less threat of tyranny from a smaller federal government.

Some liberals want to resolve the great liberal paradox by redoing the Constitution. Lewis Lapham favorably reviewed *The Frozen Republic: How the Constitution is Paralyzing Democracy*, which called for a new Constitution. Our present predicament exists partly because many have little interest, understanding, or respect for the Constitution, which is still the supreme law in America. This is partly why the rule of law has been so weakened. Unfortunately, a new Constitution today would be totally dominated by the large corporations, and the people's rights would be lost. The problem is not the Constitution, it is the misuse of power. We don't need big changes in the Constitution, we need to enforce it. Thomas Jefferson warned: "In questions of power...let no more be heard of confidence in men, but bind him down from mischief by the chains of the Constitution."

Many Americans believe big government is the main problem, and the media supports this myth. In many daily activities, abusive government officials are a serious problem; however, the threat of a one world government and the loss of all our rights is coming from the large corporations, not from the government. Progressives understand that the real problem is the large corporations and their dominance of government. Government officials are merely agents of the large corporations. While the right often speaks of CFR and TC control, sometimes describing the dangerous power of the banks, there is rarely a direct recognition that the large corporations are the real problem. Instead the Patriot movement primarily attacks problems with the government. This is the biggest weakness in the Patriot movement.

Too often the Patriot movement focuses only on oppressive government actions without understanding that the main enemy of the people is the large corporations. These are the key leaders of the CFR, TC, and related organizations. In a 1978-1979 study of CFR members, G. William Domhoff in *Who Rules America Now?*, found that 70 percent of the 100 largest corporations had at least one official in the CFR. Twenty-one of the 25 largest banks, 37 percent of the 500 largest businesses, and 16 of the 25 largest insurance companies had at least one official in the CFR. Twenty percent of the CFR members were listed in *Poor's Register of Corporations, Directors, and Executives*. Just as the Patriot movement works to restore constitutional government, a second major focus should be to restore corporate charters to the same limited status that existed in the early days of our Republic. This will help curtail corporate power.

Charles A. Reich, in *Opposing the System*, had one chapter titled "The Invisible Government." After this excellent description that anyone in the Patriot movement would benefit from studying, this liberal said there is no conspiracy.[39] While the left understands better than the right how dangerous the large corporations are, only the right carries this threat to its logical and inevitable conclusion. If the large corporations aren't stopped, a corporate police state is inevitable. This is what the right warns of, but they are called racist and extremists for saying this. Why do progressives think corporate leaders are such nice people that they wouldn't carry their quest for power to the logical conclusion? One need only study how the corporate leaders tried to establish a dictatorship in the 1930s, and what these elitists say in hundreds of publications, to understand that a dictatorship is coming. The left focuses too much on economic and institutional concepts and less on our rights being lost.

Part of the problem is that people on the right and left have an inbred dislike and even hatred of each other, so that even when they support the same positions and can benefit by working together this is rarely done. The corporate elite often play the left and right against each other, while they sit back and laugh. Divide and conquer is an old strategy. People on opposing political spectrums often won't even talk to each other. On talk radio, I have never once heard a progressive or patriot radio talk show have someone from the opposing political spectrum as a guest. People on the left and right are often drawn to attack the other, however destructive that may be. This book will probably be attacked by some on each political spectrum, because I quote from the left and right. To do this is not politically correct.

Often when people are arrested for a criminal act, professional critics of the right immediately claim these people are militia members when there is no proof of this. We have entered a period in which the militias will be attacked and blamed in numerous incidents, however little evidence there is of militia involvement. The Amtrak bombing exemplifies this trend. A message was found which the press said made this a terrorist attack tied to the militias. *U.S. News & World Report*, in an editorial, attacked the growing pattern of the press to label criminal acts as terrorism that threatens the foundations of America.[40] When the Freemen siege developed, the media called them militia extremists. The Freemen don't even call themselves a militia, and most militia groups refused to support them.

On April 19, 1996 CBS, *Evening News* described a post office assault as a militia style robbery. Perhaps soon the press will call George Washington and all patriots criminals! Will there next be militia diseases or militia hurricanes? One must never underestimate the silliness and intensity with which a government can demonize a targeted group. The *New York Times*, in describing the Russian-Chechnya war, noted "States usually mobilize public support for a war by demonizing their opponents...." The only difference in the U.S. is that the government's assault on the patriots and militias is usually with words, although this may change after the election.

When white soldiers killed a black couple, *ABC Evening News* on December 20, 1995 and the *Washington Post* on December 9, 1995 described the attack as racist and right wing extremism and then claimed the *Resister* was part of this problem, but no evidence of this was provided. The article quoted the *Resister's* attack on internationalism and U.S. policy towards Haiti and the UN and said the *Resister* supported "individual rights, strict constitutionalism, limited government...." This is what the Founders said. The *New York Times* and the *New Republic* have used the same strategy to falsely attack the *Resister*. The *New Republic* said there were "white terrorists" and a "sinister club," the Special Forces Underground that opposes "liberalism" and "internationalism."[41] Is everyone who opposes Wall Street policies a racist and extremist? The *Resister* does not publish racist material, and no one in the press has been able to prove otherwise. But it is published by soldiers in the Special Forces Underground, and the ruling elite is nervous that such soldiers are critical of their policies.

As the government has done for decades with targeted groups, it is infiltrating agent provocateurs into the militias, trying to cause violence that results in arrests and makes it easier for the press to attack the militias as dangerous radicals. The April, 1996 FBI alert about possible militia violence was associated with a threat issued by an individual from Kansas City, Missouri. This individual was ejected from militias in Kansas, Missouri, and South Dakota because of his calls for violence. Not only was this individual no longer associated with a militia, but his status is highly suspect.

Recently three people in Oklahoma were convicted of planning to bomb several groups, including Morris Dees' center. Ray Lampley, a preacher, suddenly called himself a militia leader, although the Oklahoma militia would have nothing to do with him. While Lampley and two other people were convicted of the plot, two other individuals inspired the plans and testified for the government. One of them, Richard Schrum, admitted in the *The Daily Oklahoman* newspaper that he was an FBI informant. Schrum said the FBI hired him after the Oklahoma bombing to infiltrate militias in the Southwest and that most militia members are patriots who just want to preserve the Constitution.[42] The other person involved in instigating the plot, Larry Wayne Crow, was a pilot for Tyson Foods in Arkansas. He quit his job, moved in with Lampley, and tried to form a militia and get some militia groups to commit violent acts. Crow was initially indicted, but then all charges against him were dropped. Morris Dees falsely said the militia was out to get him, when, in fact, the Feds initiated this plot which did not even involve the militia.

Another typical case of government entrapment occurred in April, 1996, when two members of a Georgia militia were arrested. Initially the press claimed they were going to bomb the Atlanta Olympics, but that assertion was withdrawn within hours. Then it was reported that there were no bombs, but the defendants Robert Starr and William McCranie supposedly had bomb-making materials. At the preliminary hearing on May 6, the defense lawyers questioned ATF agent Steven Gillis about the case in what is normally a quick and routine proceeding. Gillis admitted that government agents placed bomb-making components on Starr's property, and he wasn't sure if Starr was even aware the materials were there. There was no evidence that the defendants actually possessed or even had any knowledge of any bomb-making material. Gillis said they were able to go right to the buried material on Starr's 16 acres of land, when they obtained a search warrant, because government agents had originally planted the material. Nancy Lord, Starr's defense attorney said: "This is beyond entrapment. It is manufactured evidence. The materials were put on Mr. Starr's property without his knowledge. The whole evidence upon which this case was based was fraudulent....They have no conspiracy, they have no nexus to interstate commerce, they don't even have an explosive devise. What they have is an agent provocateur who came into a group, trying to cause trouble...."

Gillis admitted the other defendant, James McCranie, was not at any meetings where bomb building was discussed, and when a government agent started talking about bomb-making McCranie walked away saying: "I don't want to know anything about it." Gillis could not identify an agreement between anyone except government agents to commit an illegal act, so there was no conspiracy. The only people who attended bomb-building classes were government agents and possibly one, not two, defendants, and to discuss or write about bomb building is perfectly legal.

Starr, on a short-wave radio show two nights before being arrested, said he was going to expose a government set-up against him. The next day, the government obtained arrest warrants. Lord said: "Mr. Starr was arrested not because he intended to build those bombs, but because he intended not to. He intended to expose the government's confidential informants." Despite government complicity in creating this case, the judge forwarded the case to a grand jury which issued indictments, and a third militia member was also indicted. The charges include conspiracy to use weapons of mass destruction and possession of an unregistered destructive device, although the government admitted in court that the defendants wasn't even aware the material was on their property.

*The Macon Telegraph* and *Atlanta Journal Constitution* wrote several articles critical of the government's conduct in this case. Bail has been rejected for the defendants although they are respected members of the community with no criminal record. This case shows how the government harasses targeted groups. In the initial arrest there is much media attention, and later when charges are dropped, as in the Earth First case I discuss in Chapter XII, the press ignores that. The result is that people think the targeted movement is dangerous.[43]

The arrest of the Viper group in Phoenix, Arizona on July 2, 1996 may be another example of an overreaching government. CBS *Evening News* on July 2, 1996, quoting federal investigators, said an attack on government buildings wasn't imminent. Earlier that day when Bryant Gumble on NBC had asked the U.S. prosecutor in Phoenix if there was evidence that the Viper group actually planned to carry out attacks or if they were just preparing for a possible future, she refused to respond. However, as when the Georgia militia members were arrested, the government and most of the press said this was a dangerous group planning an imminent attack. Immediately after the arrests Clinton said danger was narrowly avoided, and Ray Kelly, under Secretary of the Treasury, falsely said they would be indicted to blow up federal buildings. The defendants were not charged with planning to bomb any buildings nor to overthrow the government.

Publically it was claimed that the videos show a conspiracy to bomb buildings but that wasn't shown in the charges. The charges did not even say what would be done with the explosives. In addition, why did the government rush to destroy the explosives, supposedly taken as evidence? Why was there a rush to destroy this evidence? As in the Georgia case, was this evidence planted by the government? Reportedly the gernades were inert and the rockets were toy weapons. The government case was so weak that at the preliminary hearing the judge agreed to free six of the 12 defendants until the trial despite the governments claim that these were dangerous terrorists.

On July 9, ABCs *Nightline*, usually a harsh critic of the right, admitted that the government made many strong charges against this group, the press fully supported this, and then the charges filed in court weren't nearly as serious as what the government initially told the press about this group. An ATF agent testified at the preliminary hearing that the government was absolutely certain there was no plan to bomb any building. The agent even said they didn't warn anyone of a possible threat because there was no immediate danger from this group.

As in the Georgia case, it is too early yet to tell if the Feds also planted evidence such as weapons in the Viper case. Several months ago the Viper group was approached by two government agent provocateurs to identify certain buildings to attacked in the future. This group refused to support this. Why are the Feds encouraging people to attack government buildings? At least one Fed tried to get this group to pass out Aryan Nation literature, but they refused.

In the 1970s, when agent provocateurs infiltrated the left there was an uproar in the national media and supposedly the Federal police stopped such illegal acts. Today, as the secret government tightens its control over all levels of society, there is a loud silence from the press and Congress about this infiltration program. Although an ATF agent testified in the Georgia case that the government manufactured the evidence and there was no proof linking the two defendants to the bomb-making material, the press refused to discuss this. Members of the national press attended the preliminary hearing, but the results were not reported. *Newsweek* May 6, 1996, just before the hearing, falsely claimed that pipe bombs existed and the Olympics were targeted. A free press is essential to have a free society, but it must be a press that has some connection with the truth. Our press is used as a propaganda tool by the corporate elite and government.

Rarely does the national media intelligently discuss the issues that concern millions of people in the militias and Patriot movement. Few in the national media ask if there is any truth to what is believed by these people. Few want to look at the deeper causes of the developing militia movement. Few want to acknowledge that the militias have historically played an important part of our heritage. Instead, certain patriot positions were stated, such as concerns about the UN, without analysis except for the comment that these views were paranoid and extremist. People representing the militias and Patriot movement are rarely allowed to speak in the national media. Only the corporate approved version of events is allowed to be heard.

Instead of intelligently discussing the many issues relevant to the patriot community, the press continues to demonize the right. To the corporate-national media what they decide is politically correct can be discussed. When other views on the right or left are introduced, it doesn't matter how many tens of millions of people hold such views; they are deemed to be dangerous, extremists, and racists. Attack the messenger to avoid discussing the message. The more powerful a movement becomes, the more nervous the government becomes, and the more intense is the attack. Governments always act this way. The Democrats call Republican attempts to weaken government power extremism, while the right calls environmentalists extremist crazies. Those who supported democracy in Nazi Germany were called extremists. Over 200 years ago, people like George Washington and Thomas Jefferson were called patriots, but to the British they were dangerous radicals. Vietnam War protesters were called communist inspired, Goldwater might have used the nuclear bomb, Gore Vidal was an anti-Semite, Perot was paranoid, and Buchanan is a neo-Nazi. The real sin of these people is that they threatened establishment control. Why have many liberals forgotten this lesson?

That genuine political dissent is so demonized increasingly alienates millions of people from the political system. Tens of millions of people are so disgusted with politics that they won't vote. There have been times in our past when people would have said we should explore why many people are so angry, perhaps correcting excesses. We saw this during the soul searching of the civil rights movement, but now the response of the Washington crowd is to call protesters racists and paranoid, passing more laws to take away more rights. Criticism of the government is called criticism of the nation. Political extremism is a label often applied to attack beliefs that those in power don't like. Openly and fully debating issues, including problems that have been ignored, and advocating unpopular positions gives our society the variety and vitality needed to function as a free society. Justice Brandeis said: "Repression breeds hate; hate menaces stable government; the path of safety lies in the opportunity to discuss freely supposed grievances and proposed remedies." The main unifying wish of those in the Patriot movement and the militias is to see the Constitution restored and to return to the teachings of people like George Washington and Thomas Jefferson. To the ruling elite these are very dangerous concepts.

# Chapter XVIII

# Murder As A Political Act

"Make yourself sheep and the wolves will eat you."
                                        Benjamin Franklin

The Kennedy assassination was "an act of overthrowing the government....A whole new form of government is going to take over the country."
                                        Jack Ruby

Murder or assassination for political gain is one more way the secret government maintains control. Many others besides the Kennedys and Martin Luther King have been assassinated. A favorite way to kill people is a bullet to the head and then have it called a suicide. This is an especially suspicious form of death when the local authorities then act in an unprofessional manner. Arranging an accident, often with a plane or car, is another method used to kill people. With so many suspicious suicides especially around Clinton, perhaps there is a new disease that doctors haven't yet isolated. Sufficiently irritate the secret government and you may find yourself dead, with it promptly called an accident or suicide.

I will only briefly discuss the deaths of the Kennedys and Martin Luther King, because that material has been reviewed by so many. Killing prominent political leaders made it easier to control and direct people towards tighter gun control and surveillance supposedly to prevent crime and terrorism. An excellent summary of the many people who died mysteriously after President Kennedy's death is provided in *High Treason*, by Groden and Livingstone. One person in the London *Sunday Times* said the odds were 100,000 trillion to one that so many witnesses would die so soon after the assassination. At least 21 witnesses died soon after President Kennedy's death, some violently or under mysteries circumstances. The authorities said some of these people killed themselves while others, such as Richard R. Carr, were threatened and attacked for years. Carr fought off two murder attempts.

Shortly before Robert Kennedy was killed, several people saw Sirhan, his convicted murderer, with a woman who wore a polka-dot dress. Such a person ran from the shooting, telling an elderly couple that they had just shot Kennedy. Was this woman Sirhan's controller? In 1993 National Public Radio aired a documentary entitled *The RFK Tapes*, suggesting that Sirhan Sirhan was brainwashed and set up so that the real killer(s) of Robert Kennedy could escape. There was reference to Dr. William Bryan, Jr., a California sex therapist, now deceased, who supposedly conducted hypnosis for the CIA. Several years ago A&E aired a documentary in which this same therapist bragged to two witnesses that he was part of the team that programed Sirhan, preparing him for the Kennedy hit.

Many have presented evidence that the L.A. Police Department (LAPD) was heavily infiltrated by the CIA. The LAPD obviously harassed witnesses to change their story to fit the official version, and the murder investigation was botched. It also destroyed the trial evidence, and the coroner's autopsy said Kennedy was shot from no more than three inches behind his head. However, many said Sirhan was at least three feet in front of Kennedy. Retired LAPD sergeant Paul Schraga, the first cop to arrive at the shooting, believes a conspiracy occurred and that right-wing zealots in this department's elite intelligence unit were involved in the assassination.[1]

In September, 1989 the BBC presented a documentary, *Who Killed Martin Luther King*, with evidence of government involvement in the murder. The House Select Committee on Assassinations (HSCA) in 1979 concluded that there was probably a conspiracy to kill Dr. King. A government agent testified before the HSCA that "We were operating an intensive vendetta against Dr. King in an effort to destroy him." Harold Weisberg, through documents obtained from the Freedom of Information Act (FOIA), found many irregularities in the FBI's investigation of King's death. Information released showed that the CIA had been very interested in Dr. King since the 1960s. Shortly after King's death, his mother was shot dead. She attended the autopsy and could have testified about discrepancies in the official version of events.

Charles Stephens lived in the boarding house from which James Earl Ray supposedly shot King. He testified that he saw Ray running down the hall just after hearing a rifle shot. His wife said he was drunk and outside when he claimed to have seen Ray. She also said Ray was not in the boarding house that day. When she refused to testify as the authorities wanted, she was threatened and told to shut up. Then she was put into a mental institution for 10 years, although she had no history of mental illness. Recently Jules Ron Kimble, a convicted murderer, admitted being very involved in King's death, and that the conspiracy involved the FBI, CIA, and the mob. Kimble confirmed that Ray was involved in the plot, but said he was set up to take the fall for the killing. Kimble has a long record of mob involvement and CIA and FBI contacts.

According to the HSCA report Myron Billett, the trusted chauffeur of mafia boss Sam Giancana, drove him and Gambino to a meeting in upstate New York in 1968 to meet people identified as representatives of the FBI and CIA. They offered $1 million to have King killed. Billett said Sam Giancana replied: "Hell no, not after you screwed up the Kennedy deal like that." Two weeks after Billett gave this information in an interview, he died of emphysema, as expected.

After John McFerren, a black grocery store owner, told what he knew about the King death he was beaten, robbed, and shot at. Bill Sartor, an investigative reporter, working on a book about the mob and King's death infiltrated the mob in Memphis and New Orleans. He died mysteriously in Texas while finishing the book. The cause of death could not be confirmed after two autopsies.[2]

In the last years of his life, Malcolm X often attacked the government, especially U.S. foreign policy, and he was under constant government surveillance. Two weeks before his murder, he was barred from reentering France. After his death a prominent North African diplomat told an American reporter that French intelligence was informed by the CIA that they were going to kill Malcolm X, and France didn't want it to happen on their soil. After his death the local police said protection had been offered but that Malcolm X had rejected it. Alex Haley questioned this and reported that Malcolm X repeatedly asked for police protection.

Shortly after Malcolm X was murdered in 1965, Leon Ameer, the New England representative for the group Malcolm X headed, announced that he had proof of who really killed Malcolm X, saying they were from Washington. The next day he was found dead. The police said he died of an epileptic fit, but his wife said a complete medical checkup a month before had produced no evidence of epilepsy. Perhaps it was political epilepsy! In 1979 one of the three men convicted in the death of Malcolm X admitted that someone involved in the assassination was an FBI agent in the Nation of Islam.

A fifth prominent political leader who died during this period was Walter Reuther, head of the United Auto Workers (UAW). He died May 9, 1970 when his chartered plane crashed because of a faulty altimeter. One and a half years earlier he had almost died in an identical accident. The National Transportation Safety Board found seven abnormalities in the altimeter, strongly suggesting there was sabotage, yet the final report ignored this evidence. There were no other defects in the plane nor was there evidence of pilot error. These small planes are constantly inspected so it is unbelievable that seven defects would not have been detected. The family believes Reuther was murdered. Over the years there were various attempts to kill the Reuther brothers, and the police barely investigated these assaults. Ralph Winstead spent eight years working for the UAW investigating these assassination attempts and died in what was called an accident in 1957. For years Reuther effectively promoted progressive causes as a powerful labor leader. A strong critic of the Vietnam War, he was at the top of Nixon's enemy list. Three months before Reuther died Egil Krogh, a Nixon aide later arrested as a Watergate burglar, obtained the FBI file on Reuther. When interviewed about this in 1985, Krogh said he didn't remember this. To this day the government won't release many documents on Reuther and those released are mostly inked out. What is there to hide?[3]

In 1955 the House Committee on Un-American Activities subpoenaed many actors and musicians, looking for a communist conspiracy in the entertainment industry. Much of the wrath of the McCarthy era was directed against people in Hollywood. People in the entertainment industry have a unique capacity and opportunity to stir the people, so it is always important for a police state to control and direct artists.

Over the years some have speculated about the suspicious deaths of Janis Joplin, Jimmy Hendrix, and Jim Morrison. This occurred when the government was very concerned about Vietnam War protests and the power of musicians to awaken the people. A few years ago there was a low-budget film, *Beyond the Doors*, with the theme that these people were deliberately killed by a special government commando unit because they were considered a threat to the government. This film was discussed on the television show, *A Current Affair*, December 1, 1989. Morrison was allegedly found dead on July 5, 1970 by his girlfriend Pamela Courson while visiting Paris. He was buried two days later, with the cause of death listed as a heart attack although he was only 27. No friends except Courson ever saw the body. There was no police report, no doctor present, and no autopsy. When Courson filed a death certificate on July 7, she said there were no living relatives; yet Morrison's family lived in Virginia.[4]

John Lennon was killed because he supported the peace movement and was again getting active politically. Mae Brussell, an expert on the illegal activities of the secret government, reported years ago that the government killed Lennon and other rock musicians. Various musicians who died under suspicious circumstances include Tim Buckley, Jim Croce, Mama Cass Elliot, Duane Allman, Phil Oakes, Brian Epstein manager of the Beetles, Michel Jeffery manager for Jimi Hendrix, and Donald Jackson manager for the Grateful Dead. The full list is quite long.

William Sullivan was third-in-command of the FBI in charge of the domestic intelligence division until Hoover fired him in 1971. Sullivan became a strong critic of the FBI and was testifying against various FBI agents involved in illegal domestic surveillance activities. He was also writing a book, *The Bureau*, about the FBI. On November 9, 1977 the 18-year-old son of a state policeman killed Sullivan, just when he was to speak before the HSCA. Sullivan was supposedly mistaken for a deer even though the rifle had a telescopic sight. The killer received a $500 fine and his hunting license was suspended for 10 years. In 1977 six top officials of the FBI died within six months.[5] In 1978 Regis Kennedy, an FBI agent who may have been involved in both Kennedy's deaths, testified before the HSCA. He died soon after.

In the early 1980s Rudy Lozano was a union organizer who effectively united blacks, Latinos, and whites to support progressive issues. One day a biker stopped by his home and asked for a drink of water. Lozano was shot in front of his children and nothing was stolen. Paramedics thought they might be able to save him but the police blocked their aid because "evidence might be destroyed" and he died. There had been various death threats.

Steven Carr, one more player in the contra arms and drug smuggling operation, was going to testify before Congress. He had seen the arms shipments and cocaine smuggling and had been involved in a plot to attack the American embassy in Costa Rica. After a short sentence in a Florida jail for his involvement in these activities, he fled to California because he feared being murdered. He was killed on December, 1986 in Van Nuys, California. According to leaked police reports Carr supposedly said that he swallowed three bags of cocaine. Three autopsies disagreed on key points; however, they agreed there was no sign he had swallowed three bags of cocaine. There were numerous other conflicting facts about the body. Despite the numerous discrepancies, the case was officially closed in April, 1987. A reporter was told by Peter Glibbery, an American then jailed in Costa Rica, that a CIA operative warned him the CIA killed Carr and he had better shut up.

Like Karen Silkwood, Dorothy Legarreta died in a mysterious car accident in 1988. Her briefcase, which contained previously secret government documents obtained in a class action lawsuit, was missing. According to the tow-truck driver it was discarded because it was damaged, but this violated the law. Legarreta was writing a book about secret radiation experiments on people. In 1982 she had found the notorious letter from Joseph Hamilton comparing human radiation experiments in the U.S. to the Buchenwald death camp experiments.[6]

In 1989 Wilford Draper signed an affidavit that he had been coerced and terrified by FBI agents and prosecutors to provide false evidence against Leonard Peltier, the prominent Indian political prisoner. In October, 1990 he was murdered by unknown assailants.

On August 10, 1991 the body of Joseph Daniel Casolaro was found in Martinsburg, W.V. with his wrists slashed. Casolaro met someone concerning his investigation of a major government conspiracy he called the Octopus, a network of people associated with the U.S. Justice Department's improper use of Inslaw software, Iran-contra, BCCI, gun smuggling, and drug trafficking. Two months before his death, Casolaro told his brother if he died in an accident, "don't believe it." He had received numerous death threats.

As often happens in these cases, the police labeled the death a suicide, and the family strongly disagreed. On August 11, 1992 the House Judiciary Committee criticized the suicide ruling and listed many irregularities. Casolaro's body was embalmed before his family was notified which also made an autopsy less effective. Under West Virginia law next of kin have to be notified before a body can be embalmed. Evidence left in the room made it easy to reach Casolaro's relatives, but they weren't contacted for two days. The room in which he died was not sealed by the police, so a cleaning woman sanitized it; his notes, including a draft of his book on the Octopus, were never found; and a person Casolaro was seen speaking to was never identified. Many feel he was killed because of what he discovered and the book he was writing. When you study the secret government and its activities, it can be fatal.

On January 31, 1991 Alan D. Standorf was murdered. He worked for the National Security Agency and had provided information to Casolaro. Jack Anderson feels that the death's of two other reporters may be connected to their investigation of the same Octopus organization. British researcher Jonathan Moyle was found March, 1990 hanged in the closet of his hotel room in Santiago, Chile. He was investigating Chilean arms dealer Carlos Cardoen, a prominent figure in the Inslaw case. On July 29, 1991 Larence Ng, a reporter for the London *Financial Times*, was found shot dead in Guatemala City. He was investigating a BCCI connection to arms sales in Guatemala.

The Chicago investigator, Sherman Skolnick, said in recent years 41 federal grand jury witnesses in the Inslaw case have been murdered. A *Media Bypass* article identified up to 40 people murdered so that the Justice Department would keep control of the Inslaw PROMIS software.[7] This included Gail Spiro and her three children who were shot in the head on November 1, 1992 in California. The death squads that work for the secret government also kill children. Three days later her husband Ian Spiro, was found with a bullet in the head, and the police promptly said he killed himself and his family. A week later the family gardener was also found with a bullet in the head. Perhaps the police will claim that Spiro came back from the dead to kill his gardener. Spiro, associated with the CIA, was collecting documents for a grand jury investigating the Inslaw case. The Inslaw software, taken over by the U.S. Justice Department after it forced Inslaw into bankruptcy, has been sold to many foreign intelligence agencies and banks with a back door. This provides ready access to extensive information, and this software makes it easy to track people, which is why so many people have been killed. On February 14, 1994 lawyers for Inslaw said the Justice Department has its own secret intelligence agency.

Numerous people associated with President Clinton have died in recent years. Clinton was placed in power by the secret government which controls both political parties, and they are merely protecting their investment in him. Many of these deaths have been discussed by Nicholas A. Guarino in *Murder, Bank Fraud, Drugs, and Sex, The Clinton Chronicles Book* edited by Patrick Matrisciana, and an article by Troy Underhill in *Media Bypass* February, 1995.

The death of White House deputy counsel Vince Foster July 20, 1993 aroused considerable controversy. In 1994 the Fiske report said this was a suicide. However, the *The New York Post* in early 1994 did a series of articles showing many strange events surrounding this death and the resulting investigation. In the spring of 1994 various television stations including WGN in Chicago presented information that Foster was murdered. The park police, not the FBI, investigated Foster's death. One day before Foster died the head of the FBI William Sessions was abruptly fired and given a few hours to clear his desk. Previously Sessions told Clinton he would resign when a replacement was found. Sessions said the White House interfered in the investigation of Foster's death. Various sources state that Sessions established an elite unit in the FBI to investigate Bush and Clinton corruption. This is why he was fired and his reputation attacked. While various newspapers said Foster was depressed, none explained what these burdens were that drove him to suicide. According to the investigating authorities, White House counsel Bernard Nussbaum kept them from examining documents concerning Foster's death, and Foster's personal diary and personal papers were removed.[8]

Standard investigation procedures were not followed in Foster's death. In the summer of 1994 a reporter for The London *Daily Telegraph* discovered that no authorities had spoken to people in the homes abutting Ft. Mercy Park where Foster's body was found. Key witnesses gave contradictory statements, and it is not even certain that Foster died in Ft. Mercy Park. Little blood was found, the body was laid out as if in a coffin, and they couldn't even find the bullet or bone fragments from the exit wound in Foster's skull. Was this a miraculous bullet as in President Kennedy's assassination? And in 1995 Miquel Rodriquez and Bill Duffy, chief investigators to special Whitewater prosecutor Kenneth Starr, resigned because they were not allowed to conduct a proper investigation of Foster's death. There was almost no publicity about these resignations. Experienced investigators using laboratory tests have concluded that Foster did not kill himself, and he did not die in Fort Marcy Park.

Patrick Knowlton saw people with Foster in the park, but his statements were changed by the FBI. After an October 22, 1995 article about this in the London *Sunday Telegraph*, Knowlton was subpoenaed to testify before Starr's grand jury hearing. In the days before his testimony, he was tailed by numerous people and at least one car belonged to the federal government. In 1996 the National Security Agency revealed, in response to a FOIA request, by the *Washington Weekly* that it had 700 documents about Foster but they couldn't be released for national security reasons. Some claim Foster was killed partly because he was involved in espionage.

Perhaps the most accurate comment on the death of Foster came from Webster Hubbel. Now in prison, this criminal controlled the U.S. Justice Department for Clinton as Associate Attorney General. He told a partner of the Rose law firm: "Don't believe a word you hear. It was not suicide. It couldn't have been."[9] On October 25, 1995 three world renown handwriting experts announced that the Foster suicide note was a forgery. There is a tremendous amount of information available showing suspicious circumstances with Foster's death. Interested parties should contact the Western Journalism Center (1-800-952-5595).

On July 30, 1992 C. Victor Raider II and his son died in a plane crash near Anchorage, Alaska in good weather. Raiser had been finance co-chairman for Clinton's presidential campaign, but he became disillusioned and left. That made him a potential threat. On June 22, 1993 the partially decomposed body of Paul Wilcher, a Washington lawyer investigating government corruption, was found.

The cause of death was not determined. He was investigating drug and gun running from Mena, Arkansas, the Waco massacre, and the October surprise conspiracy in the 1980 election. Three weeks before his death, he sent Janet Reno a 99 page affidavit of his findings. Jon Walker fell, or was pushed to his death on August 15, 1993 from the top of a building in Arlington, Virginia. He was an investigator for the Resolution Trust Corporation (RTC). In March, 1992 he contacted the Kansas City RTC office stating that he had information regarding the Clintons, Whitewater Development, and the Madison Guaranty Savings and Loan.

Jerry Parks headed the firm in charge of Clinton's security in Arkansas during the 1992 race. He was murdered September 26, 1993 in Little Rock in a professional hit. According to Park's son, his father investigated Clinton in the 1980s and the material gathered, which allegedly included pictures of Clinton with various women, was stolen from the family home in July 1993. The family said Parks was being followed before he was murdered. According to Park's wife, he was owed $80,000 for the security provided for Clinton's campaign. When payment was delayed, Park threatened to take his evidence to the press. Parks was paid $80,000 in July, 1994. Much of this story received prominent coverage in the London *Sunday Telegraph* but not in the U.S. Parks' son told the *Sunday Telegraph*, "I believe they had my father killed to save Bill Clinton's career." In the fall of 1994 two members of the Arkansas State Police Criminal Investigation Division told their superiors they had sufficient evidence to indict a former employee of a senior member of the Clinton White House for Parks murder. Their request for the indictment was denied.

Ed Willey had managed Clinton's presidential campaign finance committee and was reportedly involved in money laundering. On November 30, 1993 he was found hanged. On March 3, 1994 Ronald Rogers, a dentist from Arkansas was killed when his plane exploded in the air. Rogers reportedly had sensitive information involving Whitewater. The next day he was supposed to meet Ambrose Pritchard, a reporter for the London *Daily Telegraph* based in Washington, D.C.

Kathy Ferguson, died May 11, 1994 from a bullet in her right temple in Sherwood, Arkansas. A note was found by her body, and police called it a suicide. None of her friends believed she killed herself. Five days before, her ex-husband Danny Ferguson, an Arkansas state trooper was named as a codefendant in the sexual harassment suit involving Clinton. She told co-workers Clinton was mad at her ex-husband for bringing him a woman (perhaps Paula Jones) who refused his sexual advances. Women rarely use a gun to kill themselves, and Ferguson worked at a hospital so she could have easily obtained pills. Bill Shelton, Ferguson's boyfriend was found shot in the head on her grave June 12, 1994. A note was again found, and the police promptly called it a suicide. Then there is the June 23, 1993 death of Stanley Huggins, reportedly from viral pneumonia. In 1987 Huggins led an investigation of the Madison Guaranty Savings and Loan, which is part of the Whitewater probe.[10]

Many people are scared by the invisible government, so they lie or remain silent. William Cooper a retired Naval Intelligence officer and author of *Behold A Pale Horse* left the service partly because he was disgusted with many of the secret documents concerning illegal activities, such as the murder of President Kennedy, that he had seen. After his discharge he tried to provide information to a reporter. In his book Cooper describes two attempts on his life. After the second attempt, while recovering in a hospital, two men visited him and said that if he didn't shut up the third attempt would be successful. He then shut up for 16 years.[11] Sally Perdue, a former Miss Arkansas, told Evans-Pritchard that she had an affair with Clinton. She was threatened with violence if she repeated her accusations and a shotgun shell was found on the seat of her jeep.

In 1992 former LAPD detective Mike Rothmiller wrote *L.A. Secret Police*, which described the secret surveillance activities of the LAPD. He was almost killed after he started investigating certain alleged drug smugglers working for the CIA. After being shot, Rothmiller was disabled, but the police department denied him a pension or any benefits. Rothmiller had one suspect trailed by the IRS. The suspect went from L.A. directly to the White House.

At times family members or close friends are threatened or killed if a person doesn't shut up. Basil Abbott started flying illegal drugs into the U.S. for the DEA in 1973. He was jailed and then, after being released, tried to get the press to investigate this corruption. While he was in prison his wife, fleeing back to her native Sweden in fear of her life, was killed in Berlin. The reach of the secret government is world wide.[12]

Abbott's friend, CIA agent Robert Corson, prepared to go public about CIA drug operations. He was found dead in an El Paso motel. Terry Reed was forced to take his wife and young children into hiding because they were all threatened. Lester K. Coleman, a former Defense Intelligence Agency agent, revealed too much publicly about the Lockerbie plane crash, so he had to flee the country because of threats to kill him and his family, including three young children.

On June 23, 1993, and again on November 3, 1994, CBS's *Eye to Eye* presented a story about the death in 1991 of Colonel James Sabow third in command at the Marine Corps Air Station in El Toro, California and a decorated Vietnam War hero. Sabow was charged with improperly using a plane, and he wanted a court martial to present charges that the base was being used to smuggle guns to South America with illegal drugs brought back on the return flights. One morning he was found dead at his home from a shotgun blast. The authorities promptly called it a suicide, but his family and friends called it murder. A private investigator found that there were no fingerprints on the shotgun found by his body, which was not possible unless Sabow wore gloves, which was not the case. Someone else pulled the trigger. Relatives filed a suit against the Navy and Marine Corps claiming a conspiracy to cover-up his murder. The family hired forensic experts who labeled the death a murder with the body moved to look like a suicide. When *Newsweek* ran a full page article on Sabow's death and other suspicious deaths in the military, they did not print the statement by Sabow about the air base being used to import illegal drugs.[13]

In December, 1993 the *Philadelphia Inquirer* did a four part series about suspicious deaths in the military that were called suicides. There were 3,375 cases of suicide in the military from 1979 to 1993, with relatives in at least 60 cases challenging the results. In one "suicide" a soldier was found shot in the head with his hat stuffed in his mouth, handcuffs attached to his wrist, and radio cable around his neck. In 10 of 40 cases investigated, family members said the deceased person had told them about drug or weapons smuggling. Chad Langford's death was called a suicide. Ten days earlier he had told his father his life had been threatened during an undercover drug investigation. The Army said Chad arranged his own death so it would look like murder. The report could not confirm that Chad's fingerprints were on the gun or even if he had fired the gun, and other fingerprints were found on his personal items.[14]

I am not suggesting that every falsely claimed suicide in the military was a cover-up for illegal activities such as drug smuggling, but the murder of James Sabow is not the only instance of a decent American losing his life when he tried to stop criminal government activities. What happened to Colonel Sabow will happen to many honest officers, if the secret government succeeds in its plan to establish a police state.

Sometimes people who write controversial books die before the book is released. In early August, 1993 Ron Rummell, also known as Creston, was found dead in a Portland, Oregon park. He had been shot through the mouth and was supposedly holding a gun in his hands. The police called it a suicide and cremated the body the next day, without an autopsy and without notifying relatives. He published *Alien Digest* and was close friends with people who publish *Revelations of Awareness*. Both publications release radical information on the secret government and the UFO phenomenon. On June 2, 1995 Fox TV discussed this death because he was writing a book on the supposed suicide and accidental death of over 30 British scientists working on top secret projects in the British defense industry. These projects included mind control, star wars, and planting devices in the brain without the recipient being aware of this. In some of these "suicides" the victims were found with their hands and feet bound. While the U.S. press has otherwise refused to cover this story, the British press has had broad coverage with members of parliament calling for an investigation. Reporters like Tony Collins call it a conspiracy, especially since the authorities have shown no concern. A similar case involved William LeMaster, president of the failed Indian Springs State Bank, a CIA and mob front. Hours after his body was found he was cremated, and there was no autopsy.

The case of Frank Olson was reviewed on NBCs' *Unsolved Mysteries* September 25, 1994. In 1953 Olson was a germ warfare expert working at Fort Detrick, with the CIA also involved in this research. Congressional hearings in 1975 revealed that Olson was given LSD without his knowledge as part of the CIA's secret MK ULTRA program involving mind control. Olson promptly became very disorientated and depressed and told his wife he wanted to quit his job. He became a security risk to the CIA.

Within days he was taken to New York City to see a psychiatrist and was pushed or fell from the thirteenth story of a Manhattan hotel. It is strange that a top government scientist who was considered to be suicidal should stay on the thirteenth floor of a hotel. His roommate Robert Lashbrook, a CIA scientist, was very uncooperative with the police. Just after the fall he called a number and, according to the hotel night manager, said: "Well, he's gone." The other party responded, "That's too bad." Lashbrook did not call the police or an ambulance. A superficial examination of Olson was done and his death was labeled a suicide. The autopsy said there were multiple lacerations on the face and scalp, but in July, 1994 another autopsy could not find these lacerations which you would expect if Olson had fallen through a window as claimed. Instead, the extensive injuries on the face and body suggested that Olson had been beaten before his death. On November, 28, 1994 it was announced that the autopsy strongly suggested Olson was murdered. There is now an attempt to get Congress to reopen the investigation.

Don Smith was gunned down by two passing cars at 2 a.m. on July 15, 1995 while walking his dog. He had been expecting trouble and was able to return 16 shots. Minutes after a doctor at the hospital announced that he was well on the way to recovery, he died. Smith was a militia member, editor of a newsletter *Writ Rap*, and expert in the law, who made many enemies handling 80 to 100 cases at a time. Most of his suits were directed against government agencies.

The government has the ability to kill people by using drugs to cause cancer, heart attacks, or strokes that make it appear natural.[15] Documents released by the FOIA show that, by 1954, the CIA had perfected the means to give people cancer.[16] An article in the April 2, 1979 *Miami Herald* discussed the CIA's use of diseases to kill people. The CIA probably experimented on terminally ill cancer patients under the guise of legitimate medical research to perfect this technology, although healthy victims were probably also used. Anatoliy Golitsyn, an ex-senior KGB agent, said the communists also developed poisons that could be applied by direct physical contact and would leave no trace, so death would be attributed to natural causes.[17] Many intelligence agencies use these chemicals.

In 1978 a German court convicted a person for murdering his wife by placing in her food a chemical that gave her cancer. Experts at the trial testified that the chemical left no trace in the victim's body after a few hours. This poison was fairly well known, so the judge would not allow it to be identified.[18] The New York *Daily News* on October 6, 1979 reported that a biologist Steven Harper poisoned a family of five with a cancer causing agent.

Hoover died suddenly during a political struggle with Nixon and the CIA, just two weeks before the shooting of George Wallace. That shooting probably ensured that Nixon would be reelected. A report in the *Harvard Crimson* said the Senate Ervin Committee received evidence that break-ins of Hoover's apartment were led by Gordon Liddy and certain Cubans also allied with the CIA. A poison of the thyon-phosphate genre that induces fatal heart attacks was reportedly placed about Hoover's personal toilet articles. A spokesman for the Senate Intelligence Committee said they had evidence that E. Howard Hunt, a former CIA agent, had planned to kill Jack Anderson with an untraceable poison obtained from a former CIA doctor.[19]

Mae Brussel died of cancer under mysterious circumstances. An aggressive reporter, she quit her radio show because of death threats. The Indian teacher Bhagwan Rajneesh was arrested by federal authorities on October 28, 1985. Soon after he was constantly ill and suffered premature aging. Tests in London showed possible poisoning with a heavy metal probably thallium.

David Yallop in *In God's Name* presented evidence that Pope John Paul I was murdered because he wanted to return the church to its humble beginnings and break the power of the Vatican bank, which has long been allied to the mafia. The pope died of a heart attack but no autopsy was performed. The Vatican falsely claimed that church law prevented conducting an autopsy, as many wanted. There are many other strange events surrounding this death.

James A. Weyer had beaten the IRS in several major cases, including the Phil Marsh case in San Francisco, by quoting IRS regulations. Four days after he returned home from the Marsh case, he died from a heart attack. He was 53 and in excellent health.

Numerous people associated with Iran-contra met an early death. Navy Lt. Commander Alexander Martin was the accountant for the Iran-contra and drug operations. He said that of about 5,000 people involved in these operations, 400 have reportedly committed suicide, died from natural causes, or died accidentally. Often there was no death certificate, and in 187 cases, the bodies were cremated before the families were notified. In 1983 George Perry, a former GM executive linked to the Iran-contra arms smuggling, was found with three bullets in his head. The CIA and State Department would not cooperate with the New York investigators.[20] Senators examined CIA head William Casey's medical records and autopsy to see if he died of natural causes.[21] Oliver North, during his Iran-contra testimony, revealed that U.S. agents were holding Iranians as hostages to prevent a double-cross. When an American hostage wasn't released as agreed, an Iranian prisoner had a heart attack. A double-cross meant a heart attack.[22]

Cyrus Hashemi, an Iranian arms dealer who tried to assist in the arms-for-hostages deal, died mysteriously in London. Documents filed in federal court claim U.S. Customs agents believe Hashemi was killed by federal agents to keep secret the arms-for-hostages deal. Officially he died from a virulent form of leukemia diagnosed two days before his death, but a chemical or radiation injection or spray may have been used.[23]

Another suspicious death occurred when Willie Velasquez died in 1988. *Newsweek* called his death untimely! Velasquez was extremely effective in registering Hispanic voters and was going to be deputy campaign manager for the Dukakis presidential campaign. Reporters said his death weeks after he suddenly became ill from a virulent form of cancer damaged Dukakis's chances to win Texas and California.[24]

On August 8, 1989 Frank Chikane, an anti-apartheid leader and general-secretary of the South African Council of Churches, said tests at the University of Wisconsin showed someone tried to poison him by contaminating his clothes with a toxic chemical. The *Baltimore Sun* recently reported that South Africa's Truth Commission had seen evidence that in 1985 a CIA agent, Millard Shirley, came to South Africa to work for Telcom, the government communications agency. He brought "highly classified Pentagon manuals on psychological warfare." This included a recipe for prussic acids which when inhaled caused a massive coronary leaving few traces.

In November, 1989 *Playboy* interviewed an admitted hit-man who reported that certain people died of stomach cancer while imprisoned because of their food. In prison death by unknown causes is 50 times more common than in the general population.[25] Wilhelm Reich, a prominent psychiatrist and researcher who was jailed by the FDA, died in prison of "heart complications" two months before his parole. A manuscript he wrote in prison disappeared, and he told his wife that when he asked for an aspirin he was instead given two pink pills. Jack Ruby quickly developed cancer and died while in prison after killing Lee Harvey Oswald.

While assassination techniques have certainly changed over the decades, the old-fashioned hands-on approach is still used. Bob Fletcher of the Montana Militia got entangled with the CIA when his toy company was taken over for gun smuggling, and there was an attempt on his life. Someone drove a car through a wall in Fletcher's house. When that didn't hurt him the person got out of the car and in an apologetic manner shook Fletcher's hand several times and touched him on the back of the neck. About 18 hours later, Fletcher had a major heart attack which tests showed had been chemically induced. A dust that is absorbed through the skin was used.[26]

With many of these deaths you cannot be certain if the death was murder or a natural or accidental death, which is why these methods are very effective. Various federal operatives will threaten or kill people using a variety of techniques. Books like *Operation Mind Control* document that mind control techniques and drugs are used, sometimes even on children, to make people become assassins. If the country one day learns how many people have been murdered by the secret government there will be a great shock. The Constitution offers little protection against our death squads.

Chapter XIX

# Radiation Biological and Chemical Experiments on People

"The fallout settled on virtually uninhibited land."
Atomic Energy Commission (AEC)

"The more complete the despotism, the more smoothly all things move on the surface."
Elizabeth Stanton

On December 7, 1993 Energy Secretary Hazel O'Leary announced that some people were exposed to radiation in various government-supported experiments. In late June, 1994 the Energy Department said that until 1989, about 1,200 people took part in 48 undisclosed radiation experiments, often without even being warned of the dangers. On October 21, 1994 the President's Advisory Committee on Human Radiation Experiments revealed that there had been many more intentional releases of radiation into the air than had previously been known. Instead of 13 known releases there were hundreds of deliberate releases. The committee also announced that there had been many more experiments on people between 1944 and 1974 than had previously been announced.

That Secretary of Energy Hazel O'Leary stepped forward is the main reason why this story received national coverage. O'Leary was probably influenced by Eileen Welsome's three-part series, "The Plutonium Experiment" in *The Albuquerque Tribune* November 15-17, 1993. Previously there was only limited coverage of these sanctioned atrocities, although considerable material was available by 1986.[1] In 1969 *The Archives of General Psychiatry* discussed radiation experiments involving humans. The *Washington Post* gave brief coverage to a similar story in 1971. In 1980 Congress issued a report "The Forgotten Guinea Pigs," concluding that "the AEC chose to secure, at any cost, the atmospheric nuclear weapons testing program rather than to protect the health and welfare of the residents of the area who lived downwind from the site."[2] In 1981 *Mother Jones* reported that NASA-funded radiation experiments took place for 14 years at Oak Ridge Institute an AEC clinic.[3] In 1986 Rep. Edward Markey failed to get the government to release documents on these experiments. He released a report "American Nuclear Guinea Pigs" detailing government human radiation experiments on nearly 700 people, saying that "American citizens thus became nuclear calibration devices for experimenters run amok...." The victims "were captive audiences or populations that some experimenters frighteningly might have considered 'expendable.'"[4]

On December 15, 1994, the *New York Times* reported that, as early as 1947, fear of lawsuits, bad publicity, and poor labor relations motivated officials to keep secret radiation experiments on people. These experiments were not isolated events. They were part of a broad and planned program that was debated at the highest levels of government. National security was often not a primary concern.[5] On January 18, 1995, it was reported that some people injected with radioactive material, including plutonium, were not even terminally ill. They often did not have "cancer, and may not even have been chronically ill. They were doing experiments of unknown risk on people who potentially had a full, long life ahead of them." One victim was 18 years old. Often people were not informed that they were being experimented on.[6] In February, 1995 the Energy Department's Office of Human Radiation Experiments reported that 9,000 Americans, including children and newborns were used in 154 radiation tests on humans. Retarded children were fed radioactive breakfast cereal, prisoners had their testicles irradiated, and pregnant women were given radioactive iron. Some children were given radioactive injections, while the parents were told they were being given vitamin supplements. On August 19, 1995 the Energy Department said 16,000 people were in these radiation experiments.[7] The total number of victims is probably much higher than 16,000, but CIA and military records are not available for review. By the early 1960s, 500,000 radioisotopes had been distributed to doctors and universities.[8]

That many of these people weren't told they were exposed to radiation violated the Nuremberg Code established in response to Nazi atrocities. The victims were usually poor, uneducated, often black, and had a low IQ. Testimony revealed that some victims experienced extreme pain. Lenore Fenn testified that she watched an unsedated Jacob Leftin in agony when his skull was opened exposing the brain. A doctor told her he "would not remember the pain as pain." To this day a doctor involved in this atrocity defends his work just as Nazi doctors did. The U.S. government has sanctioned the torture of its citizens in the name of national security. How far we have fallen to allow this foreign government in Washington, D.C. to so abuse us. And similar radiation experiments continue today. The president's investigating committee said that of 125 recent government-funded human research proposals, 31 percent were "ethically unacceptable." In 1995, 1,077 institutions received almost $5 billion for research projects.[9]

Since this story first broke, the CIA said it found only one instance of radiation testing on humans. However, Scott Breckenridge, a former CIA official, said that in 1972 Dr. Sidney Gottlieb, head of the chemical section of the CIA's Technical Services Division, destroyed many files including secret human radiation experiments.[10] In 1975 the Rockefeller Commission said the CIA may have conducted radiation experiments on people.

In 1994 a scientist interviewed on television defended using humans in radiation experiments because it benefited science. Hitler would have been proud of this scientist. One can only imagine what other experiments are now being conducted in the name of science and national security, which we may learn about in 30 or 50 years. For every revelation we read about, how many secrets are being kept? The Human Radiation Experiment Committee's final report on October 1, 1995 only recommended compensating people in a few experiments, found little fault with those conducting these experiments, and did not even recommend attempting to contact and notify the victims.

From the late 1940s until 1979, between 250,000 to 400,000 military personnel and 150,000 civilians participated in 626 U.S. nuclear explosions. This included 235 atmospheric tests. Other victims included over 200,000 U.S. troops who were stationed by Hiroshima and Nagasaki after World War II. Government experts said there was no danger from exposure to radiation in these cities.

Starting in 1951 about 57,000 American troops were stationed in the open, a few miles from nuclear test sites and were then ordered to march towards the test site usually minutes after the explosion.[11] The 1989 movie *Nightbreakers* showed actual footage of American troops in this situation. Many of these troops got very ill years later from this exposure, but the government resisted recognizing a relationship to the tests to help these victims. Oscar Rosen, a commander of the National Association of Atomic Veterans, said: "They didn't have to use us as guinea pigs in the nuclear warfare experiments and then discard us like expendable rats."[12] Another victim, after years of severe illnesses, said: "All I have ever asked is to live like other people. But I cannot help blaming the Government for subjecting me to nuclear testing without warning me of the potential consequences and I will always wonder why it happened."[13]

It is estimated that five million Americans were exposed to toxic levels of radiation because of various government programs. Our soldiers were not given proper protection during exposure to nuclear tests. They were not volunteers, and they were never given accurate information as to the dangers involved. These soldiers rarely received medical testing once they left the military, and usually their records were lost or destroyed. By the late 1970s, many military personnel complained about their radiation-related sicknesses, and this became an issue in the media and in Congress.

Marine Major Charles Broudy was directly exposed to radiation from nuclear testing. Before he died in 1977 at age 57 of a rare lymphoma, he and his wife filed a lawsuit against the government. After his death the lawsuit was consolidated with 43 similar suits. The 9th U.S. Circuit Court of Appeals rejected the claims, and the U.S. Supreme Court refused to hear the case. The Veterans Administration (VA) also rejected these claims, because it refused to link these problems to their exposure to radiation from these tests, although this has somewhat changed. Finally in 1988 Pat Broudy and others convinced Congress to pass the Radiation Exposed Veterans Compensation Act that provided veterans with compensation for 13 types of cancer.[14]

Even with this new law, specific standards must be met for veterans to receive up to $75,000, and other disability payments must then be discontinued. Veterans cannot sue the government under the 1950 *Feres* decision because such suits would inhibit "military necessity" and "national security."[15] Senator John Warner sponsored an amendment giving contractors at the Nevada tests sites the same immunity that the federal government has. And under a 1988 law, 38 U.S.C. 5904, strict limits are placed on the right of veterans to use lawyers in appeals before the VA Board of Veterans Appeals. Civilians can collect up to $50,000, but few people filing claims have received any money, and usually the amount paid has been quite small. By 1993 14,374 military veterans exposed to these tests had filed radiation-related claims, but the VA had verified a relationship of their sickness to the tests in only 1,250 cases.[16] The government continues to require proof of exposure to radiation that is difficult to prove with the poor record keeping. The government's solution is to keep calling for more tests while the victims continue dying.

In 1965 the U.S. Public Health Service suggested testing the increase in leukemia deaths near the tests sites in southeastern Utah. The AEC said no because this might jeopardize nuclear testing, cause adverse public reaction, and result in lawsuits. When a House subcommittee investigated these tests in 1979, they received testimony that the American people were never told the truth about the dangers of these open-air nuclear tests, and that hundreds of thousands of citizens were treated like guinea pigs. In the 1950s people did not understand the health dangers from radiation released from nuclear explosions, and these tests were presented as safe, patriotic necessities. Fallout was especially concentrated in rural areas of Nevada, Utah, and northern Arizona, where death from leukemia became increasingly common. According to a report released by the Government Accounting Office, the government deliberately released radioactive material into populated areas to study fallout patterns and the rate of radioactive decay.[17]

If you want to understand why so many people fear and hate the federal government, especially in the western states read *American Ground Zero: The Secret Nuclear War*. Here are the words and photos of many victims of open air nuclear testing. Read how the Feds destroyed the lives of people like Claudia B. Peterson who said: "I see what they've done. I see I've lost a child. I've lost my sister....I see people dying young from brain tumors and leaving families, and the sorrow, and the suffering....They are killing us for their own purposes." Josephone Simkins said: "I feel we were really used, and I'll never trust our government again....It's amazing to me that the government could lie that thoroughly....They've kept lying and they finally admitted that they caused these problems." Ken Pratt said: "(When my son) was born, his face was a massive hole. I could see down his throat...and it was horrible. I wanted to die. I wanted him to die." Glenna Orton said: "We've got a Constitution and a Bill of Rights that entitles us all to life, liberty, and the pursuit of happiness. We have been used for guinea pigs and I just really resent it....I think they've taken some of my freedom away. This is kind of like Russia." Irma Thomas summed it up best: "We trusted our government, but they considered us expendable...."

The federal government exposed millions of Americans to these tests in the name of national security. The AEC in top secret documents said Utah was "a low-use segment of the population." During the testing the AEC worked very hard to convince everyone that the tests were safe, despite sudden and widespread cancer and mental retardation. Women were often told their cancer was caused by neurosis or "housewife syndrome." The government invited people to come and see the pretty mushroom cloud, because it was all so safe! Eisenhower reportedly said: "We can afford to sacrifice a few thousand people out there in the interest of national security." Where in the Constitution does it say that thousands of Americans can be injured or killed by the federal government in the name of national security? I haven't found such a hidden clause in the Constitution that allows this, and the press never asks about this.

Part of the problem has been the callous attitude of the AEC. Thomas Murray an AEC Commissioner said: "We must not let anything interfere with (these) tests—nothing." The AEC even encouraged people to watch nuclear tests to keep a positive attitude about the peaceful atom. Dotte Troxell was in a serious radiation accident in 1957 while working at an AEC plant. After developing serious radiation sickness, she was transferred to an AEC clinic and operated on. When she awoke and asked what had been done to her, the doctors told her they couldn't tell her because of national security![18]

A typical and disturbing way in which the government deals with citizens is presented in *The Myths of August*, by former Rep. Stewart Udall. As a lawyer Udall tried to get government compensation for uranium miners and people who lived downwind from nuclear tests. Udall was certain that once the government understood how people's lives had been damaged, there would be just compensation from the authorities. During his investigation, he obtained documents which showed that the government knew uranium mining would be extremely dangerous if there wasn't proper ventilation in the mines. Such ventilation was never done, and the miners were never informed of the danger. Udall, also a former Secretary of the Interior, uncovered information that while the government was telling the American people open air nuclear testing was quite safe, it had secret documents depicting the side effects of such nuclear testing including cancer, genetic damage, and death. According to Udall, this was a classic cover-up. I listened to him being interviewed, expressing his deep shock that the government would admit no wrong and help these victims.[19]

The government has strongly fought all lawsuits filed concerning nuclear testing or uranium mining. In 1987 *U.S. v. Allen* reversed a lower court ruling making the government immune from such lawsuits. In 1990, the Radiation Exposure Compensation Act gave civilian victims some compensation, after the courts blocked any restitution. The Bush Justice Department worked very hard to defeat this bill. The recent revelations of government radiation tests on people has brought numerous lawsuits. Federal Judge Sandra Beckwith refused to dismiss one suit because the defendants "treated at least 87 of it's citizens as though they were laboratory animals."

The government has been as contemptuous of animals and property rights, as it has been with the lives of American citizens. In 1953, 4,500 sheep died in Utah and Nevada after being exposed to fallout from a nuclear test. The government denied any responsibility. The ranchers lost a 1956 court case, but they won in 1982 after 20,000 pages of AEC documents were released suggesting that the government was aware all along that the testing had killed the sheep. A 1980 House committee investigation concluded that the AEC had participated in a sophisticated cover-up. There was evidence that the sheep were exposed to much higher levels of radiation than the government would publicly acknowledge. The judge ruled that "fraud was committed by the U.S. Government when it lied, pressured witnesses and manipulated the processes of the court." However, this verdict was thrown out on appeal.[20] The appeals court judge had worked for a law firm that represented the Los Alamos National Laboratory, the directors of the atomic tests.

During the many years of open air nuclear testing in the West, newspapers rarely questioned the safety of what was happening. A classic example of media bias in covering the nuclear industry was *What Happened*, which aired March 16, 1993, on the Three Mile Island accident. Owned by GE, a manufacturer of nuclear power plants, this NBC show said most people are now content. Debbie Baker, who was interviewed for the show, was very angry because they took out of context what she said and gave a false impression of her opinion. Her son was born with Down's syndrome after the accident, and she was paid $1.1 million by Metropolitan Edison the local utility. There were almost 200 similar settlements, but none of this was discussed on the show. When asked why no experts critical of nuclear energy appeared on the show, a producer said the program was entertainment not journalism.[21]

The story is the same with the nuclear weapons industry. "Nothing in our past compares to the official deceit and lying that took place in order to protect the nuclear industry. In the name of national security, politicians and bureaucrats ran roughshod over democracy and morality. Ultimately, the Cold Warriors were willing to sacrifice their own people in their zeal to beat the Russians."[22] "Hanford (nuclear weapons plant in Washington state) and the other bomb factories were allowed to endanger their neighbors and foul the environment because government scientists and officials didn't trust the people they served. Coming out of World War II, the government maintained its wartime claim to extraordinary secrecy....For their part, everyday citizens, motivated by fear of the Soviet menace and of an awesome technology, abdicated their responsibility to determine the national interest in a time of peace."[23]

On July 11, 1990, Energy Secretary James D. Watkins said at a press conference there was clear evidence that thousands of innocent civilians had been exposed to dangerous levels of radiation near government nuclear weapons complexes. Government documents released partly through the FOIA show that, since the 1940s, government scientists had been concerned that civilians were being exposed to dangerous levels of radiation by the nuclear weapons industry. There were numerous instances where government officials deliberately concealed or ignored serious problems. One local citizen by the Hanford nuclear weapons plant said that while the world criticized the Soviet Union for not telling the world about the Chernobyl accident, our own government had kept the people in the dark for over 40 years! By 1993, over 4,000 people had become plaintiffs in a lawsuit against GE, Du Pont, and Rockwell, the prime contractors at Hanford.

Throughout the development and use of atomic energy the public was usually deceived and lied to, leaving the credibility of the government in doubt. "All along the government, under all administrations, has been extremely tender of the interests of corporations, feeling that they need to be protected for the sake of economic stability."[24] How the welfare of the people was affected was rarely considered, except when they were occasionally aroused.

There is little understanding of the long term effects on the millions of people exposed to radiation. Government funded studies usually show a low incident of cancer for people downwind of nuclear tests, while privately funded studies show exactly the opposite. When statistics are used to identify the causes of cancer, radiation is never listed. With so many nuclear tests and releases of radiation from nuclear energy sites we have all been exposed to levels of radiation that may be quite toxic. The *Journal of the American Medical Association* recently reported that baby boomers are three times as likely to have cancer as their grandparents. One in three people will die of cancer in the U.S. The *Boston Globe* reported on January 9, 1994 that, according to the International Physicians for the Prevention of Nuclear War, there have been 6,290,000 deaths worldwide from exposure to nuclear radiation.[25]

John Gofman, M.D., a scientist who studies radiation and health, found in 1969 that the government manipulated statistics and underestimated by at least 20 times the risk of cancer from radiation. He said there is no safe level of radiation. The head of the AEC told Gofman they would "get him." He lost his funding at the Livermore Laboratory, and the National Cancer Society refused to fund his research. Gofman has seen so many government cover-ups that he doesn't "consider the Department of Energy a credible agency." Alice Stewart, another radiation scientist, found years ago that exposure to radiation in low doses was far more dangerous than was understood. Few wanted to believe her research, and she had difficulty getting funding.[26]

Approximately 150,000 Americans were deliberately exposed to mustard gas and other chemicals during and after World War II. They were forced to take part in these tests, threatened with prison if they violated the test secrecy, and were given no follow-up medical care even when they got sick. Amazingly, many were given "man-break" tests deliberately designed to expose the soldiers to levels of gas that would definitely cause illnesses. The intention was to test the equipment and to study how well the injured victims could function. Chemical poisons were often applied directly to the victims bodies to test the results.

These veterans rarely got aid from the VA, because there were no official records about these tests. For almost 50 years, there was an official policy of denying that the tests even took place. In 1980 the National Academy of Sciences studied the long-term effects of exposure to chemical-warfare agents for 6,720 soldiers who had participated in these experiments between 1955-1975. There was a statistical correlation between chronic exposure to mustard gas and cancer. One report said at least 4,000 soldiers suffered serious injuries from these tests. In 1991 CBS's *60 Minutes* reported on this cover-up, and Rep. Porter Goss tried to get benefits for four participants of U.S. Navy mustard-gas tests. The standards required by the VA to provide help were lowered; however, problems continue because records are often incomplete or missing.

In the 1950s soldiers were given chemical and biological warfare (CBW) agents at Fort Detrick, Md. These troops staged a sitdown strike to learn what they were being given so they were replaced by Seventh-Day Adventists volunteers. The documentary, *Bad Trip in Edgewood*, described how over 7,000 U.S. troops were exposed to gases and injections often with no advance warning. Powerful mind control drugs, such as PCP or angel dust and LSD, were used. During the 1950s and 1960s, 740 soldiers and 900 civilians were given LSD. The troops were never told what they were taking, and they were ordered not to tell anyone about these tests. There was no follow-up medical care, and some of these victims suffered serious physical and mental problems, including nervous breakdowns and epilepsy. Even people in mental hospitals were given mind altering drugs without their consent, and at least one person, Harold Blauer, died shortly after being given a mescaline derivative. Years later his family learned what happened, and after a 15 year lawsuit, they won $750,000. There were many lawsuits, and in one Supreme Court decision, a dissenting judge compared the Edgewood tests to Nazi experiments. Australia, Canada, and England conducted similar tests during World War II, as depicted in a 1989 Australian documentary, *Keen As Mustard*. At least 1,000 Canadians were injured and several thousand Australians now receive disability payments, because of injuries suffered during these tests.[27]

During World War II the Japanese developed CBW weapons that were widely used against China, and they seriously considered sending them to the U.S. in balloons. Some balloons did reach the U.S. with conventional weapons killing at least one person. Over 12,000 people died from these Japanese experiments, including some U.S. prisoners of war. On August, 15, 1995 NBC's *Dateline* had a story on these tests. One American veteran who was a victim said they received little help and "our government has betrayed us." The U.S. didn't arrest the Japanese who conducted these tests in Manchuria. Instead "we helped cover-up the human experimentation" in exchange for receiving its data.[28] The U.S. has for years worked on perfecting CBW weapons.

During World War II the U.S. was prepared to use various gases against the enemy if U.S. troops were attacked with such weapons, but this was never done. In one incident, over 600 U.S. troops were treated for mustard gas exposure when a German plane bombed Bari Harbor, Italy on December 2, 1943. A damaged U.S. ship accidently released mustard gas, killing 83 troops and almost 1,000 local citizens.[29] The U.S. made and sent Phosgene gas to England in 1941, and it almost used poison gas on Iwo Jima and Japan. The U.S. and England planned to attack six German cities with anthrax bombs that would have killed half the population, but production delays blocked this plan. The widespread use of Agent Orange and other CBW agents during the Vietnam War continues to cause great suffering for millions of people.[30]

For years the CIA, in 200 medical schools and mental hospitals, gave diseases and chemicals to citizens without their knowledge. The government also released CBW agents in many U.S. cities including N.Y., Washington, D.C., and San Francisco to see how people were effected. In 1950 in San Francisco, 11 people were hospitalized and one person died in an experiment. Relatives of the deceased victim learned in a lawsuit that the U.S. conducted 300 open air biological attacks across the U.S. between 1950 and 1969. In 1955 the CIA released the whooping cough virus in Palmetto, Florida. At least 12 people died. The Army Chemical Corps released mosquitoes by Carver Village, an entirely black town, to see if they could carry and spread yellow and dengue fever. The tests were a success and many people got sick and some died. There were over 40 germ warfare tests against American citizens. In 1966, the Army dispensed a bacteria in the New York City subways. In 1968, the CIA almost poisoned the water supply of the FDA headquarters in Washington. In 1969, over a four month period, cadmium sulfide was sprayed 115 times in Maryland. Total insanity! During a 1977 congressional investigation, the Army admitted conducting hundreds of open air experiments with toxic agents.[31]

In June, 1994 members of Minnesota's congressional delegation tried to get answers from the Army about tests of CBW warfare agents over unsuspecting Minneapolis residents in 1953. The Army said one agent used, zinc cadmium, was considered harmless, but more recent studies have shown it may cause cancer. Three women who were exposed to the tests recently came forward to report a pattern of sterility, miscarriages, and birth defects.[32] On July 18, 1995, NBC's *Dateline* investigated this atrocity. The tests were conducted by a school, and it ruined the health of many.

As documented in *Bad Blood*, by James H. Jones, in the notorious "Tuskegee Study," 412 black American sharecroppers near Tuskegee, Alabama were studied for 40 years, starting in the early 1930s. None of them were ever told they had syphilis, because the U.S. Public Health Service wanted to watch the disease develop. Symptoms included insanity, paralysis, blindness, and death, but they were never given penicillin although that was an effective treatment. That would have interfered with the study. The program ended in 1972 when a federal employee went to the press after his private complaints starting in 1966 went unanswered.

The victims received no help until eight months later, just as congressional hearings began.

In 1931 numerous Puerto Ricans were deliberately injected with cancer in an experiment led by Cornelius Rhoads of the Rockefeller Institute, and 13 died. Rhoads wrote in a letter: "The Puerto Ricans are the dirtiest, laziest, most dangerous and thievish race of men ever inhabiting this sphere....I have done my best to further the process of extermination by killing off eight and transplanting cancer into several more....All physicians take delight in the abuse and torture of the unfortunate subjects." This letter was given by the recipient to the Puerto Rican Nationalist Party. Rhoads was investigated but, although he never denied writing the letter, the prosecutor said Rhoads was just "a mentally ill person or a man with few scruples," so he was never prosecuted. During World War II, Rhoads headed two large chemical warfare projects, he had a seat on the AEC, and he headed the Sloan-Kettering Institute for Cancer Research. Later when many National Party members were imprisoned, they were exposed to radiation, burning, poisoning, and experimental drugs.[33] Here we see the mentality of certain people in the secret government. Carefully reflect on this and the great concern the corporate elite have today about the population explosion. How many people are there like Rhoads, and what would they do in a world dictatorship?

The U.S. has a long history of using CBW agents and experimental drugs on prisoners. The birth control pill was first given to Puerto Rican and Haitian women. An American doctor gave Philippine prisoners beriberi and the plague. In 1915, 12 prisoners in Mississippi were given pellagra, while in the 1940s over 400 Chicago prisoners were given malaria. Prisoners in Philadelphia were exposed to dioxin between 1965 and 1968. As with laboratory animals these tests are done to develop weapons or new drugs for the public. During the Nuremberg trials, Nazi doctors defended their atrocities by citing some of these American experiments.[34]

There have also been experiments to use genetics as a weapon.[35] By 1962, 40 scientists were working just on genetics at the U.S. Army biological warfare laboratories.[36] In 1969 Congress heard testimony about the advantages of this research. "Within the next 5 to 10 years it would be possible to produce a synthetic biological agent, an agent that does not naturally exist and for which no natural immunity could have been acquired....It would probably be possible to make a new infective micro-organism which could differ in certain important respects from any known disease-causing organisms. Most important of these is that it might be refractory to the immunological and therapeutic processes upon which we depend to maintain our relative freedom from infectious disease."[37] Within a few years, the AIDS epidemic began. There is much literature available, such as the works by Alan Cantwell, Jr., M.D. and Robert Strecker, M.D., stating that this germ was deliberately created, probably at Fort Detrick, but that subject goes beyond the scope of this book. Some researchers like Drs. Garth and Nancy Nicholson feel genetic research to develop CBW weapons has continued for years.[38] A lawsuit in 1987 forced the Department of Defense to admit that CBW research was taking place in 127 sites about the U.S. Some of these sites are using recombinant DNA techniques.

The Gulf War Syndrone (GWS) is associated with Iraqi CBW and vaccines given to U.S. troops. *Time* magazine said, in late May, 1994, evidence was presented before a Senate committee showing that the U.S. government approved the sale to Iraq of CBW agents that may have caused GWS.[39] *Spider's Web*, by Alan Friedman, describes this secret U.S. assistance to Iraq. Recently released documents suggest that troops were exposed to CBW agents and there is a cover-up. Eleven pages released in late January, 1995 by the Pentagon through the FOIA show that various CBW attacks on our troops were identified during the war and bombed-out Iraqi chemical facilities were located. There were over 1,000 chemical alarms during the war but these were all supposedly false reports. Yet the military still buys these alarms because they work so well. Former Senator Riegle held hearings and issued two reports stating that U.S. and British troops made at least 21 contacts with chemical agents and there is a cover-up. This report said the allies bombed 18 chemical, 12 biological, and 4 nuclear facilities. The government continues to deny this exposure, which limits proper medical treatment.[40] As with Agent Orange, the government often calls GWS psychological and denies there is a physical problem. In September, 1995, Iraq admitted having a much larger germ-warfare program than had previously been acknowledged,[41] and in June, 1996 the Pentagon finally admitted that some U.S. troops were exposed to Iraqi chemical weapons during the Gulf War when a munitions facility was destroyed.

Marianne Gasior, a Pittsburgh lawyer, has gathered extensive evidence about U.S. corporations providing CBW agents to Iraq before the war, and she has received death threats. Released Pentagon documents show that the U.S. knew Iraq was receiving CBW toxins from various U.S. companies before the war.[42] Peter Kawaja has identified companies in Boca Raton, Florida and Houston, Texas that, in conjunction with U.S. intelligence, illegally produced poisons that were exported to Iraq. Kawaja was working with two of these firms as a security specialist, and when he became suspicious he went to the CIA and FBI. He was told that these people were terrorists who were going to be arrested. He gathered evidence that U.S. politicians and intelligence agents were improperly working with these companies. On July 16, 1990, he sent a message about this to the National Security Agency. Soon eight armed federal agents, without showing a search warrant, raided his business seizing documents. This "evidence" was sealed under a war powers act because of national security, and he started receiving the first of many death threats.

Under the Biological Weapons Convention of 1972, it is illegal to make, experiment with, distribute, or sell germs for warfare. Kawaja believes that James Baker III, George Bush, and John Deutch (now head of the CIA) have business ties to U.S. firms that provided CBW agents to Iraq. Kawaja filed a lawsuit in federal court against various federal agents for obstruction of justice, misleading a federal grand jury, threatening a witness, and other charges. Part of the government defense was that it has an ongoing investigation and it has immunity. On October 19, 1995 the suit was dismissed, so perhaps the Feds do have the right to commit crimes that kill thousands of Americans.[43] Since large U.S. corporations supported the enemy during World War II, it should not surprise the objective observer that similar activities continue today. The Justice Department, under Bush and Clinton, has refused to bring charges against these corporations.

While CBS's *60 Minutes* on March 12, 1994 said over 50,000 Gulf War veterans are sick, some feel the number is much higher. Joyce Riley, a nurse active in helping those with GWS, said 7,000 Gulf War veterans have died and over 200,000 are sick.[44] These ill troops would have difficulty defending the U.S. The Senate has found evidence that GWS is contagious with 78 percent of the spouses and 25 percent of the children affected.[45] GWS is airborne and spreads by non-. ual but continued close contact. One Senate committee last year found that 65 pt cent of the children conceived by Gulf War veterans have birth defects.

The vaccines and drugs U.S. troops were given before going to the Gulf violated the Nuremberg Code. People aren't supposed to be given experimental drugs even during war without their informed consent. The Pentagon said it wasn't possible to get informed consent from combat troops so it obtained a waiver from the FDA to give the troops these chemicals. Soldiers who resisted the injections were forcibly given them, which is unethical and unlawful. The *New York Times* called these troops guinea pigs.[46] In 1996 Clinton's Advisory Committee on Gulf War Veterans Illnesses said the waiver obtained from the FDA should become permanent.

The military has treated people investigating GWS quite harshly. An Army reservist, Dr. Yolanda Huet-Vaughn, refused to give these experimental vaccines per the Nuremberg Code and she was court-martialed. Sentenced to 30 months in jail, this mother of three children was released after eight months. U.S. Department of Agriculture scientist Dr. Jim Moss was fired for investigating DEET, an insect repellant, to see if it was connected to the GWS. Soldiers, like Navy Reserve Capt. Julia Dyckman who gathered evidence on GWS, have been harassed by the military. Some Gulf veterans in the National Guard have been discharged for complaining about illnesses, and the records of many Gulf veterans have been deliberately destroyed.[47]

Drs. Nancy and Garth Nicholson have isolated one of the biological causes of GWS, and have successfully treated many.[48] It is a laboratory modified mycoplasma, as shown by the highly unusual DNA sequence, and was probably given to troops during the vaccines. Over the years, few have researched mycoplasma, the laboratories in the U.S. studying it often had Iraqi technicians, and mycoplasma is a highly classified germ warfare agent. Two weeks before the Gulf War started, the U.S. Commerce Department stopped shipping mycoplasma to the Iraqi Atomic Energy Commission. The CIA and Defense Intelligence Agency (DIA) tried to stop the Nicholsons' work. DIA agents went to their hospital warning them to stop their research, but they refused. Publication of their articles has been blocked, and their mail, phones, and faxes have been repeatedly intercepted.

Through a contact in the Justice Department, Garth Nicholson heard there is a secret eugenics directive in various East Coast laboratories, and friends at several laboratories confirmed this. Perhaps this is why U.S. troops were given these toxic vaccines. The Nicholsons also have evidence that these illegal toxins were tested in certain prisons. Information was leaked to them partly because some people involved in these criminal activities got sick, and they came to the Nicholsons for treatment. Although they have given interviews to the national media, each report was suppressed.[49] Garth Nicholson has written 400 scientific papers, edited 13 books, been nominated for the Nobel prize, and is editor or associate editor of 13 scientific and medical journals.

Methyl Tertiary Butyl Ether (MTBE) is a highly toxic chemical that the EPA is forcing states and cities to use in gasoline, and the percentage of MTBE that goes into gasoline is being increased. Oil companies are promoting this chemical to increase their profits. It evaporates in the air causing serious respiratory, neurological, and allergic problems. Readily soluble in water, it is now found in ground water. A prominent Italian scientist, Dr. Maltoni, found that MTBE caused cancer in animals. Dangerous chemical reactions, such as formaldehyde and tertiary butyl formate occur when MTBE is used. When it was introduced in Fairbanks, Alaska up to 50 percent of the population promptly got sick. The Centers for Disease Control (CDC) brought in doctors who said MTBE was the cause. The EPA rejected these findings, and blocked the CDC from conducting further investigations. The governor ordered removal of the chemical in all gasoline sold in the state, despite EPA threats to withdraw federal funds, and symptoms promptly disappeared. The same thing happened in Missoula, Montana and Stamford, Connecticut although fewer people were affected than in Alaska. Over 16,000 people signed petitions to remove MTBE from gasoline sold in New Jersey, and this poison has been banned in N.C. and parts of Pennsylvania and New York.[50]

Millions of Californians have been exposed to the pesticide malathion through widespread airborne spraying. This was supposedly done to protect crops, and there are plans to use it in other states. Other methods of medfly control have been underutilized, while malathion was mainly sprayed over populated areas, not over crops. In 1989-1990, 509,583 pounds of malthion were used. It causes numerous health problems, and its toxicity greatly increases when used as a spray. Malathion is in the chemical family developed by I.G. Farben to subdue or kill people, and it was used in the concentration camps.[51] In the summer of 1988, *The Oregonian* did a nine-part series about CIA front companies such as Evergreen Helicopters. Through a front company, the CIA was directly involved in spraying malathion over Southern California. Why is the CIA interested in exposing millions of citizens to this poison? Why does the government allow the widespread use of pesticides that are so toxic to our health?

Fluoridated water causes diseases such as Down's Syndrome, heart, kidney, cancer, bone, and liver problems.[52] Eleven European countries and 200 U.S. cities have banned its use. Court cases have established the toxic effects of fluoridation. In the 1970s Congress was shocked to learn that the National Cancer Institute (NCI) had never tested fluoride for cancer. The NCI took 12 years to conduct these tests, which demonstrated a sharply higher incident of bone and joint cancer in regions with water fluoridation. The U.S. hip-fracture rate is now the world's highest and even the *Journal of the American Medical Association* magazine on August 12, 1992 blamed water fluoridation.

Nazi and Soviet researchers found that fluoride created a docile, sheep-like obedience and demeanor, so it was used in prison camps. Charles Perkins was sent to Germany by the U.S. to help run I.G. Farben, the giant chemical corporation, after World War II. In 1954 he wrote the Lee Foundation for Nutritional Research: "The German chemists worked out an ingenious and far-reaching plan of mass control....Sodium fluoride occupied a prominent place....The real purpose behind water fluoridation is to reduce the resistance of the masses to domination, control, and loss of liberty." Today many tranquilizer drugs like daladorm are made from fluoride compounds. In a recent government report "The Revolution in Military Affairs and Conflict Short of War" future strategies are suggested. Drugged food would be supplied to Cuba to subdue the population and lower the incident of anti-government activity.

There is a second purpose behind the introduction of fluoride. The fluoride found in nature is calcium fluoride, while the type used in our water is sodium fluoride, which is a waste product from the aluminum industry. In the past there were numerous lawsuits over this poison, so the aluminum industry used propaganda, money, and political influence to turn a chemical used in rat poison into a product we all needed. Then large corporations could sell a toxic waste and earn more profit. The aluminum giant ALCOA was owned by Andrew Mellon, and its chief attorney Oscar R. Ewing took a senior public health job in Washington in 1946 to promote water fluoridation. The Safe Water Foundation is working to stop fluoridation.[53]

In recent years food irradiation has become increasingly common. Foods are exposed to radiation supposedly to kill various microorganisms. This may preserve food longer, but it also damages the chemical structure of food creating free radicals including benzene which causes cancer. Irradiating food also causes mutations in viruses and bacteria in food, producing more resistant strains, and some vitamins and nutrients are destroyed. A 1979 review of food irradiation literature found hundreds of adverse effects in animals.[54] Animals fed irradiated food develop kidney damage, lowered growth rates, lowered birth rates, tumors, immune system damage, and genetic mutations. Government committees ignored this evidence because of political pressure to approve food irradiation. At a recent food irradiation conference sponsored by the World Health Organization, the U.S. worked to expand food irradiation. The FDA reviewed 441 studies and eliminated all but five of them because of poor quality. Even these five studies had problems, but this weak evidence was used to approve further food irradiation. Radiation is also used to sterilize medical equipment, sanitary napkins, and tampons.[55] As with fluoridation the radiation used to irradiate food is an industry waste product. Food and Water, Inc. has been leading the fight to stop food irradiation.[56]

As with fluoride in water and radiation in food, sewage sludge is another industrial waste that has been added to our food supply. Farmers are using toxic sewage sludge as a fertilizer to grow crops. The Environmental Protection Agency (EPA) has already reclassified sewer sludge as an unregulated fertilizer, and it is being sold commercially with no monitoring. This sewage may contain highly toxic chemicals and biological toxins, but it increases corporate profits. The EPA has provided $300,000 to the Water Environment Federation (WEF) "to educate the public" about the "beneficial uses" of sludge. The WEF, which is the industry lobby group for sewage treatment plants, and the EPA want farmers and food processors to use sewage sludge as a "beneficial fertilizer." The water industry says sewage is not toxic and calls it "biosolids."[57] The book, *Toxic Sludge Is Good For You*, discusses this outrage.

A fourth atrocity that will shortly be perpetrated against the American people is the introduction of genetically engineered foods that contains genes derived from fish, insects, pigs, viruses, and bacteria. The FDA will not require labels on genetically engineered foods, although such foods has already injured people. Genetically engineered soybeans, mixed with a brazil nut protein, caused a severe allergic reaction. No one is sure that this food will be safe, and mixing human and animal or insect genes may cause many problems in the coming decades. However, the biotech industry has sufficient political power to manipulate the government to increase profits.

Bovine Growth Hormone (BGH) has recently been added to milk, and the Monsanto Corporation took legal action to scare small companies into not labeling their milk BGH free. Cows fed BGH get udder infections and more antibiotics are used, which get into our food supply. Some cows even die.[58] BGH increases milk production, which will force small farms out of business, and help shift milk

production to South America to raise corporate profits as NAFTA un-
[ is being used to help introduce other genetically engineered foods. The
Union of Concerned Scientists issued a report calling for this to be stopped until
the ecological consequences are understood. The long-term health effects are also
not understood. The European Council of Ministers has banned BGH use until
2000, and the Pure Food coalition has been fighting to remove this chemical from
milk.[59]

Aspartame used in Nutra Sweet™ is another chemical associated with the
Nazis. The Pentagon once listed it as a prospective biochemical weapon. Researchers have connected this chemical with a remarkable number of illnesses. A
study by the National Institutes of Health, *Adverse Effects of Aspartame*, listed
167 reasons not to take it. It erodes memory, depresses intelligence, and is another
substance that helps subdue and control a population. Alex Constantine has
documented numerous ties between Monsanto Corporation, the main patent holder
of aspartame, the CIA, and Nazi corporations involved in germ warfare.[60] A
consumer group has released *The Deadly Deception* and is working to ban this
chemical.[61]

The government is deliberately exposing us to more and more chemical,
radiation, and biological agents. With the corporate elite so concerned about population growth, are there deliberate plans to reduce the world's population through
the use of various poisons? In examining these insidious programs, consider the
horrific statements made by individuals in Chapter IV about our overpopulated
planet. People should get involved to stop these deadly programs.

# Chapter XX

# Restoring Constitutional Government

"The spirit of resistance to government is so valuable on occasion that I wish it to be always kept alive....What country can preserve its liberties if its rulers are not warned from time to time that its people preserve the spirit of resistance."
Thomas Jefferson

"There will never be a free and enlightened State until the State comes to recognize the individual as a higher and independent power, from which all its own power and authority are derived, and treats him accordingly....Government is best which governs least."
Henry David Thoreau

Three major issues now face the American people. First, how long will it take for the people to fully awaken to the corruption and treason that has continued for so many years. How many people have to be awakened before there is a massive response. People don't yet realize how bad things are partly because the news is so controlled and censored. A Republic can gradually be destroyed from apathy and indifference. For change to take place people must first recognize that there is a problem. Jerry Brown said: "The increasing enslavement of the people is only possible because people don't see what is happening." The one world government would destroy all that America has stood for.

In 1990 I took a three week group tour of the Soviet Union. Just after arriving I asked our Soviet tour guide if she was a member of the communist party. She responded as if I had insulted her. Every government guide and many local people we spoke to disliked or hated the communist party because of what it had done to the country. I concluded that the entire system would soon collapse, so I wasn't surprised when this happened the next year.

I now have a similar feeling regarding the disgust that millions feel about what is happening to America. Too many things have gone wrong with the economic, political, spiritual, and social fabric of the nation, and word is getting out. This doesn't necessarily mean that the entire system will collapse, although that wouldn't surprise me, but I do believe that things cannot continue too much longer as they are. Either those promoting the one world government will attempt to seize all guns, to establish an open dictatorship, and start arresting thousands of people, or the people and the military will restore the Constitution. More and more people are disgusted with politics as usual in America.

While in the Soviet Union I met a few people who thought communism and the Soviet Union were wonderful. People supposedly had all the freedoms one could want, with a high standard of living. This is what the government and the media said, so how could it be otherwise? In America we receive the same assurances from the state and the national media, so how can one disagree? However, the problem for the government is that it has lost control of information.

Second, what will the people do when they realized how dangerous the federal government has become? All our rights are now threatened, and the economic fabric of the country has been seriously weakened. This is the first generation that will not do as well economically as the previous generation, and the middle class is increasingly threatened economically. Millions of Americans are having serious problems getting decent jobs. Yet for most people, economic conditions are not that severe, certainly not to a degree that history has shown would cause a revolution. However, the American revolution is perhaps the only successful revolution in history that took place even though there was general economic well-being. Americans are used to freedom.

We have a new situation that is unique to history. As the Tofflers have said in *The Third Wave*, it is now much easier to access much more information. Today, we live in an age of mass communications with computers, faxes, and portable phones. While the main forms of mass communications are controlled by the corporate elite, it is possible to get messages out in many other ways such as at meetings, talk radio, bulletin boards, and through the alternative press in journals and books. Because of desktop publishing in the mid 1980s, many new small presses opened so much more information on many topics now gets published. As people learn the truth, the corrupt power structure is crumbling.

The third and most important issue is, will the people wake up before it is too late? Will enough people wake up to what is happening in time to prevent an open dictatorship. Over the decades the elitists have often said they want to establish a one world government in the future. The corporate elite may move beyond gradually tighten control over the people, because many want to dismantle the federal government, and resistance to the new world order is growing. On September 14, 1994 David Rockefeller addressed a UN function declaring "But this present 'window of opportunity,' during which a truly peaceful and interdependent World Order might be built, will not be open for long. Already there are powerful forces at work that threaten to destroy all of our hopes and efforts to erect an enduring structure of global cooperation."[1] Recently, in the context of enhancing UN power, Arthur Schlesinger, Jr. said: "We are not going to achieve a new world order without paying for it in blood as well as in words and money."[2]

For years influential people have said phony excuses, as done with the two world wars and the depression, should be used to enhance government power to create the one world government. For instance, the U.S. State Department commissioned a study (contract No. SCC 28270) *A World Effectively Controlled by the United Nations* by Lincoln Bloomfield. The study said a world government would take hundreds of years to evolve naturally, but a crisis, a "series of sudden, nasty, and traumatic shocks" such as a war, could bring about a world government in short order. Excuses discussed include: economic collapse, diseases, terrorism, racial riots, food shortages, or another war. These and other threats are openly debated among the ruling elite, and they will probably use some combination of threats to achieve control. The sharp rise in oil prices may be an early sign of what is coming. Some claim that the militias will be attacked and martial law will be declared. One cannot state exactly when a phony emergency will be created, but if Clinton is reelected there may well be an economic catastrophe to enhance government power. In addition, there is already a severe world-wide grain shortage from a drought, a wheat fungus is destroying much of our wheat crop, and the *Wall Street Journal* recently said we may soon be required to sign up with one store and one restaurant annually to buy all our food from for the coming year. If this article is not a parody as is claimed, are you prepared for this control?[3] Reportedly, people in the military are not prepared to live in such a controlled society.

There are powerful elements in the military determined to uphold the Constitution and protect the people. Many officers now understand the treason and corruption that has taken place for many years. Gary Allen, in several books, said senior military intelligence officers were aware of the corporate international network that seeks to enslave the world. The military may openly intervene, perhaps after a period of intense civil strife, to arrest key political, business, and media leaders charging them with treason and sedition. It may shock some to speak of this, but people in the military take an oath to "support, and defend the Constitution of the United States against all enemies, foreign and domestic...." This is an oath most in the military take with great seriousness. Our government was established by the people, and if the government becomes destructive, it can be altered or abolished by the people. The first duty of a soldier is to protect the Constitution and the people.[4]

There has long been a quiet stand-off between the military and the secret government. Each watches the other with a full range of surveillance activities used. The secret government has tried to politicize the military command with officers who support the new world order. Active duty officers are allowed to serve on corporate boards. For years some senior officers have belonged to the CFR, the new head of the CIA wants full control over the military intelligence agencies' budgets, and in April, 1996 it was reported that the CIA head may appoint the heads of the other intelligence agencies.[5] CIA leadership has always been an asset of the secret government, while military intelligence is the eyes used by the military command to watch the corporate traitors. In researching this book I have more than once spoken to people in direct contact with those in the military who are determined to defend the Constitution, and I have learned that many people are aware of this stand-off. An obvious danger is that Wall Street will create another foreign war such as in Korea or the Middle East. If many U.S. troops were sent overseas, they would not be readily available to protect the people if a phony martial law was established in the U.S.

A hint of the growing anger in the military was revealed in March, 1996 when several sources, including *Strategic Investments*, said the Pentagon had completed a study of the Oklahoma bombing showing that five bombs had exploded, McVeigh was peripherally involved as a "useful idiot," and the operation had a Middle East "signature." Clinton and the FBI do not want federal agencies conducting independent investigations of that event, especially when the conclusions disagree with the party line. The death of Admiral Boorda may be one sign of tension. Boorda, who had many family ties with Oklahoma, may have quietly assisted in investigating the Oklahoma bombing cover-up. Also, Boorda was Jewish, and in Judaism suicide is strictly forbidden. The official reason for his suicide is ridiculous. About his combat V medals, Secretary of the Navy John Dalton said: "I cannot imagine why he felt it would be difficult to explain." Hopefully, in the future, independent experts will examine his "suicide notes" as with the Foster death.

That the corporate elite has long understood the problem of dealing with a loyal military is implied in the work of Samuel P. Huntington, founder and long time contributor to *Foreign Policy*. He is a key thinkers for the corporate elite. In September, 1956 in the *American Political Science Review*, he wrote an article "Civilian Control and the Constitution." He complained about the difficulty controlling the militia. In 1957 he wrote *The Soldier and the State* concerning civilian control of the military. That most officers in the U.S. military remain loyal to the Constitution is a problem the secret government has never resolved. The growing anger of the military may be one reason why so many in Congress are retiring.

Direct intervention by the military is just one possible scenario. This quiet stand-off may continue for many years. The military may refuse to act if it sees that the secret government is not willing to establish an open dictatorship, and individuals in the secret government may recognize that they could lose everything if they move beyond gradually tightening control over the people. However, the ruling elite may act because of a fear that they may be arrested and charged with treason and sedition, as more people learn of their activities. The wild card in all this is the American people. It is difficult to see how things can continue indefinitely without an explosion. The current situation is much more volatile than most Americans understand, which is one reason why the Feds were so cautious in arresting the Freeman.

Two college professors in 1977 wrote *American Politics: Policies, Power and Change* in which they predicted that corporate-banking control of America may lead to "a corporatist system in which the major corporations dominate." This will ultimately create great tension and "a general chaos." Professor Arthur Miller, in *Democratic Dictatorship*, said: "Some type of authoritarianism, perhaps of totalitarianism, seems to be inevitable....The U.S. may be on a collision course with disaster....No one should be confident that the movement can be halted...." The dictatorship that is coming under the ruling elite may be done in the name of democracy with a "Constitution of control."[6] In *The Secret Constitution and the Need for Constitutional Change*, which was done with the aid of the Rockefeller Foundation, Miller said: "Constitutional alteration will come whether or not it is liked or planned for....We need a new republic....Ours is the age of the planned society, as any number of post-World War II developments attest. No other way is possible."

We are now in a period equivalent to the early 1770s. In 1770 the British killed some colonists in Boston, and over the next few years, people gradually understood that freedom would be protected only by fighting the British. We have had Waco and Ruby Ridge. On talk radio every day the deep anger and hatred toward the federal government is obvious, and increasingly people reluctantly acknowledge that a fight is coming to stop the Feds from destroying our rights. Art Bell, a popular radio talk show host, discussed this issue on one program and many agreed with him that a fight is coming. When the American people are sufficiently aroused great and violent change can result. America was colonized by armed religious radicals, and this Republic was founded through violent revolution.

History teaches that the secret government will not back down. In 1857 Frederick Douglass warned: "Power concedes nothing without a demand. It never did, and it never will....Find out just what people will submit to and you have found out the exact amount of injustice and wrong which will be imposed upon them. These will continue until they are resisted with either words or blows, or with both. The limits of tyrants are prescribed by the endurance of those whom they oppress." The bankers and large corporations won't give up power and their agent, the Democrat/Republican party, desperately clings to big government.

Various issues may soon bring things to a head. The nation is already bankrupt with gimmicks being used to delay and deny this reality. Soon interest payments for the national debt will be larger than all income taxes collected. There is no ability to repay the principle. Medicare and the social security system can not continue much longer without major changes. Senator Bob Kerrey said: "We are on a course toward national bankruptcy." By 2012, he believes, there will be absolutely no money left for education, highways, children's programs, or national defense. According to the Bipartisan Commission on Entitlement and Tax Reform, by 2003 entitlements and interest payments on the debt will rise from 61 to 72 percent of the budget and take the entire federal budget by 2012.[7] The 1995 budget states that in the next generation the tax rate will be 82 percent. According to Alice Rivlin director of the budget office, by 2030 the debt will increase $4.1 trillion a year. No nation can survive this.

Blinded by a lust for money and power, the government continues taking actions that angers the people. Whether under health reform or immigration control, the push for a national I.D. continues. CIA drug trafficking, and scandals like the S&L crisis, Iran-contra, and Whitewater continue. The 1994 election showed that the American people want less government intrusion in their lives. Instead many new edicts and bills are presented that tighten control over the people. This has caused growing disillusionment with our political system. GATT and NAFTA seriously threaten U.S. sovereignty. Our patent laws are being changed to support transnational corporations. To support the Omnibus Counter-Terrorism Act, FBI director Louis Freeh recommended supervising any groups "advocating social or political change." This law destroys part of the Bill of Rights. Few congressmen got calls from constituents urging passage of this bill while many citizens tried to block it. On April 15, 1996 Anthony Lewis in the *New York Times* said there was "no need or public demand" for its passage.

Federal power continues to grow, despite Clinton's claim that the era of big government is over. There is little response from government representatives to the just demands of the people. On the one hand you have an increasingly oppressive and nervous government with utterly ruthless elements. Opposing them are millions of citizens, many armed, who are determined to protect the Constitution. The drive to register and then seize all guns continues unabated, and millions of Americans will not allow this to happen. Whenever you demonize and deny political expression to millions of people, anger builds and a violent response becomes increasingly possible. If Clinton wins reelection and the Democrats capture both houses, a period of direct confrontation will be much more likely.

Recently, a federal judge illegally banned the distribution of a book, *Why We Will Never Win the War on AIDS*, by Bryan Ellison and Peter Duesberg, and then he ordered its destruction. The establishment doesn't want the people to learn the truth about AIDS.[8] As in Nazi Germany, book burning will become increasingly common in the new world order. Judicial tyranny is a growth industry.

A sign of what is coming is Rep. Schumer's bill H.R. 2580. This CFR member wants to stop what he calls "baseless conspiracy theories regarding the government...." While such speech is protected by the First Amendment, the secret government is getting increasingly nervous as the Patriot movement grows. In addition, on November 16, 1993 the Religious Freedom Restoration Act became Public Law 103-141. This law declares that "governments should not substantially burden religious exercise without compelling justification." For over 200 years we had full religious freedom under the First Amendment. Now suddenly the government quietly passes a law, in violation of the Constitution, which authorizes it to block religious expression if it feels justified. In *FDR, My Exploited Father-in-Law*, C.B. Dall said the corporate elite "now plan to uproot and to gradually destroy the Spiritual background of all people. Initially, Christianity is the prime target, then Judaism, then *all* other religions! That bleak program is absolutely necessary for them...to make assembly-line puppets out of us, the many."[9]

In education, the Careers Act (H.R. 1617 and S 143) has already passed both houses and is in committee. Federal control will replace state authority in the education system with a national data bank, a national employment service, and apprentice system to train and employ people, per the dictates of the corporations. Computers will track everyone. Backed by the Carnegie Foundation, this law would create a cradle-to-grave national employment system that would be loved in any communist nation.

When you also consider the hundreds of thousands of people jailed for marijuana violations and a similar number of people whose assets have been forfeited, often without even being charged with a crime, you begin to appreciate why so many people fear and hate the federal government. Moreover, the open air nuclear tests and radiation medical experiments killed and injured millions of people. One reason why the federal government is so hated in the western states is because so many Americans died from exposure to nuclear tests that the government for years said were quite safe. The town mortician in St. George, Utah, which is near an atmospheric nuclear testing site, buried many children who died of leukemia. He said, "They done to us what the Russians couldn't do." Yet journalists for media giants ask how people can be angry at the federal government! Each one of these victims has friends and relatives, and the anger is building. Ask a Japanese American, an American Indian, or many black Americans if the federal government can be trusted.

A California newspaper the *Mountain Messenger* frustrated with continued government intrusions said: "We Americans are a proud and independent people and we tend to resent anyone telling us what we must do and what we must think. We will tend to go along with the government, but only up to a point and for a great many proud and independent Americans, that point has been reached and is very nearly surpassed." *Media Bypass* and the *Washington Report* said numerous sources believe we are now in the lull before a storm that may be the greatest upheaval since the Civil War.[10] However, if many more politicians resign and the press is filled with charges of corruption, examine whether corporate leaders are also indicted and jailed. The secret government may attempt to deflect the people's anger by sacrificing some crooked politicians.

People like William Greider, in *Who Will Tell the People*, and the books by Kevin Phillips explain how the people are today powerless and cut off from the political decision-making processes in America. What they do not really discuss is that, once a government represents the moneyed interests instead of the people, that government can become extremely dangerous. It is not just that the people have become politically powerless, *our rights are being lost*. It is time to stop trusting the federal government and recognize that it has become the enemy of the people. To change reality, it must first be accepted.

Gore Vidal is one of the few prominent social commentators who understands the growing potential for a police state and a violent response. "Unfortunately, the people are without alternatives. That is what makes the situation so volatile and potentially dangerous."[11] "We are now in a prerevolutionary time....In due course, something on the order of the ethnic rebellions in the Soviet Union or even of the people's uprising in China will take place here. Too few have ripped off too many for too long. Opinion (mass media) can no longer disguise the contradiction at the heart of conservative-corporate opinion. The corporate few are free to do what they will, while the many are losing their freedoms at a rapid rate." When discussing the growing loss of our freedoms Vidal said "Should the few persist in their efforts to dominate the private lives of the many, I recommend force as a means of changing their minds."[12]

Wesley A Riddle, Professor of History at West Point, said: "If some do not recognize their impeding slavery, it is because the tyrant who steals our freedoms is subtle, multifaceted, sometimes benevolent, and wears the mask of a smiling bureaucrat and government social worker, who has your supposed best interest in mind....The liberty we have gotten is not the ordered sort the Founders intended. It serves no purpose nor ends but our own destruction. We witness now the onset of social chaos sanctioned by government, without the consent of the people to do it." This officer concluded by saying the Constitution may have been "circumvented" to serve the elites, and we are heading towards "national suicide."[13]

In 1957 Senator George W. Malone spoke in Congress about the illegal Federal Reserve: "I believe that if the people of this nation fully understood what Congress has done to them over the past 49 years, they would move on Washington, they would not wait for an election....It adds up to a preconceived plan to destroy the economic and social interdependence of the U.S." Charles A. Reich, in *Opposing the System*, said the present system cannot continue much longer and protests and demonstrations are probably coming as the large corporations increasingly destroy our heritage.[14] I agree with Reich that these protests should "unite rather than divide" to succeed. This is partly why I feel the left and right must unite to stop the large corporations.

In 1861 President Lincoln told Father Chiniquy that he was aware of the secret power of financial interests that were dedicated to overthrowing the government and if the people ever awoke to the evil intents of these people "the revulsion would be comparable to that which swept France" during its revolution.[15] On November 21, 1864 Lincoln wrote William Elkin stating: "I see in the near future a crisis approaching that unnerves me and causes me to tremble for the safety of my country....Corporations have been enthroned and an era of corruption in high places will follow, and the money power of the country will endeavor to prolong its reign by working upon the prejudices of the people until all wealth is aggregated in a few hands, and the Republic is destroyed. I feel at this moment more anxiety for the safety of my country than ever before even in the midst of war."

Gary Phillips has spent his career in the U.S. Immigration and Naturalization Service (INS). This head of the Seattle INS discovered that the Sixteenth Amendment was never properly ratified, so he has refused to pay income taxes since 1993. Phillips said: "What I see going on in this country scares me to death, it makes pre-revolution France look like Sunday School. If it boils over, anybody in government will be seen as the enemy and punishment will come at the hands of the mob."

Time and again throughout history the ruling class has wanted one thing—to own and control everything and everyone. The ruling elite look on the American people with utter contempt and arrogance, so they do not understand how widespread and deep is the people's anger at the growing federal tyranny. If the right to bear arms is suddenly removed, the dictatorship would be at hand, and the people have a right to defend themselves against tyranny. It is absolutely essential that the people not be disarmed. The Constitution and Bill of Rights are sacred documents that above all else must be protected.

While I feel people should understand how volatile things now are, I am not calling for violence. I have reached many conclusions about our present predicament with some sadness, believing that all life is precious and recognizing the failure of our political system. I prefer that a new political party develop, that enough people awaken in time, so the Constitution can be restored through the normal political process; but that may no longer be possible. Courts rarely respect the Constitution and our legal system has become an organ of corporate power that only the rich can afford. There is rampant vote fraud and the large corporations control the press, Congress, and the executive branch.

Throughout this book I have made numerous suggestions that people can follow. It may be wise in the tradition of the civil rights movement and anti-war protests to have huge marches on Washington, D.C. and other cities to demand in a nonviolent manner that the Constitution be followed and that government be returned to the people. About 22 states have now approved term limits.[16] Removing the grip of professional politicians, lobbyists, and cash from dominating politics is essential. There must be campaign finance reform and term limits, but no constitutional convention, for all politicians, as well as more use of the initiative, referendum, and recall of public officials. There should also be national elections to decide key issues, as is done in some states and in Switzerland. Direct voting gives the people a more direct say in government. Also, elections should take place on weekends as in many countries.

Many issues discussed in this book relate to the potential rise of a third party. One poll described Americans as "a disbelieving electorate almost out of patience." However, third parties are suppressed through harassment and manipulation of the election laws. Economic issues are important, but the continued loss of our rights and spiritual values will be the basis for a third party movement in America. Get involved with the Patriot movement and a third party such as the Libertarian Party, especially if it aggressively works to restore the Constitution. In a third party there is the nucleus for a revitalized America to restore the principles of constitutional government. Candidates like Charles Collins will increasingly step forward and be supported by the people. Attacking the Federal Reserve and supporting a return to constitutional government, Collins was forced out of the Republican party in a manner that would warm the heart of any fascist.

In 1994, 62 percent of the electorate didn't vote. If the people are given more political power, they will become more involved in politics. What the country needs is a new populist party to restore the Constitution and end corporate influence. Millions of people are ready for this. A Patriot-Christian populist coalition could dismantle the federal government while protecting constitutional rights and Christian values. Global capitalism should be replaced by restoring Jeffersonian democracy. The Christian right is increasingly disgusted with the Republican party which takes them for granted.

Workers and minority groups should abandon the Democratic party, as it has abandoned them. The Democratic party is desperately clinging to the New Deal, constantly calling Republican plans to shrink government right wing extremism, while proclaiming that it also wants less government. Clinton has taken up the Republican call for less government so he can increase government power. As the Democratic party becomes increasingly irrelevant to the issues of our time, it lashes out at what it does not understand. While many of the newly elected Republicans are a hope, the party is still controlled by Wall Street as we saw in NAFTA, GATT, and the Mexican loan, so it remains to be seen if these new members can make a difference. James Mill warned: "The benefits of the representative system are lost, in all cases, in which the interests of the choosing body are not the same with those of the community."

During the 1992 presidential campaign the key phrase used by Clinton's team was "It's the economy stupid." The economy has improved, yet Clinton and Congress have earned little respect. Clinton and the political pundits don't understand why this is so. Just after the 1994 elections I read a remarkably distorted essay by Arthur Schlesinger, Jr. in the *Wall Street Journal*.[17] He acknowledged that people were very angry but didn't understand why because the economy was doing well. The anti-government bias of the people was acknowledged, and Schlesinger called it "ideological anti-government extremism." That the federal government now has far more power than was ever envisioned by the Founders and far more power than they warned could safely be used, is ignored by the more government is better crowd. This is the extremism of the Washington elite that must end to restore constitutional government. The arrogance politicians have towards the people has helped create the anger and contempt many feel towards Washington. Now we increasingly have rights that the state defines and allows; we no longer are born with God given rights such as "Life, Liberty and the pursuit of Happiness" as described in the Declaration of Independence.

The politicians and pundits define American happiness in terms of economics, not in terms of freedom or moral values. Since the 1994 elections, I have heard numerous experts speak on the results. The concern about lost rights is never even raised in the myriad opinion polls. The most the experts can acknowledge is that many feel the federal government has too much power, but what this means is rarely discussed. What difference does it make if we earn $5.00 or $5,000 an hour if we lose all our liberties. If the Democratic/Republican party starts dismantling the federal government but refuses to remove the many laws violating the people's rights, both parties will be devastated in the coming years as happened recently in Canada and Italy.

In 1992 the public turned against the Republican party because it was very angry with politicians and wanted change. With little change and wanting less government in 1994 the people voted for the Republicans in large numbers. By 1996 little has changed, and this is deepening the people's anger and disillusionment. Tom Foley, a member of the CFR, was replaced as House speaker by CFR member Newt Gingrich. As long as the Democratic/Republican party controls Congress, different faces will make similar false promises and nothing will change. We have one national political party with two branches controlled by and representing the banks and big business. As Quigley said in *Tragedy and Hope*, even in the last century the business interests acted to control both political parties creating false debates to fool the public and conceal their influence.[18]

Ultimately the people will start voting in large numbers for third party candidates. Even Newt Gingrich agreed with this possibility just after the 1994 elections. Then a poll showed that 60 percent of the people voted to reject the Democratic party and only 18 percent felt the vote was a Republican mandate. At best the 1994 election was a qualified two year mandate for the Republicans. In the fall of 1994 a poll showed that six out of 10 Americans wanted to change our entire system of government. According to a poll by the University of Michigan, trust in government has gone from about 80 percent in 1964 to under 20 percent by 1994.

Already many political pundits have declared the Republican revolution a failure. Few government agencies have been closed and corporate welfare has barely been touched. The special interests remain in control and term limits remains a distant goal.[19] Even the budget cuts only refer to cutting the degree of growth not reversing and limiting federal spending.

A major reason why people are so angry is that "It's the Constitution stupid." Millions of Americans are witnessing their rights being lost, but the politicians are too cut off from the people to acknowledge or even understand this concern, and the corporate media is too busy telling us about the latest crime or sports event. When is the last time the politicians or media discussed how little value the Constitution has in our lives today? That our freedoms are being lost is never even discussed. Instead we hear that constitutional protections may have to be sacrificed because of crime and terrorism.

We are ruled by professional politicians who want money and power. There is no sense of integrity, ethics, or spirituality in government. Our representatives no longer respect or represent the people and our constitutional heritage. The successful politician of the future will loudly proclaim how the Constitution has been seriously weakened and that constitutional government must be restored. However, the people must watch what is actually done not just what is said.

Instead of just attacking the government to bring about needed reforms, we should restore government to its proper role by putting it under the constraints of the Constitution. Constitutional government is good government. In addition, it is an illusion to think that just by reducing government there will be more individual freedoms, because the real problem comes primarily from the large corporations not from big government. The result of the corporate take-over of our country in the 20th century has been five major wars, a crippling national debt where before there was none, crippling taxes where before there were few, loss of constitutional rule, a huge prison population, and creation of a vast bureaucracy. Even if Clinton were indicted and removed from office, as many want, little would change. The power of the secret government would remain intact, because the large corporations would just put into place another agent. Our entire political system has been corrupted and removing one or many dishonest politicians is no longer sufficient. Corporate control of the federal government must end.

There is a growing call for a spiritual transformation of public service. Jim Wallis said, in *The Soul of Politics*: "Deep in the American soul exists the conviction that politics and morality are integrally related." There needs to be a "politics of conscience." Michael Lerner, in *Jewish Renewal*, called for a return to compassion and moral integrity to restore morality to public life. Stephen Carter, in *The Culture of Disbelief*, argued that spiritual values must again become part of the debate as to what type of society we want America to be.[20] We need to understand, as individuals and as a society, that the corporate wish for more and more material wealth leads to an emptiness of the soul. We must stop thinkng that economic growth will solve all our problems. When personal happiness is so centered around material wealth, a spiritual crisis and immorality is inevitable. George Washington said at the end of his presidency: "Of all the dispositions and habits which lead to political prosperity, religion and morality are indispensable supports....Honesty is always the best policy." Thomas Jefferson said: "The whole of government consists in the art of being honest." Ethics and moral values must be restored to public service.

More people should turn to God to make wise and compassionate choices in life. If everyone were more directly experiencing God's love, there would be much less suffering and far fewer problems in the world. One way to reestablish constitutional government in America is to with pure intentions and from your heart and higher self to send light and love to the bankers, industrialists, politicians, rogue elements in the intelligence and military community and others that would destroy this Republic that they may move closer to the Divine. Love is the greatest power in the universe. If thousands of people are sending light and love to these groups, this will have a strong effect on them. Light, love, and force of arms only as a last resort, should be directed towards those promoting the new world order. As Jesus taught this is a higher path. People have a right to defend their freedoms with arms if necessary, but unless the government openly tries to remove guns from the people or uses some excuse to declare martial law, people should get more involved in the political system and also focus on educating more people to our present predicament. The militias should stand ready but not initiate armed action.

One should also understand that such positive spiritual actions while helpful may not be enough. Some would say that it is being negative to discuss what has been written in this book. There are times in life when direct actions are necessary to protect one's rights and freedoms. If people had sat back and said that God would remove Hitler or Stalin, the world would be a much worse place today. Positive spiritual reflection is always appropriate, but in this world it isn't always enough, especially when events have reached an advanced stage. We as citizens have a responsibility to ourselves, to society, and to future generations to restore the rights and freedoms which the Founders fought so hard to establish.

Shortly before his death, Anthony Sherman described a vision that George Washington had at Valley Forge. He was visited by an angel and told that "while the stars remain and the heavens send down dew upon the earth, so long shall the Republic last. The whole world united shall never be able to prevail against her. Let every child of the Republic learn to live for his God, his land and the Union." Washington was shown three great dangers to Americas survival. The first was the Revolutionary War, the second was the Civil War, and the third concerned an event that has not yet occurred.[21]

If constitutional government was restored, the nation would then face the third great danger described in Washington's vision. The European elites would see America as the great threat to establishing a one world government, so they would scheme to attack the U.S. Washington saw vast armies from Europe, Asia, and Africa attacking America with great devastation resulting. The angelic being reportedly said: "Son of the Republic, what you have seen is thus interpreted. Three great perils will come upon the Republic. The most fearful is the third...."[22] For constitutional government to be safely restored in America, the world center of the secret government, the one square mile city of London and its back up centers in Switzerland and Italy, must also be captured. Perhaps if the U.S. military intervenes it will be done in conjunction with patriots in other countries!

Historians state that one to three percent of the population fought the British in the Revolutionary War. By the 1930s the repression from Washington had gotten far worse than what our ancestors faced, and today, far more than three percent of the U.S. population understands this. While scholars like Leonard W. Levy have convincingly demonstrated that in the early years of the Republic there was little emphasis on following the teachings of the Founders, if constitutional government is to be restored today it is essential that we return to the vision of Founders for guidance. Government must again be tied to the chains of the Constitution.

Many in power, such as congressmen and judges, should not wait until the last minute to start supporting the Constitution. As the federal government increases its power and abuses the people and the Constitution and more people understand that increasingly the choice is to support the Constitution and the rule of law or to commit treason. As the corporate onslaught continues to destroy our constitutional heritage and way of life we are approaching the situation that Ulysses S. Grant described in 1861, at the start of the Civil War. Then he said: "There are but two parties now, traitors and patriots."

I believe enough people will awaken in time to prevent the new world order police state, and that we as a people can continue moving closer to God's love and grace. The human race has today reached a critical turning point. We as a people will soon undergo great advancement in our spiritual evolution, or there will be a sharp collapse in consciousness. I pray that God's grace will continue to shine on our country and that the vision of freedom and morality that the Founding Fathers so sacrificed for will once again be restored to America. What is ultimately at stake here is whether America, and indeed the entire planet, will continue under a hierarchical society, where the few rule the many, or we can exist under Divine law in a truly democratic Republic where we are all equal before God.

# Notes

## Chapter I Introduction
1 See *U.S. News &World Report,* June 13, 1994, p. 32.
2 Robert A. Heinlein, *Take Back Your Government* (N.Y: Simon & Schuster, 1992), p. 249.
3 Joe Urschel, "Sentiments Not Held Only by the Fringe," *USA Today*, May 16, 1995, p. A1, A2.
4 "State of Seige," *Newsweek*, September 18, 1995, p. 21.
5 David M. Kotz, *Bank Control of Large Corporations in the United States* (Berkeley, University of Cal. Press, 1978).
6 David Heilbroner, "The Law Goes on a Treasure Hunt," *New York Times Magazine*, Section 6, December 11, 1994, p. 73.

## Chapter II Freedom is Being Lost
1 David P. Szatinary, *Shays Rebellion: The Making of An Agrarian Insurrection* (Amherst: The University of Mass., 1980), p. 120.
2 Jerry Fresia, *Toward An American Revolution* (Boston: South End Press, 1988), p. 33-43.
3 Wesley A. Riddle, "Secession and the Moral Compact," *Vital Speeches*, August 1, 1995, p. 638.
4 Noam Chomsky, *Deterring Democracy* (N.Y: Verso, 1991), p. 365.
5 *Ibid.*, p. 369-370.
6 Gerry Spence, *From Freedom to Slavery* (N.Y: St. Martin's Press, 1993), p. 5-6, 11.
7 *Ibid.*, p. 77, 104.
8 *Ibid.*, p. 86, 149.
9 William Greider, *Who Will Tell the People* (N.Y: Simon & Schuster, 1992), p. 11-12, 61, 241.
10 Ferdinand Lundberg, *Myth of Democracy* (N.Y: Carol Publishing Group, 1989), p. 88.
11 Lewis H. Lapham, *The Wish For Kings* (N.Y: Grove Press, 1993),
 p. 27-28.
12 *Ibid.*, p. 178.
13 Gore Vidal, *The Decline and Fall of the American Empire* (Berkeley, Ca: Odonian Press, 1986-1992), p. 59.
14 Michael Novak, "Democracy, Capitalism and Morality," *Wall Street Journal*, December 27, 1994, p. A16.

## Chapter III The Secret Government
1 C.B. Dall, *FDR, My Exploited Father-in-Law* (Tulsa, Ok: Christian Crusade Publications, 1968), p. 69, 92, 108, 137, 185.
2 Elliott Roosevelt, *The Conservators* (N.Y: Arbor House, 1983), p. 320.
3 George Seldes, *1000 Americans* (N.Y: Boni & Gaer, 1947), p. 176.
4 Robert J. Groden and Harrison E. Livingtone, *High Treason* (Boothwyn, Pa: The Conservatory Press, 1989), p. 350-1.

5 To order a fascinating interview Quigley gave to a *Washington Post* reporter in 1974 send $13.30 to: Stanley Monteith P.O. Box 1835 Soquel, Ca. 95073.
6 Dall, *op. cit.*, Note 1, p. 92.
7 I Timothy 6:10 *Bible*.
8 Gary Allen, *None Dare Call It Conspiracy* (Seal Beach, Ca: Concord Press, 1971), p. 89; John A. Stormer, *None Dare Call It Treason* (Florissant, Mo: Liberty Bell Press, 1964), p. 211-2.
9 Richard Harwood, "Ruling Class Journalists," *Washington Post*, October 30, 1993, p. A21.
10 Carroll Quigley, *Tragedy and Hope* (N.Y: The MacMillian Co., 1966), p. 950.
11 *Ibid.*, p. 324, 337.
12 Elliott Roosevelt, ed., *F.D.R. His Personal Letters 1928-1945*, Vol. I (N.Y: Duell, Sloan & Pearce, 1950), p. 371-373.
13 Phyllis Schlafly and Chester Ward, *Kissinger on the Couch* (New Rochelle, N.Y: Arlington House, 1975), p. 151.
14 Frank Smyth, "My Spy Story," *Wall Street Journal*, February 22, 1996, p. A19.
15 Schlafly, *op. cit.*, Note 13, p. 146, 149-150.
16 "How the FBI's Criminal-Espionage Investigation of the CFR Was Foiled," (Wichita, Ks: Sunset Research, 1994).
17 Zbigniew Brzezinski, *Between Two Ages* (N.Y: The Viking Press, 1970), p. 72, 134.
18 David Rockefeller, "From a China Traveler," *New York Times*, August 10, 1973, p. 31.
19 Michel J. Crozier, Samuel P. Huntington, and Joji Watanuki, *The Crisis of Democracy* (N.Y: The Trilateral Commission, 1975), p. 102, 162, 173.
20 Stephen Gill, *American Hegemony and the Trilateral Commission* (Cambridge: Cambridge University Press, 1990), p. 129.
21 Cord Meyer, Jr., *Peace or Anarchy* (Boston: Little, Brown and Co., 1948), p. 67-68.
22 For a good list of members of these groups in the federal government send $1.00 to F.R.E.E. P.O. Box 33339 Kerrville, Tx. 78028. They get their information partly from checking the directors and executives in Standard & Poors Register of public corporations and from annual reports published by CFR. These groups are quite confident so they rarely hide the names of their members although their meetings are usually conducted in secret.
23 George C. Edwards and Wallace E. Walker, eds., *National Security and the U.S. Constitution* (Baltimore: The John Hopkins University Press, 1988), p. 24.
24 "Hylan Takes Stand on National Issues," *New York Times*, March 27, 1922, p. 3.
25 U.S., Congress, Senate, *Congressional Record*, February 23, 1954 Vol. 100 Part 2, p. S 2121.
26 U.S. Congress, House, Special House Committee to Investigate Tax-Exempt Foundations, Reece Committee 1954, p. 176-7.
27 Rene A. Wormser, *Foundations: Their Power and Influence* (N.Y: Devin-Adair Co., 1958). p. 317-327.
28 Barry Goldwater, *With No Apologies* (N.Y: William Morrow and Co., 1979), p. 128.
29 *Ibid.*, p. 280, 284, 285.

30 R. Buckminster Fuller, *Critical Path* (N.Y: St. Martin's Press, 1981), p. 117-119.

31 Dall, *op. cit.*, Note 1, p. 85-86.

32 Christopher Lydon, "Jimmy Carter Revealed," *Atlantic Monthly*, 240 (July, 1977), 50-7; Jeremiah Novak, "The Trilateral Connection," *Atlantic Monthly*, 240 (July, 1977), 57-9.

33 Goldwater, *op. cit.*, Note 28, p. 293.

34 See the February 24, March 23, and May 4, 1992 columns by Alexander Cockburn in *The Nation*.

35 Joseph Kraft, "School For Statesmen," *Harpers Magazine*, 217 (July, 1958), 68.

36 Antony C. Sutton, *America's Secret Establishment* (Billings, Mt: Liberty House Press, 1986).

## Chapter IV New World Order

1 Alfred M. Lilienthal, "Which Way to World Government?" *Foreign Policy Association Headline Series*, Number 83 (September-October, 1950), p. 43.

2 George W. Blount, *Peace Through World Government* (Durham, N.C: Moore Publishing Co., 1974).

3 Jean Drissell, "A Senator's View of World Order," *Transition*, III (April, 1976).

4 Arnold Toynbee, *Experiences* (N.Y: Oxford University Press, 1969), p. 110.

5 Takashi Oka, "A Crowded World: Can Mankind Survive," *Christian Science Monitor*, February 10, 1975, p. 5-6.

6 Alexander King and Bertrand Schneider, *The First Global Revolution A Report By the Council of the Club of Rome* (N.Y: Pantheon Books, 1991), p. 110-115.

7 Lincoln P. Bloomfield, "International Force in a Disarming-But Revolutionary-World," *International Organization*, XVII (Spring, 1963), 444-64; Graham T. Allison, Joseph S. Nye, Jr., and Albert Carnesale, eds., *Fateful Visions* (Cambridge, Ma: Ballinger Publishing Co., 1988), p. 211.

8 *Ibid.*, p. 212.

9 Richard Falk, "A New Paradigm for International Legal Studies: Prospects and Proposals," *Yale Law Journal*, 84 (April, 1975), 969-1021; Richard Falk, *A Study of Future Worlds* (N.Y: The Free Press, 1975).

10 U.S., Congress, Senate, Subcommittee on Foreign Relations, *Revision of the U.N. Charter*, Hearings, 81st Cong., 2d Session. February 17, 1950. (Washington, D.C: Government Printing Office, 1950), p. 494.

11 James Warburg, *The West in Crisis* (Garden City, N.Y: Doubleday & Co., 1959), p. 30.

12 Gary Allen, *Say No To the New World Order* (Seal Beach, Ca: Concord Press, 1987), p. 59-61.

13 Philip Kerr, "From Empire to Commonwealth," *Foreign Affairs*, I (December 15, 1922), 97-98.

14 John Foster Dulles, *War or Peace* (N.Y: The Macmillan Co., 1950), p. 40.

15 H.G. Wells, *Anticipations of the Reaction of Mechanical and Scientific Progress Upon Human Life and Thought"* (N.Y: Harper and Brothers, 1901), p. 322-325.

16 Bertrand Russell, *The Impact of Science on Society* (N.Y: Simon & Schuster, 1953), p. 103-105. These words appeared in the 1953 edition of this book.

17 Julian Huxley, *UNESCO: Its Purpose and Its Philosophy* (Washington, D.C: Public Affairs Press, 1947), p. 13, 15, 21.
18 Paul R. Ehrlich and Anne H. Ehrlich, *Population, Resources, Environment: Issues on Human Ecology* (San Francisco: W.H. Freeman and Co., 1970), p. 204.
19 Paul Ehrlich, *The Population Bomb* (N.Y: Ballantine, 1978), p. 17.
20 Peter Beinart, "Aid and Abet," *New Republic*, October 30, 1995, p. 23-25.
21 Michael S. Teitelbaum, "The Population Threat," *Foreign Affairs*, 71 (Winter 1992/1993), 63-78.
22 Bahgat Elnadi and Adel Rifaat, "Interview Jacques-Yves Cousteau," *The Unesco Courier*, (November, 1991), 8-13.
23 Robert Lederer, "Chemical-Biological Warfare, Medical Experiments, and Population Control," *Covert Action*, Number 28 (Summer, 1987), 33-42.
24 Warren Bennis and Philip Slater, *The Temporary Society* (N.Y: Harper & Row, Publishers, 1968), p. 44-45.
25 G.B. Chisholm, "The Reestablishment of Peacetime Society," *Psychiatry*, IX (February, 1946), p. 7, 9.
26 Garrett Hardin, "Parenthood: Right or Privilege?" *Science*, June 31, 1970, p. 427.
27 Edgar R. Chasteen, *The Case for Compulsive Birth Control* (Englewood Cliffs, NJ: Prentice-Hall, Inc., 1971), p. 79, 204.
28 Alexander Cockburn and Jeffrey St. Clair, "Slime Green," *The Progressive*, 60 (May, 1996), 18-21.
29 Laurance Rockefeller, "The Case for a Simpler Life-Style," *The Reader's Digest*, 108 (February, 1976), 61-65.
30 Barbara Marx Hubbard, "The Book of Co-Creation: The Revelation Alternative to Armageddon, Part III Manuscript 1980, p. 59-61.
31 Joyce Nelson, "Burson-Marsteller, Pax Trilateral, and the Brundtland Gang vs. the Environment," *Covert Action*, Number 44 (Spring, 1993), 26-33, 57-58.
32 Zbigniew Brzezinski, *Between Two Ages* (N.Y: The Viking Press, 1970), p. 10, 16.
33 "American Malvern," *Time*, March 16, 1942, p. 44, 46-48.
34 Edgar C. Bundy, *Collectivism in the Churches* (Wheaton Ill: The Church League of America, 1958), p. 174-7.
35 U.S., Congress, House, Foreign Affairs Committee, Subcommittee on International Operations, *U.S. Policy in the UN*, 99 Congress 1st Sess. December 4, 1985. (Washington, D.C: Government Printing Office, 1985), p. 152-157.
36 Strobe Talbott, "The Birth of the Global Nation," *Time*, July 20, 1992, p. 70-71.
37 Ross Smyth, "Towards Global Governance," *The Rotarian*, 165 (November, 1994), 67.
38 "New World Order: Consensus," *Cape Code Times*, January 28, 1993.
39 Mark Riebling, *Wedge The Secret War Between the FBI and CIA* (N.Y: Alfred A. Knopf, 1994), p. 407-409.
40 G.K. Chesterton, "Wells and the World State," in *The Collected Works of G.K. Chesterton*, ed. by Robert Royal (San Francisco: Ignatius Press, 1986), p. 215-216.
41 Testimony before the Trade Subcommittee of the House Ways and Means Committee, February 2, 1994.

42 Malachi Martin, *The Keys of this Blood* (N.Y: Simon & Schuster, 1990), p. 16.
43 Best Studios has produced 3 videos on this report. P.O. Box 69 Wheeler, Wi. 54772 (1-800-257-2672).
44 Leonard C. Lewin, *Report From Iron Mountain on the Possibility and Desirability of Peace* (N.Y: The Dial Press, Inc., 1967), p. 73.
45 Zbigniew Brzezinski, "America in the Technetronic Age," *Encounter*, XXX (January, 1968), 16-26.
46 George Bernard Shaw, *The Intelligent Woman's Guide to Socialism and Capitalism* (N.Y: Brentano's Publishers, 1928), p. 53.
47 Barry Goldwater, *With No Apologies* (N.Y: William Morrow and Co., 1979), p. 278.
48 Frank Kofsky, *Harry S. Truman and the War Scare of 1948* (N.Y: St. Martin's Press, 1993), p. 308.
49 Michael Parenti, *Inventing Reality* (N.Y: St. Martin's Press, 1986), p. 240-241.
50 "Viewpoint," *U.S. News & World Report*, May 20, 1996, p. 22.

## Chapter V Fooling the People
1 Rodney Stich, *Defrauding America* (Alamo, Ca: Diablo Western Press, Inc., 1993), p. 517.
2 Carl Bernstein, "The CIA and the Media," *Rolling Stone*, Number 250 October 20, 1977, p. 25.
3 Daniel Patrick Moynihan, "Reforming the CIA?" *Unclassified*, VI (June-August, 1994), 6-8.
4 Thomas Kuhn, *Structure of Scientific Revolutions* (Chicago: University of Chicago Press, 1970), p. 92.
5 Ray Moseley, "West's Fear of Islam Overblown," *San Francisco Examiner*, February 19, 1995, p. A13.
6 C.B. Dall, *FDR, My Exploited Father-in-Law* (Tulsa, Ok: Christian Crusade Publications, 1968), p. 22-23, 109, 140-141.
7 A K. Chesterton, *The New Unhappy Lords* (London: The Candour Publishing Co., 1965), p. 36.
8 John Sullivan, "In Considering Electronic Voting, Giuliani Faces the Fraud Factor," *New York Times*, August 26, 1995, p. A11; "Voting Early and Often," *Wall Street Journal*, December 19, 1994, p. A14.
9 Ivars Peterson, "Making Votes Count," *Science News*, October 30, 1993, p. 282.
10 Jonathan Vankin, *Conspiracies Cover-Ups and Crimes* (N.Y: Dell Publishing, 1995), p. 22-38.
11 "What National Emergency?" *The Los Angeles Daily Journal*, September 27, 1995, p. 4.
12 Eugene Schroder, *Constitution Fact or Fiction* (Cleburne, Texas: Buffalo Creek Press, 1995).
13 Ruth Marcus, "President Says He Shares the Blame for Defeats," *Washington Post*, November 10, 1994, p. A1.
14 James W. Loewen, *Lies My Teacher Told Me* (N.Y: The New Press, 1995), p. 267.

15 Mark I. Schwartz, "What Multiculturalism Did to Canada," *Wall Street Journal*, April 5, 1996, p. A9.
16 Ralph Keyes, "Did They Really Say It," *Parade Magazine*, May 16, 1993, p. 10.
17 Lewis Copeland and Lawrence W. Lamin, eds., *The World's Greatest Speeches* (N.Y: Dover Publications, Inc., 1973), p. 232-234.
18 Catherine Millard, *The Rewriting of America's History* (Camp Hill, Pa: Horizon House Publishers, 1991), p. 229, 240, 247, 258-263.
19 Elizabeth Gleick, "She Spoke Volumes," *Time*, September 25, 1995, p. 52.
20 Henry Glassie, *Passing the Time in Ballymenone: Culture and History of an Ulster Community* (Philadelphia: U. of Pennsylvania Press, 1982), p. 652.
21 Don Doig, "The Independent Jury's Secret Veto Power," *Media Bypass*, II (December, 1994), 25-29.
22 For further information 1-800-835-5879 JIFA P.O. Box 59 Helmville, Mt. 59843. Joining this organization is an excellent way to protect the people's rights.
23 Wade Lambert, "Militias Are Joining Jury-Power Activists To Fight Government," *Wall Street Journal*, May 25, 1995, p. A1, A8.
24 James Ledbetter, "Press Clips," *Village Voice*, June 13, 1995, p. A9.
25 Mort Rosenblum, "Hidden Agendas," *Vanity Fair*, 53 (March, 1990), 120.
26 Ron Harris, "Experts Say the War on Drugs Has Turned Into a War on Blacks," *San Francisco Chronicle*, April 24, 1990, p. A12.
27 Arnold C. Brackman, *The Other Nuremberg: The Untold Story of the Tokyo War Crimes Trials* (N.Y: William Morrow and Co., 1987), p. 190-195.
28 Dall, *op. cit.*, Note 6, p. 59.
29 David Boren, "The World Needs An Army on Call," *New York Times*, August 26, 1992, p. A21; Ronnie Dugger, "Create a World Army," *New York Times*, June 27, 1995, p. A15; Warren Getler, "Uncle Sam Should Strengthen U.N., Not Boss It," *Wall Street Journal*, August 20, 1992, p. A9.
30 Gerald B. Helman and Steven R. Ratner, "Saving Failed States," *Foreign Policy*, 89 (Winter, 1992-1993), 3-21.
31 Strobe Talbott, "Dealing With Anti-Countries," *Time*, December 14, 1992, p. 35.
32 Duncan Hunter, "Bosnia Becomes Anthony Lake's Laboratory," *Washington Times National Weekly*, February 12-18, 1996, p. 34.
33 Stephen D. Goose and Frank Smyth, "Arming Genocide in Rwanda," *Foreign Affairs*, 73 (September/October, 1994), 86-96.
34 Jon Stewart, "New Ways to Pay the U.N. Piper," *San Francisco Chronicle*, May 7, 1995, p. 6.
35 David A. Andelman, "The Drug Money Maze," *Foreign Affairs*, 73 (July/August, 1994), 94-108.
36 "Radiation Victims Protest Biased Investigation," *The Progressive*, 58 (December, 1994), 14.
37 Robin Rauzi, "Victims Lawyer Wants Scientist Punished for Radiation Tests," *Albuquerque Tribune*, December. 15, 1994, p. A6.
38 Glenn Alcalay, "Damage Control on Human Radiation Experiments," *Covert Action*, Number 52 (Spring, 1995), 46-47.
39 Edward S. Corwin, *Presidential Power and the Constitution* (Ithaca, N.Y: Cornel University Press, 1976), p. 143.

40 William Minter and Laurence H. Shoup, *Imperial Brain Trust: The Council on Foreign Relations and United States Foreign Policy* (N.Y: Monthly Review Press, 1977). p. 24-27.
41 Murray N. Rothbard, *America's Great Depression* (Kansas City: Sheed and Ward, Inc., 1972).
42 Gary Allen, *None Dare Call It Conspiracy* (Seal Beach, Ca: Concord Press, 1971), p. 54.
43 *Ibid.*, p. 43-5.
44 C.B. Dall, *FDR, My Exploited Father-in-Law* (Tulsa, Ok: Christian Crusade Publications, 1968), p. 49, 119-120.
45 *Ibid.*, p. 59.
46 Walter Karp, *Indispensable Enemies* (N.Y: Saturday Review Press, 1973), p. 110-111, 128.
47 Howard Zinn, *The Politics of History* (Boston: Beacon Press, 1970), p. 118-136.
48 Barton Bernstein, "The New Deal: The Conservative Achievements of Liberal Reform," in *Towards A New Past Dissenting Essays in American History*, ed. by Barton Bernstein (N. Y: Pantheon Books, 1968), p. 263-288.
49 James Petras and Steve Vieux, "The New Shape of the Imperial State," *Z Magazine*, VIII (September, 1995), 43-50.
50 Arthur Schlesinger, Jr., "In Defense of Government," *Wall Street Journal*, June 7, 1995, p. A14.
51 Ruth Simon, "How Washington Could Tip the Scales Against Investors," *Money*, XXIV (October, 1995), p. 122-124, 127-128; Jeffrey Taylor, "Congress Sends Business a Christmas Gift," *Wall Street Journal*, December 26, 1995, p. A2.
52 John J. DiIulio, Jr. and Donald F. Kettl, "Fine Print," (Washington, D.C: The Brookings Institution, 1995), p. 60.
53 William M. Bulkeley, "Get Ready for Smart Cards in Health Care," *The Wall Street Journal*, May 3, 1993, p. B11.
54 James M. Burns, "The Power to Lead," in *Reforming American Government*, editor Donald L. Robinson, (Boulder, Co: Westview Press, 1985), p. 160.
55 Michael S. Paulsen, "The Case for a Constitutional Convention," *Wall Street Journal*, May 3, 1995, p. A15.
56 Dirk Johnson, "Conspiracy Theories' Impact Reverberates in Legislatures," *New York Times*, July 6, 1995, p. A1, A12.

**Chapter VI State Rights and the Federal Government**
1 Joyce Rosenwald, "Conceived in Liberty," *Media Bypass*, III (July, 1995), 50-51.
2 Pickney G. McElwee, "The 14th Amendment to the Constitution of the United Statres and the Threat That It Poses to Our Democratic Government," *South Carolina Quarterly*, Vol II (1959), 484-519.
3 James J Kilpatrick, *The Sovereign States* (Chicago: Henry Regnery Co., 1957), p. 47.
4 David Robertson, *Debates and Other Proceedings of the Convention of Virginia* (Richmond, 1805), p. 27.
5 *Ibid.*, p. 32.

6 From a letter to Joseph C. Cabell, February 2, 1816, *The Writings of Thomas Jefferson* (Washington, D.C: Thomas Jefferson Memorial Association, 1905), Vol. 14, p. 421.

7 Alfred Adask, "Fed Fear," *AntiShyster*, V (Spring, 1995), 6.

8 Barry Goldwater, *The Conscience of A Conservative* (Shepherdsville, Ky: Victor Publishing Co., Inc., 1960), p. 16.

9 *Ibid.*, p. 21-22.

10 Daniel Yankelovich, *Coming to Public Judgment* (Syracuse, N.Y: Syracuse University Press, 1991).

11 David Schoenbrod, "It's Time Congress Took Back Its Power to Make Laws," *Wall Street Journal*, December 6, 1995, p. A21.

12 Michael Shanahan and Miles Benson, "Pork Losing Some Sheen for Voters," *San Francisco Examiner*, October 23, 1994, p. A2.

13 Jonathan Rauch, *Demosclerosis* (N.Y: Random House, 1994), p. 164.

14 Stephen Moore, "The Unconstitutional Congress," *Policy Review*, (Spring, 1995), p. 25.

15 Kevin Fedarko, "A Gun Ban is Shot Down," *Time*, May 8, 1995, p. 85.

16 Moore, *op. cit.*, Note 14, p. 22-27.

17 William F. Weld, "Release Us From Federal Nonsense," *Wall Street Journal*, December 11, 1995, p. A14; Paul C. Roberts, "Welfare: Maybe the States Can Figure Out What Works," *Business Week*, December 4, 1995, p. 21.

18 Bruce Babbitt, "States Rights for Liberals," *The New Republic*, January 24, 1981, p. 21-23.

19 Tom Bethell, "Fix Washington Before It Enslaves Us All," *Wall Street Journal*, December 2, 1994, p. A12.

20 Paul Roberts, "America's Secessionist Boom The Goodbye Whirl," *The New Republic*, November 21, 1994, p. 11-12.

21 Warren Cohen, David Hage, and Robert F. Black, "Reversing the Tide," *U.S. News & World Report*, April 3, 1995, p. 42-47, 49; Robert W. Poole Jr., "The Asset Test: A Privatization Agenda," *Reason*, IX (February, 1995), 34-36.

22 David R. Henderson, "The Case For Small Government," *Fortune*, June 26, 1995, p. 39-40.

23 Rauch, *op. cit.*, Note 13, p. 142.

24 Wesley A. Riddle, "Secession and the Moral Compact," *Vital Speeches*, August 1, 1995, p. 638.

25 To learn more contact Ken Bohnsack 1154 West Logan Street Freeport, Il. 61032 (815)-232-8737.

26 Louis Fisher, "The Curious Belief in Judicial Supremacy," *Suffolk University Law Review*, XXV (Spring, 1991), 85-116.

27 Pete Du Pont, "Pleading the Tenth," *National Review*, November 27, 1995, p. 50-53.

28 "The Tenth Amendment: A Barrier Against Congress' Grab For Power," *Judicial Watch*, III (Winter, 1995), 1-4.

29 Thomas Sowell, "Is the Constitution Superfluous?" *Forbes*, June 5, 1995, p. 61.

30 Alexis de Tocqueville, *Democracy in America*, Vol. I (N.Y: Vintage Books, 1990).

31 Richard A. Epstein, "Self Interest and the Constitution," *Journal of Legal Education*, XXXVII (June, 1987), p. 153-161.

## Chapter VII Early Signs of Treason

1 "Pacifists Pester Till Mayor Calls The Traitors," *New York Times*, March 24, 1917, p. A2; Jennings C. Wise, *Woodrow Wilson: Disciple of Revolution* (N.Y: Paisley Press, 1938), p. 647.
2 Lt. Colonel J.B. MacLean, "Why Did We Let Trotzky Go?" *MacLean's* (June, 1919), p. 34A, 66A, 66B.
3 U.S., Congress, House, Rep. McFadden *Congressional Record*, Vol. 77 Part 6 1st Sess., June 15, 1933, p. 6227.
4 Antony C. Sutton, *Western Technology and Soviet Economic Development 1917 to 1930*, Vol. I (Stanford, Ca: Hoover Institution Publications, 1968), p. 71-3, 86-91, 290-292.
5 Michael Ledeen, "A Sellout to China," *Wall Street Journal*, March 12, 1996, p. A18. The Alliance For American Innovation is taking steps to protect U.S. Patents-1100 Connecticut Ave., NW #1200 Washington, D.C. 20036-4101.
6 Carroll Quigley, *Tragedy and Hope: A History of the World in Our Time* (N.Y: The MacMillian Co., 1966), p. 938.
7 *Ibid.*, 954.
8 Antony C. Sutton, *Wall Street and the Bolshevik Revolution* (New Rochelle, N.Y: Arlington House Publishers, 1974), p. 176.
9 Max Eastman, "The Character and Fate of Leon Trotsky," *Foreign Affairs* (January, 1941), 332.
10 Gabriel Kolko, "American Business and Germany, 1930-1941," *The Western Political Quarterly*, XV (1962), 715.
11 John P. Diggins, *Mussolini and Fascism: The View from America* (Princeton, N.J: Princeton University Press, 1972); Michael Parenti, *Inventing Reality* (N.Y: St. Martin's Press, 1986), p. 115-116.
12 M.R. Montgomery, "The Press and Adolf Hitler: What the Newspapers Didn't See," *Boston Globe*, January 30, 1983, p. 10-12, 30, 32-37.
13 Antony C. Sutton, *Wall Street and the Rise of Hitler* (Seal Beach, Ca: '76 Press, 1976), p. 120-122.
14 Charles F. Ross, *NRA Economic Planning* (Indianapolis: The Principia Press, 1937), p. 37.
15 U.S., Congress, Senate, *Congressional Record*, 1933, p. 5165; Committee on Finance, *National Industrial Recovery*, Hearings 73rd Cong., 1st Sess., S. 1712 and H.R. 5755 (Washington: Government Printing Office, 1933), p. 5.
16 Jules Archer, *The Plot To Seize the White House* (N.Y: Hawthorn Books, Inc., 1973), p. 31.
17 Charles Higham, *Trading With the Enemy* (N.Y: Delacorte Press, 1983).
18 Robert Smith, *MacArthur in Korea: The Naked Emperor* (N.Y: Simon & Schuster, 1982), p. 228-235.
19 U.S., Congress, House, Special Committee on Un-American Activities, *Investigation of Nazi Propaganda Activites and Investigation of Certain Other Propaganga Activities*, 73d Cong., 2d Sess., Dec. 29, 1934. Hearings no. 73-D.C.-6, Part 1. Reported issued Feb. 15, 1935 HUAC, House Report no. 153 74 Congress, George Seldes; *1000 Americans* (N.Y: Boni & Gaer, 1947), p. 290-292.
20 Antony C. Sutton, *Wall Street and FDR* (New Rochelle, N.Y: Arlington House Publishers, 1975), p. 143-160.
21 Archer, *op. cit.*, Note 16, p. ix.
22 "Plot Without Plotters," *Time*, XXIV (December 3, 1934), p. 13-15.

23 John Spivak, *A Man In His Time* (N.Y: Horizon Press, 1967), p. 298.
24 Archer, *op. cit.*, Note 16, p. 190.
25 Archer, *op. cit.*, Note 16, p. ix.
26 U.S. Congress, Senate, *Special Committee Investigating the Munitions Industry*, Hearings, 73 Congress, 2d sess. (Washington, D.C: Government Printing Office, 1934-37); George Seldes, *Iron Blood and Profits* (N.Y: Harper & Brothers, 1934).
27 Wayne S. Cole, *Roosevelt and the Isolationists 1932-45* (Lincoln, Nebraska: U. of Nebraska Press, 1983), p. 141-162.
28 John E. Wiltz, *In Search of Peace* (Baton Rouge, La: Louisiana State University Press, 1963), p. 197-202.
29 Raymond G. Swing, "Morgan's Nerves Begin to Jump," *The Nation*, May 1, 1935, p. 504.
30 Harry Williams, *Huey Long* (N.Y: Alfred A. Knopf, 1969).
31 John T. Flynn, *The Roosevelt Myth* (N.Y: The Devin-Adair Company, 1948), p. 66.
32 Carleton Beals, *The Story of Huey P. Long* (Westport, Ct: Greenwood Press, 1935), p. 404-407.
33 Allan A. Michie and Frank Ryhlick, *Dixie Demagogues* (N.Y: Vanguard Press, 1939), p. 116.
34 Higham, *op. cit.*, Note 17, p. 167-8; U.S., Congress, *Congressional Record*, Appendix, August 20, 1942, p. A3134.
35 Charles Higham, *American Swastika* (Garden City, N.Y: Doubleday & Co., Inc., 1985).
36 John Roy Carlson, *Under Cover* (N.Y: E.P. Dutton & Co., Inc., 1943), p. 460.
37 Michele F. Stenchjem, *An American First* (New Rochelle, N.Y: Arlington House Publishers, 1976), p. 29-30.
38 Bill Kauffman, *America First* (Amherst, N.Y: Prometheus Books, 1995), p. 11, 15-21, 95-96.
39 George Seldes, *Facts and Fascism* (N.Y: In fact, Inc. 1943), p. 68, 254.
40 *Ibid.*, p. 153-4, 254, 262-4.
41 *Ibid.*, p. 68, 262.
42 Joseph Borkin, *The Crime and Punishment of I.G. Farben* (N.Y: Macmillan Publishing Co., Inc., 1978), p. 76-80.
43 R. Buckminster Fuller, *Critical Path* (N.Y: St Martin's Press, 1981), p. 104.
44 Seldes, *op. cit.*, Note 39, p. 75.
45 Seldes, *op. cit.*, Note 19, p. 153, 162; *In fact* February 1 and 8, 1942; Seldes, *op. cit.*, Note 39, p. 75; U.S., Congress, Munitions Hearings Part 12.
46 James Stewart Martin, *All Honorable Men* (Boston: Little, Brown and Company, 1950), p. 19-23.
47 John Loftus and Mark Aarons, *The Secret War Against the Jews* (N.Y: St. Martin's Press, 1994), p. 55-105.
48 David Ignatius, "Britain's War In America," *Washington Post*, September 17, 1989, p. C1, C2.
49 Martin, *op. cit.*, Note 46, p. 67-68.

50 Higham, op. cit., Note 17, p. xxiv-xxv, 188-191; "Uncle Sam and the Swastika," Archives on Audio, radio telecast, May 23, 1980, August 12, 1990, May 24, 1992, May 30, 1993. M11. Produced by Dave Emory.
51 Sutton, op. cit., Note 13, p. 128-132, 123, 83, 79, 68.
52 Martin, op. cit., Note 46, p. 79; Sutton, op. cit., Note 13, p. 149-161.
53 Martin, op. cit., Note 46, p. 277.
54 Martin, op. cit., Note 46, p. 264-6, 279-280, 288-291, 295-7.
55 Tom Bower, The Paperclip Conspiracy: The Hunt for the Nazi Scientists (Boston: Little, Brown and Co., 1987).
56 Christopher Simpson, Blowback (N.Y: Weidenfeld & Nicolson, 1988).
57 Carl Oglesby, "Reinhard Gehlen: The Secret Treaty of Fort Hunt," Covert Action, Number 35 (Fall, 1990), 8-16.
58 Martin Lee, "Hitler's Last Laugh," Propaganda Review, Number 4 (Spring, 1989), 17-21.
59 Russ Bellant, Old Nazis, the New Right and the Republican Party (Boston: South End Press, 1989); Russ Bellant, "Old Nazis and the New Right: The Republican Party and Fascists," Covert Action, Number 33 (Winter, 1990), 27-31.
60 Peter Braestrup, "GOP's 'Open Door:' Who's Coming In?" Washington Post, November 21, 1971, p. A1.
61 Lee, op. cit., Note 58, p. 21.

## Chapter VIII Rise of the Corporate State

1 Alex Carey, Taking the Risk Out of Democracy (Sydney, Australia: U. of New South Wales Press, 1995), p. 18.
2 Jonathan Rowe, "Reinventing the Corporation," The Washington Monthly, XXVIII (April, 1996), 16-23; Richard L. Grossman and Frank T. Adams, Taking Care of Business: Citizenship and the Charter of Incorporation (Cambridge, Ma: Charter, Ink, 1993).
3 William Leach, Land of Desire (N.Y: Pantheon Books, 1993), p. 3.
4 Stuart Ewen, Captains of Consciousness (N.Y: McGraw-Hill, 1976).
5 Samuel Strauss, "The Future," The Villager, April 28, 1923, p. 119.
6 Leach, op. cit., Note 3, p. xiii.
7 Walter Weyl, The New Democracy (N.Y: The Macmillan Company, 1912), p. 331.
8 Walter Karp, Buried Alive (N.Y: Henry Holt & Co., 1988), p. 164.
9 Samuel Strauss, "Things Are in the Saddle," The Atlantic Monthly, 134 (November, 1924), 577-588.
10 Samuel Strauss, "Rich Men and Key Men," The Altantic Monthly, CXL (December, 1927), 721-729.
11 G.K. Chesterton, "What of the Republic," in The Collected Works of G.K. Chesterton, ed. by Robert Royal (San Francisco: Ignatius Press, 1986), p. 588.
12 Ibid., p. 590.
13 Lewis H. Lapham, Money and Class In America (N.Y: Weidenfeld & Nicolson, 1988), p. 215.
14 Lewis H. Lapham, The Wish for Kings (N.Y: Grove Press, 1993), p. 36.
15 William H. Roberts and Edwin P. Rome, Corporate and Commercial Speech: First Amendment Protection of Expression in Business (Westport: Quorum, 1985).

16 Charles A. Reich, *Opposing the System* (N.Y: Crown Publishers, Inc., 1995, p. 41.

17 Jaye Scholl, "Giving Business the Business," *Barron's*, March 25, 1991, p. 18-19. People can now access the ethical performance of 20,000 corporations with the database provided by The Ethical Consumer Research Association 16 Nicholas St., 5th floor, Manchester M1 4EJ, U.K. This group also publishes the *Ethical Consumer* magazine.

18 Russell Mokhiber, "Underworld U.S.A.," *In These Times*, April 1, 1996, p. 14-16.

19 Richard Behar and Michael Kramer, "Something Smells Fowl," *Time*, October 17, 1994, p. 42-44.

20 Kurt Eichenwald, "Brokerage Firm Admits Crimes in Energy Deals," *New York Times*, October 28, 1994, p. A1, C13.

21 Carla Atkinson, "The New Civil War," *Public Citizen*, XI (January/February, 1991), 13-15.

22 Bruce Alpert, "Targeting 'Corporate Welfare,'" *San Francisco Examiner*, December 11, 1994, p. B3.

23 James Bovard, "Plowing Deeper," *Barrons*, April 15, 1996, p. 58.

24 Linda Grant and Robert F. Black, "Getting Business Off the Dole," *U.S. News & World Report*, April 10, 1995, p. 38; Howard Gleckman, "Welfare Cuts: Now, It's Corporate America's Turn," *Business Week*, April 10, 1995, p. 37.

25 Karen Tumulty, "Why Subsidies Survive," *Time*, March 25, 1996, p. 46-47.

26 Ralph Nader, "Easy Money," *In These Times* February 19, 1996, p. 14-17; Ruth Simon, "You're Losing Your Consumer Rights," *Money*, XXV (March, 1996), 100-111.

27 Richard J. Barnet, "Stateless Corporations: Lords of the Global Economy," *The Nation*, December 19, 1994, p. 754-757.

28 Peter Downs, "A Return to Corporate Serfdom," *Z Magazine*, V (March, 1992), 96-99.

29 Eve Pell, "Libel As A Political Weapon," *The Nation*, June 6, 1981, p. 681, 698-700.

30 Eric F. Coppolino, "Dioxin Critic Sued," *Lies Of Our Times*, V (May, 1994), 23-24.

31 "Libel and Then Some," *Muckracker*, (October, 1994), 3.

32 John Sterling, "SLAPP-Happy Corporations Get SLAPPed Back," *Earth Island Journal*, IX (Spring, 1994), 20.

33 James A. Smith, *The Idea Brokers* (N.Y: Macmillan, Inc., 1991).

34 David S. Broder and Michael Wessikopf, "Finding New Friends on the Hill," *The Washington Post National Weekly*, XI October 3-9, 1994, p. 11.

35 Herbert Schiller, *Culture, Inc The Corporate Takeover of Public Expression* (N.Y: Oxford Uiversity Press, 1989), p. 106.

36 Michael Parenti, *Land of Idols* (N.Y: St. Martin's Press, 1994), p. 94-95.

37 Hans Haacke, "Museums, Managers of Consciousness," in *Hans Haacke Unfinished Business*, ed. by Brian Wallis (Cambridge: MIT Press, 1986), p. 71.

38 David Margolick, "Albany High Court Lets Malls Restrict Leafleting," *New York Times*, December 20, 1985, p. A1, B11.

39 Scott G. Bullock, "The Mall's in Their Court," *Reason*, XXVII (August/September, 1995), 46-48.

40 "Selling to School Kids," *Consumer Reports*, 60 (May, 1995), 327-329.

41 Richard Foreman, *Leasing the Ivory Tower: The Corporate Takeover of Academia* (Boston: South End Press, 1995), p. 145; Elizabeth Fones-Wolf, *Selling Free Enterprise: The Business Assault on Labor and Liberalism* (Chicago: University of Illinois Press, 1994), p. 189-217.
42 Ron Nixon, "Truth to the Highest Bidder: Science for Sale," *Covert Action*, Number 52 (Spring, 1995), 48-53.
43 Joel Bleifuss, "With Science on Their Side," *In These Times*, October 30, 1995, p. 12-14.
44 Fones-Wolf, op. cit., Note 41.
45 Robert Pear, "Doctors Say H.M.O.'s Limit What They Can Tell Patients," *New York Times*, December 21, 1995, p. A1; Susan Brink, "How Your HMO Could Hurt You," *U.S. News & World Report*, January 15, 1996, p. 62-64.
46 Schiller *op. cit.*, Note 35, p. 67, 111, 157.
47 *Ibid.*, p. 3, 162, 163.
48 Grant McConnell, *Private Power and American Democracy* (N.Y: Alfred A. Knopf, 1966), p. 361-362.
49 Gerry Spence, *From Freedom to Slavery* (N.Y: St. Martin's Press, 1993), p. xiii-xiv, 7.
50 Arthur S. Miller, *The Modern Corporate State* (Westport, Ct: Greenwood Press, 1976), p. 115, 196, 216-217.
51 Richard Barber, *The American Corporation: Its Power, Its Money, Its Politics* (N.Y: E.P. Dutton & Co., 1970), p. 188-189.
52 Matt Murray, "Amid Record Profits, Companies Continue to Lay Off Employees," *Wall Street Journal*, May 4, 1995, p. A1, A5.
53 Arthur Schlesinger, Jr., "In Defense of Government," *Wall Street Journal*, June 7, 1995, p. A14.
54 Joel Bleifuss, "The New Abolitionists," *In These Times*, April 1, 1996, p. 12-13. Organizations formed to curtail corporate power include: The Program on Corporations, Law and Democracy P.O. Box 806 Cambridge, Ma. 02140, International Forum on Globalization P.O. Box 12218 S.F., Ca. 94112, and Share the Wealth 37 Temple Pl Boston, Ma. 02111.
55 C. Wright Mills, *Power Elite* (N.Y: Oxford U. Press, 1956).

**Chapter IX Rise of the Transnational Corporations**
1 Jeremy Brecher and Tim Costello, "The Lilliput Strategy: Taking on the Multinationals," *The Nation*, December 19, 1994, p. 757-760; Edward S. Herman, "The End of Democracy?" *Z Magazine*, VI (September, 1993), 57-62; Edward S. Herman, "Economists Versus Democracy," *Z Magazine*, VI (Dec, 1993), 54-58.
2 Bruce Rich, "Fifty Years of World Bank Outrages," *Earth Island Journal*, IX (Winter 1993-1994), 34-35; Jude Wanniski, "An IFI Question: Are Multilaterals the Solution...Or Part of the Problem?" *Wall Street Journal*, October 12, 1995, p. A22; Patricia Adams, "A Troubling Deposit at World Bank," *Wall Street Journal*, November 29, 1995, p. A14.
3 Richard J. Barnet, "Stateless Corporations: Lords of the Global Economy," *The Nation*, December 19, 1994, p. 754-757; Richard J. Barnet, *Global Dreams: Imperial Corporations and the New World Order* (N.Y: Simon & Schuster, 1994).
4 Keith B. Rickburg, "A Line of 'Big Men' Has Thrown Democracy For A Loss," *The Washington Post National Weekly*, XII January 9-15, 1995, p. 18.
5 Charles Lane, "Rabble Rousing," *The New Republic*, June 12, 1995, p. 15-16.

6 William I. Robinson, "Low Intensity Democracy: The New Face of Global Domination," *Covert Action*, Number 50 (Fall, 1994), 40-47.
7 Michel Crozier, Samuel P. Huntington, and Joji Watanuki, *The Crisis of Democracy: Report on the Governability of Democracies to the Trilateral Commission* (N.Y: New York University Press, 1975).
8 Stephen Gill, *American Hegemony and the Trilateral Commission* (Cambridge: Cambridge University Press, 1990).
9 Joseph Schumpeter, *Capitalism, Socialism and Democracy*, 2nd edition (N.Y: Harper & Row, 1947).
10 Noam Chomsky, "Rollback IV: Towards a Utopia of the Masters," *Z Magazine*, VIII (May, 1995), 18-24.
11 "Soft-soaping India," *New Statesman & Society*, January 13, 1995, p. 24-25.
12 Walker F. Todd, "Mexican Handout: Bailing Out the Creditor Class," *The Nation*, February 13, 1995, p. 193-194.
13 George J. Church, "Mexico's Troubles Are Our Troubles," *Time*, March 6, 1995, p. 34-40.
14 Martin Espinoza, "Mexico's Next Revolution," *San Francisco Bay Guardian*, February 22, 1995, p. 22-23, 25; Ken Silverstein and Alexander Cockburn, "Who Broke Mexico: The Killers and the Killing," *The Nation*, March 6, 1995, p. 306-308, 310.
15 David Asman, "Don't Cry For Argentina," *Wall Street Journal*, May 4, 1995, p. A14.
16 Walker F. Todd, "Guess Whose Banks We're Planning to Bail Out Next," *Sacramento Bee*, December 31, 1995, Forum p. 1, 6.
17 "NAFTA's Progress Next Stop South," *The Economist*, February 25, 1995, p. 29-30.
18 Henry Kissinger, "For U.S. Leadership, a Moment Missed," *Washington Post*, May 12, 1995, p. A26.
19 "In Need of Fastening," *The Economist*, May 27, 1995, p. 15-16.
20 Steven Greenhouse, "Christopher Backs Free Trade With Europe," *New York Times*, June 3, 1995, p. A5.
21 Richard N. Cooper, "A Monetary System For the Future," *Foreign Affairs*, 63 (Fall, 1984), 166-184.
22 "A Question of Motive," *The Economist*, September 30, 1995, p. 16; Rob Norton, "There Go Those Eurocrats Again," *Fortune*, September 18, 1995, p. 51.
23 James Goldsmith, *The Trap* (N.Y: Carroll and Graf Publishers, Inc., 1994).
24 U.S., Congress, Senate, Committee On Commerce, Science, and Transportation, *GATT Treaty*, Hearings, 103d Cong., 2d Sess. (Washington, D.C: Government Printing Office, 1994), p. 495, 498, 503.
25 U.S., Congress, House, Committee on Ways and Means, *GATT Treaty*, 103d Cong., 2nd Sess. June 10, 1994, (Washington, D.C: Government Printing Office, 1994), p. 131.
26 James Goldsmith, "The GATT Trap," *Earth Island Journal*, X (Winter, 1995), 32-34.
27 George J. Church, "Are We Better Off?" *Time*, January 29, 1996, p. 36-40.
28 Aaron Bernstein, "Is America Becoming More of A Class Society?" *Business Week*, February 26, 1996, p. 86-91.
29 "Cheap Labor," *Mother Jones*, XXI (January/February, 1996), 13; John Greenwald, "Cutting Off the Brains," *Time*, February 5, 1996, p. 46; Michael S.

Teitelbaum, "Too Many Engineers, Too Few Jobs," *New York Times*, March 19, 1996, p. A17.
30 Christopher Lasch, "The Revolt of the Elites and the Betrayal of Democracy," *Harpers*, 289 (November, 1994), 47.
31 Robert B. Reich, "Who Is Us?" *Harvard Business Review*, 90 (January/February, 1990), 59.
32 William Greider, "The Global Marketplace: Closet Dictator," In *The Case Against Free Trade GATT, NAFTA, and the Globalization of Corporate Power*, ed. Ralph Nader et al (Berkeley: North Atlantic Books, 1993), p. 209.
33 Lasch, *op. cit.*, Note 30, p. 49.
34 Richard G. Gardner, "The Hard Road to World Order *Foreign Affairs*, 52 (April, 1974), 558-560.
35 Jeremy Brecher, "After NAFTA: Global Village or Global Pillage?" *The Nation*, December 6, 1993, p. 685-688; Jeremy Brecher and John B. Childs, *Global Visions: Beyond the New World Order* (Boston: South End Press, 1993).
36 George Seldes, *Facts and Fascism* (N.Y: In fact, Inc., 1943), p. 49-50; "Japanese Fascism: Its Structure and Significance For Contemporary Americans," Archives on Audio, radio telecast, October 2, 1988. M26. Produced by Dave Emory.
37 Laxmi Nakarmi, "The Kiwis Are Open for Business," *Business Week*, September 25, 1995, p. 117-118; Franklin Winchester, "New Zealand From Welfare State to Utopia?" *Perceptions*, II (September/October, 1995), 10-12.

**Chapter X Rise of the National Security State: The Cold War and Democracy**

1 John W. Baer, "The Strange Origin of the Pledge of Allegiance," *Propaganda Review*, Number 5 (Summer, 1989), 36-37.
2 Walter Karp, *Buried Alive* (N.Y: Franklin Square Press, 1992), p. 13-26.
3 Bruce D. Porter, *War and the Rise of the State* (N.Y: Macmillan, 1994), p. 292-3.
4 James Madison, "Political Observations," in *Letter and Other Writings of James Madison*, Vol. IV (Philadelphia: J.B. Lippincott and Co., 1865), p. 491-2.
5 Alexis de Tocqueville, *Democracy In America*, Vol 2 (N.Y: Vintage, 1990), p. 269.
6 Porter, *op. cit.*, Note 3, p. xv.
7 Gore Vidal, *The Decline and Fall of the American Empire* (Berkeley: Odonian Press, 1992), p. 30.
8 R. Buckminster Fuller, *Critical Path* (N.Y: St Martin's Press, 1981), p. 116.
9 William A. Williams, "The Cold-War Revisionists," *The Nation*, November 13, 1967, p. 492-495.
10 H.W. Brands, *The Devil We Knew: Americans and the Cold War* (N.Y: Oxford University Press, 1993), p. vi.
11 Barton J. Bernstein, "American Foreign Policy and the Origins of the Cold War," in *Politics and Policies of the Truman Administration*, ed. by Barton J. Bernstein (Chicago: Quadrangle Books, 1970), p. 16-17.
12 "Aviation RFC," *Business Week*, January 31, 1948, p. 28, 30, 32.
13 "From Cold War to Cold Peace," *Business Week*, February 12, 1949, p. 19-20.

14 Frank Kofsky, *Harry S. Truman and the War Scare of 1948* (N.Y: St. Martin's Press, 1993), p. 308.
15 Carl Bernstein, *Loyalties: A Son's Memoir* (N.Y: Simon & Schuster, 1989), p. 197-198.
16 Kofsky, *op. cit.*, Note 14, p. 246.
17 Harold B. Hinton, "Eisenhower Scoffs at Fears of a War Started By Russia," *New York Times*, February, 6 1948, p. 1, 12.
18 "Crisis," *Wall Street Journal*, April 2, 1948, p. 4.
19 Brands, *op. cit.*, Note 10, p. 23-24.
20 Harold D. Lasswell, *National Security and Individual Freedom* (N.Y: McGraw-Hill Book Co., Inc., 1950), p. 23, 47.
21 Karp, *op. cit.*, Note 2, p. 111.
22 Michael Parenti, *Inventing Reality* (N.Y: St. Martin's Press, 1986), p. 126.
23 Stewart Udall, *The Myths of August* (N.Y: Pantheon, 1994), p. xi-xii, 7, 344, 346, 354, 357.
24 Lewis Lapham, *Wish for Kings* (N.Y: Grove Press, 1993), p. 157, 177.
25 Bill Moyers, *The Secret Government: The Constitution In Crisis* (Washington, D.C: Seven Locks Press, 1988), p. 16, 27, 54, 78, 89, 100, 101, 117.
26 Vidal, *op. cit.*, Note 7, p. 50, 63.
27 William Greider, *Who Will Tell the People* (N.Y: Simon & Schuster, 1992), p. 374-5.
28 *Ibid.*, p. 360.
29 David Wise, *The Politics of Lying* (N.Y: Random House, 1973), p. 343.
30 *Ibid.*, p. 64.
31 *Ibid.*, p. 342, 344, 345.
32 Peter Montgomery and Peter Overby, "The Fight to Know," *Common Cause Magazine*, (July/August, 1991), 17-21.
33 Lyle Denniston, "Court Nibbles Away at FOIA," *Washington Journalism Review*, XIV (March, 1992), 64.
34 Robert P. Deyling, "Judicial Deference and De Novo Review in Litigation Over National Security Information Under the Freedom of Information Act," *Villanova Law Review*, 37 (1992), 67-112.
35 Janine Jackson, "Top Secret: What the Government Isn't Telling You," *Extra*, VI (November/December, 1993), 14-16, 19.
36 EO 12937 Federal Register Nov. 15, 1994 p. 59097.
37 This publication can be ordered from: Federation of American Scientists 307 Mass. Ave., N.E. Washington, D.C. 20002.
38 Felix Morley, *Freedom and Federalism* (Indianapolis: Liberty Press, 1981), p. xx.
39 George Edwards, III and Earl W. Wallace, eds., *National Security and the U.S. Constitution* (Baltimore: The John Hopkins University Press, 1988), p. 68, 324.
40 Patrick Kennon, *The Twilight of Democracy* (N.Y: Doubleday and Co., 1995), p. 125.
41 Ann Markusen and Joel Yudken, *Dismantling the Cold War Economy* (N.Y: Harper Collins Publications, Inc., 1992).
42 William Greider, "The Country that Stayed Out in the Cold," *Rolling Stone*, Number 622 January 23, 1992, p. 19-20.
43 Robert Pollin, "Dismantling Defense: Use Conversion to Create Jobs," *The Nation*, July 12, 1993, p. 66-68.

44 David Moberg, "Conversion Inexperience," *In These Times*, December 26, 1994, p. 14-19.
45 Archibald MacLeish, "The Conquest of America," *The Atlantic Monthly*, 184 (August, 1949), 17-22.
46 Brands, *op. cit.*, Note 10, p. 224-228.

## Chapter XI The CIA and the Intelligence Community

1 Tim Weiner, "Senate Committee Receives Apology From Spy Agency," *New York Times*, August 11, 1994, p. A1, C19.
2 Tim Weiner, *Blank Check The Pentagons Black Budget* (N.Y: Warner Books, 1990), p. 7.
3 Walter Pincus, "Spy Agency Hoards Secret $1 Billion," *Washington Post*, September 24, 1995, p. A1, A22; Tim Weiner, "A Secret Agency's Secret Budgets Yield 'Lost' Billions, Officials Say," *New York Times*, January 30, 1996, p. A1.
4 Federalist 58, Final Report p. 412.
5 G. Hunt, ed., Letter to W.T. Barry, August 4, 1822, *The Writings of James Madison*, Vol. 9 (N.Y: G.P. Putnam's Sons, 1910), p. 103.
6 Weiner, *op. cit.*, Note 2, p. 24, 111.
7 Stewart L. Udall, *The Myths of August* (N.Y: Pantheon, 1994), p. 7.
8 Merle Miller, *Plain Speaking: An Oral Biography of Harry S. Truman* (N.Y: Berkeley Publishing, 1974), p. 392.
9 Steven Emerson, *Secret Warriors* (N.Y: G.P. Putnam's Sons, 1988).
10 Bill Moyers, *The Secret Government: The Constitution In Crisis* (Washington, D.C: Seven Locks Press, 1988), p. 92.
11 Verne Lyon, "Domestic Surveillance: The History of Operation CHAOS," *Covert Action*, Number 34 (Summer, 1990), 59-62.
12 "The Select Committee's Investigative Record" *The Village Voice*, February 15, 1976, p. 72-91.
13 Tim Weiner, "The Pentagon's Secret Stash," *Mother Jones*, XVII (March/April, 1992), 22-28.
14 John Stockwell, *The Praetorian Guard* (Boston: South End Press, 1991), p. 101.
15 Peter Cassidy, "The Banker Who Said No to the CIA," *The Progressive*, 56 (June, 1992), 24-25.
16 James R. Adams and Douglas Frantz, *A Full Service Bank* (N.Y: Simon & Schuster, Inc., 1992), p. 326-7.
17 "The BCCI-CIA Connection: Just How Far Did It Go?" *Newsweek*, December 7, 1992, p. 49.
18 Tom Post, Daniel Pedersen, and Steve Le Vine, "The CIA and BCCI," *Newsweek*, August 12, 1991, p. 16-19, 21; Jack Calhoun, "BCCI: The Bank of the CIA," *Covert Action*, Number 44 (Spring, 1993), 40-45.
19 Ralph Nader, "How Clinton Can Build Democracy," *The Nation*, November 30, 1992, p. 649, 652-3.
20 Pete Brewton, *The Mafia, CIA and George Bush* (N.Y: Shapolsky Publishers, Inc., 1992), p. 384, 385.
21 *Ibid.*, p. 343-357.
22 Steve Weinberg, "The Mob, the CIA and the S&L Scandal," *Columbia Journalism Review*, XXIX (November/December, 1990), 28-35; Rebecca Sims,

"Operatives and S&Ls: The CIA and Financial Institutions," *Covert Action*, Number 35 (Fall, 1990), 43-48.

23 David Corn, "The Company They Keep," *The Washington Monthly*, XXVI (July/August, 1994), 34-38.

24 David Corn, *Blond Ghost: Ted Shackley and the CIAs Crusaders* (N.Y: Simon & Schuster, 1994).

25 Marcus Raskin, "Let's Terminate the C.I.A.," *The Nation*, June 8, 1992, p. 776-7.

26 Stockwell, *op. cit.*, Note 14, p. 51-2.

27 Frank Smyth, "My Enemy's Friends," *The New Republic*, June 5, 1995, p. 18.

28 James Risen, "Congressman Under Fire for CIA Disclosures," *Los Angeles Times*, April 8, 1995, p. A1, 14.

29 Tim Weiner, "Spy Suspect Relied Deceptively On Lie Test in 1991, F.B.I. Says," *New York Times*, March 8, 1994, p. 1, 18.

30 Ronald J. Ostrow and Robert L Jackson, "CIA Overlooked Red Flag From Ameses' Bank," *Los Angeles Times*, March 12, 1994, p. A1, 16.

31 David Johnston, "Prosecutors Say Official At C.I.A. Spied For Russia," *New York Times*, February 23, 1994, p. A1.

32 Mark Almond, "The KGB and America's War on Drugs," *Wall Street Journal*, March 10, 1994, p. A18.

33 Bill Gertz, "CIA: IMF Aid to Moscow Paid Ames," *The Washington Times National Weekly*, December 4-10, 1995, p. 17.

34 "The C.I.A.'s False Intelligence," *New York Times*, November 29, 1995, p. A14.

35 Jack Anderson and Michael Binstein, "Testifying to the CIA's Arrogance," *Washington Post*, January 11, 1996, p. 10.

36 George McGovern, "We Need A Constitutional Presidency," *Parade Magazine*, August 9, 1987.

37 Jeffrey Denny, "See No Evil," *Common Cause Magazine*, XVII (July/August, 1991), 23-27, 40.

38 Rodney Stich, *Defrauding America* (Alamo, Ca: Diablo Western Press, Inc., 1993), p. 312.

39 Jack Colhoun, "Bush Administration Uses CIA To Stonewall Iraqgate Investigation," *Covert Action*, Number 42 (Fall, 1992), 40-41.

40 David Andelman, "The CIA's Trade Secret," *Worth*, II (December/January, 1994), 19.

41 Jonathan Vankin and John Whalen, *50 Greatest Conspiracies of All Time* (N.Y: A Citadel Press Book, 1995), p. 157-164.

42 Stich, *op. cit.*, Note 38, p. 286-287, 431, 517.

43 Angelo Codevilla, "Get Smart-Eliminate the CIA." *Wall Street Journal*, January 18, 1995, p. A16.

44 David Ignatius, "Reinvent the CIA," *Washington Monthly*, XXVI (April, 1994), 38; Rob Norton, "The CIA's Mission Improbable," *Fortune*, 132 (October 2, 1995), 55.

45 Raskin, *op. cit.*, Note 25, p. 776-784.

46 R. Buckminster Fuller, *Critical Path* (N.Y: St. Martin's Press, 1981), p. 116.

47 Robert Dreyfuss, "Spying For Dollars," *In These Times*, March 20, 1995, p. 24-26; Anthony L. Kimery, "The CIA: Banking On Intelligence," *Covert Action*, Number 46 (Fall, 1993), 55-59.
48 Russ W. Baker, "CIA Out of Control," *Village Voice*, September 10, 1991, p. 35-41.

**Chapter XII State and Federal Police**
1 Athan Theoharis, *From the Secret Files of J. Edgar Hoover* (Chicago: Ivan R. Dee, 1991), p. 2.
2 Mary King, *Freedom Song* (N.Y: William Morrow and Co., Inc., 1987), p. 228; Howard Zinn, "Federal Bureau of Intimidation," *Covert Action*, Number 47 (Winter 1993-1994), 27-31.
3 Louis Wolf, "Bag of Dirty Tricks," *Covert Action*, Number 47 (Winter 1993-1994), 54.
4 Ken Lawrence, "Sources and Methods: Mail Surveillance," *Covert Action*, Number 12 (April, 1981), 44-45, 48.
5 Zinn, *op. cit.*, Note 2, p. 30; Ford Rowan, *Techno Spies* (N.Y: G. P. Putnam's Sons, 1978), p. 37.
6 Frank J. Donner, *The Age of Surveillance* (N.Y: Alfred A. Knopf, 1980), p. 162-168.
7 Loch K. Johnson, *America's Secret Power* (N.Y: Oxford U. Press, 1989), p. 5.
8 Bertram Gross, *Friendly Fascism* (Boston: South End Press, 1980), p. 306.
9 Theoharis, *op. cit.*, Note 1, p. 357.
10 Manning Marable, *Race, Reform and Rebellion: The Second Reconstruction in Black America, 1945-1982* (Jackson: U. of Mississippi Press, 1984), p. 125.
11 Rex Weyler, *Blood of the Land: The Government and Corporate War Against the American Indian Movement* (N.Y: Everest House, 1982); Ward Churchill, "The Government's Propaganda War Against the American Indian Movement," *Extra*, V (October/November, 1992), 22-24.
12 Wolf, op. cit., Note 3, 55-56; William Steif, "Puerto Rico's Watergate," *The Progressive*, 56 (October, 1992), 28-31.
13 Mike Rothmiller, *L.A. Secret Police: Inside the LAPD Elite Spy Network* (N.Y: Pocket Books, 1992).
14 Jack Cheevers, "FBI Compiled Thick Dossier on Phil Burton," *The Tribune*, September 12, 1988, p. A1, A2.
15 Christopher Hitchens, "Minority Report," *The Nation*, April 25, 1987, p. 531.
16 John Stockwell, *The Praetorian Guard* (Boston: South End Press, 1991), p. 105-6.
17 Ross Gelbspan, *Break-ins Death Threats and the FBI* (Boston: South End Press, 1991); Ward Churchill and Jim Vander Wall, *Agents of Repression: the FBI's Secret War Against the Black Panter Party and the American Indian Movement* (Boston: South End Press, 1988).
18 "FDA's Strange Raid," *Seattle Post-Intelligencer*, May 11, 1992.
19 David Helvarg, *The War Against the Greens* (San Francisco, Ca: Sierra Club, 1994), p. 396.
20 *Ibid.*, p. 400, 402.
21 Judi Bari, "Fighting An FBI Frame-Up," *Earth Island Journal*, IX (Summer, 1994), 40-41.

22 Joel Bleifuss, "Dirty Tricks Are Here Again," *In These Times*, October 17, 1994, p. 12-14.

23 David Z. Nevin, "It Could Happen to Anyone," *Washington Post*, July 18, 1993, p. C7.

24 David Johnston, "Idaho Siege Report Says F.B.I. Agents Violated Procedure," *New York Times*, December 13, 1994, p. A1, A11.

25 David Johnston, "F.B.I. Leader at 1992 Standoff in Idaho Says Review Shielded Top Officials," *New York Times*, May 10, 1995, p. A15.

26 R. W. Bradford, "Still Smoldering," *Liberty*, VIII (July, 1995), 22-24.

27 "Religious Views of Some Extremists May Fuel More Violence," *Los Angeles Times*, April 29, 1995, p. B4, B5.

28 James Bovard, "The New J. Edgar Hoover," *American Spectator*, XXVIII (August, 1995), 28-35.

29 "They Swooped," *The Economist*, August 19, 1995, p. 27.

30 David A. Burnham, "Bureaucratus Gigantus vs. Tyrannosaurus Rex," *AntiShyster*, V (Spring, 1995), 14-15.

31 Lola Sherman and Jim Okerblom, "Herb Firm Polluting is Alleged," *The San Diego Union Tribune*, August 25, 1995, p. B1, B5.

32 Jack Lamb, "American Treason Busters," *Aid & Abet Police Newsletter*, II (July, 1994), 6.

33 Valerie Richardson, "No Nonsense Idaho Sheriff Tells Feds to Steer Clear," *Washington Times National Weekly*, September 4-10, 1995, p. A1, A15.

34 Michael Hedges, "ATF Hunts Down Gun, Not Criminals," The *Washington Times National Weekly*, April 24-30, 1995, p. 1, 15.

35 John D. Lewis, Jr., "American Gestapo," *Reason*, XI (April, 1980), 24-28, 44.

36 Troy Underhill and David Coker, "The Feds Raid on NAFC," *Media Bypass*, II (December, 1994), 40-45.

37 Michael Isikoff and Mark Hosenball, "One Fed's War on the FBI," *Newsweek*, September 25, 1995, p. 45.

38 Rodney Stich, *Defrauding America* (Alamo, Ca: Diablo Western Press, Inc., 1993), p. 411-4.

39 "'Framed' by the FBI," *AntiShyster*, V (Fall, 1995), 48-55.

40 Gordon Witkin, "Enlisting the Feds in the War on Gangs," *U.S. New & World Report*, March 6, 1995, p. 38-39.

41 Steven B. Rich, "The National Guard, Drug Interdiction and Counterdrug Activities, and Posse Comitatus: The Meaning and Implications of 'In Federal Service,'" *The Army Lawyer*, (June, 1994), 35-43.

42 Peter Cassidy, "Guess Who's the Enemy," *The Progressive*, 60 (January, 1996), 22-24.

43 Bill Swindell, "Militia Coordinator On Federal Payroll," *Tulsa World*, April 7, 1996, p. A15; Bill Swindell, "Militia Figure Won't Take Cash From FBI," *Tulsa World*, April 17, 1996, p. A9.

44 James Ridgeway, "The Long Arm of the Law," *Village Voice*, May 21, 1996, p. 32.

45 Mike Zielinski, "Armed and Dangerous: Private Police on the March," *Covert Action*, Number 54 (Fall, 1995), 44-50.

46 Richard Behar, "Stalked by Allstate," *Fortune*, October 2, 1995, p. 128, 130-132, 134, 136, 138, 140, 142.

47 John Connolly, "Inside the Shadow CIA," *Spy*, VI (September, 1992), 46-54; Donner, *op. cit.*, Note 6, p. 414-451.
48 David B. Kopel, "Knock, Knock," *National Review*, March 20, 1995, p. 54, 56-58.
49 David Wise, *The American Police State* (N.Y: Random House, 1976), p. 398.

**Chapter XIII Militias in American History**
1 Stephen P. Hallbrook, "The Right to Bear Arms in the First State Bills of Rights: Pennsylvania, North Carolina, Vermont, and Massachusetts," *Vermont Law Review*, X (Fall, 1985), 314.
2 William S. Fields and David T. Hardy, "The Militia and the Constitution: A Legal History," *Military Law Review*, 136 (Spring, 1992); James B. Whisker, "The Citizen-Soldier Under Federal and State Law," *West Virginia Law Review*, 94, (Summer, 1992).
3 Pauline Maier, *From Resistance to Revolution* (N.Y: Alfred A. Knopf, 1974).
4 Hallbrook, *op cit.*, Note 1, p. 314-6.
5 *Ibid.*, p. 314, 318-9.
6 Thomas M. Moncure, Jr., "Right To Bear Arms," *Lincoln Law Review*, XIX (1990), 9.
7 Daniel D. Polsby, "Second Reading," *Reason*, (March, 1996), 35.
8 Joseph Story, *Commentaries on the Constitution*, Vol. 3 (1833), p. 746-747.
9 Charles E. Stevens, *Sources of the Constitution of the United States* (N.Y: MacMillian and Co., 1894; reprint ed., Littleton, Co: Fred B. Rothman and Co., 1987), p. 223-224.
10 David Engdahl, "The New Civil Disturbance Regulations: The Threat of Military Intervention," *Indiana Law Journal*, 49 (Spring 1974), 581-617.
11 *Ibid.*, p. 597-605; Major H.W.C. Furman, "Restrictions Upon Use of the Army Imposed by the Posse Comitatus Act," *Military Law Review*, VII (January, 1960), 85-129.
12 Whisker, *op. cit.*, Note 2, p. 987.

**Chapter XIV Our Hidden Past: History of Martial Law in the U.S.**
1 "Martial Law," *Southern California Law Review*, 42 (Spring, 1969), 549.
2 Frederick B. Wiener, "Martial Law Today," *American Bar Association J.*, 55 (August 1969), 723.
3 Gabor S. Boritt, *Lincoln the War President* (N.Y: Oxford University Press, 1992), p. 152.
4 Jonathan Lurie, "Andrew Jackson, Martial Law, Civilian Control of the Military, and American Politics: An Intriguing Amalgam," *Military Law Review*, 126 (Fall, 1989), 135-145.
5 Richard F. Bensel,*Yankee Leviathan* (N.Y: Cambridge University Press, 1990), p. 140-1.
6 *Ibid.*, p. 143.
7 Robert E. Denney, *The Civil War Years* (N.Y: Sterling Publishing Co., 1994), p. 71, 104.
8 Allan Nevins, *The War For the Union: War Becomes Revolution, 1862-1863*, Vol. 3 (N.Y: Charles Scribner Sons, 1960; reprint ed., N.Y: MacMillian Publishing Co., 1992), p. 90-392.
9 Mark E. Neely, Jr., *The Fate of Liberty* (N.Y: Oxford U. Press, 1991), p. 65.

10 Charles Fairman, *The Law of Martial Law* (Chicago: Callaghan and Co., 1930), p. 43-49.
11 James G. Randall, *Constitutional Problems Under Lincoln* (Gloucester, Mass: Peter Smith, 1963), p. 183.
12 *Blacks Law Dictionary* (St. Paul, Mn: West Publishing Co., 1991), p. 97.
13 Fairman, *op. cit.*, Note 10, p. 68.
14 Frederick B. Wiener, "Militia Clause of the Constitution," *Harvard Law Review*, LIV (December 1940), 218-219.
15 F. David Trickey, "Constitutional and Statutory Basis of Governors' Emergency Powers," *Michigan Law Review*, 64 (December, 1965), 307.
16 *op. cit.*, Note 1, p. 555.

## Chapter XV Martial Law and Emergency Rule Today

1 Dave Lindorff, "Could It Happen Here?" *Mother Jones*, XIII (April, 1988), 60.
2 Richard P. Pollock, "The Mysterious Mountain," *The Progressive*, 40 (March, 1976), 12-16.
3 Keenen Peck, "The Take-Charge Gang," *The Progressive*, 49 (May, 1985), 18-24.
4 Lindorff, *op. cit.*, Note 1, p. 60.
5 Peck, *op. cit.*, Note 3, p. 18.
6 B.W. Menke, *Martial Law-Its Use in Case of Atomic Attack* (Washington, D.C. Industrial College of the Armed Forces, 1956), p. 1, 2, 44-45, 81-82.
7 Howard Witt, "Lawyers Press U.S. on Martial Law Plans For War Survival," *Chicago Tribune*, August 15, 1983, Section 1, p. 12.
8 Tim Weiner, *Blank Check The Pentagons Black Budget* (N.Y: Warner Books, 1990), p. 54-55.
9 Bruce G. Blair, "Alerting in Crisis and Conventional War," in *Managing Nuclear Operations*, ed. by Ashton B. Carter, (Washington, D.C: The Brookings Institution, 1987), p. 116-117.
10 Alfonso Chardy, "Reagan Advisers Ran 'Secret' Government," *Miami Herald*, July 5, 1987, p. 1, 14; Alfonso Chardy, "North Helped Revise Wartime Plans," *Miami Herald*, July 19, 1987, p. 17; Joe Conason and Murray Waas, "The Enemy Within," *Village Voice*, July 21, 1987, p. 14-18, 32.
11 Chardy, July 5, 1987, *op. cit.*, Note 10, p. 1, 14.
12 *Ibid.*; Chardy, July 19, 1987, *op. cit.*, Note 10, p. 17.
13 Pete Earley, "Smith Accuses FEMA of Grab for Power," *Washington Post*, September 3, 1984, p. A19.
14 Lindorff, *op. cit.*, Note 1, p. 60.
15 Peck, op. cit., Note 3, p. 23.
16 Ted Gup, "How FEMA Learned to Stop Worrying About Civilians and Love the Bomb," *Mother Jones*, XIX (January/February, 1994), 28-31, 74, 76.
17 John Stockwell, *The Praetorian Guard* (Boston: South End Press, 1991), p. 20.
18 Tom Redmond, "Garden Plot-A Sweeping Martial Law Plan Developed in the 1960s-is Alive in SF," *San Francisco Bay Guardian*, September 8, 1987, p. 17-19; "Meese Acknowledges Counter-insurgency Role," *San Francisco Bay Guardian*, February 20, 1985, p. 5.
19 Melinda Beck, *et al.*, "'We Need Drastic Measures,'" *Newsweek*, March 13, 1989, p. 21.
20 Richard Lacayo, "Lock 'Em Up," *Time*, Febuary 7, 1994, p. 50-53.

21 Frank Lalli, "How Gramm Coddles Criminals, Not Investors," *Money*, XXIII (December, 1994), 5.
22 Robert Sherrill, "Ruthless Ambition Phil Gramm's Trail of Sleaze," *The Nation*, March 6, 1995, p. 301-306.
23 Karl Ross, "In Puerto Rico's War on Drugs, Combat Troops Reinforce Police," *Washington Post*, June 30, 1994, p. A3.
24 Robert S. Rivkin, *The Rights of Servicemen* (N.Y: Richard W. Baron, 1973), p. 104-109.
25 U.S., Congress, House, *Congressional Record*, June 9, 1994, p. H 4256-4258.
26 Rowan Scarborough, "American Medic is Poised to Snub United Nations Uniform," *Washington Times*, September 4-10, 1995, p. 17.
27 Peter Cassidy, "Silent Coup in Cyberspace," *Covert Action*, Number 52 (Spring, 1995), 54-56.
28 Weiner, *op. cit.*, Note 8, p. 121.
29 John Loftus and Mark Aarons, *The Secret War Against the Jews* (N.Y: St. Martin's Press, 1994), p. 181-196.
30 James Bamford, *The Puzzle Palace* (Boston: Houghton Mifflin Co., 1982), p. 366-367.
31 John Markoff, "FBI Wants Advanced System to Vastly Increase Wiretapping," *New York Times*, November 2, 1995, p. A1, C5.
32 Paul B. Carroll and Dianne Solis, "Reporter's Notebook: In Mexico, Corruption Fight Stirs Skepticism," *Wall Street Journal*, November 29, 1995, p. A11.
33 Frank J. Donner, *The Age of Surveillance* (N.Y: Alfred A. Knopf, 1980), p. 244-248.
34 Philip Colangelo, "The Secret FISA Court: Rubber Stamping on Rights," *Covert Action*, Number 53 (Summer, 1995), 43-49; James Bamford, *The Puzzle Palace* (Boston: Houghton Mifflin Co., 1982), p. 367-379.
35 Wayne Biddle, "Tapping Phone Records: They've Got Your Number," *The Nation*, October 26, 1992, p. 467, 468, 470.
36 Ford Rowan, *Techno Spies* (N.Y: G. P. Putnam's Sons, 1978), p. 152.
37 Lee Hockstader, "U.S. Offers Russians New Joint War Games, Research" *Washington Post*, May 6, 1994, p. A32.
38 William F. Jasper, "Fact and Fiction," *The New American*, October 31, 1994, p. 4-8, 25-31.
39 U.S., Congress, Senate, *Congressional Record*, November 5, 1993 p. S 15183.
40 Eric Schmitt, "Guardsmen Fight Cuts By Pentagon," *New York Times*, December 26, 1995, p. A1, A13.
41 Gregory Vistica, "Gangstas' in the Ranks," *Newsweek*, July 24, 1995, p. 48.
42 William Cooper, *Behold A Pale Horse* (Sedona, Az: Light Technology Publishing, 1991).
43 Dennis Cuddy, Ph.D., *The Road to Socialism and the New World Order* (Highland City, Fl: Florida Pro Family Forum, Inc., 1995), p. 77.

**Chapter XVI The Oklahoma Bombing**
1 Mary Anne Weaver, "Children of the Jihad," *The New Yorker*, June 12, 1995, 40-47.

2 Eleanor Randolph, "Prosecutors in Terrorism Trial 'Vent' Star Witness's Trouble With the Truth," *Washington Post*, March 13, 1995, p. A6.

3 James C. McKinley, Jr., "After the Trial, Many Questions Remain," *New York Times*, October 2, 1995, p. A10.

4 Ralph Blumenthal, "Tapes Depict Proposal to Thwart Bomb Used in Trade Center Blast," *New York Times*, October 28, 1993, p. A1, B3.

5 Elizabeth Gleick, "Something Big is Going to Happen," *Time*, May 8, 1995, p. 50.

6 Kevin Johnson, "No Racing Fuel in Okla. Bomb," *USA Today*, August 3, 1995, p. A2.

7 Jo Thomas, "Little Used Law Becomes A Lever," *New York Times*, August 29, 1995, p. A1, A9.

8 _____, "Sightings of John Doe No. 2: In Blast Case, Mystery No. 1," *New York Times*, December 3, 1995, p. 1, 22.

9 Melinda Liu, "A Case Built On a Web of Damning Detail," *Newsweek*, July 3, 1995, p. 28.

10 George J. Church, "A Two-Bit Conspiracy," *Time*, August 21, 1995, p. 25.

11 Jon Rappoport, *Oklahoma City Bombing The Suppressed Truth* (Los Angeles: Blue Press, 1995), p. 45-46; Richard A. Serrano, "Second Witness at Odds With Oklahoma Blast Theory," *Los Angeles Times*, September 8, 1995, p. A38.

12 Lawrence W. Myers, "A Closer Look," *Media Bypass*, III (December, 1995), 33-37; Lawrence W. Myers, "FBI Leaks Threaten Fair Trial for Kaczynski, Others Accused," *Media Bypass*, IV (June, 1996), 16-18.

13 William F. Jasper, "Explosive Evidence of a Cover-Up," *New American*, August 7, 1995, p. 4-7, 21-27.

14 Ted Gunderson, *The Gunderson Report on the Bombing of the Alfred P. Murrah Federal Building Oklahoma City, Oklahoma* April 19, 1995.

15 Scott Sandlin, "White Sands A Car Bomb Laboratory," *Albuquerque Journal*, July 16, 1995, p. A1.

16 William F. Jasper, "Were There Two Explosions?" *New American*, June 12, 1995, p. 15-7.

17 J.D. Cash and Jeff Holladay, "Feds Try to Discount 2nd Bomb Explosion," *McCurtain Daily Gazette*, June 4, 1995, p. 1, 2.

18 Jeff Holladay and J.D. Cash, "Secondary Explosion Revealed in Murrah Blast," *McCurtain Daily Gazette*, May 4, 1995, p. 1, 2.

19 William F. Jasper, "Seismic Support," *New American*, August 7, 1995, p. 13-16.

20 People interested in examining the scientific arguments in the debate can get a video for $15.00 from the Geophysical Society of Oklahoma City, P.O. Box 12163, Oklahoma City, Ok. 73157.

21 J.D. Cash and Jeff Holladay, "ATF's Explanation Disputed," *McCurtain Daily Gazette*, July 30, 1995, p. 1, 12.

22 Jeff Holladay, "Bomb Probe Beginning Today May Answer Questions," *McCurtain Daily Gazette*, May 5, 1995, p. 1.

23 J.D. Cash and Jeff Holladay, "Witnesses Confirm Explosives, Second Explosion," *McCurtain Daily Gazette*, June 25, 1995, p. 1, 2.

24 _____, "Worker Helped Remove Munitions, Missle from Murrah Building," *McCurtain Daily Gazette*, July 7, 1995, p. 1, 2.

25 _____, "Murrah Film Provokes New Call for Investigation," *McCurtain Daily Gazette*, September 10, 1995, p. 1, 2.
26 *Ibid.*, p. 1, 2.
27 J.D. Cash, "Feds Violated Explosives Law," *McCurtain Daily Gazette*, May 18, 1995, p. 1, 2.
28 Tom Morganthau, *et al.*, "Still Holes in the Case," *Newsweek*, August 21, 1995, p. 29.
29 Dave Hogan, "If He'd Been at Work...Former Portlander Says," *The Oregonian*, April 20, 1995, p. A9.
30 Arnold Hamilton, "Book Plot Parallels Bombing," *Dallas Morning News*, June 11, 1995, p. 46A.
31 Sherry Koonce, "Bombing Leaves Family Worried For Older Sister," *The Panola Watchman*, April 23, 1995, p. A1, A6.
32 Rapopport, *op. cit.*, Note 11, p. 66.
33 Cash, *op. cit.*, Note 21, p. 1, 12.
34 Lawrence W. Myers, "OKC Bombing Grand Jurors Claim 'Cover-Up,'" *Media Bypass*, III (November, 1995), 44-48.
35 Kevin Johnson, "A 'Terrible' Turn in Bomb Case," *USA Today*, October 19, 1995, p. 3A.
36 Morganthau, *op. cit.*, Note 28, p. 29.
37 Church, *op. cit.*, Note 10, p. 22-26.
38 Kevin Johnson, "Bombing Case Now Moves Into the Courtroom," *USA Today*, August 7, 1995, p. 8A.
39 Myers, *op. cit.*, Note 34, p. 44-48.
40 Ambrose Evans-Pritchard and Andrew Gimson, "Did Agents Bungle U.S. Terror Bomb?" *The Sunday Telegraph*, May 17, 1996, p. 26.
41 J.D. Cash and Jeff Holladay, "McVeigh, White Supremacists, German Linked by FBI Agent's Memo," *McCurtain Daily Gazette*, March 21, 1996, p. 1, 2.
42 Tim Kelsey, "British Link to U.S. Bomb Massacre," *London Sunday Times*, February 4, 1996, p. 1, 22.
43 J.D. Cash and Jeff Holladay, "FBI Ignored Lawman's Elohim City Information," *McCurtain Sunday Gazette and Broken Bow News*, April 14, 1996, p. 1, 12.
44 _____, "Is Tulsa Resident John Doe No. 2?" *McCurtain Daily Gazette*, February 27, 1996, p. 2, 4.
45 "Mystery Surrounds German's Link to Bombing," *McCurtain Sunday Gazette and Broken Bow News*, February 4, 1996, p. 1, 12.
46 William F. Jasper, "New Charges of OKC Cover-Up," *New American*, November 27, 1995, p. 6.
47 Evans-Pritchard, *op. cit.*, Note 40, p. 26.
48 James C. McKinley, Jr., "After the Trial, Many Questions Remain," *New York Times*, October 2, 1995, p. A10; Morganthau, *op. cit.*, Note 28, p. 29.

**Chapter XVII Recent Attacks on the Militias and Patriot Movement**
1 John Harwood, "Equal Hostility: Women Are Angry at Government Too," *Wall Street Journal*, May 12, 1995, p. A1, A14; Katy Kelly, "Women Find Niche in Militias," *USA Today*, May 16, 1995, p. 6D.

2 Bill Wallace, "A Call to Arms," *San Francisco Chronicle*, March 12, 1995, p. 1, 5.
3 Alan W. Bock, "Weekend Warriors," *National Review*, May 29, 1995, p. 41.
4 Wallace, *op. cit.*, Note 2, p. 1, 5.
5 Keith Schneider, "Fearing A Conspiracy, Some Heed a Call to Arms," *New York Times*, November 14, 1994, p. A12.
6 Mike Tharp, "The Growing Militias: Thunder on the Far Right," *U.S. News & World Report*, May 1, 1995, p. 36.
7 Rebecca Shelton, "The New Minutemen," *Kansas City New Times*, February 22, 1995.
8 Jill Smolowe, "Enemies of the State," *Time*, May 8, 1995, p. 58-64, 66, 68-69.
9 Jesse Walker, "The Populist Rainbow," *Chronicles*, (March, 1996), 25-27; Jonathan Karl, "Birds of a Feather? White Militia Bigs Like Farrakhan," *New York Post*, October 19, 1995.
10 Jonathan Vankin, *Conspiracies Cover-Ups and Crimes* (N.Y: Dell Publishing, 1995), p. xiii.
11 These shows take place several times a year. Preparedness Shows P.O. Box 25454 Salt Lake City, Utah 84125 (801-265-8828).
12 Schneider, *op. cit.*, Note 5, p. A12.
13 Albert R. Hunt, "Stop Encouraging the Crazies," *Wall Street Journal*, April 27, 1995, p. A15.
14 Mack Tanner, "Extreme Prejudice," *Reason*, XXVII (July, 1995), 45.
15 Virginia I. Postrel, "Fighting Words," *Reason*, XXVII (July, 1995), 4, 6, 7.
16 Psychiatrists' Forum "Health Care: Air or Software?" *Clinical Psychiatry News*, (October, 1994), 22.
17 Mark Potok and Katy Kelly, "Militia Movement Draw: A Shared Anger, Fear," *USA Today*, May 16, 1995, p. D16.
18 Joe Urschel, "Sentiments Not Held Only by the Fringe," *USA Today*, May 16, 1995, p. A1, A2.
19 Alfred Adask, "Fed Fear," *AntiShyster*, V (Spring, 1995), 3-6.
20 Richard Morin, "Anger at Washington Cools in Aftermath of Bombing," *Washington Post*, May 18, 1995, p. A1, A14.
21 Charles V. Zehren, "Vitriolic Reaction to Militia Stance Shocks Lawmaker," *The Boston Globe*, July 9, 1995, p. 16.
22 Noam Chomsky, "Democracy's Slow Death," *In These Times*, November 28, 1994, p. 25-28.
23 David Barsamian, "Militias and Conspiracy Theories," *Z Magazine*, VIII (September, 1995), 29-35.
24 David Helvarg, *The War Against the Greens* (San Francisco, Ca: Sierra Club, 1994), p. 364-5.
25 David Helvarg and Alexander Cockburn, "Exchange," *The Nation*, August 14/21, 1995, p. 150.
26 Robert Perkinson, "Oklahoma Fallout," *Z Magazine*, VIII (July/August, 1995), 8-11.
27 Erik Davis, "The Right Wing Hunkers Down on Line: Barbed Wire Net," *Village Voice*, May 2, 1995, p. 28.
28 "Maine Novelist Organizes a Populist 'Militia,'" *New York Times*, February 19, 1996, p. A7.

29 "Militia Roundup," *The Progressive*, 59 (August, 1995), 6; "Militias-Ness," *The Nation*, July 17/24, 1995, p. 74.
30 Paul Glastris, "Patriot Games," *Washington Monthly*, XXVII (June, 1995), 23-26.
31 Michael Kelly, "The Road to Paranoia," *The New Yorker*, June 19, 1995, p. 60-75.
32 Chip Berlet and Matthew N. Lyons, "Militia Nation," *The Progressive*, 59 (June, 1995), 22-25.
33 Marc Cooper, "Camouflage Days, E-Mail Nights," *The Nation*, October 23, 1995, p. 464-466.
34 Alexander Cockburn, "Beat the Devil: Who's Left? Who's Right?" *The Nation*, June 12, 1995, p. 820-821.
35 _____, "Beat the Devil: Liberals as Cops, Liberals as Bombers," *The Nation*, June 26, 1995, p. 911.
36 Barbara Dority, "Is the Extremist Right Entirely Wrong?" *The Humanist*, 55 (November/December, 1995), p. 12-15.
37 Mack Tanner, "Extreme Prejudice," *Reason*, XXVII (July, 1995), 42-50.
38 Steven Stark, "Right Wing Populism," *Atlantic Monthly*, 277 (February, 1996), 19-20, 28-29.
39 Charles A. Reich, *Opposing the System* (N.Y: Crown Publishers, Inc. 1995), p. 52.
40 Stephen Budiansky, "One More Leap for Nuttiness," *U.S. News & World Report*, October 23, 1995, p. 14-15.
41 Philip Shenon, "U.S. Army Says Rightist Militias May Be Recruiting Elite Troops," *New York Times*, March 22, 1996, p. A1, 12; "Notebook," *New Republic*, January, 1, 1996, p. 8.
42 Robby Trammell, "Informant Proud of Role in Arrests of Bomb-Plot Suspects," *The Daily Oklahoman*, November 15, 1995, p. 1-2; Doug Ferguson, "'Prophet,' Ex-Corporate Pilot Indicted in Bombing Plot," *The Daily Oklahoman*, November 16, 1995, p. 12.
43 Audrey Post, "Magistrate Delays Ruling to Examine Evidence More Closely," *The Macon Telegraph*, May 7, 1996, p. A1, 10; Audrey Post, "Starr, McCranie Plead Not Guilty in Federal Court," *The Macon Telegraph*, May 31, 1996, p. B1.

**Chapter XVIII Murder as a Political Weapon in America**
1 William W. Turner and John Christian, *The Assassination of Robert F. Kennedy. A Searching Look at the Conspiracy and Coverup, 1968-1978* (N.Y: Random House, 1978); "And Now, Who Shot R.F.K.?" *Time*, 141 (June 7, 1993), p. 45.
2 John Edginton and John Sergeant, "The Murder of Martin Luther King Jr.," *Covert Action*, Number 34 (Summer, 1990), 21-27.
3 Michael Parenti and Peggy Noton, "The Wonderful Life and Strange Death of Walter Reuther," *Covert Action*, Number 54 (Fall, 1995), 37-43.
4 Jerry Hopkins and Danny Sugerman, *No One Here Gets Out Alive* (N.Y: Warner Books, 1980).
5 Robert J. Groden and Harrison E. Livingtone, *High Treason* (Boothwyn, Pa: The Conservatory Press, 1989), p. 125-126.
6 Geoffrey Sea, "The Radiation Story No One Would Touch," *Columbia Journal Review*, XXXII (March/April 1994), 37-40.

7 Karen Lee Bixman, "Obstruction of Justice: Exposing the Inslaw Scandal and Related Crimes," *Media Bypass*, III (June, 1995), 33-37.

8 Michael Kitchen, "Who Killed Vince Foster?" *Soldier of Fortune*, XIX (June, 1994), 45-47; Ambrose Evans-Pritchard, "A Death That Won't Die," *The American Spectator*, XXVIII (November, 1995), 35-38.

9 Gregory Jaynes, "The Death of Hope," *Esquire*, 120 (November, 1993), 86.

10 "Whitewater: Curiouser," *The Economist*, July 9, 1994, p. 29-30.

11 William Cooper, *Behold A Pale Horse* (Sedona, Az: Light Technology Publishing, 1991), p. 27.

12 Rodney Stich, *Defrauding America* (Alamo, Ca: Diablo Western Press, Inc., 1993), p. 306-9, 535.

13 Nina Archer Biddle, "He Didn't Commit Suicide," *Newsweek*, CXXIV (September 19, 1994), p. 35.

14 David Zucchino, "The Suicide Files: Death in the Military," *The Philadelphia Inquirer*, December 19-22, 1993.

15 Stich, *op. cit.*, Note 12, p. 406.

16 "Tribute to the Late Mae Brussell," Archives on Audio, radio telecast, M27 E and F. Produced by Dave Emory.

17 Anatoliy Golitsyn, *New Lies For Old* (N.Y: Dodd, Mead & Co., 1984), p. 352.

18 "Deadly Drug Kept Secret," *San Francisco Chronicle*, April 15, 1978, p. 35.

19 U.S. Congress, Senate, *Intelligence Committee* Final Report, Book IV, p. 136. 1975; United Press, September 23, 1975; Groden, *op. cit.*, Note 5, p. 364.

20 Ralph Blumenthal, "An Upstate Murder in 1983 is Reported Linked to Iran Arms Smuggling," *New York Times*, December 2, 1986, p. A15.

21 "Casey Death Probes Reported," *San Francisco Chronicle*, July 20, 1987, p. 8.

22 *The Tower Commission Report* (N.Y: Times Book and Bantam Books, 1987), p. 169.

23 "Mysterious Death of Iranian Arms Dealer Under Investigation," *San Jose Mercury News*, June 13, 1987, p. 21A.

24 "Loss of a Leader," *Newsweek*, July 11, 1988, p. 5.

25 "The Hit on Jimmy Hoffa," *Playboy*, XXXVI (November, 1989), 62-64, 74-77, 165-166.

26 Michael Kelly, "The Road to Paranoia," *The New Yorker*, LXXI (June 19, 1995), p. 72.

## Chapter XIX Radiation, Biological, and Chemical Experiments on People

1 Emily G. Harris, "Human Radiation Tests: An Old Story Finally Makes the Front Page" *Extra*, VII (May/June, 1994), 19-20; Geoffrey Sea, "The Radiation Story No One Would Touch," *Columbia Journal Review*, XXXII (March/April, 1994), 37-40; Debra D. Durocher, "Rereporting the News," *American Journalism Review*, XVI (March, 1994), 34-37.

2 Thomas Saffer and Orville Kelly, *Countdown Zero* (N.Y: Penguin Books, 1982), p. 309.

3 "Informed Consent," *Mother Jones*, VI (September/October, 1981), 31-37.

4 U.S. Congress, House, Subcommittee on Energy, Conservation and Power, *American Nuclear Guinea Pigs: Three Decades of Radiation Experiments on U.S.*

*Citizens*, Hearing, October 1986, (Washington, D.C: Government Printing Office, 1986), p. 2.
5 Philip J. Hilts, "Inquiry on Radiation Tests Links U.S. Secrecy to Fear of Lawsuits," *New York Times*, December 15, 1994, p. A14; Tod Ensign and Glenn Alcalay, "Duck and Cover(up): U.S. Radiation Testing on Humans," *Covert Action*, Number 49 (Summer, 1994), 28-35.
6 Philip J. Hilts, "Healthy People Secretly Poisoned in 40's Test," *New York Times*, January 19, 1995, p. A13.
7 "Radiation Experiment Number Is Doubled by U.S., to 16,000," *New York Times*, August 20, 1995, p. A13.
8 Douglas Pasternak and Peter Cary, "Tales From the Crypt," *U.S. News & World Report*, September 18, 1995, p. 70, 77-78, 80-82.
9 *Ibid.*, p. 80.
10 Tim Weiner, "CIA seeks Documents From its Radiation Tests," *New York Times*, January 5, 1994, p. A11.
11 Harvey Wasserman and Norman Solomon. *Killing Our Own* (N.Y: Dell Publishing Co., Inc., 1982), p. 71.
12 Mary Manning, "Atomic Vets Battle Time," *The Bulletin of the Atomic Scientist*, 51 (January/February, 1995), 54-60.
13 Wasserman, *op. cit.*, Note 11, p. 72.
14 Deborah Hastings, "Widow Battles for Truth on Radiation," *San Francisco Chronicle*, January 23, 1994, p. B1.
15 Allan Favish, "Radiation Injury and Atomic Veterans: Shifting the Burden of Proof on Factual Causation," *Hastings Law Journal*, XXXII (March, 1981), 933-974.
16 Robert Dvorchak, "Deadly Cloud Hangs Over A Bomb Test," *Marin Independent Journal*, April 3, 1994, p. A10.
17 General Accounting Office, "Nuclear Health and Safety: Examples of Post World War II Radiation Releases at U.S. Nuclear Sites," RCED 94-51 FS, November, 1993.
18 Sea, *op. cit.*, Note 1, p. 38.
19 Stewart L. Udall, *The Myths of August* (N.Y: Pantheon, 1994).
20 R. Jeffrey Smith, "Atom Bomb Tests Leave Infamous Legacy," *Science*, 218, October 15, 1982, p. 266-269.
21 Karl Grossman, Three Mile Island: "They Say Nothing Happened" *Extra*, VI (July/August, 1993), 6.
22 Michael D'Antonio, *Atomic Harvest* (N.Y: Crown Publishing Group, 1993), p. xii.
23 *Ibid.*, p. 6-7.
24 Ferdinand Lundberg, *Myth of Democracy* (N.Y: Carol Publishing Group, 1989), p. 87.
25 John Downey, "We Are All Downwinders," *Lies of Our Times*, (April, 1994), 14-19.
26 Carole Gallagher, *American Ground Zero: The Secret Nuclear War* (Cambridge, Ma: MIT Press, 1993), p. 325-333; Gayle Greene, "Daughter of Time," *In These Times*, April 29, 1996, p. 17-19.
27 Karen Freeman, "The Unfought Chemical War," *The Bulletin of the Atomic Scientist*, 47 (December, 1991), 30-39.

28 Nicholas Kristof, "Japan Confronting Gruesome War Atrocity," *New York Times*, March 17, 1995, p. A1, 4; Sheldon H. Harris, *Factories of Death* (N.Y: Routledge, 1994).

29 Karen Freeman, "The VA's Sorry, The Army's Silent," *The Bulletin of the Atomic Scientists*, 49 (March, 1993), 39-43.

30 Ken Lawrence, "The History of U.S. Bio-Chemical Killers," *Covert Action*, Number 17 (Summer, 1982), 5-7; Robert Lederer, "Chemical-Biological Warfare, Medical Experiments, and Population Control," *Covert Action*, Number 28 (Summer, 1987), 33-42.

31 Louis Wolf, "This Side of Nuclear War: The Pentagon's Other Option," *Covert Action*, Number 17 (Summer, 1982), 16-17.

32 "Biological War Testing in 1953 by Army Probed," *San Francisco Examiner*, June 26, 1994.

33 Lederer, *op. cit.*, Note 30, p. 36.

34 *Ibid.*, p. 35; Jessica Mitford, *Kind and Usual Punishment: The Prison Business* (N.Y: Alfred A. Knopf, 1973), p. 138-167.

35 Jeanne McDermott, *The Killing Winds: The Menace of Biological Warfare* (N.Y: Arbot House, 1987); Charles Piller, "DNA-Key to Biological Warfare?" *The Nation*, December 10, 1983, p. 585, 597-600; Charles Piller and Keith R. Yamamoto, *Gene Wars: Military Control Over the New Genetic Technologies* (N.Y: William Morrow, 1988).

36 Robert Harris and Jeremy Paxman, *A Higher Form of Killing* (N.Y: Hill and Wand, 1982), p. 241.

37 U.S., Congress, House, Testimony before a sub-committee of the House Committee on Appropriations, Department of Defense Appropriations for 1970, Washington, 1969.

38 Alfred Adask, "Gulf War Illness," *AntiShyster*, V (Summer, 1995), p. 17-22.

39 "Informed Sources," *Time*, June 6, 1994, p. 13.

40 Dennis Bernstein, "Gulf War Syndrome: The Cover-up Unravels," *San Francisco Bay Guardian*, April 5, 1995, p. 19; Dennis Bernstein, "Gulf War Syndrome Covered Up Chemical and Biological Agents Exposed," *Covert Action*, Number 53 (Summer, 1995), 6-12.

41 Stephen J. Hedges, *et al.*, "Baghdad's Dirty Secrets," *U.S. News & World Report*, September 11, 1995, p. 41-43.

42 Kenneth Timmerman, "The Iraq Papers," *New Republic*, January 29, 1996, p. 12, 14-15; Stephen R. Weissman, "A Culture of Deference," (N.Y: Basic Books, 1995), p. 181.

43 To contact Peter Kawaja 4338 Sugar Pine Drive Boca Raton, Fl. 33487 (407) 241-8407.

44 For assistance contact: American Gulf War Veterans Association 3506 Highway 6 South #117 Sugarland, Tx. 77478-4401 (713)-587-5437.

45 Marlene Cimons, "Gulf War Syndrome May Be Contagious, Survey Shows," *Los Angeles Times*, October 21, 1994, p. A4.

46 George J. Annas and Michael A. Grodin, "Our Guinea Pigs in the Gulf," *New York Times*, January 3, 1991, p. A21.

47 Bernstein, *Covert Action, op. cit.*, Note 40, p. 11-12.

48' The Nicholsons will do a free test for those in need. Dr Garth Nicholson, University of Texas M.D. Anderson Cancer Center, 1515 Holcomb Bl, Houston, Tx. 77030. (713)-792-7477.

49 Alfred Adask, "Gulf War Illness," *AntiShyster*, V (Summer, 1995), 17-22.

50 To learn more about stopping MTBE contact Oxybusters of Texas Guy Baird 412 Monterrey Victoria, Tx. 77904. Phone 713-905-7567 To complain to the EPA call 800-621-8431.

51 Lisabeth Hush, "A Preference For Poison: Malathion...The Drug War Continues," *Perceptions*, I (Spring, 1994), 6-11.

52 Val Valerian, "On the Toxic Nature of Fluorides," *Perceptions*, II (September/October, 1995), 30-32, 34, 36-37.

53 The Safe Water Foundation 6439 Taggart Rd. Delaware, Ohio 43015 (614)-548-5340.

54 John Stauber and Sheldon Rampton, "The Public Relations Industry's Secret War on Activists," *Covert Action*, Number 55 (Winter 1995), 18-26, 57; Joel Bleifuss, "Slinging Sludge," *In These Times*, June 10, 1996, p. 12-13.

55 Will Fantle, "BGH Hotline Helps Farmers," *The Progressive*, 59 (July, 1995), 6.

56 Pure Food 1130 17th St. #300 Washington, D.C. 20036 1-800-451-7670.

57 Alex Constantine, "NutraSweet TM, the NutraPoison," *Prevailing Winds*, Number 1, p. 40-49.

58 Aspartame Consumer Safety Network P.O. Box 780634 Dallas, Tx. 75378. Phone 214-352-4268.

59 J. Barna, "Compilation of Bioassay Data on the Wholesomeness of Irradiated Food Items," *Acta Alimentaria*, VIII (1979), 205.

60 Sharon Begley and Elizabeth Roberts, "Dishing Up Gamma Rays," *Newsweek*, January 27, 1992, p. 52; Susan Meeker-Lowry, "From Irradiation To Electronic Pasteurization," *Z Magazine*, IX (May, 1996), 34-40.

61 Food and Water, Inc. RR 1, Box 114 Marshfield, Vt. 05658-9702. Phone 802-426-3700.

## Chapter XX Restoring Constitutional Government

1 "Excerpts From Remarks by David Rockefeller," *BCUN Briefing*, VIII (1994), p. 1

2 Arthur Schlesinger, Jr., "Back to the Womb?" *Foreign Affairs*, 74 (July/August, 1995), 8.

3 Karl-Otto Liebmann, "Blueprint for Managed Foodcare," *Wall Street Journal*, January 10, 1996, p, A14.

4 Lt. Colonel Thomas H. Reese, "An Officer's Oath," *Military Law Review*, (July, 1964), p. 5-41; Edward M. Coffman, "The Army Officer and the Constitution," *Parameters*, XVII (September, 1987), 2-12.

5 Douglas Waller, "Master of the Game," *Time*, May 6, 1996, p. 41-43.

6 Arthur Miller, *Democratic Dictatorship The Emergent Constitution of Control* (London: Greenwood Press, 1981), p. xi, xiv, 184.

7 "A Course Toward National Bankruptcy," *U.S. New & World Report*, August 22, 1994, p. 10.

8 Save the AIDS Book Legal Defense Fund 4141 Ball Road #157 Cypress, Ca. 90630 (805) 681-9988.

9 C.B. Dall, *FDR, My Exploited Father-in-Law* (Tulsa, Ok: Christian Crusade Publications, 1968) p. 59.

10 Jim R. Norman, "The Still Before the Storm," *Media Bypass*, III (December, 1995), 22-26.

11 Gore Vidal, "The Union of the State," *The Nation*, December 26, 1994, p. 789-790, 792.

12 _____, *The Decline and Fall of American Empire* (Berkeley, Ca: Odonian Press, 1992), p. 50-52, 57.

13 Wesley A. Riddle, "Secession and the Moral Compact," *Vital Speeches of the Day*, August 1, 1995, p. 635-639.

14 Charles A. Reich, *Opposing the System* (N.Y: Crown Publishers, Inc., 1995), p. 5, 151-3.

15 Timothy G. Beckley and Arthur Crockett, *Prophecies of the Presidents* (New Brunswick, N.J: Inner Light Publications, 1992), p. 94.

16 Peter A. Brown, "Term Limits Are Changing How State Governments Run," *San Francisco Examiner*, August 28, 1994, p. A7.

17 Arthur Schlesinger, Jr., "Election '94: Not Realignment but Dealignment," *Wall Street Journal*, November 16, 1994, p. A34.

18 Carroll Quigley, *Tragedy and Hope: A History of the World in Our Time* (N.Y: The MacMillian Co., 1966), p. 73.

19 Paul A. Gigot, "So How Much of a Revolution is This, Really?" *Wall Street Journal*, October 27, 1995, p. A14; Kevin Phillips, "The Champagne's Gone Flat," *Washington Post National Weekly*, August 14-20, 1995, p. 23.

20 Wray Herbert, "The Spirit of Politics," *U.S. News & World Report*, November 14, 1994, p. 115-116, 118.

21 Wesley Bramshaw, "Washington's Dream," *National Tribune*, December, 1880, p.1.

22 Beckley, *op. cit.*, Note 15, p.13-14.

# Bibliography

Adams, Frank T. *Taking Care of Business: Citizen and the Charter of Incorporation.* Cambridge, Ma: Charter, Ink, 1993.

Adams, James R, and Douglas Frantz. *A Full Service Bank.* N.Y: Simon & Schuster, Inc., 1992.

Allen, Gary. *None Dare Call It Conspiracy.* Seal Beach, Ca: Concord Press, 1971.

_____.*The Rockefeller File.* Seal Beach, Ca: '76 Press, 1976.

_____.*Say No To the New World Order.* Seal Beach, Ca: Concord Press, 1987.

Allison, Graham, Albert Carnesale, and Joseph Nye, Jr. *Fateful Visions.* Cambridge, Ma: Ballinger Publ. Co., 1988.

Archer, Jules. *The Plot To Seize the White House.* N.Y: Hawthorn Books, Inc., 1973.

Baker, Jeffrey A. *Cheque Mate: The Game of Princes.* St. Petersburg, Fl: Group I-The Baker Group, Inc., 1993.

Barber, Richard J. *The American Corporation: Its Power, Its Money, Its Politics.* N.Y: E. P. Dutton & Co., Inc., 1970.

Barnet, Richard J. and John Cavanagh. *Global Dreams Imperial Corporations and the New World Order.* N.Y: Simon & Schuster, 1994.

Beaty, Jonathan, and S.C. Gwaynne. *The Outlaw Bank BCCI.* N.Y: Random House, 1993.

Beckley, Timothy G., and Arthur Crockett. *Prophecies of the Presidents.* New Brunswick, N.J: Inner Light Publications, 1992.

Bellant, Russ. *Old Nazis, the New Right and the Republican Party.* Boston: South End Press, 1989.

Bensel, Richard F. *Yankee Leviathan.* N.Y: Cambridge University Press, 1990.

Bernstein, Barton J. "American Foreign Policy and the Origins of the Cold War." In *Politics and Policies of the Truman Administration,* edited by Barton J. Bernstein. Chicago: Quadrangle Books, 1970.

_____. "The New Deal: The Conservative Achievements of Liberal Reform." In *Towards A New Past: Dissenting Essays in American History,* edited by Barton J. Bernstein. N.Y: Pantheon Books, 1968.

Blair, Bruce G. "Alerting in Crisis and Conventional War." In *Managing Nuclear Operations,* edited by Ashton B. Carter. Washington, D.C: The Brookings Institution, 1987.

Blount, George W. *Peace Through World Government.* Durham, N.C: Moore Publishing Co., 1974.

Boritt, Gabor S. *Lincoln the War President.* N.Y: Oxford University Press, 1992.

Bosworth, Allan R. *America's Concentration Camps.* N.Y: W.W. Norton and Co. Inc., 1967.

Bower, Tom. *The Paperclip Conspiracy: The Hunt for the Nazi Scientists.* Boston: Little, Brown and Co., 1987.

Boyd, Steven R. *Alternative Constitutions for the United States.* Westport, Ct: Westport, 1992.

Brackman, Arnold C. *The Other Nuremberg The Untold Story of the Tokyo War Crimes Trials*. N.Y. William Morrow and Co., 1987.

Brands, H.W. *The Devil We Knew: Americans and the Cold War*. N.Y: Oxford University Press, 1993.

Brecher, Jeremy, and Tim Costello. *Global Village or Global Pillage*. Boston: South End Press, 1994.

Brecher, Jeremy, and John B. Childs. *Global Visions: Beyond the New World Order*. Boston: South End Press, 1993.

Brewton, Pete. *The Mafia, CIA and George Bush*. N.Y: Shapolsky Publishers, Inc., 1991.

Brzezinski, Zbigniew. *Between Two Ages*. N.Y: The Viking Press, 1970.

Bundy, Edgar C. *Collectivism in the Churches*. Wheaton, Ill: The Church League of America, 1958.

Carlson, John Roy. *Under Cover*. N.Y: E.P. Dutton & Co., Inc., 1943.

Chesterton, A.K. *The New Unhappy Lords*. London: The Candour Publishing Co., 1965.

Chesterton, G.K. "What of the Republic?" In *The Collected Works of G. K. Chesterton What I Saw in America*, Vol XXI, edited by Robert Royal San Francisco: Ignatius Press, 1990.

Chomsky, Noam. *Deterring Democracy*. N.Y: Verso, 1991.

_____.*World Orders Old and New*. N.Y: Columbia U. Press, 1994.

Churchill, Ward, and Jim Vander Wall. *Agents of Repression: the FBI's Secret War Against the Black Panter Party and the American Indian Movement*. Boston: South End Press, 1988.

Clark, Grenville, and Louis Sohn. *Introduction to World Peace Through World Law*. Chicago: World Without War Publications, 1958.

*.World Peace Through World Law*. Cambridge, Mass: Harvard University Press, 1966.

Cole, Wayne S. *Roosevelt and the Isolationists, 1932-45*. Lincoln, Neb: University of Nebraska Press, 1983.

_____.*Senator Gerald P. Nye and American Foreign Relations*. Minneapolis: The University of Minnesota Press, 1962.

Coleman, John. *Conspirators' Hierarchy: The Story of the Committee of 300*. Bozeman, MT: America West Publishers, 1992.

Constantine, Alex. *Blood, Carnage and the Agent Provocateur*. Los Angeles, 1993.

Corn, David. *Blond Ghost: Ted Shackley and the CIAs Crusades*. N.Y: Simon & Schuster, 1994.

Corwin, Edward S., and Richard Loss. *Presidential Power and the Constitution*. Ithaca, N.Y: Cornell University Press, 1976.

Courtney, Kent, and Phoebe Courtney. *America's Unelected Rulers*. New Orleans, La: A Conservative Society of American Publication, 1962.

Crozier, Michel J., Samuel P. Huntington, and Joji Watanuki. *The Crisis of Democracy*. N.Y: The Trilateral Commission, 1975.

Cuddy, Dennis L, and Robert H. Goldsborough. *The New World Order: Chronology and Commentary*. Baltimore, Md: The American Research Foundation, Inc., 1992.

_____.*The New World Order: A Critique and Chronology*. St. Louis: America's Future, 1992.

_____.*President Clinton Will Continue The New World Order*. Oklahoma City, Ok: Southwest Radio Church, 1993.

_____.*The Road to Socialism and the New World Order*. Highland City, Fl: Florida Pro Family Forum, Inc., 1995.

_____. *Secret Records Revealed*. Marborough, N.H: The Plymouth Rock Foundation, 1994.

Dall, C.B. *FDR, My Exploited Father-in-Law*. Tulsa, Ok: Christian Crusade Publications, 1968.

D'Antonio, Michael. *Atomic Harvest*. N.Y: Crown Publishing Group, 1993.

Denney, Robert E. *The Civil War Years*. N.Y: Sterling Publishing Co., 1994.

Diggins, John P. *Mussolini and Fascism: The View from America*. Princeton, N.J: Princeton University Press, 1972.

Domhoff, G. William. *Who Rules America Now?* Englewood Cliffs, N.J: Prentice-Hall, Inc., 1983.

Donner. Frank. J. *The Age of Surveillance*. N.Y: Alfred A. Knopf, 1980.

Dulles, John Foster. *War or Peace*. N.Y: The Macmillian Co., 1950.

Edwards III, George C., and Wallace E. Walker., eds. *National Security and the U.S. Constitution*. Baltimore: The John Hopkins University Press, 1988.

Ehrlich, Paul. *The Population Bomb*. N.Y: Ballantine, 1978.

Emerson, Steven. *Secret Warriors*. N.Y: G.P. Putnam's Sons, 1988.

Epperson, A. Ralph. *Clinton's Conspiracy*. Tucson, Az: Publius Press, 1992.

Ewen, Stuart. *Captains of Consciousness*. N.Y: McGraw-Hill, 1976.

Fairman, Charles. *The Law of Martial Law*. Chicago: Callaghan & Co., 1930.

Falk, Richard. *A Study of Future Worlds*. N.Y: The Free Press, 1975.

Flynn, John T. *The Roosevelt Myth*. N.Y: The Devin-Adair Company, 1948.

Fones-Wolf, Elizabeth. *Selling Free Enterprise: The Business Assault on Labor and Liberalism*. Chicago: University of Illinois Press, 1994.

Foreman, Richard. *Leasing the Ivory Tower: The Corporate Takeover of Academia*. Boston: South End Press, 1995.

Fresia, Jerry. *Toward An American Revolution*. Boston: South End Press, 1988.

Fuller, R. Buckminster. *Critical Path*. N.Y: St Martin's Press, 1981.

Gallagher, Carole. *American Ground Zero: The Secret Nuclear War*. Cambridge, Ma: MIT Press, 1993.

Gelbspan, Ross. *Break-ins Death Threats and the FBI: the Covert War Against the Central American Movement*. Boston: South End Press, 1991.

George, John., and Laird Wilcox. *Nazis, Communists, Klansmen, and Others on the Fringe*. Buffalo, N.Y: Prometheus Books, 1992.

Gill, Stephen. *American Hegemony and the Trilateral Commission*. Cambridge: Cambridge University Press, 1990.

Glick, Brian. *War At Home*. Boston: South End Press, 1989.

Goldsmith, James. *The Trap*. N.Y: Carroll and Graf Publishing, Inc., 1994.

Goldwater, Barry. *The Conscience of A Conservative*. Shepherdsville, Ky: Victor Publishing Co., Inc., 1960.

_____.*With No Apologies*. N.Y: William Morrow and Co., 1979.

Golitsyn, Anatoliy. *New Lies For Old*. N.Y: Dodd, Mead & Co., 1984.

Greider, William. *Who Will Tell the People*. N.Y: Simon & Schuster, 1992.

Groden, Robert J., and Harrison E. Livingtone. *High Treason*. Boothwyn, Pa: The Conservatory Press, 1989.

Gross, Bertram. *Friendly Fascism*. Boston: South End Press, 1980.

Haacke, Hans. "Museums, Managers of Consciousness." In *Hans Haacke Unfinished Business*, edited by Brian Wallis. Cambridge: MIT Press, 1986.

Habermas, Jurgen. *The Structural Transformation of the Public Sphere.* Cambridge: MIT Press, 1962.

Hacker, Andrew, ed. *The Corporation Take-Over.* Garden City, N.Y: Anchor Books, 1965.

Halperin, Morton H., and Daniel Hoffman. *Freedom vs. National Security.* N.Y: Chelsea House Publishers, 1977.

Harmon, Willis W., and O.W. Markley, eds. *Changing Images of Man.* Elmsford, N.Y: Pergamon Press, 1982.

Harris, Robert, and Jeremy Paxman. *A Higher Form of Killing.* N.Y: Hill and Wand, 1982.

Harris, Sheldon. *Factories of Death: Japanese Secret Biological Warefare Projects in Manchuria and China 1932-45 and the American Cover-Up.* N.Y: Routledge, 1994.

Heinlein, Robert A. *Take Back Your Government.* N.Y: Simon & Schuster, 1992.

Helvarg, David. *The War Against the Greens.* San Francisco, Ca: Sierra Club, 1994.

Higham, Charles. *American Swastika.* Garden City, N.Y: Doubleday & Co., Inc., 1985.

_____. *Trading With the Enemy.* N.Y: Delacorte Press, 1983.

Hopkins, Jerry, and Danny Sugerman. *No One Here Gets Out Alive.* N.Y: Warner Books, 1980.

Hunt, Linda. *Secret Agenda.* N.Y: St. Martin's Press, 1991.

Johnson, Loch K. *America's Secret Power The CIA in a Democratic Society.* N.Y: Oxford University Press, 1989.

Karp, Walter. *Buried Alive.* N.Y: Franklin Square Press, 1992.

_____. *Indispensable Enemies.* N.Y: Saturday Review Press, 1973.

_____. *Liberty Under Siege.* N.Y: Henry Holt & Co., 1988.

Kauffman, Bill. *America First.* Amherst, N.Y: Prometheus Books, 1995.

Kennedy, James R., and Walter D. Kennedy. *The South Was Right.* Gretna, La: Pelican Publishing Co., 1991.

Kennon, Patrick E. *The Twilight of Democracy.* N.Y: Doubleday, 1995.

Kidd, Devvy. *Ever Wonder Why: Project '93.* Boulder, Co: Wayv, 1993.

Kilpatrick, James J. *The Sovereign States.* Chicago: Henry Regnery Co., 1957.

King, Alexander, and Bertrand Schneider. *The First Global Revolution A Report By the Council of the Club of Rome.* N.Y: Pantheon Books, 1991.

King, Mary. *Freedom Song.* N.Y: William Morrow and Co., Inc., 1987.

Kofsky, Frank. *Harry S. Truman and the War Scare of 1948.* N.Y: St. Martin's Press, 1993.

Kotz, David M. *Bank Control of Large Corporations in the United States.* Berkeley: University of California Press, 1978.

Kuhn, Thomas S. *The Structure of Scientific Revolutions.* Chicago: University of Chicago Press, 1970.

Lang, Tim, Kathleen Tucker, and Tony Webb. *Food Irradiation Who Wants It.* Rochester, Vt: Thorsons Publishers, Inc., 1987.

Lapham, Lewis H. *Money and Class In America.* N.Y: Weidenfeld & Nicolson, 1988.

_____.*The Wish For Kings*. N.Y: Grove Press, 1993.

LaPierre, Wayne R. *Guns, Crime, and Freedom*. Washington, D.C: Regnery Publishing, Inc., 1994.

Lasch, Christopher. *Betrayal of Democracy*. N.Y: W.W. Norton & Co., 1995.

Lasswell, Harold D. *National Security and Individual Freedom*. N.Y: Da Capo Press, 1971.

Leach, William. *Land of Desire*. N.Y: Pantheon Books, 1993.

Leffler, Melvyn P. *A Ponderance of Power: National Security, the Truman Administration and the Cold War*. Stanford, Ca: Stanford U. Press, 1991.

Levy, Leonard W. *Original Intent and the Framers Constitution*. N.Y: MacMillan Publishing Co., 1988.

Lewin, Leonard C. *Report From Iron Mountain on the Possibility and Desirability of Peace*. N.Y: The Dial Press, Inc., 1967.

Litchfield, Michael. *It's A Conspiracy*. Berkeley: Earth Works Press, 1992.

Loewen, James W. *Lies My Teacher Told Me*. N.Y: The New Press, 1995.

Loftus, John, and Mark Aarons. *The Secret War Against the Jews*. N.Y: St. Martins Press, 1994.

Lowe, Janet. *The Secret Empire*. Homewood, Ill: Business One Irwin, 1992.

Lundberg, Ferdinand. *Myth of Democracy*. N.Y: Carol Publishing Group, 1989.

Maier, Pauline. *From Resistance to Rebellion*. N.Y: Alfred A. Knopf, 1974.

Markusen, Ann, and Joel Yudken. *Dismantling The Cold War Economy*. N.Y: Harper Collins Publications, Inc., 1992.

Martin, James S. *All Honorable Men*. Boston: Little, Brown and Co., 1950.

Martin, Malachi. *The Keys of This Blood*. N.Y: Simon & Schuster, 1990.

Matrisciana, Patrick, Ed. *The Clinton Chronicles Book*. Hemet, Ca: Jeremiah Books, 1994.

Mayer, Milton. *They Thought They Were Free*. Chicago: The University of Chicago Press, 1955.

McConnell, Grant. *Private Power and American Democracy*. N.Y: Alfred A. Knopf, 1966.

McDermott, Jeanne. *The Killing Winds: The Menace of Biological Warfare*. N.Y: Arbot House, 1987.

Mead, Walter Russell. *Mortal Splendor The American Empire in Transition*. Boston: Houghton Mifflin Co., 1987.

Menges, Constantine. *Inside the National Security Council*. N.Y: Simon & Schuster, 1988.

Menke, B.W. *Martial Law—Its Use in Case of Atomic Attack*. Washington, D.C: Industrial College of the Armed Forces, 1956.

Meyer, Jr., Cord. *Peace or Anarchy*. Boston: Little, Brown and Co., 1948.

Milkis, Sidney M. *The President and the Parties*. N.Y: Oxford University Press, 1993.

Millard, Catherine. *The Rewriting of America's History*. Camp Hill, Pa: Horizon House Publishers, 1991.

Miller, Arthur S. *Democratic Dictatorship The Emergent Constitution of Control*. Westport, Ct: Greenwood Press, 1981.

_____.*The Modern Corporate State*. Westport, Ct: Greenwood Press, 1976.

_____.*The Secret Constitution and the Need for Constitutional Change*. Westport, Ct: Greenwood Press, 1987.

Miller, Merle. *Plain Speaking An Oral Biography of Harry S. Truman*. N.Y: Berkeley, Publishing Corp., 1974.

Mills, C. Wright. *Power Elite*. N.Y: Oxford U. Press, 1956.

Minter, William, and Laurence H. Shoup. *Imperial Brain Trust: The Council on Foreign Relations and United States Foreign Policy*. N.Y: Monthly Review Press, 1977.

Mitford, Jessica. *Kind and Usual Punishment: The Prison Business*. N.Y: Alfred A. Knopf, 1973.

Mokhiber, Russell. *Corporate Crime and Violence*. San Francisco: Sierra Club, 1988.

Morley, Felix. *Freedom and Federalism*. Indianapolis: Liberty Press, 1981.

Moyers, Bill. *The Secret Government: The Constitution In Crisis*. Washington, D.C: Seven Locks Press, 1988.

Munro, William B. *The Invisible Government*. N.Y: The MacMillan Co., 1928.

Neely, Jr., Mark E. *The Fate of Liberty*. N.Y: Oxford University Press, 1991.

Nevins, Allan. *The War For the Union: War Becomes Revolution, 1862-1863*, Vol. 3 (N.Y: Charles Scribners Sons, 1960).

Ortega Y Gasset, Jose. *The Revolt of the Masses*. N.Y: W.W. Norton & Co., 1932.

Parenti, Michael. *Inventing Reality*. N.Y: St. Martin's Press, 1986.

_____.*Land of Idols*. N.Y: St. Martin's Press, 1994.

Phillips, Kevin. *Arrogant Capital*. N.Y: Little Brown & Co., 1994.

_____.*Boiling Point*. N.Y: Random House, 1993.

Piller, Charles, and Keith R. Yamamoto. *Gene Wars: Military Control Over the New Genetic Technologies*. N.Y: William Morrow, 1988.

Pool, James, and Suzanne Pool. *Who Financed Hitler*. N.Y: The Dial Press, 1978.

Porter, Bruce D. *War and the Rise of the State*. N.Y: Macmillan, 1994.

Pye, A. Kenneth. *The Use of Troops in Civil Disturbances in the United States*. Durham, N.C: Duke University, 1982.

Quigley, Carroll. *The Anglo-American Establishment*. N.Y: Books in Focus, 1981.

_____.*Tragedy and Hope: A History of the World in Our Time*. N.Y: The MacMillian Co., 1966.

Randall, James G. *Constitutional Problems Under Lincoln*. Gloucester, Mass: Peter Smith, 1963.

Rappoport, Jon. *Oklahoma City Bombing The Suppressed Truth*. Los Angeles: Blue Press, 1995.

Rauch, Jonathan. *Demosclerosis*. N.Y: Random House, 1994.

Reich, Charles A. *Opposing the System*. N.Y: Crown Publishers, Inc., 1995.

Robertson, Pat. *The New World Order*. Dallas: Word Publishing, 1991.

Robinson, Donald L., ed. *Reforming American Government*. Boulder, Co: Westview Press, 1985.

Roosevelt, Elliot. *The Conservators*. N.Y: Arbor House, 1983.

Rossiter, Clinton. *Constitutional Dictatorship*. N.Y: Harcourt, Brace & World, Inc., 1948.

Rothbard, Murray N. *America's Great Depression*. Kansas City: Sheed and Ward, Inc., 1963.

Rothmiller, Mike. *L.A. Secret Police: Inside the LAPD Elite Spy Network.* N.Y: Pocket Books, 1992.

Rowan, Ford. *Techno Spies.* N.Y: G. P. Putnam's Sons, 1978.

Russell, Bertrand. *The Impact of Science on Society.* N.Y: Simon & Schuster, 1953.

Saffer, Thomas H, and Orville E. Kelly. *Countdown Zero.* N.Y: G.P. Putnam's Sons, 1982.

Schiller, Herbert I. *Culture Inc. The Corporate Takeover of Public Expression.* N.Y: Oxford University Press, 1989.

Schlafly, Phyllis, and Chester Ward. *Kissinger on the Couch.* New Rochelle, N.Y: Arlington House, 1975.

Schroder, Eugene. *Constitution Fact or Fiction.* Cleburne, Tx: Buffalo Creek Press, 1995.

Schultz, Bud, and Ruth Schultz. *It Did Happen Here.* Berkeley: University of California Press, 1989.

Schumpeter, Joseph A. *Capitalism, Socialism, and Democracy.* N.Y: Harper & Brothers Publishers, 1942.

Seldes, George. *Facts and Fascism.* N.Y: In fact, Inc., 1943.

_____.*Iron Blood and Profits.* N.Y: Harper and Brothers Publishers, 1934.

_____.*1000 Americans.* N.Y: Boni & Gaer, 1947.

Simpson, Christopher. *Blowback.* N.Y: Weidenfeld & Nicolson, 1988.

Skousen, W. Cleon. *The Naked Capitalist.* Salt Lake City: W. Cleon Skousen, 1971.

Smith, James A. *The Idea Brokers.* N.Y: Macmillan, Inc., 1991.

Smoot, Dan. *The Invisible Government.* Boston: Western Islands, 1962.

Spence, Gerry. *From Freedom to Slavery.* N.Y: St. Martin's Press, 1993.

Spivak, John. *A Man In His Time.* N.Y: Horizon Press, 1967.

Sprague, Dean. *Freedom Under Lincoln.* Boston: Houghton Mifflin Co., 1965.

Stenehjem, Michele F. *An American First.* New Rochelle, N.Y: Arlington House Publishers, 1976.

Stevens, Charles E. *Sources of the Constitution of the United States.* N.Y: MacMillian and Co., 1894. reprinted Littleton, Co: Fred B. Rothman and Co., 1987.

Stich, Rodney. *Defrauding America.* Alamo, Ca: Diablo Western Press, Inc., 1993.

Stockwell, John. *The Praetorian Guard.* Boston: South End Press, 1991.

Stormer, John A. *None Dare Call It Treason.* Florissant, Mo: Liberty Bell Press, 1964.

Sutton, Antony C. *Wall Street and FDR.* New Rochelle, N.Y: Arlington House Publishers, 1975.

_____.*Wall Street and the Bolshevik Revolution.* New Rochelle, N.Y: Arlington House Publishers, 1974.

_____.*Wall Street and the Rise of Hitler.* Seal Beach, Ca: '76 Press, 1976.

_____.*Western Technology and Soviet Economic Development 1917 to 1930,* Vol. I. Stanford, Ca: Hoover Institution Publications, 1968.

_____.*Western Technology and Soviet Economic Development 1945 to 1965,* Vol. III. Stanford, Ca: Hoover Institution Publications, 1973.

Szatinary, David P. *Shays Rebellion: The Making of An Agrarian Insurrection.* Amherst: The University of Mass., 1980.

Theoharis, Athan. *From the Secret Files of J. Edgar Hoover.* Chicago: Ivan R. Dee, 1991.

Tiefer, Charles. *The Semi-Sovereign Presidency.* Boulder, Co: Westview Press, 1994.

Tocqueville, Alexis de. *Democracy In America.* N.Y: Vintage, 1990.

Toynbee, Arnold. *Experiences.* N.Y: Oxford U. Press, 1969.

Turner, William W., and John Christian. *The Assassination of Robert F. Kennedy: A Searching Look at the Conspiracy and Cover-up, 1968-1978.* N.Y: Random House, 1978.

Udall, Stewart L. *The Myths of August.* N.Y: Pantheon, 1994.

Uhl, Michael, and Tod Ensign. *GI Guinea Pigs.* N.Y: Playboy Press, 1980.

Vankin, Jonathan, and John Whalen. *50 Greatest Conspiracies of All Time.* N.Y: Carol Publishing Group, 1995.

Vankin, Jonathan. *Conspiracies Cover-Ups and Crimes.* N.Y: Dell Publishing, 1995.

Vidal, Gore. *At Home.* N.Y: Random House, Inc., 1982.

_____.*The Decline and Fall of the American Empire.* Berkeley, Ca: Odonian Press, 1992.

_____.*The Second American Revolution.* N.Y: Random House, Inc. 1976.

Warburg, James. *The West in Crisis.* Garden City, N.Y: Doubleday & Co., 1959.

Wasserman, Harvey, and Norman Solomon. *Killing Our Own.* N.Y: Dell Publishing Co., Inc., 1982.

Weiner, Tim. *Blank Check The Pentagons Black Budget.* N.Y: Warner Books, 1990.

Weyl, Walter. *The New Democracy.* N.Y: The Macmillan Company, 1912.

Weyler, Rex. *Blood of the Land: The Government and Corporate War Against the American Indian Movement.* N.Y: Everest House, 1982.

Williams, T. Harry. *Huey Long.* N.Y: Alfred A. Knopf, 1969.

Wiltz, John E. *In Search of Peace.* Baton Rouge, La: Louisiana State University Press, 1963.

Wise, David. *The American Police State.* N.Y: Random House, 1976.

_____.*The Politics of Lying.* N.Y: Random House, 1973.

Woodward, Bob. *Veil: The Secret Wars of the CIA, 1981-1987.* N.Y: Simon & Schuster, 1987.

Wormser, Rene A. *Foundations: Their Power and Influence.* N.Y: Devin-Adair Co., 1958.

Yankelovich, Daniel. *Coming to Public Judgment.* Syracuse, N.Y: Syracuse University Press, 1991.

Zinn, Howard. *The Politics of History.* Chicago: University of Illinois Press, 1970.

# Index